CHINESE SHAR-PEI
KW-156

Photography: Isabelle Francais, Bruce K. Harkins, Palmer Photos, Robert Pearcy, and Skibinski Photography.

Drawings by *Scott Boldt, Richard Crammer, Richard Davis, Andrew Prendimano, John Quinn, and Alexandra Suchenka.*

Front endpapers: *Uniqueness and personality perhaps explain the extraordinary upsurge of popularity for the Chinese Shar-pei in recent times. These dogs are owned by Gerald and Patricia Brown.*

Title page: *Affectionate and expressive, the Chinese Shar-pei makes a wonderfully pleasing and endearing companion. Owners, Gerald and Patricia Brown.*

Distributed in the UNITED STATES by T.F.H. Publications, Inc., One T.F.H. Plaza, Neptune City, NJ 07753; in CANADA to the Pet Trade by H & L Pet Supplies Inc., 27 Kingston Crescent, Kitchener, Ontario N2B 2T6; Rolf C. Hagen Ltd., 3225 Sartelon Street, Montreal 382 Quebec; in CANADA to the Book Trade by Macmillan of Canada (A Division of Canada Publishing Corporation), 164 Commander Boulevard, Agincourt, Ontario M1S 3C7; in ENGLAND by T.F.H. Publications Limited, Cliveden House/Priors Way/Bray, Maidenhead, Berkshire SL6 2HP, England; in AUSTRALIA AND THE SOUTH PACIFIC by T.F.H. (Australia) Pty. Ltd., Box 149, Brookvale 2100 N.S.W., Australia; in NEW ZEALAND by Ross Haines & Son, Ltd., 18 Monmouth Street, Grey Lynn, Auckland 2, New Zealand; in SINGAPORE AND MALAYSIA by MPH Distributors (S) Pte., Ltd., 601 Sims Drive, #03/07/21, Singapore 1438; in the PHILIPPINES by Bio-Research, 5 Lippay Street, San Lorenzo Village, Makati Rizal; in SOUTH AFRICA by Multipet Pty. Ltd., 30 Turners Avenue, Durban 4001. Published by T.F.H. Publications, Inc. Manufactured in the United States of America by T.F.H. Publications, Inc.

T.f.H
10/9/90

CHINESE SHAR-PEI

ANNA KATHERINE NICHOLAS

Much indebted to the efforts of a handful of Shar-pei enthusiasts devoted to saving the breed from destruction, owners today are ever so fortunate to have these delightful and dignified fellows to share their homes and lives with. K. Derrick Paulus is the owner of these two Shar-pei.

Contents

Origin and Early History of the Chinese Shar-Pei

The Chinese Shar-Pei is one of the earliest breeds of dog known to man, although not always by that name. The dogs considered the progenitors of this modern breed were in existence as long ago as some twenty centuries, having been a definite type since the Han Dynasty (ca. 220 AD). Thus, in common with most Chinese breeds, its roots are deeply buried in the sands of time.

That these dogs were held in high esteem is undeniable, for very many artifacts featuring these hippopotamus-resembling canines have been found by archeologists who have frequently referred to them as "Tomb Dogs." The resemblance in this statuary is quite clear, including the unique blunt muzzle and other facial characteristics which set these dogs apart from others. We know that at least one statue of a "Tomb Dog" has been, and quite probably still is, displayed in the Avery Brundage Collection at the Asian Art Museum, San Francisco, California.

The most widely expressed belief regarding the origin of these dogs is that they were native to the South China Sea area; more specifically, a small town named Dah Let in the province of Kwong Tung. Another theory is that the dogs actually originated in Tibet or in northern China and were known there prior to their appearance in Dah Let. Who is to say for certain after all these years?

The forebears of the Shar-Pei have been described as being a great deal larger than the dogs we now know of this breed, weighing on the average about 165 pounds.

Our modern Shar-Pei has inherited many of the original dog's characteristics. Standing 18 to 20 inches at the withers, this unique dog, unlike any other under the canine sun, combines all the distinctive hippo-like features which set him apart from all other types of dog. China has developed some of dogdom's most unique breeds, a tradition in which the Shar-Pei definitely plays his part!

As a breed, the Shar-Pei started out as a working farm dog. He was owned by the Chinese peasant to whom he was extremely useful. Generations of Shar-Pei have distinguished themselves as guard dogs, herders, and companion dogs. Then as now, they were loyal, reliable, alert, and intelligent— exactly what the peasants, many living in isolated areas, needed for the protection of themselves and their property.

Facing page: *Exotic and extraordinary, the Chinese Shar-pei expands the Orient's already existing list of exceptional breeds. Owners, Gerald and Patricia Brown.*

"SERVICE DOG" OR "FIGHTING DOG"

So well did the early Shar-Pei ancestors fulfill their duties that they became known as "Service Dogs." For hundreds of years they were also known as "Chinese Fighting Dogs." It has been explained, however, that this is not truly an accurate description of the breeds employment, for although he was occasionally used for pit fighting, he was more commonly used for service-oriented functions.

The early Shar-Pei has been especially praised for his herding talents, and the success he enjoyed hunting game in China.

As "Fighting Dogs," these early ancestors of the Shar-Pei evidently were not overly successful against other breeds. The principal interest in

This handsome dog is Down-Homes China Souel who was imported from Matgo Law in Hong Kong by Ernest Albright of Pleasant Hill, California.

developing this aspect of their personality came about in Canton, a city close to Dah Let. Here the sporting and gambling elements were attached. With little in those days to be offered for amusement, some of the gamblers turned their attention towards developing the fighting talents of the dogs. The poverty-stricken peasants of the area were ready and willing to participate in whatever might be available to help put a bit of gold in their pockets.

The Chinese Fighting Dogs were well-equipped in several ways for the activity—the same features which made them successful hunters were also helpful in this capacity. The looseness of skin which enabled a dog, even with his skin in the grip of an opponent's teeth, to twist and attack the other animal served as a protection to his internal organs, creating a nearly impenetrable buffer from his attacker's grip.

The principal distinguishing characteristic of the Shar-Pei *is* his coat; but not its *looseness* so much as its *texture* for which the breed was named, "Shar-Pei" meaning "sand skin." This coat is extremely rough and bristly in texture, most uncomfortable in the mouth of another canine or wild animal.

His small, deep-set eyes make the Shar-Pei less vulnerable to eye injuries; similarly, his tiny ears present little area for painful injury.

Standing proud at three months of age, this is Tail's End Kinni Kinnick, owned by Ann Coleman of Tail's End Shar-Pei.

The formation of the teeth make them a powerful weapon, the curved canine scimitars, once clasped on an opponent, are extremely difficult to escape. For generations now the Shar-Pei has been bred for "scissors" bite as have the majority of dog breeds.

The story goes that eventually the gamblers "discovered" the Western fighting dogs which surpassed the Chinese dogs in weight and proficiency. It has been said that, although physically well-equipped for combat, the Shar-Pei did not appear to have much heart to fight, being basically friendly and amiable. In reality, it took intensive training and the help of stimulants to persuade him to fight in the pits. Actually, the Shar-Pei was much happier at home fending off intruders on his master's property than matching power and wits with other dogs in a pit.

With less interest in the fighting dog lifestyle, these fine animals returned to their original roles of farm and family dog. Actually it was only a comparitively small number of them who had been involved in the pits, as many peasants who relied on them for protection were appalled to see their reliable pets and protectors

killed or maimed in this manner.

Interestingly, although we have seen references to Chinese Fighting Dogs upon occasion, as of 1960 (and we doubt that they have since done so), no official recognition of them as a breed has been included in the registry of any governing kennel club or leading kennel council.

It is difficult to comprehend, as one considers the escalating rise in popularity of the Chinese Shar-Pei and of Shar-Pei owners and fanciers, that less than two decades ago, during the late 1960s, the number of Shar-Pei had become so alarmingly small that complete extinction seemed both imminent and unavoidable. *The Guinness Book of World Records* noted this fact by listing the Shar-Pei as "the rarest breed of dog in the world," a dubious honor considering what the

Offspring of two wondrously celestial Champion parents, this is Alpha Devil's Promenade at three months of age. He is owned by Ann Coleman, Tail's End Shar-Pei.

possible outcome might have been. For without question, had that trend been permitted to continue, there would by now be no Shar-Pei left for the animal lovers of the world to enjoy.

THE PEOPLE'S REPUBLIC OF CHINA

The Communist Party takeover of China created a catastrophic situation for all dogs there. The Communistic viewpoint precludes the "wasting of food" on dogs; thus levied heavy taxation on the ownership of even one. Taxation was periodically increased until, by the late 1940s, there was hardly a dog left to be seen in

China. This definitely hit the poverty-stricken peasants hard. The maintaining of a dog had now become a major expenditure, it took hardly any time at all to reduce the numbers of Shar-Pei to practically zero. It seemed like the beginning of the end for the breed, the first step down the road of the Shar-Pei's trip into extinction.

THE CONTRIBUTION OF MATGO LAW

Having observed the outcome of the Communist Party's rule in China on the nation's dog population, a great friend of the Shar-Pei, Matgo Law, feared that Hong Kong might one day also be taken over by the People's Republic. To him it was unthinkable that a similar destruction of dogs might be repeated in Hong Kong. Determined to protect and assure a future for his beloved breed, a man who did not believe in sitting passively and watching such horrors take place, Law decided that prompt and decisive action on behalf of the Shar-Pei must take place.

Having seen at one time a magazine article featuring the names of endangered breeds, Law wrote a letter to an American magazine in hopes of what might develop. This letter extolled the qualities of the Shar-Pei, included a picture or two, and asked if any American dog lovers might be willing to help save a breed. The letter went out to the magazine with faint hope, as Mr. Law was far from confident that there would be any reply whatsoever. How elated he must have been when the response added up to more than 200 people not only willing but eager to pick up the challenge

An exceptional puppy at the House of Sheng Li. Owner-bred by R.L. and Vicky Teshera.

and rescue the Shar-Pei from potential destruction.

Consequently, the amount of Shar-Pei breeding in Hong Kong was not sufficient to even make a dent in the number of orders. However, there was some breeding stock in Hong Kong (one would imagine that some of the Chinese owners may have gotten some of their dogs into the hands of the Hong Kong breeders when the new tax laws tightened on dog owners on the Communist mainland). There were other breeders, we are sure, in addition to Mr. Law in Hong Kong.

Patiently and/or pensively, Astra peers into the camera. Owners, R.L. and Vicky Teshera.

EVOLUTION OF THE PRESENT-DAY SHAR-PEI

We understand that, as of the present time, there still are a few Shar-Pei dogs of the original Chinese lines left in China. It has been said that the modern Shar-Pei, as we know the breed today, is not descended purely from Chinese stock, but that

somewhere along the line an outcross or two was introduced. The breeds included most frequently as probabilities are the Chow Chow, the Bull Mastiff, the Boxer, and the Bull Terrier. Simply observing the breeds, one can note similarities between the Shar-Pei and the Chow Chow, and even members of the Mastiff family (scaled down to a far smaller size). There are decidedly mutual characteristics between Chows and the Shar-Pei; and between Shar-Pei and certain of the Mastiffs. Where this crossbreeding might have occurred is difficult to say.

Joseph Chan, who was born and raised in Macau, lives in California but still spend time in China. Mr. Chan, writing for the American magazine *Dog World,* tells his readers that he keeps in constant touch with the remaining Shar-Pei owners in Macau. His feeling, as stated in the article and to me in conversation, is that, "Due to the political climate from the early 1950 period through the mid-1960s, the only place for Hong Kong people to obtain Shar-Pei was from Macau. At that time in Hong Kong, Shar-Pei were non-existent". Mr. Chan mentions that there are experienced breeders in the United States who have suspected that the Shar-Pei is a modified breed, and his comment on this is "that they were right all along. This mixed breed consists of the Chinese Shar-Pei bred to

Sound and handsome, this beautifully balanced Shar-pei is owned by Dianne Barlow. The heavy bone and flawless head are marks of his exquisite type. He is Ch. Alpha Artic Gorilla Remington.

the Bull Mastiff, Chow Chow, Bulldog, Boxer, and Bull Terrier.''

We will leave it to the reader to reach his own decision on this matter. The writer's personal comment is that if such *did* take place, it is a rather common practice in establishing and improving a breed; and I daresay that there are very few breeds of dog who have come down through the ages without an outcross or two somewhere along the way to "set" certain characteristics, to improve others, to establish size, etc.

THE CHINESE STANDARD FOR THE SHAR-PEI

Mr. Chan has given us permission to use parts of his translated interpretation of the true Chinese Standard for Shar-Pei, which is especially intriguing. The Chinese custom is to refer to the most commonly known similar shape or form to describe each part of the dog. Also, the first eight parts of the Chinese Standard are given in sequence which when recited in Cantonese are in the form of a poem.

What the Chinese standard, as translated, calls for is as follows:

WU-LO HEAD—The shape of a Wu-Lo melon, (like a pear). Heavy and round at the bottom (skull); tapered at the top (muzzle).

CLAM SHELL EAR—Ear similar to small clam shell. Thick and

small.

BUTTERFLY NOSE—There is a cookie in Guangzhou, China, called "butterfly" of similar appearance to a front view of the dog's nose, with a very wide nostril. The dog's nose should be big (wide) and blunt.

PAE PAH LEGS—The Pae Pah is a musical instrument shaped like a ham. The hind legs should be thick, muscled, and straight without any angulation.

SHRIMP BACK—Back is strong and flexible, no dip behind withers. The croup is flat, not steep or round. In normal posture, the back is slightly arched, almost straight. The difference between the roach back and the shrimp back is that the shrimp back is flexible while the roach back remains permanent.

IRON-WIRE TAIL—Tail should be stiff and thin at the base like a piece of cable, high set on the back. Preferably the tail makes a tight round curl; so tight that a small hole, like a coin, forms in the center of this tail. To the Chinese, the correct tail is of great importance.

GRANDMA FACE—Describes the facial wrinkling, just a little like "Granny's." The face should not be overly wrinkled.

IRON PELLET TONGUE— Bluish black color like an iron pellet. In China, a "flowered" tongue is acceptable.

WATER BUFFALO NECK— Strong and of medium length, with a small amount of dewlap, like a water buffalo.

WUN FISH BODY—A common fish in Kwong Tung Province describes body that is, like this fish, not too round nor too flat in rib cage. Dry and firm. Skin tight without wrinkles except in the withers area. When skin is grabbed and pulled away from body it should be extremely loose.

FACING SKY ANUS—Tail set so high on back that the anus protrudes slightly and faces upwards. Has noticeable rim.

HORSE'S REAR END—Broad, muscular, well-developed, like that of a horse.

Ch. Commodity of Tail's End is owned by Ann Coleman. She is a cream female of noteworthy type who is both a Group winner and a Best of Breed winner.

These three horsecoat puppies of Fingertail Charmin have certainly cornered the market on irresistibility and charm. They are owned by Jo Ann Webster.

DRAGON LEG—Front legs wide-spaced to side of body forming very wide chest.

GARLIC FEET—Thick, firm, well-knuckled. Resembles garlic bulb with toes forming the garlic cloves.

MOTHER FROG MOUTH—Muzzle short, wide, tapered to blunt wedge triangle. When opened, corners of mouth wider than placement of eyes.

ROOF TILE MOUTH—Longer than the preferred Mother Frog Mouth. Muzzle strong, round in shape. Resembles Chinese Roof Tile.

IRON TOENAIL—Bluish black.

RUSTY BLACK—Color of a black dog's coat which should be dull, not shiny, with tips of hair ending in reddish brown, like rust.

FIVE (POINT) RED—This does not refer to coat color, but to five areas of the body which may be red or pink on dogs of diluted pigmentation (meaning coat colors of red, light fawn, cream, or white). These parts are the nose, eye rims, tongue, toenails, and anus.

In China, the two preferred coat colors would appear to be rusty black and dark fawn.

Development of the Shar-Pei Outside China

THE SHAR-PEI IN THE UNITED STATES

A warm, highly enthusiastic reception greeted the Shar-Pei as they began arriving from Hong Kong into the United States. The moment dog lovers saw them they wanted to own one; and obviously the supply was limited, leaving many would-be owners waiting patiently for their puppies to be born.

America loves the new, the different, and the chance to be in on the start of something important. The Shar-Pei covers all these categories. Plus very definitely it can be said of this breed "that to know one is to love one" as only a short acquaintance is needed before one starts to appreciate the intelligence and marvelous disposition of these dogs.

What a fortunate day it was for the future of this breed when Mr. and Mrs. Ernest Albright of California became attracted to it. The Albrights had partially retired at just about the time Matgo Law's letter describing the plight of the Shar-Pei appeared in the American press. Additionally, they had been seriously considering involving themselves in dog breeding but had not decided on a particular breed.

The news of the Shar-Pei appealed to them instantly and they decided to take on this project.

Mr. Albright started to wage a "Shar-Pei Publicity Campaign" that turned out to be enormously successful. His dogs were shown and discussed on television and in the press. Additionally, he spent untold hours in discussion of the breed with interested parties, sharing his knowledge and understanding of the breed. Mr. Albright's efforts for the breed in the U.S. and Mr. Law's work in Hong Kong both were entirely successful and blossomed within an amazingly short length of time. Prior to the breed's actually arriving in America, their popularity mushroomed as many

A pup of promise, this is Tzo Tzo's Mamie of Tail's End photographed at two and a half months of age. She is owned by Ann Coleman.

Lounging away the afternoon, here lies House of Treasures Oprah with House of Treasures Mason—although shown here with less flurry and chatter than usual, they are ofttimes filled with uninterruptable activity. Bred by Barbara and Gary Roche.

visitors to Hong Kong who saw them either returned with a puppy or ordered one. Among these were numerous prominent U.S. judges and other visitors to the Orient. The first this writer knew of them was through the John Pattersons, noted Basset Hound breeders and popular multiple breed judges, who brought back pictures of the new dogs that they were going to breed. These dogs brought the Pattersons great pleasure, and they have continued to be favorites of the family.

The Albrights, whose dogs are known as the Ho Wun Chinese Shar-Pei, received their first two during the early 1970s. Their breeding program took off in 1974. The Board of Governors of the

Shar Pei Club of America have recently passed a Resolution that Albright be recognized as an Honorary Lifetime Director and President Emeritus as an expression of thanks, respect, and admiration of a job well-done. Albright had previously served as founder member, president, and director of the Shar Pei Club of America from 1974 to 1981.

ALBRIGHT'S DISTINGUISHED SHAR-PEI

Albright's famous dogs are the handsome stud dog Chin China Souel, who was born in Hong Kong from Chinese stock. Mui-Chu helped promote the breed's popularity when she was featured on the cover of *Popular Dogs*

Magazine in 1973. Ming Yun, from the first Albright homebred litter, became a quite well-known television star by her appearance with David Frost, Garry Moore, and on such widely viewed programs as *To Tell The Truth* and *Good Morning, America.* Shima, another Albright dog, was a star for a Japanese movie on television in 1979. Ting helped to publicize the breed in Canada by making guest appearances at a school exhibit, the large and prestigious Metropolitan Kennel Club Dog Show, and as the subject of numerous newspaper stories. Fawn appeared in 600 newspapers and magazines and at Canada's Metropolitan Kennel Club in 1978. Tibet who did stunts for Johnny Carson on *The Tonight Show* in March, 1979, was invited by Betty White to her show and received a wide range of press coverage. On reviewing all this, one must comment that Mr. Albright really does know how to run an advertising campaign; and that such wide coverage must have made every person in the North American countries realize that the Shar-Pei's future was to be a bright one!

The Chinese Shar-Pei Club of America is the National Parent Specialty for the breed. It is the responsibility of this organization to keep the registry until the breed is admitted into the American Kennel Club Stud Book, at which point the records are turned over to A.K.C. The Shar-Pei Club also holds specialty shows, match shows, and other competitive events for the breed. They award the title "Champion" to any Shar-Pei having acquired the requisite number of points to earn this distinction. All of the dogs pictured in this book who bear titles have gained them from the CSPCA.

THE ROAD TO TAKE

There will be new worlds to conquer when the Shar-Pei receives its own breed classification as being fully recognized by the American Kennel Club. The first breakthrough came in the admittance of the breed to the Miscellaneous Class at dog shows. This became effective on May 4, 1988.

The following step will be admittance to the Stud Book when the required number of Shar-Pei have been CSPCA-registered. We understand that now about 40,000 Shar-Pei are already listed in the registry. And finally comes the breed's own classification as an American Kennel Club-recognized breed at dog shows. This is exciting to contemplate as many breeders are truly producing dogs of tremendous quality.

A gentleman deserving high praise from the Shar-Pei fancy is William W. Morison, who has been the registrar for the Chinese Shar-Pei Club of America since 1978 and was the chairman of

Owned by Steve Peloso, this is House of Treasures Mason, a remarkable example of a fawn horse coat male.

committee that negotiated the consolidation of the two existing Shar-Pei clubs. As further proof of his dedication to the breed, he consented to take on the added responsibility of becoming membership secretary in 1984. Mr. Morison is a native Californian having been born and raised in the Bay area.

Throughout the United States, there are many affiliated clubs to the National, all with busy, ambitious program schedules. Fun, education, and good exposure of the breed are among the purposes of these organizations. These clubs hold specialty shows (sometimes two annually) and support the breed at rare breed shows in which the Shar-Pei has done quite spectacularly.

In the East, the Northeastern Shar-Pei Club is an especially involved organization, and we believe is the first for the breed whose members have supported temperament tests for their dogs, a number of whom have earned TT degrees.

Those wishing to inquire about a Shar-Pei club in their area or any other aspect of the breed and its ownership should contact the Shar-Pei Club of America, Inc., at 9705 East 80th Street, Raytown, Missouri. Also, information can be sought from the Shar-Pei Club of America's Registry address, 55 Oak Court, Danville, California, 94526.

Development Outside China

A thorough study of the Standard of Perfection as drawn up by the Chinese Shar-Pei Club of America, effective May, 1988, is most helpful, as familiarity with this detailed description will help familiarize the reader with the desirable and the less desirable physical characteristics of this breed.

SHAR-PEI AROUND THE WORLD

Although there could be but little argument that Hong Kong and the United States have been the seats of the greatest activity in the Shar-Pei world recently, we are pleased to know that the breed is being popularized and working towards official recognition in other important strongholds of dog lovers, too.

Australia, for example, has a nucleus of people "into" the Shar-Pei, working hard to benefit the breed with official recognition being their desired goal.

Canada was rather in the "fringe benefit" area of Mr. Albright's publicity campaign in the states. Much that was written about the breed in the U.S. was read and studied there; the dogs were displayed at important Canadian dog shows, and the day may not be too far off when Shar-Pei fanciers shall receive word from the Canadian Kennel Club that official recognition is nearing.

We have heard little on the subject of the Shar-Pei in Great Britain so far: but we feel safely assured that there is interest in that country, too.

Tibet, Taiwan, and the

This red brush male is Fingertail Yunny. The Shar-pei is loved for his mellow disposition and gentle manner. Owner, Jo Ann Webster.

Peering prophetically over the formidable vastness of the outside world, this is Cra-Jack's H.O.T. Sugar at three months. A cream dilute from House of Treasures.

Philippines have been mentioned as strongholds which the breed enjoys.

But there is still a long way to go! Let us not forget that the breed only first started to attract attention in the early 1970s. We expect big things for the Shar-Pei and its friends in the future. Wait and see!

AMERICAN STANDARD

The following is the American Standard for the Chinese Shar-Pei by the Chinese Shar-Pei Club of America, Inc.

GENERAL APPEARANCE—An alert, dignified, active, compact dog of medium size and substance, square in profile, close-coupled, the well-proportioned head slightly but not overly large for the body. The

short, harsh coat, the loose skin covering the head and body, the small ears, the "hippopotamus" muzzle shape and the high set tail impart to the Shar-Pei a unique look peculiar to him alone. The loose skin and wrinkles covering the head, neck and body are superabundant in puppies but these features may be limited to the head, neck and withers in the adult.

HEAD—Large, slightly but not overly, proudly carried and covered with profuse wrinkles on the forehead continuing into side wrinkles framing the face. SKULL—Flat and broad, the stop moderately defined, the length from nose to stop is approximately the same as from stop to occiput. MUZZLE—One of the distinctive

With dazzling promise, this is Remington's Arctic Stardust owned by Dianne Barlow.

features of the breed. It is broad and full with no suggestion of snipiness. The lips and top of muzzle are well padded and may cause a slight bulge at the base of the nose. NOSE—Large and wide and darkly pigmented, preferably black but any color nose conforming to the general coat color of the dog is acceptable. In dilute colors, the preferred nose is self-colored. Darkly pigmented cream Shar-Pei may have some light pigment either in the center of their noses or on their entire nose. TEETH—Strong, meeting in a scissors bite. Deviation from a scissor bite is a major fault. EYES—Dark, small, almond-shaped and sunken, displaying a scowling expression. In the dilute-colored dogs, the eye color may be lighter. EARS—Extremely small, rather thick, equilateral triangles in shape, slightly rounded at the tips, edges of the ear may curl. Ears lie flat against the head, are set wide apart and forward on the skull, pointing toward the eyes. The ears have the ability to move. Pricked ears are a disqualification. TONGUE, ROOF OF MOUTH, GUMS AND FLEWS—Solid bluish black is preferred in all coat colors except in dilute colors, which have a solid lavender pigmentation. A spotted tongue is a major fault. A solid pink tongue is a disqualification. (Tongue colors may lighten due to heat stress; care must be taken not to confuse dilute pigmentation with a pink tongue).

BODY—Proportion: The height

Head study of Ch. Meiting Sheng Li of the House of Sheng Li. Owners, R.L. and Vicky Teshera.

of the Shar-Pei from the ground to the withers is approximately equal to the length from the point of breastbone to the point of rump. NECK—Medium length, full and set well into the shoulders. There are moderate to heavy folds of loose skin and abundant dewlap about the neck and throat.

BACK—Short and close-coupled, the topline dips slightly behind the withers, slightly rising over the short, broad loin. CHEST—Broad and deep with the brisket extending to the elbow and rising slightly under the loin. CROUP—Flat, with the base of the tail set extremely high, clearly exposing an uptilted anus. TAIL—The high set tail is a characteristic feature of the Shar-Pei. The tail is thick and round at the base, tapering to a fine point and curling over or to either side of the back. The absence of a complete tail is a disqualification.

FOREQUARTERS—Shoulders: Muscular, well-laid back and sloping. Forelegs: When viewed from the front, straight, moderately spaced, with elbows close to the body. When viewed from the side, the forelegs are straight, the pasterns are strong and flexible. The bone is substantial but never heavy and is of moderate length. FEET—Moderate in size, compact, and firmly set, not splayed. Removal of front dewclaws is optional.

HINDQUARTERS—Muscular, strong, and moderately angulated. The metatarsi (hocks) are short, perpendicular to the ground, and parallel to each other when viewed from the rear. Hind dewclaws must be removed.

COAT—The extremely harsh coat is one of the distinguishing features of the breed. The coat is absolutely straight and offstanding on the main trunk of the body but generally lies somewhat flatter on the limbs. The coat appears healthy without being shiny or lustrous. Acceptable coat lengths may range from the extremely short "horse coat" up to the "brush coat," not to exceed one inch in length at the withers. A soft coat, a wavy coat, a coat in excess of 1 inch in length at the withers, or a coat that has been trimmed is a major fault. The Shar-Pei is shown in its natural state.

COLOR—Only solid colors are acceptable. A solid-colored dog may have shading, primarily darker down the back and on the ears. The shading must be variations of the same body color (except in sables) and may include darker hairs throughout the coat. The following colors are disqualifying faults: albino, brindle, parti-color (patches), spotted (spots, ticked, roaning), and a tan-pointed pattern (typical black and tan or saddled).

GAIT—The movement of the Shar-Pei is to be judged at a trot. The gait is free and balanced with the feet tending to converge on a center line of gravity when the dog moves at a vigorous trot. The gait combines good forward reach and a strong drive in the hindquarters. Proper movement is essential.

SIZE—The preferred height is 18 to 20 inches at the withers. The preferred weight is 40 to 55 pounds. The dog is usually larger and more square-bodied than the bitch but both appear well proportioned.

TEMPERAMENT—Regal, alert, intelligent, dignified, lordly, scowling, sober, and snobbish; essentially independent and somewhat standoffish with strangers, but extreme in his devotion to his family. The Shar-Pei stands firmly on the ground with a calm, confident stature.

A champion at eight months of age, this is Ch. Meiting Sheng Li—his five-point major wins included among them Best of Breed. He is owned by R.L. and Vicky Teshera.

MAJOR FAULTS:
1. Deviation from a scissor bite
2. Spotted tongue
3. A soft coat, a wavy coat, a coat in excess of 1 inch in length at the withers or a coat that has been trimmed.

DISQUALIFYING FAULTS:
1. Pricked ears
2. Solid pink tongue
3. Absence of a complete tail
4. Not a solid color, i.e.: albino; brindle; parti-colored (patches); spotted (including spots, ticked or roaning); tan-pointed pattern (including typical black and tan or saddled patterns).

HONG KONG STANDARD

In addition to the Chinese and American Standards for the Shar-Pei, there also exists the Hong Kong Standard which is somewhat different. The writer believes you will find the color qualifications of the Hong Kong Standard most fascinating reading as they are more specific than the American Standard (A.K.C.—1988). This standard was translated by Matgo Law.

COLOR—Whole colors—black,

red, deep fawn, light fawn, and cream frequently shaded, (the underpart of tail and back of thighs of a lighter color) but not in patches or parti-colored. This is what the Standard says about colors: "The Shar-Pei should always be a solid color, never parti-colored. Shadings in the blacks and fawns are very common and not indicative of parti-colors. Parti-colors, brindle and black and tans should definitely be penalized and certainly not used in breeding programme." Matgo S.H. Law. March 1980.

Black: Often shaded; nose black, born black; quite easily turn to a rusted-grey color in long exposure to sunshine.

Fawn: Deeper or lighter shade of cinnamon (in American Chow's language); often shaded; nose black; is born flesh-color and turns black in about a week's time. Most common color.

Red: Also shaded, but not so distinctive as blacks or fawns; nose black; deep red color is not common.

Cream: Shaded; fawn ears and always associated with brick-colored nose with black rim (this is why this color should be deep brown and tongue color should be completely blue-black, as blue-black as the blacks and fawns.

Dilute: Theoretically cream is a dilute color but the writer tried to distinguish the following described color variety from the 'creams' and termed it 'dilute.' The coat color is a deeper tone of reddish cream; the color of 'hot cream' in the language of Persian Cat breeders. The nose color is lighter brick-colored (lighter than the creams) without dark pigment around the rim. Eye color is usually lighter and the main difference is the tongue color—a shade of overall light-purple instead of solid blue-black. If the overall color pattern is not diluted to an excessive degree, this color is acceptable.

Rust: An overall rusty-grey (not a seasonal rusted-black color and much lighter overall color than the former); the intermixture of black and fawn hairs; shaded, darker along the top of the back, fawn-rusty on legs; the overall appearance of a whole color effect is maintained and no suggestion of distinctive border between darker and lighter color regions. Nose black.

Chocolate: A whole chocolate color with a chocolate nose and yellowish eyes; tongue color is light-purple; it is whole colored, therefore, acceptable. The writer has so far seen only one of this color, born from both black parents.

Except those specially mentioned, the tongue color of all these varieties should be completely blue-black. The stronger and deeper pigments being favored.

His wistful expression tainted by a subdued complacency makes the Chinese Shar-pei a most intriguing animal. Owners, Gerald and Patricia Brown.

Character, Personality and Temperament

Almost certainly it was the strangeness of his appearance that first attracted your attention to the Shar-Pei. A dog so different is immediately eye-catching, leading the onlooker to want to learn more about the breed.

It takes only a very short period of acquaintance before you become enthralled with the Shar-Pei's many splendid qualities, and to find that the unique physical characteristics are actually only the tip of the iceberg where the merits of a Shar-Pei are concerned.

Shar-Pei owners with speed and efficiency will explain to you in detail that this is the breed of the future. They reveal that dogs are delightful in temperament, and that once you have owned one, you never again will be satisfied with any other breed. An intelligent dog, he is of reliable and even disposition, adoring of his family and friends. With strangers possible initial aloofness quickly becomes a friendly wag. His alertness makes him a competent watchdog. He is playful and comical in his antics, thus a source of amusement and cheer.

Devoted to home and family, Shar-Pei are affectionate to the entire family rather than just selecting one person on whom to shower affection. They get on well with children, and are not hard to handle (if the introductions are properly made) with other pets in the household.

Shar-Pei owners have commented that their dogs are close to humans in their reactions and understanding; they are quiet and non-destructive. That they do not have the urge to wander far afield is another asset. However, this does not mean that they should be permitted to wander on their own. Furthermore, an obviously valuable and exotic dog is in constant peril of being stolen for profit.

Shar-Pei fanciers are zealous in protecting the friendliness and good disposition of their dogs. To this end, all puppies are "socialized" from earliest puppyhood, played with, petted, and loved. It is important to the future self-confidence and disposition of any dog that he feel secure and loved and that his natural inclination towards a happy association with the world be encouraged throughout his growing up period.

POTENTIAL MEDICAL PROBLEMS OF THE SHAR-PEI

The ownership of a Shar-Pei, as is the case with any breed of dog, should never be undertaken without a sense of responsibility. It is quite easy to be intrigued by and fall in love with almost any puppy. But when bringing one home, it should be remembered that this is a commitment for the duration of the puppy's hopefully long lifetime. Also, in the case of the Shar-Pei, it is a comparative

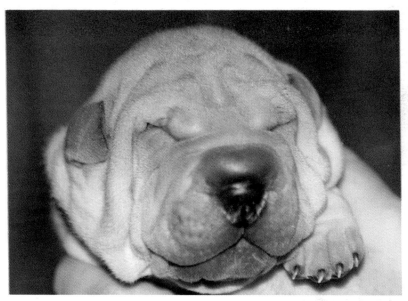

The condition affecting this puppy is known as entropion—it is a defect which requires serious attention by a vet or an experienced breeder. The puppy in this photo belongs to Jo Ann Webster who is one such breeder who has successfully performed the "tacking" procedure on her own.

"new breed" and consequently brings with it some problems which have not yet been completely solved.

Hip dysplasia is a serious condition of which you must be aware. If you are at all planning to use your Shar-Pei as a stud dog or a brood bitch, it is a necessity that you deal with a breeder who is involved with an x-ray program to ascertain the status of the dog you are getting in this regard.

Entropion is a condition in which the edges of the eyelids roll inward, thus bringing the lashes into contact with the eyeball. If left uncorrected, the constant irritation of the lashes rubbing on the eyeball becomes both uncomfortable and dangerous to the eye; thus a simple operation of "tacking" the eyelids should be performed. Some long-time breeders are able to perform this "tacking" themselves. But I strongly advise that it be attended to promptly by a *veterinarian,* and given attention even if the puppy is only a few weeks old. Neglect of this condition can lead to an eye ulcer with the possible loss of the eye to follow. Be on the watch for this with any Shar-Pei you purchase.

There is also a situation involving some Shar-Pei's mouths.

An excellent example of how a future champion appears at eight weeks of age! This is Ch. Hillie's Roisin-Rua Gung Ho (Rosie) owned by Alice Lawler.

In this case the lower lip of the dog has a tendency to roll in over the teeth of the lower jaw, making eating difficult and in severe cases requiring surgical attention.

Another problem area is the breed's tendency toward skin trouble which is certainly not illogical when one considers the number of wrinkles the dogs have. Many breeders have been working on this and have found that mange is *not* involved, as has sometimes been rumored. They believe that it is caused by an allergy to certain foods. Several breeders have expressed an opinion on this, and the concensus is that foods with cornmeal and those with beet sweetening should be avoided. As with human allergies, it can sometimes take a bit of "doing" to track down the culprit. But canine nutritionists have been at work, and you can get the latest "findings" from your veterinarian or an experienced breeder. Again, the breed has not been established for that long and there is still much to learn. Fortunately, breeders are working their hardest to eliminate these problems and will undoubtedly do so in relatively few generations.

Selecting Your Dog

Now that you have decided which dog breed suits your needs, your lifestyle, and your own temperament, there will be much to consider before you make your final purchase. Buying a puppy on impulse may only cause heartbreak later on; it makes better sense to put some real thought into your canine investment, especially since it is likely that he will share many happy years with you. Which individual will you choose as your adoring companion? Ask yourself some questions as you analyze your needs and preferences for a dog, read all that you can about your particular breed, and visit as many dog shows as possible. At the shows you will be surrounded by people who can give you all the details about the breed you are interested in buying. Decide if you want a household pet, a dog for breeding, or a show dog. Would you prefer a male or female? Puppy or adult?

If you buy from a breeder, ask him to help you with your decision. When you have settled on the dog you want, discuss with him the dog's temperament, the animal's positive and negative aspects, any health problems it might have, its feeding and grooming requirements, and whether the dog has been immunized. Reputable breeders will be

willing to answer any questions you might have that pertain to the dog you have selected, and often they will make themselves available if you call for advice or if you encounter problems after you've made your purchase.

A well-balanced pup, this is Gung Ho's Ping Ki Li, owned by Alice Lawler and Peggy Kastner. This youngster is shown taking Best of Breed in a Juniors' competition, handled by Alicia Kastner.

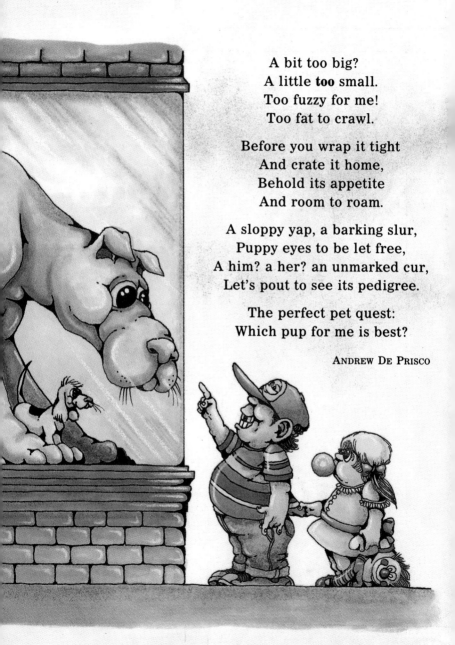

A bit too big?
A little **too** small.
Too fuzzy for me!
Too fat to crawl.

Before you wrap it tight
And crate it home,
Behold its appetite
And room to roam.

A sloppy yap, a barking slur,
Puppy eyes to be let free,
A him? a her? an unmarked cur,
Let's pout to see its pedigree.

The perfect pet quest:
Which pup for me is best?

ANDREW DE PRISCO

Selecting Your Dog

Most breeders want to see their dogs placed in loving, responsible homes; they are careful about who buys their animals. So as the dog's new owner, prepare yourself for some interrogation from the breeder.

WHERE TO BUY

You can choose among several places to buy your dog. Many people think of their local pet shop as the first source for buying a puppy, and very often they're right; you should remember, however, that a pet shop cannot possibly stock all breeds of dog. If your pet shop does not carry the type of dog you desire, there are other places to look. One is a kennel whose business is breeding show-quality dogs; such kennels may have extra pups for sale. Another source is the one-dog owner who wants to sell the puppies from an occasional litter to pay the expenses of his small-scale breeding operation. To find such kennels and part-time breeders and hobbyists, check the classified section of your local newspaper or look in your telephone directory.

Whichever source you choose, you can usually tell in a very short time whether the puppies will make healthy and happy pets. If they are clean, plump, and lively, they are probably in good health. At the breeder's you will have the advantage of seeing the puppies' dam and perhaps their sire and other relatives. Remember that the mother, having just raised a demanding family, may not be looking her best; but if she is sturdy, friendly, and well-mannered, her puppies should be too. If you feel that something is lacking in the care or condition of the dogs, it is better to look elsewhere than to buy hastily and regret it afterward. Buy a healthy dog with a good disposition, one that has been

These two outstanding puppies face very promising futures. At seven months, Fingertail Teaberry H.O.T., a five point red male, sitting on the left of three-month-old Ch. Pai Gei's H.O.T. Stuff, a red brushcoat female. They are owned by Gary and Barbara Roche.

Noted for her outstanding movement is Ch. Gold's Taffy Apple Hau Jou owned by Gayle Gold of the House of Gold.

properly socialized and likes being around people.

If you cannot find the dog you want locally, write to the secretary of the national breed club or kennel club and ask for names of breeders near you or to whom you can write for information. Puppies are often shipped, sight unseen, from reputable breeders. In these instances, pictures and pedigree information are usually sent beforehand to help you decide.

Breeders can supply you with further details and helpful guidance, if you require it. Many breed clubs provide a puppy referral service, so you may want to look into this before making your final decision.

PET OR SHOW DOG

Conscientious breeders strive to maintain those desirable qualities in their breed. At the same time, they are always working to improve on what they have already achieved, and they do this by referring to the breed standard of perfection. The standard describes the ideal dog, and those animals that come close to the ideal are generally selected as show

Owners of purebred dogs too often forget that all breeds of dog are interrelated. The ancient canine that is the believed ancestor of all dogs is known as Tomarctus. As packs traveled and inhabited various lands, types evolved through the process of adaptation. Later, as dogs and man joined forces, type became further diversified. This chart sketches one commonly accepted theory of the domesticated dog's development. Where does your dog fit in? With a few exceptions, dogs evolve or change as a result of a specific functional need.

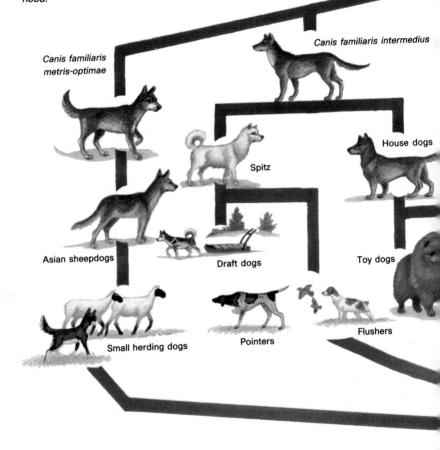

Canis familiaris intermedius

Canis familiaris metris-optimae

House dogs

Spitz

Asian sheepdogs

Draft dogs

Toy dogs

Small herding dogs

Pointers

Flushers

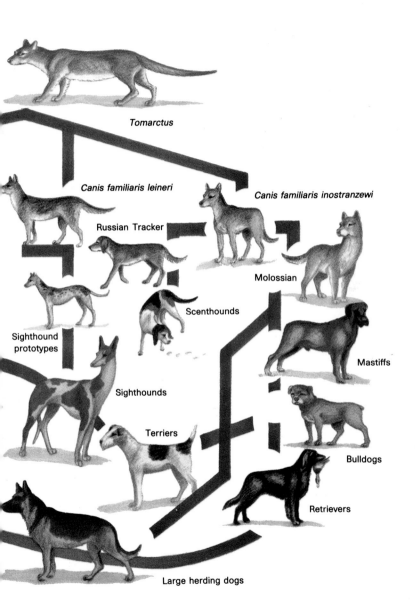

Tomarctus

Canis familiaris leineri

Canis familiaris inostranzewi

Russian Tracker

Molossian

Scenthounds

Mastiffs

Sighthound prototypes

Sighthounds

Terriers

Bulldogs

Retrievers

Large herding dogs

stock; those that do not are culled and sold as pets. Keep in mind that pet-quality purebred dogs are in no way less healthy or attractive than show-quality specimens. It's just that the pet may have undesirable features (such as ears that are too large

A champion of unsurpassable acclaim, Ch. Gold's Black Magic owner-bred by Gayle and Marty Gold sired 22 champions. He was highly praised for his wonderful temperament and the consistent sparkle of his progeny.

or eyes that are the wrong color for its breed) which would be faults in the show ring. Often these so-called "flaws" are detectable only by experienced breeders or show judges. Naturally the more perfect animal, in terms of its breed standard, will cost more—even though he seems almost identical to his pet-quality littermate.

If you think you may eventually want to show your dog or raise a litter of puppies, by all means buy the best you can afford. You will save expense and disappointment later on. However, if the puppy is strictly to be a pet for the children, or a companion for you, you can afford to look for a bargain. The pup which is not show material, or the older pup for which there is often less demand, or the grown dog which is not being used for breeding are occasionally available and offer opportunities to save money. Remember that your initial investment may be a bargain, but it takes good food and care— and plenty of both—to raise a healthy, vigorous puppy through its adulthood.

Facing page: *A notable trait of the Shar-pei is the purple tongue which is very visible on this specimen. This handsome dog is owned by Valerie E. Fiorella.*

Selecting Your Dog

The price you pay for your dog is little compared to the love and devotion he will return over the many years he'll be with you. With proper care and affection, your pup should live to a ripe old age; thanks to modern veterinary science and improvements in canine nutrition, dogs today are better maintained and live longer. It is not uncommon to see dogs living well into their teens.

Generally speaking, small dogs live longer than big ones. With love and the proper care any dog will live to its optimum age. Many persons, however, opt for a particular breed because of its proven longevity. This, of course, is purely a personal decision.

MALE OR FEMALE

If you intend to breed your dog someday, by all means buy a female. You can find a suitable mate without difficulty when the time comes, and you'll have the pleasure of raising a litter of puppies. If you don't want to raise puppies, however, your female should be spayed so that she will remain a healthy, lively pet. Similarly, a male purchased as a pet, rather than as a stud

This illustration of the dog's skeleton and vital organs reveals the distinctive construction of the dog. Veterinary medicine, largely devoted to the better health of your dog, continues to make advances that promise even greater canine longevity.

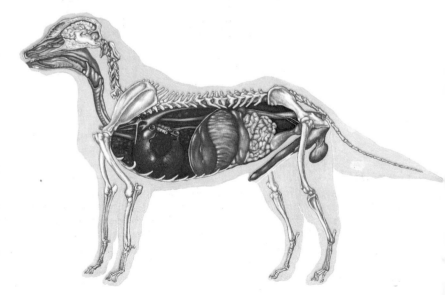

According to some astrologers, dogs too are affected by their zodiac sign. If you follow the stars, be sure to select a dog born under a sky compatible with that of your birth date.

dog, should be castrated. The female is smaller than the male and generally quieter. She has less tendency to roam in search of romance, but a properly trained male can be a charming pet and has a certain difference in temperament that is appealing to many people. Male versus female is chiefly a matter of personal choice; both make fine companions.

ADULT OR PUP

Whether to buy a grown dog or a young puppy is another question. It is surely an undeniable pleasure to watch your dog grow from a lively pup to a mature, dignified dog. If you don't have the time to spend on the more frequent meals, housebreaking, and other training a puppy needs in order to become a dog you can be proud of, then choose an older, partly-trained adolescent or a grown dog. If you want a show dog, remember that no one, not even an expert, can predict with one hundred percent accuracy what a puppy will be like when he grows up. The dog may seem to exhibit show potential *most* of the time, but six months is the earliest age for the would-be exhibitor to select a prospect and know that its future is in the show ring.

If you have a small child, it is best to get a puppy big enough to defend itself, one not less than four or five months old.

Older children will enjoy playing with and helping to take care of a baby pup; but at less than four months, a puppy wants to do little else but eat and sleep, and he must be protected from teasing and overtiring. You cannot expect a very young child to understand that a puppy is a fragile living being; to the youngster he is a toy like his

This wonderful, huggable bundle is Fingertail Bumble, certain to tumble her way into the hearts of a number of judges. Owner, Jo Ann Webster.

House of Treasures Oprah taking the first steps toward her championship.

stuffed dog. Children, therefore, must learn how to handle and care for their young pets.

We recommend you start with a puppy so that you can raise and train it according to the rules you have established in your own home. While a dog is young, its behavior can be more easily shaped by the owner, whereas an older dog , although trainable, may be a bit set in his ways.

WHAT TO LOOK FOR IN A PUPPY

In choosing a puppy, assuming that it comes from healthy, well-bred parents, look for one that is friendly and outgoing. The biggest pup in the litter is apt to be somewhat coarse as a grown dog, while the appealing "runt of the litter" may turn out to be a timid shadow—or have a Napoleonic complex! If you want a show dog and have no experience in choosing a prospect, study the breed standard and listen carefully to the breeder on the finer points of show conformation. A breeder's prices will be in accord with his puppies' expected worth, and he will be honest with you about each pup's potential because it is to his own advantage. He wants his top-quality show puppies placed in the public eye to reflect glory on him—and to attract future buyers. Why should he sell a potential show champion to someone who just wants a pet?

Now that you have paid your money and made your choice, you are ready to depart with puppy, papers, and instructions. Make sure that you know the youngster's feeding routine, and take along some of his food. For the trip home, place him in a comfortable, sturdy carrier. Do not drive home with a puppy on your lap! If you'll be travelling for a few hours, at the very least bring along a bottle of water from the breeder and a small water dish.

PEDIGREE AND REGISTRATION

Owners of puppies are often misled by sellers with such ruses as leading the owner to believe his dog is something special. The term *pedigree papers* is quite different from the term *registration papers*. A pedigree is nothing more than a statement made by the breeder of the dog;

Dog shows are fascinating to both the participants and the spectators. If you have never attended a dog show, you are missing an important part of the canine world. This is the Crufts Show in England.

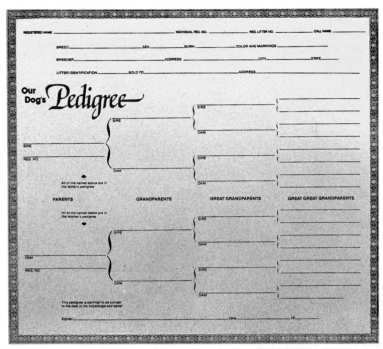

Pedigree papers can trace a dog's lineage back several generations. They do not, however, guarantee that a puppy is of good quality or sound health.

and it is written on special pedigree blanks, which are readily available from any pet shop or breed club, with the names of several generations from which the new puppy comes. It records your puppy's ancestry and other important data, such as the pup's date of birth, its breed, its sex, its sire and dam, its breeder's name and address, and so on. If your dog has had purebred champions in his background, then the pedigree papers are valuable as evidence of the good breeding behind your dog; but if the names on the pedigree paper are meaningless, then so is the paper itself. Just because a dog has a pedigree doesn't necessarily mean he is registered with a kennel club.

Registration papers from the American Kennel Club or the United Kennel Club in the United States or The Kennel Club of Great Britain attest to the fact that the mother and father of your puppy were purebred dogs of the breed represented by your puppy and that they were registered with a particular club. Normally every registered dog also has a complete pedigree available. Registration papers, which you receive when you buy a puppy, merely enable you to register your puppy. Usually the breeder has registered only the litter, so it is the new owner's responsibility to register and name an individual pup. The papers should be filled out and sent to the appropriate address printed on the application, along with the fee required for the registration. A certificate of registration will then be sent to you.

Pedigree and registration, by the way, have nothing to do with licensing, which is a local regulation applying to purebred and mongrel alike. Find out what the local ordinance is in your town or city and how it applies to your dog; then buy a license and keep it on your dog's collar for identification.

This handsome Shar-pei is Ch. Blackwitch's Charlie Jenning. He finished his championship at less than one year of age. Owner, May Jennings.

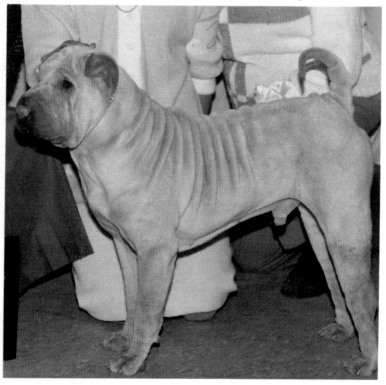

The New Family Member

Taking Winners here at Windy City All-Breed Match, this is Ch. Stroh's Brewed at Blackwitch. Owner, Denise A. Beagle, Blackwitch Farms.

At long last, the day you have all been waiting for, your new puppy will make its grand entrance into your home. Before you bring your companion to its new residence, however, you must plan carefully for its arrival. Keep in mind that the puppy will need

The New Family Member

time to adjust to life with a different owner. He may seem a bit apprehensive about the strange surroundings in which he finds himself, having spent the first few weeks of life with his dam and littermates, but in a couple of days, with love and patience on your part, the transition will be complete.

First impressions are important, especially from the puppy's point of view, and these may very well set the pattern of his future relationship with you. You must be consistent in the

A crate, for home and travel, is standard equipment and makes an excellent gift for the new dog owner.

way you handle your pet so that he learns what is expected of him. He must come to trust and respect you as his keeper and master. Provide him with proper care and attention, and you will be rewarded with a loyal companion for many years. Considering the needs of your puppy and planning ahead will surely make the change from his former home to his new one easier.

ADVANCE PREPARATION

In preparing for your puppy's arrival, perhaps more important than anything else is to find out from the seller how the pup was maintained. What brand of food was offered and when and how often was the puppy fed? Has

the pup been housebroken; if so, what method was employed? Attempt to continue whatever routine was started by the person from whom you bought your puppy; then, gradually, you can make those changes that suit you and your lifestyle. If, for example, the puppy has been paper trained, plan to stock up on newspaper. Place this newspaper toilet facility in a selected spot so that your puppy learns to use the designated area as his "bathroom." And keep on hand a supply of the dog food to which he is accustomed, as a sudden switch to new food could cause digestive upsets.

Another consideration is sleeping and resting quarters. Be sure to supply a dog bed for your pup, and introduce him to his special cozy corner so that he

A warm bed, equipped with a ticking clock, chew bone, and safe dog toy, can help a pup feel secure and welcome in its new home.

knows where to retire when he feels like taking a snooze. You'll need to buy a collar (or harness) and leash, a safe chew item (such as Nylabone® or Gumabone®), and a few grooming tools as well. A couple of sturdy feeding dishes, one for food and one for water, will be needed; and it will be necessary, beforehand, to set up a feeding station.

FINDING A VETERINARIAN

An important part of your preparations should include finding a local veterinarian who can provide quality health care in the form of routine check-ups, inoculations, and prompt medical attention in case of illness or an emergency. Find out if the animal you have selected has been vaccinated against canine diseases, and make certain you secure all health certificates at the time of purchase. This information will be valuable to your veterinarian, who will want to know the puppy's complete medical history. Incidentally, don't wait until your puppy becomes sick before you seek the services of a vet; make an appointment for your pup before or soon after he takes up residence with you so that he starts out with a clean bill of health in his new home.

CHILDREN AND PUPPIES

Prepare the young members of the household on pet care. Children should learn not only to love their charges but to respect them and treat them with the consideration one would give all living things. It must be emphasized to youngsters that the puppy has certain needs, just as humans have, and all family members must take an active role in ensuring that these needs are met. Someone must feed the puppy. Someone must walk him a couple of times a day or clean up after him if he is trained to relieve himself on newspaper. Someone must groom his coat, clean his ears, and clip his nails from time to time. Someone

must see to it that the puppy gets sufficient exercise and attention each day.

A child who has a pet to care for learns responsibility; nonetheless, parental guidance is an essential part of his learning experience. Many a child has been known to "love a pet to death," squeezing and hugging the animal in ways which are irritating or even painful. Others have been found guilty of teasing, perhaps unintentionally, and disturbing their pet while the animal is eating or resting. One must teach a child, therefore, when and how to gently stroke and fondle a puppy. In time, the child can learn how to carefully pick up and handle the pup. A dog should always be supported with both hands, *not* lifted by the scruff of the neck. One hand placed under the chest, between the front legs, and the other hand supporting the dog's rear end will be comfortable and will restrain the animal as you hold and carry him. Always demonstrate to children the proper way to lift a dog.

BE A GOOD NEIGHBOR

For the sake of your dog's safety and well being, don't allow him to wander onto the property of others. Keep him confined at all times to your own yard or indoors where he won't become a nuisance. Consider what

Evident in this photo, the adult Shar-pei is much less wrinkled than the Shar-pei puppy although no less irresistible.

Many dangers lurk around the house. Keep all poisonous substances and sharp objects away from your curious pup.

dangers lie ahead for an unleashed dog that has total freedom of the great outdoors, particularly when he is unsupervised by his master. There are cars and trucks to dodge on the streets and highways. There are stray animals with which to wrangle. There are poisons all around, such as car antifreeze in driveways or toxic plants and shrubs, which, if swallowed, could prove fatal. There are dognappers and sadistic people who may steal or bring harm to your beloved pet. In short, there are all sorts of nasty things waiting to hurt him. Did you know that if your dog consumes rotting garbage, there is the possibility he could go into shock or even die? And are you aware that a dog left to roam in a wooded area or field could become infected with any number of parasites if he plays with or ingests some small prey, such as a rabbit, that might be carrying these parasitic organisms? A thorn from a rosebush imbedded in the dog's foot pad, tar from a newly paved road stuck to his coat, and a wound inflicted by a wild animal all can be avoided if you take the precaution of keeping your dog in a safe enclosure where he will be protected from such dangers. Don't let your dog run loose; he is likely to stray from home and get into all sorts of trouble.

Clockwise from upper right: *pokeweed, jimson weed, foxglove,* and *yew.* If ingested, a toxic plant can be dangerous to your dog.

The New Family Member

GETTING ACQUAINTED

Plan to bring your new pet home in the morning so that by nightfall he will have had some time to become acquainted with you and his new environment. Avoid introducing the pup to the family around holiday time, since all of the extra excitement will only add to the confusion and frighten him. Let the puppy enter your home on a day when the

Resist the temptation to handle him too much during these first few days. And, if there are other dogs or animals around the house, make certain all are properly introduced. If you observe fighting among the animals, or some other problem, you may have to separate all parties until they learn to accept one another. Remember that neglecting your other pets while

routine is normal. For those people who work during the week, a Saturday morning is an ideal time to bring the puppy to his new home; this way he has the entire weekend to make adjustments before being left alone for a few hours, come Monday morning.

Let the puppy explore, under your watchful eye of course, and let him come to know his new home without stress and fear.

Pictured here as a puppy, Ch. Temple Toi Talala—a Shar-pei of particular promise owned by Ann Coleman, Tail's End Shar-Pei.

Facing page: *The appeal and charm of the Chinese Shar-pei puppy are seemingly unending. Defying description and sensibility, these two puppies exemplify such ineffability.*

showering the new puppy with extra attention will only cause animosity and jealousy. Make an effort to pay special attention to the other animals as well.

On that eventful first night, try not to give in and let the puppy sleep with you; otherwise, this could become a difficult habit to break. Let him cry and whimper, even if it means a night of restlessness for the entire family. Some people have had success with putting a doll or a hot water bottle wrapped in a towel in the puppy's bed as a surrogate mother, while others have placed a ticking alarm clock in the bed to simulate the heartbeat of the pup's dam and littermates. Remember that this furry little fellow is used to the warmth and security of his mother and siblings, so the adjustment to sleeping alone will take time. Select a location away from drafts and away from the feeding station for placement of his dog bed. Keep in mind, also, that the bed should be roomy enough for him to stretch out in; as he grows older, you may need to supply a larger one.

Prior to the pup's arrival, set up his room and partition it the way you would to keep an infant out of a particular area. You may want to keep his bed, his feeding station, and his toilet area all in the same room—in separate locations—or you may want to set the feeding station up in your kitchen, where meals for all family members are served. Whatever you decide, do it ahead of time so you will have that much less to worry about when your puppy finally moves in with you.

Above all else, be patient with your puppy as he adjusts to life in his new home. If you purchase a pup that is not housebroken, you will have to spend time with the dog—just as you would with a small child—until he develops proper toilet habits. Even a housebroken puppy may feel nervous in strange new surroundings and have an occasional accident. Praise and encouragement will elicit far better results than punishment or scolding. Remember that your puppy wants nothing more than to please you, thus he is anxious to learn the behavior that is required of him.

Feeding Requirements

Perhaps more than any other single aspect of your dog's development, proper feeding requires an educated and responsible dog owner. The importance of nutrition on your dog's bone and muscle growth cannot be over emphasized.

Soon after your puppy comes to live with you, he will need to be fed. Remember to ask the seller what foods were given to the youngster and stay with that diet for a while. It is important for the puppy to keep eating and to avoid skipping a meal, so entice him with the food to which he is accustomed. If you prefer to switch to some other brand of dog food, each day begin to add small quantities of the new brand to the usual food offering. Make the portions of the new food progressively larger until the pup is weaned from his former diet.

What should you feed the puppy and how often? His diet is really quite simple and relatively inexpensive to prepare. Puppies need to be fed small portions at frequent intervals, since they are growing and their activity level is high. You must ensure that your pup gains weight steadily; with an adult dog, however, growth slows down and weight must be regulated to prevent obesity and a host of other problems. At one time, it was thought that home-cooked meals were the answer, with daily rations of meat,

The canine digestive system is adapted for omnivorous eating habits. Canines require both animal and vegetable matter for good health.

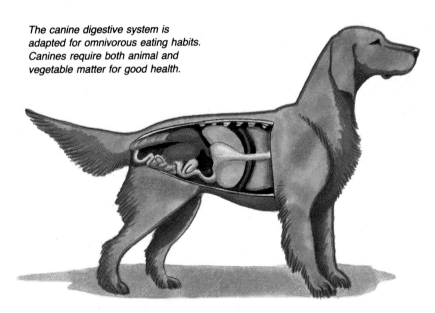

Feeding Requirements

vegetables, egg yolk, cereal, cheese, brewer's yeast, and vitamin supplements. With all of the nutritionally complete commercial dog food products readily available, these time-consuming preparations really are unnecessary now. A great deal of money and research has resulted in foods that we can serve our dogs with confidence and pride; and most of these commercial foods have been developed along strict guidelines according to the size, weight, and age of your dog. These products are reasonably priced, easy to find, and convenient to store.

THE PUPPY'S MEALS

After a puppy has been fully weaned from its mother until approximately three months of age, it needs to be fed four times a day. In the morning and evening offer kibble (dog meal) soaked in hot water or broth, to which you have added some canned meat-based food or fresh raw meat cut into small chunks. At noon and bedtime feed him a bit of kibble or whole-grain cereal moistened with milk (moistening, by the way, makes the food easier to digest, since dogs don't typically chew their food). From three to six months, increase the portion size and

The famous Ernest Albright portrayed here with some of his foundation Shar-pei of the 1970s. In 1986, Albright was elected President Emeritus and Honary Lifetime Director of the Shar-Pei Club of America, the organization he founded in 12 years prior.

An extraordinary specimen, this is three-month-old Remington's Earth Angel, possibly one of the most outstanding puppies to be produced at this kennel.

offer just three meals—one milk and two meat. At six months, two meals are sufficient; at one year, a single meal can be given, supplemented with a few dry biscuits in the morning and evening. During the colder months, especially if your dog is active, you might want to mix in some wheat germ oil or corn oil or bacon drippings with the meal to add extra calories. Remember to keep a bowl of cool, fresh water on hand always to help your dog regulate its body temperature and to aid in digestion.

From one year on, you may continue feeding the mature dog a single meal (in the evening, perhaps, when you have your supper), or you may prefer to divide this meal in two, offering half in the morning and the other half at night. Keep in mind that while puppies require foods in small chunks, or nuggets, older dogs can handle larger pieces of food at mealtime. Discuss your dog's feeding schedule with your veterinarian; he can make suggestions about the right diet for your particular canine friend.

COMPARISON SHOPPING

With so many fine dog-food products on the market today, there is something for

Feeding Requirements

everyone's pet. You may want to serve dry food "as is" or mix it with warm water or broth. Perhaps you'll choose to combine dry food with fresh or canned preparations. Some canned foods contain all meat, but they are not complete; others are mixtures of meat and grains, which have been fortified with additional nutrients to make them more complete and balanced. There are also various packaged foods that can be served alone or as supplements and that can be left out for a few hours without spoiling. This self-feeding method, which works well for dogs that are not prone to weight problems, allows the animal to serve himself whenever he feels hungry. Many people who work during the day find these dry or semi-moist rations convenient to use, and these foods are great to bring along if you travel with your dog.

Be sure to read the labels carefully before you make your dog-food purchases. Most

Pet shops offer a large selection of quality bowls that are efficient and affordable. Offered in a wide variety of colors, bowls are easy to coordinate.

Vegetables, grains, meats and dairy products are all vital components of your dog's diet. Fortunately, commercial dog foods are nutritionally balanced and easily digestible.

reputable pet-food manufacturers list the ingredients and the nutritional content right on the can or package. Instructions are usually included so that you will know how much to feed your dog to keep him thriving and in top condition. A varied, well-balanced diet that supplies the proper amounts of protein, carbohydrate, fat, vitamins, minerals, and water is important to keep your puppy healthy and to guarantee his normal development. Adjustments to the diet can be made, under your veterinarian's supervision, according to the individual puppy, his rate of growth, his activity level, and so on. Liquid or powder vitamin and mineral supplements, or those in tablet form, are available and can be given if you need to feel certain that the diet is balanced.

The Shar-Pei's unique appearance and delightful disposition have made the breed quite in vogue in recent times. Here Legibach's Lady Prunella at six months of age enjoys some very special attention. Owners, Pat and Gina Leone.

DEVELOPING GOOD EATING HABITS

Try to serve your puppy his meals at the same time each day and in the same location so that he will get used to his daily routine and develop good eating habits. A bit of raw egg, cottage cheese, or table scraps (leftover food from your own meals) can

Feeding your dog need not be a messy chore, provided that non-tipping, easy-clean bowls are used for each meal.

be offered from time to time; but never accustom your dog to eating human "junk food." Cake, candy, chocolate, soda, and other snack foods are for people, not dogs. Besides, these foods provide only "empty" calories that your pet doesn't need if he is to stay healthy. Avoid offering spicy, fried, fatty, or starchy foods; rather, offer leftover meats, vegetables, and gravies. Get in the habit of feeding your puppy or your grown dog his *own* daily meals of dog food. If ever you are in doubt about what foods and how much to serve, consult your veterinarian.

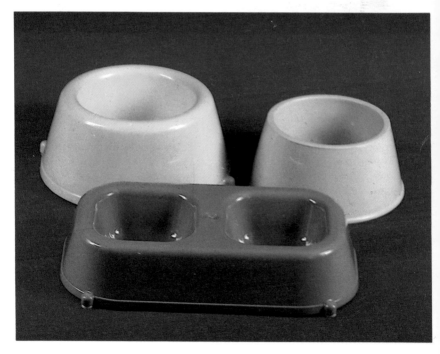

Feeding Requirements

A pet nurser enables you to feed pups that have difficulty nursing from their mother and also helps with the weaning process.

FEEDING GUIDELINES

Some things to bear in mind with regard to your dog's feeding regimen follow.

- Nutritional balance, provided by many commercial dog foods, is vital; avoid feeding a one-sided all-meat diet. Variety in the kinds of meat (beef, lamb, chicken, liver) or cereal grains (wheat, oats, corn) that you offer your dog is of secondary importance compared to the balance or "completeness" of dietary components.

- Always refrigerate opened canned food so that it doesn't spoil. Remember to remove all uneaten portions of canned or moistened food from the feeding dish as soon as the pup has finished his meal. Discard the leftover food immediately and thoroughly wash and dry the feeding dish, as a dirty dish is a breeding ground for harmful germs.

- When offering dry foods, always keep a supply of water on hand for your dog. Water should be made available at all times, even if dry foods are not left out for self-feeding. Each day the water dish should be washed with soap and hot water, rinsed well, and dried; a refill of clean, fresh water should be provided daily.

- Food and water should be served at room temperature, neither too hot nor too cold, so that it is more palatable for your puppy.

- Serve your pup's meals in sturdy hard-plastic, stainless steel, or earthenware containers, ones that won't tip over as the dog gulps his food down. Some bowls and dishes are weighted to prevent spillage, while others fit neatly into holders which offer support. Feeding dishes should be large enough to hold each meal.

- Whenever the nutritional needs of your dog change—

that is to say, when it grows older or if it becomes ill, obese, or pregnant; or if it starts to nurse its young—special diets are in order. Always contact your vet for advice on these special dietary requirements.

- Feed your puppy at the same regular intervals each day; reserve treats for special

given the chance, he will accept and relish every in-between-meal tidbit you offer him. This pampering will only put extra weight on your pet and cause him to be unhealthy in the long run.

- Do not encourage your dog to beg for food from the table while you are eating your meals.

occasions or, perhaps, to reward good behavior during training sessions.

- Hard foods, such as biscuits and dog meal, should be offered regularly. Chewing on these hard, dry morsels helps the dog keep its teeth clean and its gums conditioned.
- Never overfeed your dog. If

Metal bowls are long lasting and easy to clean. Feeding and water bowls should be washed with soap and warm water and then rinsed on a regular basis.

FEEDING CHART

Age and No. of Feedings Per Day	Weight in Lbs.	Weight in Kg.	Caloric Requirement kcal M.E./Day
Puppies—Weaning to 3 months Four per day	1–3 3–6 6–12 12–20 15–30	.5–1.4 1.4–2.7 2.7–5.4 5.4–9.1 6.8–13.6	124–334 334–574 574–943 943–1384 1113–1872
Puppies—3 to 6 months Three per day	3–10 5–15 12–25 20–40 30–70	1.4–4.5 2.3–6.8 5.4–11.3 9.1–18.2 13.6–31.8	334–816 494–1113 943–1645 1384–2352 1872–3542
Puppies—6 to 12 months Two per day	6–12 12–25 20–50 40–70 70–100	2.7–5.4 5.4–11.3 9.1–22.7 18.2–31.8 31.8–45.4	574–943 943–1645 1384–2750 2352–3542 3542–4640
Normally Active Adults One or two per day	6–12 12–25 25–50 50–90 90–175	2.7–5.4 5.4–11.3 11.3–22.7 22.7–40.8 40.8–79.4	286–472 472–823 823–1375 1375–2151 2151–3675

This chart presents general parameters of a dog's caloric requirements, based on weight. The total caloric intake comes from a complete, balanced diet of quality foods. To assist owners, dog food companies generally provide the nutritional information of their product right on the label.

Accommodations

Puppies newly weaned from their mother and siblings should be kept warm at all times. As they get older, they can be acclimated gradually to cooler temperatures. When you purchase your dog, find out from the seller whether he is hardy and can withstand the rigors of outdoor living. Many breeds have been known to adapt well to a surprising number of invest in a crate for him to call his "home" whenever he needs to be confined for short intervals. You might plan to partition off a special room, or part of a room, for your pooch; or you may find that a heated garage or finished basement works well as your dog's living quarters. If your breed can tolerate living outside, you may want to buy or build him his own dog house with an

environments, so long as they are given time to adjust. If your pup is to be an indoor companion, perhaps a dog bed in the corner of the family room will suffice; or you may want to

A bed for your dog gives him a place to call his own. His bed should be placed in a warm, dry, draft-free location.

Accommodations

attached run. It might be feasible to place his house in your fenced-in backyard. The breed that can live outdoors fares well when given access to some sort of warm, dry shelter during periods of inclement weather. As you begin thinking about where your canine friend will spend most of his time, you'll want to consider his breed, his age, his temperament, his need for exercise, and the money, space, and resources you have available to house him.

THE DOG BED

In preparing for your puppy's arrival, it is recommended that a dog bed be waiting for him so that he has a place to sleep and rest. If you have provided him with his own bed or basket, ensure that it is placed in a warm, dry, draft-free spot that is private but at the same time near the center of family activity. Refrain from placing his bed near the feed and water dishes or his toilet area. You may want to give your puppy something with

Dog beds come in a variety of sizes and styles and are easily acquired at your local pet shop. Choose one that will accommodate your puppy when he has reached his full-grown size.

Use discretion when giving your dog a toy. Children's toys are not puppies' toys. A pup can easily remove and ingest a button-eye, causing serious complications and even death.

which to snuggle, such as a laundered towel or blanket or an article of old clothing. Some dogs have been known to chew apart their beds and bedding, but you can easily channel this chewing energy into more constructive behavior simply by supplying him with some safe toys or a Nylabone® pacifier for gnawing. Pet shops stock dog beds, among other supplies that you might need for your pup. Select a bed that is roomy, comfortable, and easy to clean, keeping in mind that you may have to replace the smaller bed with a larger one as the puppy grows to adulthood. Remember to clean and disinfect the bed and sleeping area from time to time, as these can become parasitic playgrounds for fleas, lice, mites, and the like.

Accommodations

THE CRATE

Although many dog lovers may cringe at the mere mention of the word *crate*, thinking of it as a cage or a cruel means of confinement, this handy piece of equipment can be put to good use for puppies and grown dogs alike. Even though you may love your dog to an extraordinary degree, you may not want him to have free rein of the house, particularly when you are not home to supervise him. If used properly, a crate can restrict your dog when it is not convenient to have him underfoot, *i.e.,* when guests are visiting or during your mealtimes.

A surprising number of dog owners, who originally had negative feelings about crating their dogs, have had great success using crates. The crate itself serves as a bed, provided it is furnished with bedding material, or it can be used as an indoor dog house. Not all dogs readily accept crates or being confined in them for short intervals, so for these dogs, another means of restriction must be found. But for those dogs that do adjust to spending

Crates allow for safe and easy travel and aid in the housebreaking process. Crates come in a variety of sizes, styles and colors.

time in these structures, the crate can be useful in many ways. The animal can be confined for a few hours while you are away from home or at work, or you can bring your crated dog along with you in the car when you travel or go on vacation. Crates also prove handy as carriers whenever you have to transport a sick dog to the veterinarian.

Most crates are made of sturdy wire or plastic, and some of the collapsible models can be conveniently stored or folded so that they can be moved easily from room to room or from inside the house to the yard on a warm, sunny day. If you allow your puppy or grown dog to become acquainted with its crate by cleverly propping the door open and leaving some of his favorite toys inside, in no time he will come to regard the crate as his own doggie haven. As with a dog bed, place the crate away from drafts in a dry, warm spot; refrain from placing food and water dishes in it, as these only crowd the space and offer opportunity for spillage.

If you need to confine your puppy so that he can't get into mischief while you're not home, remember to consider the animal's needs at all times. Select a large crate, one in which the dog can stand up and move around comfortably; in fact, bigger is better in this context.

The crate you choose for your dog should be appropriately sized. A crate can provide the new pet with a sense of security and belonging. Easily accessible, crates are an inexpensive, sensible investment.

Never leave the animal confined for more than a few hours at a time without letting him out to exercise, play, and, if necessary, relieve himself. Never crate a dog for ten hours, for example, unless you keep the door to the crate open so that he can get out for food and water and to stretch a bit. If long intervals of confinement are necessary, consider placing the unlatched crate in a partitioned section of your house or apartment.

Crates have become the answer for many a dog owner faced with the dilemma of either getting rid of a destructive dog or living with him despite his bad habits. People who have neither the time nor the patience to train their dogs, or to modify undesirable behavior patterns, can at least restrain their pets during the times they can't be there to supervise. So long as the crate is used in a humane fashion, whereby a dog is confined for no more than a few hours at any one time, it can figure importantly in a dog owner's life. Show dogs, incidentally, learn at an early age that much time will be spent in and out of crates while they are on the show circuit. Many canine celebrities are kept in their crates until they are called to ringside, and they spend many hours crated to and from the shows.

THE DOG HOUSE

These structures, often made of wood, should be sturdy and

Consider your dog's present and fully grown size before purchasing the proper crate for him.

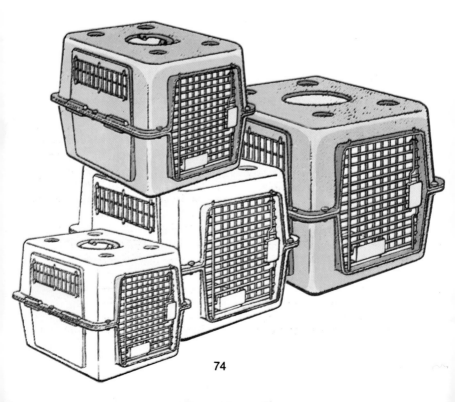

Commercial dog houses are designed for comfort and pest control.

offer enough room for your dog to stretch out in when it rests or sleeps. Dog houses that are elevated or situated on a platform protect the animal from cold and dampness that may seep through the ground. Of the breeds that are temperature hardy and will live outdoors, some are housed outside during the daytime only; others are permanent outdoor residents day and night, all year 'round.

If your intention is to have a companion that lives out-of-doors, it will be necessary to provide him with a more elaborate house, one that really protects him from the elements. Make sure the dog's house is constructed of waterproof materials. Furnish him with sufficient bedding to burrow into on a chilly night and provide extra insulation to keep out drafts and wet weather. Add a partition (a kind of room divider which separates the entry area from the main sleeping space) inside his house or attach a swinging door to the entrance to help keep him warm when he is inside his residence. The swinging door facilitates entry to and from the dog house, while at the same time it provides protection, particularly from wind and drafts.

Some fortunate owners whose yards are enclosed by high fencing allow their dogs complete freedom within the boundaries of their property. In these situations, a dog can leave his dog house and get all the exercise he wants. Of course such a large space requires more effort to keep it clean. An alternative to complete backyard freedom is a dog kennel or run which attaches to or surrounds the dog's house. This restricts some forms of movement, such as running, perhaps, but it does provide ample room for walking, climbing, jumping, and stretching. Another option is to fence off part of the yard and place the dog house in the enclosure. If you need to tether your dog to its house, make certain to use a fairly long lead so as not to hamper the animal's need to move and exercise his limbs.

A thick drape hung over the entrance to the dog's house will prevent drafts, thus keeping your dog warm and dry.

CLEANLINESS

No matter where your dog lives, either in or out of your home, be sure to keep him in surroundings that are as clean and sanitary as possible. His excrement should be removed and disposed of every day without fail. No dog should be forced to lie in his own feces. If your dog lives in his own house, the floor should be swept occasionally and the bedding should be changed regularly if it becomes soiled. Food and water dishes need to be scrubbed with hot water and detergent and rinsed well to remove all traces of soap. The water dish should be refilled with a supply of fresh water. The dog and his environment must be kept free of parasites (especially fleas and mosquitoes, which can carry disease) with products designed to keep these pests under control. Dog crates need frequent scrubbing, too, as do the floors of kennels and runs. Your pet must be kept clean and comfortable at all times; if you exercise strict sanitary control, you will keep disease and parasite infestation to a minimum.

Just as grooming and bathing keep your dog in a healthy condition, regular cleaning and disinfecting of his living area are important for his overall health. Many dogs that suffer from depression are subjected to

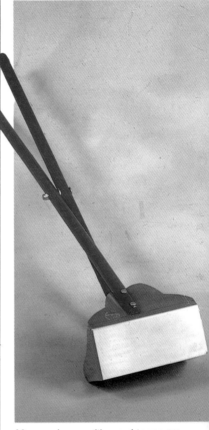

More and more cities and towns are requiring dog owners to clean up after their pets. Commercial pooper scoopers can make the clean-up easy and efficient. They are also helpful for backyard sanitation.

poorly maintained quarters. Your dog's physical and psychological well being are closely related. A clean dog is a healthy and happy dog.

Accommodations

EXERCISE

A well-balanced diet and regular medical attention from a qualified veterinarian are essential in promoting good health for your dog, but so is daily exercise to keep him fit and mentally alert. Dogs that have been confined all day while their owners are at work or school need special attention. There should be some time set aside make this daily ritual more pleasant both for themselves and their canine companions by combining the walk with a little "roughhousing," that is to say, a bit of fun and togetherness.

Whenever possible, take a stroll to an empty lot, a playground, or a nearby park. Attach a long lead to your dog's collar, and let him run and jump and tone his body through

Large outdoor pens are used by many breeding, boarding, and medical professionals. Always inspect the facility before leaving your dog in any professional's care.

each day for play—a romp with a family member, perhaps. Not everyone is lucky enough to let his dog run through an open meadow or along a sandy beach, but even a ten-minute walk in the fresh air will do. Dogs that are house-bound, particularly those that live in apartments, need to be walked out-of-doors after each meal so that they can relieve themselves. Owners can aerobic activity. This will help him burn calories and will keep him trim, and it will also help relieve tension and stress that may have had a chance to develop while you were away all day. For people who work Monday through Friday, weekend jaunts can be especially beneficial, since there will be more time to spend with your canine friend. You might

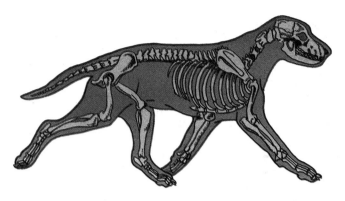

Responsible breeding practices, regular exercise, and proper nutrition all contribute to sound bone development.

want to engage him in a simple game of fetch with a stick or a rubber ball. Even such basic tricks as rolling over, standing on the hindlegs, or jumping up (all of which can be done inside the home as well) can provide additional exercise. But if you plan to challenge your dog with a real workout to raise his heart rate, remember not to push him too hard without first warming up with a brisk walk. Don't forget to "cool him down" afterwards with a rhythmic trot until his heart rate returns to normal. Some dog owners jog with their dogs or take them along on bicycle excursions.

At the very least, however, play with your dog every day to keep him in good shape physically and mentally. If you can walk him outdoors, or better yet run with him in a more vigorous activity, by all means do it. Don't neglect your pet and leave him confined

The knee joint is also known as the stifle joint. It is formed by the articulation of the upper and lower leg.

Accommodations

for long periods without attention from you or time for exercise.

EXERCISING FOR YOU AND YOUR DOG

Dogs are like people. They come in three weights: overweight, underweight, and the correct weight. It is fair to say that most dogs are in better shape than most humans who own them. The reason for this is that most dogs accept exercise without objection—people do not! Follow your dog's lead towards exercise and the complete enjoyment of the outdoors—your dog is the ideal work-out partner. There are toys at your local pet shop which are designed just for that purpose: to allow you to play and exercise with your dog. Here are a few recommended exercise toys for you and your dog.

Flying discs can make exercise exciting.

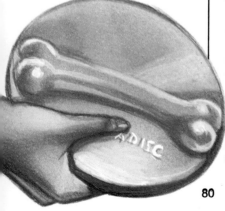

Frisbee® Flying Discs*

Who hasn't seen or heard of a Frisbee® flying disc? This flying-saucer–like toy is available in three or more sizes. The small size is 10 cm (4″); the medium size is about 15 cm (6″) and the larger size is 23 cm (9″). The size of the flying disc has little to do with the size of the dog—small puppies chase anything; some larger dogs chase nothing. The advantage of the larger disc is that it is the same size as the toy made for humans only! Start with the size that you think is best suited for your dog. What is much more important is the material from which the flying disc is made; *soft un-chew-worthy plastic flying discs are not good for dogs.*

Most people play with these polyethylene discs and use these same discs to play with their dogs. Polyethylene plastic discs usually last an hour or so. Every time the dog grabs it, his teeth dig into the cheap plastic, leaving an imprint. In a short while the disc is not useable— and even worse, it may be dangerous, since the dog can break off a chunk and swallow it, or the distorted disc can swerve out of control and hit someone.

*Frisbee® is a trademark of the Kransco Company, California, and is used for their brand of flying disc.

Be sure that you do not throw the flying disc where your dog can injure himself. Open spaces where cars are not permitted or a park are most ideal.

Nylon Discs

Your pet shop will have a nylon disc that has a dog bone molded into the top of it. While this may look silly at first, the advantage is simple. When a typical Frisbee® lands on a flat surface, the dog may be unable to grasp it with its mouth or turn it over with its paw. Thus frustrated, the dog loses interest in the game and you will have to fetch it yourself. The nylon disc with the bone molded into the top of it allows the dog the option of flipping it over with its paw or grasping it with its mouth. It also has more capacity; thus you can use it as a food or water dish on these outings. The nylon disc may also be flavored and scented, besides being annealed, so your dog can find it more easily if it gets lost in the woods or high grass.

Accommodations

Polyurethane Flexible Floppy Flying Discs

The greatest advance in flying discs came with the manufacture of these discs from polyurethane. The polyurethane is so soft that it doesn't hurt you, your dog, or the window it might strike accidentally. Only very, very rarely can it break a window—usually one that was already cracked. The polyurethane Gumadisc® is floppy and soft. It can be folded

Gumabone® flying discs are proven safe and durable for dogs. The soft, pliable texture and the scent impregnation make these discs loved by dogs.

and fits into your pocket. It is also much tougher than cheap plastics, and most pet shops guarantee that it will last ten times longer than cheap plastic discs.

With most flying discs made for dogs comes an instruction booklet on how to use the disc with your canine friend. Basically, you play with the dog and the disc so the dog knows the disc belongs to him. Then you throw it continuously, increasing the distance, so that the dog fetches it and brings it back to you.

The exercise for you comes in when your dog stops fetching it, or when you have a partner. The two of you play catch. You stand as far apart as available space allows—usually 30–35 m (100 feet) is more than enough room. You throw the disc to each other, arousing your dog's interest as he tries to catch it. When the disc is dropped or veers off, the dog grabs it and brings it back (hopefully). Obviously you will have to run to catch the disc before your dog does.

There are contests held all over the world where distance, height, and other characteristics are measured competitively. Ask your local pet shop to help you locate a Frisbee® Club near you.

*Frisbee® is a trademark of the Kransco Company, California, and is used for their brand of flying disc.

Many owners complain that plastic flying discs are destroyed quickly by their dogs, making an otherwise fun pastime an expensive outing. Flying discs made of annealed nylon are proven to last longer and thereby provide hours of enjoyable, affordable exercise for you and your dog.

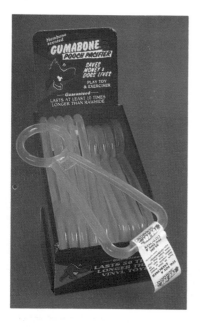

Tug Toys

A tug toy is a hard rubber, cheap plastic, or polyurethane toy which allows a dog and his owner to have a game of tug-o-war. The owner grips one end while the dog grips the other— then they pull. The polyurethane flexible tug toy is the best on the market at the present time. Your pet shop will have one to show you. The polyurethane toys are clear in color and stay soft forever. Cheap plastic tug toys are indisputably dangerous, and the hard-rubber tug toys get brittle too fast and are too stiff for most dogs; however, there *is* a difference in price—just ask the advice of any shop operator.

Most every dog loves a challenging tug of war. Tug toys of sturdy polyurethane and strong cotton floss are favorites of many dogs.

Balls made of annealed nylon make fetching safe, pleasing and hygienic for your dog. Their virtually indestructible construction prevents the dog from tearing pieces of the ball and ingesting them, and the appealing scent inspires an enthusiastic retrieve. When worn, as shown here, nylon balls should be replaced with new ones.

Balls

Nobody has to tell you about playing ball with your dog. The reminder you may need is that you should not throw the ball where traffic might interfere with the dog's catching or fetching of it. The ball should not be cheap plastic (a dog's worst enemy as far as toys are concerned) but made of a substantial material. Balls made of nylon are practically indestructible, but they are very hard and must be rolled, never thrown. The same balls made of polyurethane are great—they bounce and are soft. The Nylabone® and Gumabone® balls are scented and flavored, and dogs can easily find them when lost.

Other manufacturers make balls of almost every substance, including plastic, cotton, and wood. Billiard balls, baseballs, tennis balls, and so on, have all been used by dog owners who want their dogs to play with them in a game of catch. A strong caveat is that you use only those balls made especially for dogs.

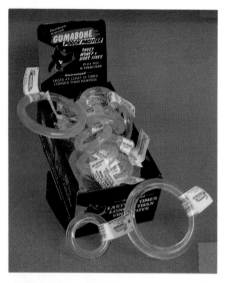

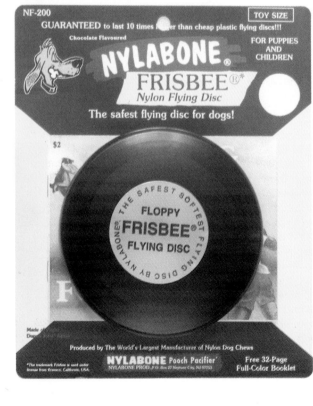

With the variety of safe, exercise-oriented chew products available, there is little excuse for a sedentary, plaque-infested existence to persist in an otherwise healthy dog.

Housebreaking and Training

Housebreaking can be the groundwork on which all future training is based. The two most commonly recommended methods involve paper training and crate training. When paper training is used, owners often employ litter boxes lined with paper to limit the area and make clean-up fast and easy.

HOUSEBREAKING

The new addition to your family may already have received some basic house training before his arrival in your home. If he has not, remember that a puppy will want to relieve himself about half a dozen times a day; it is up to you to specify where and when he should "do his business." Housebreaking is your first training concern and should begin the moment you bring the puppy home.

Ideally, puppies should be taken outdoors after meals, as a full stomach will exert pressure on the bladder and colon. What goes into the dog must eventually come out; the period after his meal is the most natural and appropriate time. When he eliminates, he should be praised, for this will increase the likelihood of the same thing happening after every meal. He should also be encouraged to use the same area and will probably be attracted to it after frequent use.

Some veterinarians maintain that a puppy can learn to urinate and defecate on command, if properly trained. The advantage of this conditioning technique is that your pet will associate the act of elimination with a particular word of your choice rather than with a particular time or place which might not always be convenient or available. So whether you are visiting an unfamiliar place or don't want to go outside with your dog in sub-zero temperatures, he will still be able to relieve himself when he hears the specific command word. Elimination will occur after this "trigger" phrase or word sets up a conditioned reflex in the dog, who will eliminate anything contained in his bladder or bowel upon hearing it. The shorter the word, the more you can repeat it and imprint it on your dog's memory.

Your chosen command word should be given simultaneously with the sphincter opening events in order to achieve perfect and rapid conditioning. This is why it is important to familiarize yourself with the tell-tale signs preceding your puppy's elimination process. Then you will be prepared to say the word at the crucial moment. There is usually a sense of urgency on the dog's part; he may follow a sniffing and circling pattern which you will soon recognize. It is important to use the command in his usual area only when you know the puppy

can eliminate, i.e., when his stomach or bladder is full. He will soon learn to associate the act with the word. One word of advice, however, if you plan to try out this method: never use the puppy's name or any other word which he might frequently hear about the house—you can imagine the result!

Finally, remember that any training takes time. Such a conditioned response can be obtained with intensive practice with any normal, healthy dog over six weeks of age. Even Pavlov's salivating dogs required fifty repetitions before the desired response was achieved. Patience and persistence will eventually produce results—do not lose heart!

Indoors, sheets of newspapers can be used to cover the specific area where your dog should relieve himself. These should be placed some distance away from his sleeping and feeding area, as a puppy will not urinate or defecate where he eats. When the newspapers are changed, the bottom papers should be placed on top of the new ones in order to reinforce the purpose of the papers by scent as well as by sight. The puppy should be praised during or immediately after he has made use of this particular part of the room. Each positive reinforcement increases the possibility of his using that area again.

When he arrives, it is advisable to limit the puppy to one room, usually the kitchen, as it most likely has a linoleum or easily washable floor surface. Given the run of the house, the sheer size of the place will seem overwhelming and confusing and he might leave his "signature"

PATIENCE, PERSISTENCE, AND PRAISE

As with a human baby, you must be patient, tolerant, and understanding of your pet's mistakes, making him feel loved and wanted, not rejected and isolated. You wouldn't hit a baby for soiling his diapers, as you

An anchored lead can be the solution to a yard without a fence.

on your furniture or clothes! There will be time later to familiarize him gradually with his new surroundings.

would realize that he was not yet able to control his bowel movements; be as compassionate with your canine infant. Never rub his nose in his excreta. Never indulge in the common practice of punishing him with a rolled-up newspaper. Never hit a puppy with your hand. He will only become "hand-shy" and learn to fear you. Usually the punishment is meted out sometime after the offense and loses its efficacy, as the bewildered dog cannot connect the two events. Moreover, by association, he will soon learn to be afraid of you and anything to do with newspapers—including, perhaps, that area where he is *supposed* to relieve himself!

Most puppies are eager to please. Praise, encouragement, and reward (particularly the food variety) will produce far better results than any scolding or physical punishment. Moreover, it is far better to dissuade your puppy from doing certain things, such as chewing on chair legs or other furniture, by making those objects particularly distasteful to him. Some pet shops stock bitter apple sprays or citronella compounds for application to furniture legs. If these are ineffective, you could smear them with a generous amount of hot chili sauce or cayenne pepper mixed with petroleum jelly, for example. This would make it seem as if the object itself was administering the

From the moment you bring your dog home, the rules of the house must be enforced to ensure a consistently obedient home companion.

Professionals cite that housebreaking on newspapers can cause some dogs to believe that it is always okay to excrete on papers, regardless of location. Housebreaking pads are used by many cautious owners.

punishment whenever he attempted to chew it. He probably wouldn't need a second reminder!

Remember that the reason a dog has housebreaking or behavior problems is because his owner has allowed them to develop. This is why you must begin as you intend to continue, letting your dog know what is acceptable and unacceptable behavior. It is also important that you be consistent in your demands; you cannot feed him from the dining room table one day and then punish him when he begs for food from your dinner guests.

TRAINING

You will want the newest member of your family to be welcomed by everyone; this will not happen if he urinates in every room of the house or barks all night! He needs training in the correct forms of behavior in this new human world. You cannot expect your puppy to become the perfect pet overnight. He needs your help in his socialization process. Training greatly facilitates and enhances the relationship of the dog to his owner and to the rest of society. A successfully trained dog can be taken anywhere and behave well with anyone. Indeed, it is that one crucial word—*training*—which can transform an aggressive animal into a peaceful, well-behaved pet. Now, how does this "transformation" take place?

Some owners of small dogs use a figure-eight-style harness as a means of restraint.

Collars should always be worn, with identification tag and license attached.

WHEN AND HOW TO TRAIN

Like housebreaking, training should begin as soon as the puppy enters the house. The formal training sessions should be short but frequent, for example, ten to fifteen minute periods three times a day. These are much more effective than long, tiring sessions of half an hour which might soon become boring. You are building your relationship with your puppy during these times, so make them as enjoyable as possible. It is a good idea to have these sessions *before* the puppy's meal, not after it when he wouldn't feel like exerting himself; the dog will then associate something pleasurable with his training sessions and look forward to them.

THE COLLAR AND LEASH

Your puppy should become used to a collar and leash as soon as possible. If he is very

The variety of canine collars and leashes available surely allows for the personal touch.

young, a thin, choke-chain collar can be used, but you will need a larger and heavier one for training when he is a little older. Remember to have his name and address on an identification tag attached to his collar, as you don't want to lose your pet if he

A choke collar can be an effective training tool when used properly.

should happen to leave your premises and explore the neighborhood!

Let the puppy wear his collar until he is used to how it feels. After a short time he will soon become accustomed to it and you can attach the leash. He might resist your attempts to lead him or simply sit down and refuse to budge. Fight him for a few minutes, tugging on the leash if necessary, then let him relax for the day. He won't be trained until he learns that he must obey the pull under any circumstance, but this will take a few sessions. Remember that a dog's period of concentration is short, so LITTLE and OFTEN is the wisest course of action—and

patience is the password to success.

GIVING COMMANDS

When you begin giving your puppy simple commands, make them as short as possible and use the same word with the same meaning at all times, for example, "Heel," "Sit," and "Stay." You must be consistent; otherwise your puppy will become confused. The dog's name should prefix all commands to attract his attention. Do not become impatient with him however many times you have to repeat your command.

A good way to introduce the "Come" command is by calling the puppy when his meal is

94

ready. Once this is learned, you can call your pet to you at will, always remembering to praise him for his prompt obedience. This "reward," or positive reinforcement, is such a crucial part of training that a Director of the New York Academy of Dog Training constructed his whole teaching program upon the methods of "Love, Praise, and Reward." Incidentally, if you use the command "Come," use it every time. Don't switch to "Come here" or "Come boy," as this will only confuse your dog.

It is worth underlining the fact that punishment is an ineffective teaching technique. We have already seen this in housebreaking. For example, if your pup should run away, it

A puppy's collar should be light and comfortable, yet still effectively secure the dog.

would be senseless to beat him when he eventually returns; he would only connect the punishment with his return, not with running away! In addition, it is unwise to call him to you to punish him, as he will soon learn not to respond when you call his name.

A lead that allows for a sure, comfortable grip is a training necessity. Introduce your new dog to the lead slowly. When he becomes comfortable with it, training can begin.

Housebreaking and Training

SOME SPECIFIC COMMANDS

"Sit" This is one of the easiest and most useful commands for your dog to learn, so it is a good idea to begin with it. The only equipment required is a leash, a collar, and a few tasty tidbits. Take your dog out for some exercise before his meal. After about five minutes, call him to you, praise him when he arrives,

A popular item with owners who love to walk their dogs is the harness. The harness fits comfortably around the dog's forequarters and displaces the pressure of the owner's tug on the lead.

and slip his collar on him. Hold the leash tightly in your right hand; this should force the dog's head up and focus his attention on you. As you say "Sit" in a loud, clear voice, with your left hand press steadily on his rump until he is in a sitting position. As soon as he is in the correct position, praise him and give him the tidbit you have in your hand. Now wait a few minutes to let him rest and repeat the routine. Through repetition, the dog soon associates the word with the act. Never make the lesson too long. Eventually your praise will be reward enough for your puppy. Other methods to teach this command exist, but this one, executed with care and moderation, has proven the most effective.

"Sit-Stay/Stay" To teach your pet to remain in one place or "stay" on your command, first of all order him to the sitting position at your side. Lower your left hand with the flat of your palm in front of his nose and your fingers pointing downwards. Hold the leash high and taut behind his head so that he cannot move. Speak the command "Sit-stay" and, as you are giving it, step in front of him. Repeat the command and tighten the leash so the animal cannot follow you. Walk completely around him, repeating the command and keeping him motionless by holding the leash at arm's length above him to check his movement. When he remains in this position for about fifteen seconds, you can begin the second part of the training. You will have to exchange the leash for a nylon cord or rope about twenty to thirty feet long. Repeat the whole routine from the beginning and be ready to prevent any movement towards you with a sharp "Sit-stay." Move around him in ever-widening circles until you are about fifteen feet away from him. If he still remains seated, you can pat yourself on the back! One useful thing to remember is that the dog makes associations with what you say, how you say it, and what you do while you are saying it. Give this command in a firm, clear tone of voice, perhaps using an admonishing forefinger raised, warning the dog to "stay."

Two training accessories especially common with obedience trial enthusiasts are the hurdle (above) and the dumbbell (below). To see dogs performing with these and other field accessories, attend an obedience competition. Remember that training requires consistency and commitment, but the rewards are well worth the effort.

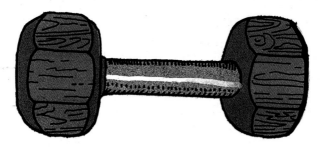

Housebreaking and Training

"Heel" When you walk your dog, you should hold the leash firmly in your right hand. The dog should walk on your left so you have the leash crossing your body. This enables you to have greater control over the dog.

Let your dog lead you for the first few moments so that he fully understands that freedom can be his if he goes about it properly. He already knows that when he wants to go outdoors the leash and collar are necessary, so he has respect for the leash. Now, if he starts to pull in one direction while walking, all you do is *stop walking.* He will walk a few steps and then find that he can't walk any further. He will then turn and look into your face. *This is the crucial point!* Just stand there for a moment and stare right back at him . . . now walk another ten feet and stop again. Again your dog will probably walk to the end of the leash, find he can't go any further, and turn around and look again. If he starts to pull and jerk, just stand there. After he quiets down, bend down and comfort him, as he may be frightened. Keep up this training until he learns not to outwalk you.

Once the puppy obeys the pull of the leash, half of your training is accomplished. "Heeling" is a necessity for a well-behaved dog, so teach him to walk beside you, head even with your knee.

Nothing looks sadder than a big dog taking his helpless owner for a walk. It is annoying to passers-by and other dog owners to have a large dog, however friendly, bear down on them and entangle dogs, people, and packages.

To teach your dog, start off walking briskly, saying "Heel" in a firm voice. Pull back with a sharp jerk if he lunges ahead, and if he lags repeat the command and tug on the leash, not allowing him to drag behind. After the dog has learned to heel at various speeds on leash, you

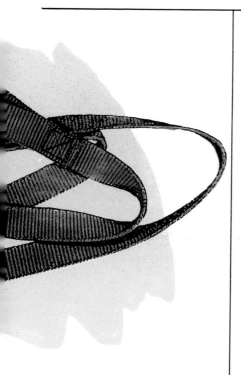

The lead is an essential tool for teaching such commands as "heel," "come," and "down."

can remove it and practice heeling free, but have it ready to snap on again as soon as he wanders.

"Come" Your dog has already learned to come to you when you call his name. Why? Because you only call him when his food is ready or when you wish to play with him or praise him. Outdoors such a response is more difficult to achieve, if he is happily playing by himself or with other dogs, so he must be trained to come to you when he is called. To teach him to come, let him reach the end of a long lead, then give the command, gently pulling him towards you at the same time. As soon as he associates the word *come* with the action of moving towards you, pull only when he does not respond immediately. As he starts to come, move back to make him learn that he must come from a distance as well as when he is close to you. Soon you may be able to practice without a leash, but if he is slow to come or actively disobedient, go to him and pull him toward you, repeating the command. Always remember to reward his successful completion of a task.

"Down" Teaching the "down" command ideally begins while your dog is still a pup. During puppyhood your dog frequently will lie down, as this position is one of the dog's most natural positions. Invest some time, and keep close watch over your pup. Each time he begins to lie, repeat in a low convincing tone the word "down." If for the first day of training, you concur a majority of the dog's sitting with your commands and continue

99

with reinforcement and moderate praise your pup should conquer the "down" command in no time.

Teaching the "down" command to a mature dog likely will require more effort. Although the lying position is still natural to a dog, his being forced into it is not. Some dogs may react with fear, anger, or confusion. Others may accept the process and prove quick learners. Have your

For the dog that responds with anger or aggression, attach a lead (and a muzzle) and have the dog sit facing you at a close distance. There should be a J-loop formed by the lead. With moderate force, relative to the size and strength of your dog, step on the J-loop, forcing the dog down, while repeating the command "down" in a low forceful tone. When the dog is down, moderate praise should

Threats and physical punishment have no place in the canine training process. The keys to effective training are patience, persistence, and praise.

dog sit and face you. If he is responsive and congenial, gently take his paws, and slowly pull them towards you; give the "down" command as he approaches the proper position. Repeat several times: moderate reinforcement of this procedure should prove rewardingly successful.

be given. If the dog proves responsive, you may attempt extending his legs to the "down" position—leaving the muzzle on, of course. Daily reinforcement of the training method will soon yield the desired results. The keys to remember are: patience, persistence, and praise.

Behavior Modification

"Problems with the Barking Dog" and "Aggressive Behavior and Dominance" are extracts from the veterinary monograph *Canine Behavior* (a compilation of columns from *Canine Practice,* a journal published by Veterinary Practice Publishing Company).

PROBLEMS WITH THE BARKING DOG

One of the most frequent complaints about canine behavior is barking. Aside from the biting dog, the barking dog is probably the pet peeve of many non-dog owners. I know of at least one city in which owners of dogs that bark excessively, and for which there are complaints on file, are required to take steps to eliminate the barking.

Canine practitioners are drawn into problems with barking when they are asked for their advice in helping an owner come up with a solution or, as a last resort, when they are requested to perform a debarking operation or even euthanasia. In this column I will deal with some of the factors that apparently cause dogs to bark and suggest some corrective approaches.

Barking is, of course, a natural response for many dogs. They have an inherited predisposition to bark as an alarm when other dogs or people approach their territory. Alarm barking makes

A problem facing many dog owners is excessive vocalization. Fortunately, a number of correctives have proven successful.

many dogs valuable as household watchdogs and is not necessarily undesirable behavior. With a different vocal tone and pattern, dogs bark when they are playing with each other. On occasion dogs have a tendency to bark back at other dogs or join in with other barking dogs.

In addition to inherited barking tendencies, dogs can also learn to bark if the barking is followed, at least sometimes, by a reward. Thus dogs may bark when they wish to come in the house or to get out of a kennel. Some dogs are trained to bark upon hearing the command "speak" for a food reward.

One of the first approaches to

take when discussing a barking problem is to determine if the behavior is a manifestation of a natural (inherited) tendency or is learned behavior which has been rewarded in the past.

Can Barking Be Extinguished?
Extinction, as a way of eliminating a behavioral problem, may be considered when it is clear that the behavior has been learned and when one can identify the specific rewarding or reinforcing factors that maintain the behavior.

For example, the dog that barks upon hearing the command "speak" is periodically rewarded with food and praise. If a dog is never, ever given food or praise again when it barks after being told to "speak," it will eventually stop this type of barking. This is the process of extinction and it implies that the

Reward in the form of treats is often effective.

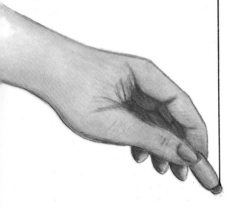

behavior must be repeated but never again rewarded.

A more practical example of the possible use of extinction would be in dealing with the dog that apparently barks because, at least occasionally, it is allowed in the house. By not allowing the dog in the house until the barking has become very frequent and loud, the owners may have shaped the barking behavior to that which is the most objectionable. If the dog is never allowed in the house again when barking, the barking should eventually be extinguished—at least theoretically.

How Should Punishment Be Used? Sometimes it is not feasible to attempt to extinguish barking even if it seems to be the case that the behavior was learned. This brings up the advisability of punishment. Clients who seek advice in dealing with a barking problem may already have employed some type of punishment such as shouting at the dog or throwing something at it. That this type of punishment is ineffective is attested to by the fact that the client is seeking advice. By shouting at a dog or hitting, a person interferes with what effect the punishment may have on the behavior itself through the arousal of autonomic reactions and escape attempts or submissive responses by the dog.

The Water Bucket Approach

I am rather impressed by the ingenuity of some dog owners in coming up with ways to punish a dog for barking without being directly involved in administering the punishment. One such harried dog owner I talked to, who was also a veterinarian, was plagued by his dog's barking in the kennel commencing at about 1:30 a.m. every night. A platform to hold a bucket of water was constructed over the area of the kennel in which the dog usually chose to bark. Through a system of hinges, ropes, and pulleys, a mechanism was devised so that the dog owner could pull a rope from his bedroom window, dumping a bucket of water on the dog when he started to bark. The bucket was suspended such that once it was dumped, it uprighted itself and the owner could fill it again remotely by turning on a garden hose. After two appropriate dunkings, the dog's barking behavior was apparently eliminated.

With a little ingenuity, a bucket attached to a trap door can be constructed. Soaking the dog in this surprising manner can possibly extinguish a bad barking habit. Always take into consideration the weather conditions, the health and age of your dog, and the cause of the barking problem before embarking on the water-bucket cure.

In advising a client on the type of punishment discussed above, keep in mind one important consideration. From the time the owner is ready to administer punishment for barking, every attempt should be made to punish all undesirable barking from that point on and not to allow excessively long periods of barking to go unpunished. Thus it may be necessary to keep a dog indoors when away unless the dog will be punished for barking when the owner is gone.

Behavior Modification

Alternative Responses Barking dogs are, and probably always will be, one of the enduring problems of dog owners. Barking is relatively effortless, and it is such a natural response for many dogs that it is admittedly hard to eliminate with either punishment or a program of conditioning non-barking. In some instances it may be advisable to forget about eliminating barking and to suggest that the problem be dealt with by changing the circumstances which lead to barking. For example, a dog that barks continuously in the backyard while the owners are away may not bark if left in the house while they are gone. But the problem of keeping the dog in the house may be related to inadequate house training or the dog's shedding hair or climbing onto the furniture. It may be easier to correct these latter behavioral problems than it is to change the barking behavior.

Especially for aggressive dogs, muzzles can prevent both injuries and lawsuits.

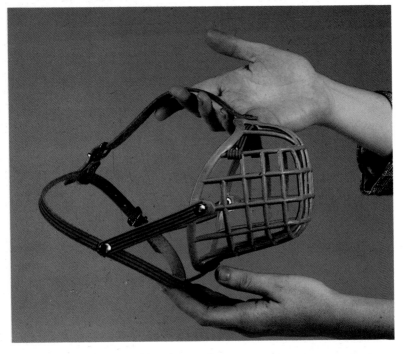

AGGRESSIVE BEHAVIOR AND DOMINANCE

Aggressiveness can have many causes. Determining what kind of aggression an animal is manifesting is a prerequisite to successful treatment of the behavior. A frequent problem that is presented to the practitioner is one of aggression related to dominance.

Dogs, which are social animals, have a hierarchal system of dominance within their pack. This predisposition to take a dominant or submissive position relative to fellow canines also occurs in relationship to people. Only in unusual situations would a submissive dog threaten a dominant animal, and almost never would it physically assault its superior. The dominant dog, however, frequently threatens submissive individuals to maintain its position. In a household setting, a person may be the object of threats, and when the person backs off, the dog's position is reassured. The aggressive behavior is also reinforced, and when behavior is reinforced it is likely to recur.

Case History The following is a typical case history of a dog presented for aggression stemming from dominance.

Max was a two-year-old intact male Cocker Spaniel. He had been acquired by Mr. Smith, one year prior to his owner's marriage, as a puppy. He liked and was well liked by both Mr. and Mrs. Smith. He frequently solicited and received attention from both people. However, several times over the last few months, Max had snapped at Mrs. Smith and repeatedly growled at her. A detailed anamnesis revealed that such incidents usually occurred in situations where the dog wanted his own way or did not want to be bothered. He would growl if asked to move off a chair or if persistently commanded to do a specific task. He growled if Mrs. Smith came between him and a young female Cocker Spaniel acquired a year ago. He also refused to let Mrs. Smith take anything from his possession.

Behavior Modification

Max never showed any of these aggressive behaviors toward Mr. Smith or strangers. Admittedly he did not have much opportunity to demonstrate such behaviors toward strangers. A description of the dog's body and facial postures and circumstances under which the

Dogs can become possessive of their playthings or aggressive in defense of their territory.

aggression occurred did not indicate that this was a case of fear-induced aggression, but rather one of assertion of dominance.

Mrs. Smith's reaction to the aggression was always to retreat, and, hence, the dog was rewarded for his assertiveness. She had never physically disciplined the dog and was afraid to do so. To encourage her to physically take control of the dog would likely have resulted in her being bitten. The dominance-submissive relationship had to be reversed in a more subtle manner.

Instructions to Client Mrs. Smith was instructed to avoid all situations which might evoke any aggressive signs from Max. This was to prevent any further reinforcement of his growling and threats.

Both she and her husband were not to indiscriminately pet or show affection towards the dog. For the time being, if Max solicited attention from Mr. Smith, he was to ignore the dog. Mrs. Smith was to take advantage of Max's desire for attention by giving him a command which he had to obey before she praised and petted him. She was also to take advantage of high motivation levels for other activities whenever such situations arose. Max had to obey a command before she gave him anything—

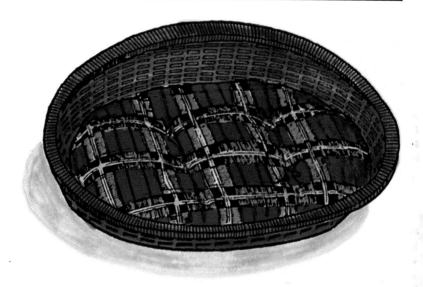

before she petted him, before she let him out or in, etc.

Mrs. Smith also was to assume total care of the dog and become "the source of all good things in life" for Max. She was to feed him, take him on walks, play with him, etc.

Mrs. Smith also spent 5–10 minutes a day teaching Max simple parlor tricks and obedience responses for coveted food rewards as well as praise. These were entirely fun and play sessions—but within a few days the dog had acquired the habit of quickly responding to commands. And this habit transferred over to the non-game situations.

Results Within a few weeks,

The dog's bed can become an object of possession. The dog can come to perceive it as his territory, not allowing others to come near. In such instances behavior modification may be necessary.

Max had ceased to growl and threaten Mrs. Smith in situations that he previously had. He would move out of her way or lie quietly when she would pass by him. She could order him off the furniture and handle the female Cocker Spaniel without eliciting threats from Max.

Mrs. Smith still felt that she would not be able to take the objects from Max's possession. Additional instructions were

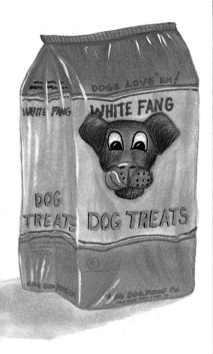

A dog comes to associate the pleasure of receiving a treat with the action immediately preceding it. Treats are effective in shaping behavior and building a relationship with your pet when they are used judiciously and in moderation.

given to her. She then began placing a series of objects at progressively closer distances to the dog while the dog was in a sit-stay position. After she placed the object on the floor for a short time, she would pick it up. If the dog was still in a sit-stay (which it always was), he received a reward of cheese and verbal praise. Eventually the objects were to be placed and

removed from directly in front of the dog. At first she was to use objects that the dog did not care much about and then progressively use more coveted items. This was what she was supposed to do, but before she actually had completed the program she called in excitedly to report that she had taken a piece of stolen food and a household ornament from Max's mouth. And he didn't even object! She said she had calmly told Max to sit. He did. He was so used to doing so, in the game and other situations, that the response was now automatic. She walked over, removed the item from his mouth, and praised him.

Mrs. Smith did resume the systematic presentation of objects and put the dog on an intermittent schedule of food and praise reinforcement during the practice sessions. Mr. Smith again began interacting with Max.

A progress check six months later indicated Max was still an obedient dog and had definitely assumed a submissive position relative to both of his owners. The dominance hierarchy between Max and Mrs. Smith had been reversed *without resorting to any physical punishment.* Mrs. Smith was instructed to reinforce her dominance position by frequently giving Max a command and reinforcing him for the appropriate response.

Summary The essential elements in treatment of such cases are as follows. First, of course, there must be a correct diagnosis of what kind of aggressive behavior is occurring. During the course of treatment, the submissive person(s) should avoid all situations that might evoke an aggressive attitude by the dog. All other family members should totally ignore the dog during the treatment interim. The person most dominated by the dog should take over complete care of the dog in addition to spending 5–10 minutes a day teaching the dog tricks or simple obedience commands (sit-stay is a useful one to gain control of the dog in subsequent circumstances). These should be fun-and-games situations. Food rewards are highly recommended in addition to simple praise.

The person submissive to the dog should take the opportunity to give the dog a command, which must be obeyed, before doing anything pleasant for the dog.

It must be emphasized to the owner that no guarantee can be made that the dog will never threaten or be aggressive again. What is being done, as with all other aggression cases, is an attempt to reduce the likelihood, incidence, and intensity of occurrence of the aggressive behavior.

DESTRUCTIVE TENDENCIES

It is ironical but true that a dog's destructive behavior in the home may be proof of his love for his owner. He may be trying to get more attention from his owner or, in other cases, may be expressing his frustration at his owner's absence. An abundance

Some crates have wire-mesh fronts while others do not. The primary consideration in choosing a crate is its ventilation.

of unused energy may also contribute to a dog's destructive behavior, and therefore the owner should ensure that his dog has, at least, twenty minutes of vigorous exercise a day.

As a dog's destructive tendencies may stem from his desire to get more attention from his owner, the latter should devote specific periods each day to his dog when he is actively interacting with him. Such a period should contain practice obedience techniques during which the owner can reward the dog with his favorite food as well as praise and affection.

Planned departure conditioning is one specific technique which has been used to solve the problem of destructive tendencies in a puppy. It eventually ensures the dog's good behavior during the owner's absence. A series of

Not just great recreational devices to channel doggie tensions, the Gumabone® products have been scientifically proven to reduce tartar and plaque build-up. These products are available in many shapes and sizes. Gumabone® products should be replaced regularly when they become excessively worn.

short departures, which are identical to real departures, should condition the dog to behave well in the owner's absence. How is this to be achieved? Initially, the departures are so short (2–5 minutes) that the dog has no opportunity to be destructive. The dog is always rewarded for having been good when the owner returns. Gradually the duration of the departures is increased. The departure time is also varied so that the dog does not know when the owner is going to return. Since a different kind of behavior is now expected, it is best if a new stimulus or "atmosphere" is introduced into the training sessions to permit the dog to distinguish these departures as different from previous departures when he was destructive.

This new stimulus could be the sound of the radio or television. The association which the dog will develop is that whenever the "signal" or "stimulus" is on, the owner will return in an unknown

A safe tug toy.

period of time and, if the dog has not been destructive, he will be rewarded. As with the daily owner-dog interaction, the food reward is especially useful.

If the dog misbehaves during his owner's absence, the owner should speak sternly to him and isolate him from social contact for at least thirty minutes. (Puppies hate to be ignored.) Then the owner should conduct another departure of a shorter time and generously reward good behavior when he returns. The owner should progress slowly enough in the program so that once the departure has been initiated, the dog is never given an opportunity to make a mistake.

If planned departures are working satisfactorily, the departure time may gradually be extended to several hours. To reduce the dog's anxiety when left alone, he should be given a "safety valve" such as the indestructible Nylabone® to play with and chew on.

A proven safe chew product.

Health Care

From the moment you purchase your puppy, the most important person in both your lives becomes your veterinarian. His professional advice and treatment will ensure the good health of your pet. The vet is the first person to call when illness or accidents occur. Do *not* try to be your own veterinarian or apply human remedies to canine diseases. However, just as you would keep a first aid kit handy for minor injuries sustained by members of your family at home, so you should keep a similar kit prepared for your pet.

First aid for your dog would consist of stopping any bleeding, cleaning the wound, and

Even in your own back yard, injuries can occur.

preventing infection. Thus your kit might contain medicated powder, gauze bandages, and adhesive tape to be used in case of cuts. If the cut is deep and bleeding profusely, the bandage should be applied very tightly to help in the formation of a clot. A tight bandage should not be kept in place longer than necessary, so take your pet to the veterinarian immediately.

Walking or running on a cut pad prevents the cut from healing. Proper suturing of the cut and regular changing of the bandages should have your pet's wound healed in a week to ten days. A minor cut should be covered with a light bandage, for you want as much air as possible to reach the wound. Do not apply wads of cotton to a wound; they will stick to the area and may cause contamination.

You should also keep some hydrogen peroxide available, as it is useful in cleaning wounds and is also one of the best and simplest emetics known. Cotton applicator swabs are useful for applying ointment or removing debris from the eyes. A pair of tweezers should also be kept handy for removing foreign bodies from the dog's neck, head or body.

Nearly everything a dog might contract in the way of sickness has basically the same set of symptoms: loss of appetite, diarrhea, dull eyes, dull coat,

When emergencies occur, it pays to be prepared. A first-aid kit, well stocked with common sense medical accessories and tools, is helpful to have available at all times.

warm and/or runny nose, and a high temperature. Therefore, it is most important to take his temperature at the first sign of illness. To do this, you will need a rectal thermometer which should be lubricated with petroleum jelly. Carefully insert it into the rectum, holding it in place for at least two minutes. It must be held firmly; otherwise there is the danger of its being sucked up into the rectum or slipping out, thus giving an inaccurate reading. The normal temperature for a dog is between 101° and 102.5°F. If your pet is seriously ill or injured in an accident, your veterinarian will advise you what to do before he arrives.

SWALLOWING FOREIGN OBJECTS

Most of us have had experience with a child swallowing a foreign object. Usually it is a small coin; occasionally it may be a fruit pit or something more dangerous. Dogs, *as a general rule,* will not swallow anything which isn't edible. There are, however, many dogs that swallow pebbles or small shiny objects such as pins, coins, and bits of cloth and plastic. This is especially true of dogs that are offered so-called "chew toys."

Chew toys are available in many sizes, shapes, colors and materials. Some even have whistles which sound when the dog's owner plays with it or when the dog chomps on it quickly. Most dogs attack the whistle first, doing everything possible to make it stop squeaking. Obviously, if the whistle is made of metal, a dog can injure its mouth, teeth, or tongue. Therefore, *never* buy a "squeak toy" made with a metal whistle.

Other chew toys are made of vinyl, a cheap plastic which is soft to the touch and pliable. Most of the cute little toys that are figures of animals or people are made of this cheap plastic. They are sometimes hand-painted in countries where the cost of such labor is low. Not only is the paint used dangerous to dogs, because of the lead content, but the vinyl tears easily and is usually destroyed by the dog during the first hour. Small bits of vinyl may be ingested and cause blockage of the intestines. You are, therefore, reminded of these things before you buy anything vinyl for your dog!

Very inexpensive dog toys, usually found in supermarkets and other low-price venues, may be made of polyethylene. These are to be avoided completely, as this cheap plastic is, for some odd reason, attractive to dogs. Dogs destroy the toy in minutes and sometimes swallow the indigestible bits and pieces that come off. Most pet shops carry only safe toys.

WHAT TOYS ARE SAFE FOR DOGS?

Hard Rubber Toys made of hard rubber are usually safe for dogs, providing the toy is made of 100% hard rubber and not a compound of rubber and other materials. The rubber must be "virgin" and not re-ground from old tires, tubes, and other scrap rubber products. The main problem with rubber, even 100% virgin rubber, is that it oxidizes quickly, especially when subjected to the ultraviolet rays of the sun and a dog's saliva. The rubber then tends to be brittle, to crack, to dust off, and to be extremely dangerous to dogs that like swallowing things.

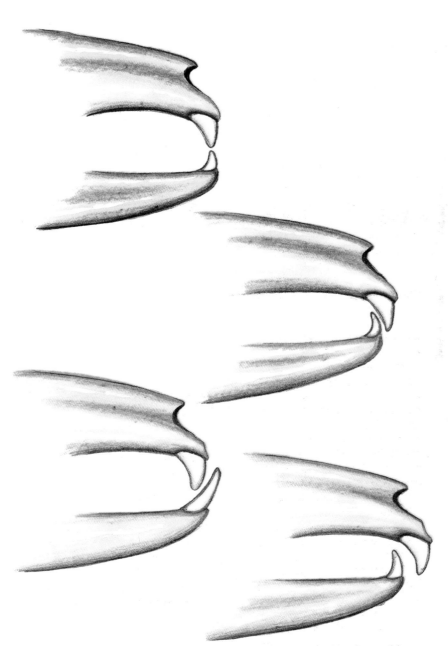

From top to bottom, *the four common bite types are: (a) level, (b) scissors, (c) un-dershot, and (d) overshot. Different breeds have different bite types and one bite type may be desirable in your breed and most undesirable in another.*

Health Care

Nylon Toys Toys made of nylon could well be the safest of all toys, *providing the nylon is annealed.* Nylon that is not annealed is very fragile ,and if you smash it against a hard surface, it might shatter like glass. The same is true when the weather is cold and the nylon drops below freezing. Thus far there is only one line of dog toys that is made of annealed virgin nylon—Nylabone®. These toys are not only annealed but they are flavored and scented. The flavors and scents, such as hambone, are undetectable by humans, but dogs seem to find them attractive.

Some nylon bones have the flavor sprayed on them or molded into them. These cheaper bones are easy to detect—just smell them. If you discern an odor, you know they are poorly made. The main

The inherent need to chew is strong in dogs of all ages. The canine's constant chewing of his favorite chew products will necessitate their regular replacement. When a bone becomes frayed, it's time to replace it.

problem with the nylon toys that have an odor is that they are not annealed and they "smell up" the house or car. The dog's saliva dilutes the odor of the bone, and when he drops it on your rug, this odor attaches itself to the rug and is quite difficult to remove.

Annealed nylon may be the best there is ,but it is not 100% safe. The Nylabone® dog chews are really meant to be Pooch Pacifiers®. This trade name indicates the effect intended for the dog, which is to relieve the tension in your excited puppy or adult dog who is left alone or wants to "spite" you. Instead of chewing up the furniture or some other object, he chews up his Nylabone® instead. Many dogs ignore the Nylabone® for weeks, suddenly attacking it when they have to relieve their doggie tensions.

Some dogs may have jaws strong enough to chomp off a piece of Nylabone®, but this is extremely rare. *One word of caution:* the Nylabone® should be replaced when the dog has chewed down the knuckle. Most dogs slowly scrape off small slivers of nylon which pass harmlessly through their digestive tract. The resultant frizzled bone actually becomes a toothbrush.

One of the great characteristics of nylon bones is that they can be boiled and

The Gumaknot® is the favorite chew item of many dogs.

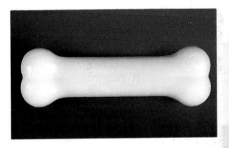

Above: *The Nylabone® is an effective, proven-safe therapeutic device.* **Below**: *The Gumaball® is useful for outside recreation, exercise, and tooth care.*

Doggie treats come in a wide variety of sizes, shapes, and flavors. While they can be useful as rewards and occasional tidbits, they do not satisfy the dog's need to chew. Treats are best used for what they are intended—as treats.

sterilized. If a dog loses interest in his Nylabone®, or it is too hard for him to chew due to his age and the condition of his teeth, you can cook it in some chicken or beef broth, allowing it to boil for 30 minutes. Let it cool down normally. It will then be perfectly sterile and re-flavored for the next dog. *Don't try this with plastic bones, as they will melt and ruin your pot.*

Polyurethane Toys Toys made of polyurethane are almost as good as nylon bones—but not quite. There are several brands on the market: ignore the ones which have scents that you can discern. Some of the scented polyurethane bones have an unbearable odor after the scent has rubbed off the bone and onto your rug or car seat. Again, look for the better-quality polyurethane toy. Gumabone® is

a flexible material, the same as used for making artificial hearts and the bumpers on automobiles, thus it is strong and stable. It is not as strong as Nylabone®, but many dogs like it because it is soft.

The most popular of the Gumabone® products made in polyurethane are the tug toys, balls, and Frisbee® flying discs. These items are almost clear in color, have the decided advantage of lasting a long time, and are useful in providing exercise for both a dog and his master or mistress.

Whatever dog toy you buy, be sure it is high quality. Pet shops, as a rule, carry the better-quality toys, while supermarkets seem to be concerned only with price. Of course there may be exceptions, but you are best advised to ask your local pet shop operator—or even your veterinarian—what toys are suitable for *your* dog.

In conclusion, if your dog is a swallower of foreign objects, don't give him anything cheap to chew on. If he swallows a coin, you can hardly blame the Treasury! Unless your dog is carefully supervised, use only the largest size Nylabone®, and replace it as soon as the dog chews down the knuckles. *Do not let the dog take the Nylabone® outdoors.* First of all he can hide and bury it, digging it up when his tensions rise. Then, too, all nylon becomes more brittle when it freezes, even Nylabone®.

IF YOUR PET SWALLOWS POISON

A poisoned dog must be treated instantly; any delay could cause his death. Different poisons act in different ways and require different treatments. If you know the dog has swallowed an acid, alkali, gasoline, or kerosene, do not induce vomiting. Give milk to dilute the poison and rush him to the vet. If you can find the bottle or container of poison, check the label to see if there is a recommended antidote. If not, try to induce vomiting by giving him a mixture of hydrogen peroxide and water. Mix the regular drugstore strength of hydrogen peroxide (3%) with an equal part of water, but do not attempt to pour it down your dog's throat, as that could cause inhalation pneumonia. Instead, simply pull the dog's lips away from the side of his mouth, making a pocket for depositing the liquid. Use at least a tablespoonful of the mixture for every ten pounds of your dog's

Handling a dog who is sick or injured requires skill. To protect yourself from being bitten, you should first secure the dog's muzzle with a slow, cautious motion, if no safety muzzle is available. Then the animal can be treated or transported as required.

weight. He will vomit in about two minutes. When his stomach has settled, give him a teaspoonful of Epsom salts in a little water to empty the intestine quickly. The hydrogen peroxide, on ingestion, becomes oxygen and water and is harmless to your dog; it is the best antidote for phosphorus, which is often used in rat poisons. After you have administered this emergency treatment to your pet and his stomach and bowels have been emptied, rush him to your veterinarian for further care.

DANGER IN THE HOME

There are numerous household products that can prove fatal if ingested by your pet. These include rat poison, antifreeze, boric acid, hand soap, detergents, insecticides, mothballs, household cleansers,

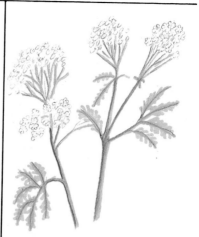

Water hemlock is one of the many poisonous plants that can cause serious complications if ingested by a canine.

bleaches, de-icers, polishes and disinfectants, paint and varnish removers, acetone, turpentine, and even health and beauty aids if ingested in large enough quantities. A word to the wise should be sufficient: what you would keep locked away from your two-year-old child should also be kept hidden from your pet.

There is another danger lurking within the home among the household plants, which are almost all poisonous, even if swallowed in small quantities. There are hundreds of poisonous plants around us, among which are: ivy leaves, cyclamen, lily of the valley, rhododendrons, tulip bulbs, azalea, wisteria, poinsettia

Suburban backyards are often fertile grounds for a variety of flowering plant types. Many of these pretty-to-the-eye plants can be harmful to a canine. Lily-of-the-valley is attractive and popular in some climates; it is, however, poisonous if ingested and should not be cultivated near the dog's living area.

Lactrodectus mactans, *better known as the black widow spider, is said to possess venom over 15 times as toxic as many rattlesnakes'. This spider most commonly occurs in warm climates. Owners are encouraged to inspect the dog's living area periodically for such lethal inhabitants.*

leaves, mistletoe, daffodils, delphiniums, foxglove leaves, the jimson weed—we cannot name them all. Rhubarb leaves, for example, either raw or cooked, can cause death or violent convulsions. Peach, elderberry, and cherry trees can cause cyanide poisoning if their bark is consumed.

There are also many insects that can be poisonous to dogs such as spiders, bees, wasps, and some flies. A few toads and frogs exude a fluid that can make a dog foam at the mouth—and even kill him—if he bites too hard!

There have been cases of dogs suffering nicotine poisoning by consuming the contents of full ashtrays which thoughtless smokers have left on the coffee table. Also, do not leave nails, staples, pins, or other sharp objects lying around. Likewise, don't let your puppy play with plastic bags which could suffocate him. Unplug, remove, or cover any electrical cords or wires near your dog. Chewing live wires could lead to severe mouth burns or death. Remember that an ounce of prevention is worth a pound of cure: keep all potentially dangerous objects out of your pet's reach.

Bufo marinus, *the giant toad, is a very large species of toad that, when provoked, will produce a secretion that is toxic if ingested. The giant toad can potentially be a canine killer.*

VEHICLE TRAVEL SAFETY

A dog should never be left alone in a car. It takes only a few minutes for the heat to become unbearable in the summer, and to drop to freezing in the winter.

A dog traveling in a car or truck should be well behaved. An undisciplined dog can be deadly in a moving vehicle. The dog should be trained to lie on the back seat of the vehicle. Allowing your dog to stick its head out of the window is unwise. The dog may jump or it may get something in its eye. Some manufacturers sell seat belts and car seats designed for dogs.

Traveling with your dog in the back of your pick-up truck is an unacceptable notion and dangerous to all involved.

PROTECT YOURSELF FIRST

In almost all first aid situations, the dog is in pain. He may indeed be in shock and not appear to be suffering, until you move him. Then he may bite your hand or resist being helped at all. So if you want to help your dog, help yourself first by tying his mouth closed. To do this, use a piece of strong cloth four inches wide and three feet long, depending on the size of the dog. Make a loop in the middle of the strip and slip it over his nose with the knot under his chin and over the bony part of his nose.

Pull it tight and bring the ends back around his head behind the ears and tie it tightly, ending with a bow knot for quick, easy release. Now you can handle the dog safely. As a dog perspires through his tongue, do not leave the "emergency muzzle" on any longer than necessary.

ADMINISTERING MEDICINE

When you are giving liquid medicine to your dog, it is a good idea to pull the lips away from the side of the mouth, form a lip pocket, and let the liquid trickle past the tongue. Remain at his side, never in front of the dog, as he may cough and spray you with the liquid. Moreover, you must never pour liquid medicine while the victim's tongue is drawn out, as inhalation pneumonia could be the disastrous result.

Medicine in pill form is best administered by forcing the dog's mouth open, holding his head back, and placing the capsule as far back on his tongue as you can reach. To do this: put the palm of your hand over the dog's muzzle (his foreface) with your fingers on one side of his jaw, your thumb

An injured dog can bite, rather unintentionally. A make-shift muzzle can be used in the case of an emergency. A tie or a torn piece of cloth can suffice.

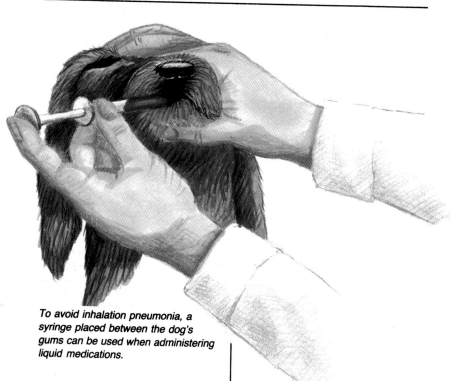

To avoid inhalation pneumonia, a syringe placed between the dog's gums can be used when administering liquid medications.

on the other. Press his lips hard against his teeth while using your other hand to pull down his lower jaw. With your two fingers, try to put the pill as far back on the dog's tongue as you can reach. Keep his mouth and nostrils closed and he should be forced to swallow the medicine. As the dog will not be feeling well, stroke his neck to comfort him and to help him swallow his medicine more easily. Do keep an eye on him for a few moments afterward, however, to make certain that he does not spit it out.

IN CASE OF AN ACCIDENT

It is often difficult for you to assess the dog's injuries after a road accident. He may appear normal, but there might be internal hemorrhaging. A vital organ could be damaged or ribs broken. Keep the dog as quiet and warm as possible; cover him with blankets or your coat to let his own body heat build up. Signs of shock are a rapid and weak pulse, glassy-eyed appearance, subnormal temperature, and slow capillary refill time. To determine the last symptom, press firmly against the dog's gums until they turn white. Release and count the number of seconds until the gums return to their normal color. If it is more than 2–3 seconds, the dog may be going into shock. Failure to return to the reddish pink color indicates that the dog may be in serious trouble and needs immediate assistance.

If artificial respiration is required, first open the dog's mouth and check for obstructions; extend his tongue and examine the pharynx. Clear his mouth of mucus and blood and hold the mouth slightly open. Mouth-to-mouth resuscitation involves holding the dog's tongue to the bottom of his mouth with one hand and sealing his nostrils with the other while you blow into his mouth. Watch for his chest to rise with each inflation. Repeat every 5–6 seconds, the equivalent of 10–12 breaths a minute.

If the veterinarian cannot come to you, try to improvise a stretcher to take the dog to him.

To administer pills, simply press the dog's lips against his teeth until he opens his mouth. Then place the pill as far back on the tongue as possible. Now hold the dog's mouth closed and see that the dog has swallowed. Praise him for his cooperation.

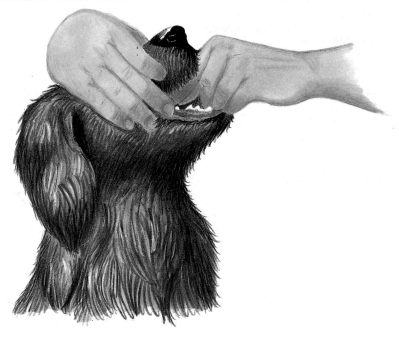

Health Care

To carry a puppy, wrap him in a blanket that has been folded into several thicknesses. If he is in shock, it is better to pick him up by holding one hand under his chest, the other under the hindquarters. This will keep him stretched out.

It is always better to roll an injured dog than to try and lift him. If you find him lying beside the road after a car accident, apply a muzzle even if you have to use someone's necktie to make one. Send someone for a blanket and roll him gently onto

Known as Elizabethan collars, these devices can be purchased at a pet store or provided by your veterinarian to prevent the dog from complications resulting from excessive licking or chewing.

it. Two people, one on each side, can make a stretcher out of the blanket and move the dog easily.

If no blanket is available and the injured dog must be moved, try to keep him as flat as possible. So many dogs' backs are broken in car accidents that one must first consider that possibility. However, if he can move his hind legs or tail, his spine is probably not broken. Get medical assistance for him immediately.

It should be mentioned that unfortunate car accidents, which can maim or kill your dog, can be avoided if he is confined at all times either indoors or, if out-of-doors, in a fenced-in yard or

Nightshade (left) and larkspur (right) are two plants that are poisonous when ingested. Many dogs eat small amounts of wild grass, which is often harmless if not sprayed with pesticides; however, the owner must be cautious that poisonous plants are not growing in the grass, for they can be accidentally consumed.

some other protective enclosure. *Never* allow your dog to roam free; even a well-trained dog may, for some unknown reason, dart into the street—and the result could be tragic.

If you need to walk your dog, leash him first so that he will be protected from moving vehicles.

PROTECTING YOUR PET

It is important to watch for any tell-tale signs of illness so that you can spare your pet any unnecessary suffering. Your dog's eyes, for example, should normally be bright and alert, so if the haw is bloodshot or partially covers the eye, it may be a sign of illness or irritation. If your dog has matter in the corners of his eyes, bathe them with a mild eye wash; obtain ointment or eye drops from your veterinarian to treat a chronic condition.

If your dog seems to have something wrong with his ears which causes him to scratch at them or shake his head, cautiously probe the ear with a cotton swab. An accumulation of wax will probably work itself out. Dirt or dried blood, however, is indicative of ear mites or infection and should be treated immediately. Sore ears in the summer, due to insect bites, should be washed with mild soap and water, then covered with a soothing ointment and wrapped in gauze if necessary. Keep your pet away from insects until his ears heal, even if this means confining him indoors.

Health Care

INOCULATIONS

Periodic check-ups by your veterinarian throughout your puppy's life are good health insurance. The person from whom your puppy was purchased should tell you what inoculations your puppy has had and when the next visit to the vet is necessary. You must make certain that your puppy has been vaccinated against the following infectious canine diseases: distemper, canine hepatitis, leptospirosis, rabies, parvovirus, and parainfluenza. Annual "boosters" thereafter provide inexpensive protection for your dog against such serious diseases. Puppies should also be checked for worms at an early age.

DISTEMPER

Young dogs are most susceptible to distemper, although it may affect dogs of all ages. Some signs of the disease are loss of appetite, depression, chills, and fever, as well as a watery discharge from the eyes and nose. Unless treated promptly, the disease goes into advanced stages with infections of the lungs, intestines, and nervous system. Dogs that recover may be impaired with paralysis, convulsions, a twitch, or some other defect, usually spastic in nature. Early inoculations in puppyhood

While the vet is inspecting your dog, secure him around the base of his neck and the tuck of his abdomen.

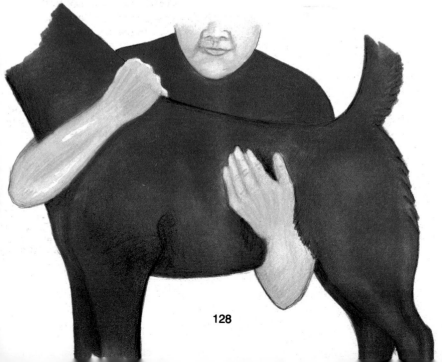

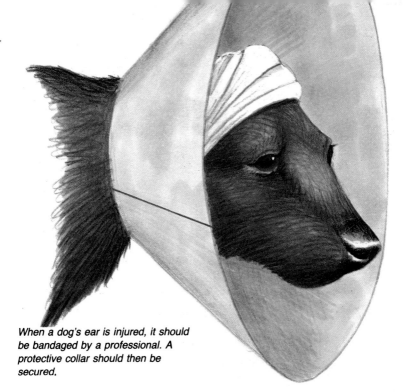

When a dog's ear is injured, it should be bandaged by a professional. A protective collar should then be secured.

should be followed by an annual booster to help protect against this disease.

CANINE HEPATITIS

The signs of hepatitis are drowsiness, vomiting, loss of appetite, high temperature, and great thirst. These signs may be accompanied by swellings of the head, neck, and abdomen. Vomiting may also occur. This disease strikes quickly, and death may occur in only a few hours. An annual booster shot is needed after the initial series of puppy shots.

LEPTOSPIROSIS

Infection caused by either of two serovars, *canicola* or *copehageni* is usually begun by the dog's licking substances contaminated by the urine or feces of infected animals. Brown rats are the main carriers of *copehageni*. The signs are weakness, vomiting, and a yellowish discoloration of the jaws, teeth, and tongue, caused by an inflammation of the kidneys. A veterinarian can administer the bacterins to protect your dog from this disease. The frequency of the doses is determined by the risk factor involved.

RABIES

This disease of the dog's central nervous system spreads by infectious saliva, which is transmitted by the bite of an infected animal. Of the two main classes of signs, the first is "furious rabies," in which the dog shows a period of melancholy or depression, then irritation, and finally paralysis. The first period can be from a few hours to several days, and during this time the dog is cross and will change his position often, lose his appetite, begin to lick, and bite or swallow foreign objects. During this phase the dog is spasmodically wild and has impulses to run away. The dog acts fearless and bites everything in sight. If he is caged or confined, he will fight at the bars and possibly break teeth or fracture his jaw. His bark becomes a peculiar howl. In the final stage, the animal's lower jaw becomes paralyzed and hangs down. He then walks with a stagger, and saliva drips from his mouth. About four to eight days after the onset of paralysis, the dog dies.

The second class of symptoms is referred to as "dumb rabies" and is characterized by the dog's walking in a bearlike manner with his head down. The lower jaw is paralyzed and the dog is unable to bite. It appears as if he has a bone caught in his throat.

If a dog is bitten by a rabid animal, he probably can be saved if he is taken to a veterinarian in time for a series of injections. After the signs appear, however, no cure is possible. The local health

Rats are the carriers of many diseases, including leptospirosis.

department must be notified in the case of a rabid dog, for he is a danger to all who come near him. As with the other shots each year, an annual rabies inoculation is very important. In many areas, the administration of rabies vaccines for dogs is required by law.

PARVOVIRUS

This relatively new virus is a contagious disease that has spread in almost epidemic proportions throughout certain sections of the United States. It has also appeared in Australia, Canada, and Europe. Canine parvovirus attacks the intestinal tract, white blood cells, and heart muscle. It is believed to spread through dog-to-dog contact, and the specific course of infection seems to come from fecal matter of infected dogs. Overcoming parvovirus is difficult, for it is capable of existing in the environment for many months under varying conditions and temperatures, and it can be transmitted from place to place on the hair and feet of infected dogs, as well as on the clothes and shoes of people.

Vomiting and severe diarrhea, which will appear within five to seven days after the animal has been exposed to the virus, are the initial signs of this disease. At the onset of illness, feces will be light gray or yellow-gray in

It is believed that mice can carry the early-stage deer ticks that may be carriers of the dreaded lyme disease.

color, and the urine might be blood-streaked. Because of the vomiting and severe diarrhea, the dog that has contracted the disease will dehydrate quickly. Depression and loss of appetite, as well as a rise in temperature, can accompany the other symptoms. Death caused by this disease usually occurs within 48 to 72 hours following the appearance of the symptoms. Puppies are hardest hit, and the virus is fatal to 75 percent of puppies that contract it. Death in

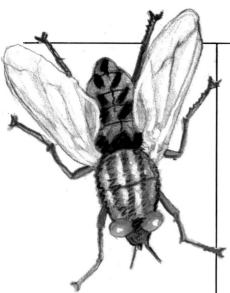

Stable fly: a painful bite.

puppies can be within two days of the onset of the illness.

A series of shots administered by a veterinarian is the best preventive measure for canine parvovirus. It is also important to disinfect the area where the dog is housed by using one part sodium hypochlorite solution (household bleach) to thirty parts of water and to keep the dog from coming into contact with the fecal matter of other dogs.

Deer tick: a carrier of lyme.

LYME DISEASE

Known as a bacterial infection, Lyme disease is transmitted by ticks infected with a spirochete known as *Borrelia burgdorferi*. The disease is most often acquired by the parasitic bite of an infected deer tick, *Ixodes dammini*. While the range of symptoms is broad, common warning signs include: rash beginning at the bite and soon extending in a bullseye-targetlike fashion; chills, fever, lack of balance, lethargy, and stiffness; swelling and pain, especially in the joints, possibly leading to arthritis or arthritic conditions; heart problems, weak limbs, facial paralysis, and lack of tactile sensation. Although there is no known cure-all, tetracycline and some other drugs have been prescribed with various degrees of success. If you suspect that your dog has Lyme disease, contact your vet immediately.

PARAINFLUENZA

Parainfluenza, or infectious canine tracheobronchitis, is commonly known as "kennel cough." It is highly contagious, affects the upper respiratory system, and is spread through direct or indirect contact with already diseased dogs. It will readily infect dogs of all ages that have not been vaccinated or that were previously infected. While this condition is definitely one of the serious diseases in dogs, it is self-limiting, usually lasting only two to four weeks. The symptoms are high fever and intense, harsh coughing that brings up mucus. As long as your pet sees your veterinarian immediately, the chances for his complete recovery are excellent.

EXTERNAL PARASITES

A parasite is an animal that lives in or on an organism of another species, known as the host, without contributing to the well-being of the host. The majority of dogs' skin problems are parasitic in nature and an estimated 90% of puppies are born with parasites.

Ticks can cause serious problems to dogs where the latter have access to woods, fields, and vegetation in which large numbers of native mammals live. Ticks are usually found clinging to vegetation and attach themselves to animals

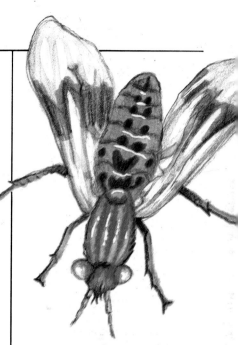

Deer fly: a welt-inducing bite.

passing by. They have eight legs and a heavy shield or shell-like covering on their upper surface. Only by keeping dogs away from tick-infested areas can ticks on dogs be prevented.

The flea is the single most common cause of skin and coat problems in dogs. There are 11,000 kinds of fleas which can transmit specific disorders like tapeworm and heartworm or transport smaller parasites onto your dog. The common tapeworm, for example, requires the flea as an intermediate host for completion of its life cycle.

A female flea can lay hundreds of eggs and these will become adults in less than three weeks. Depending on the temperature

Brown dog tick: a common parasite.

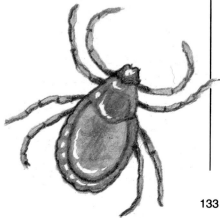

The bite of a single flea can cause an irritation that spreads quickly over the surface of the skin. For flea prevention, the dog and his living quarters should be treated regularly.

and the amount of moisture, large numbers of fleas can attack dogs. The ears of dogs, in particular, can play host to hundreds of fleas.

Fleas can lurk in crevices and cracks, carpets, and bedding for months, so frequent cleaning of your dog's environment is absolutely essential. If he is infected by other dogs, then have him bathed and "dipped," which means that he will be put into water containing a chemical that kills fleas. Your veterinarian will advise which dip to use, and your dog must be bathed for at least twenty minutes. These parasites are tenacious and remarkably agile creatures; fleas have existed since prehistoric times and have been found in arctic as well as tropical climates. Some experts claim that fleas can jump 150 times the length of their bodies; this makes them difficult to catch and kill. Thus, treating your pet for parasites without simultaneously

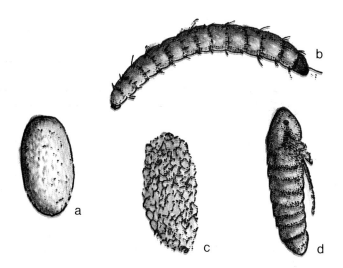

The life cycle of the flea: (a) egg (b) larvae (c) cocoon (d) pupae. If allowed to persist on the dog, fleas will build nests and reproduce, quickly infesting the dog. Regular brushing accompanied by anti-flea applications should suffice to eliminate the flea problem.

treating the environment is both inefficient and ineffective.

INTERNAL PARASITES

Four common internal parasites that may infect a dog are: roundworms, hookworms, whipworms, and tapeworms. The first three can be diagnosed by laboratory examination of the dog's stool, and tapeworms can be seen in the stool or attached to the hair around the anus. When a veterinarian determines what type of worm or worms are present, he then can advise the best treatment.

Roundworms, the dog's most common intestinal parasite, have a life cycle which permits complete eradication by worming twice, ten days apart. The first worming will remove all adults and the second will destroy all subsequently hatched eggs before they, in turn, can produce more parasites.

A dog in good physical condition is less susceptible to worm infestation than a weak dog. Proper sanitation and a nutritious diet help in preventing worms. One of the best preventive measures is to have clean, dry bedding for the dog, as this diminishes the possibility of reinfection due to flea or tick bites.

Health Care

Heartworm infestation in dogs is passed by mosquitoes. Dogs with this disease tire easily, have difficulty in breathing, and lose weight despite a hearty appetite. Administration of preventive medicine throughout the spring, summer, and fall months is advised. A veterinarian must first take a blood sample from the dog to test for the presence of the disease, and if the dog is heartworm-free, pills or liquid medicine can be prescribed.

Heartworm life cycle: a carrier mosquito bites a dog and deposits microfilariae; the filariae travel through the dog's blood stream, lodging in the heart to reproduce. The carrier dog is later bitten by an uninfected mosquito, which thereby acquires uninfectious microfilariae, develops the microfilariae to an infectious stage, bites and infects another dog.

CANINE SENIOR CITIZENS

The processes of aging and gradual degenerative changes start far earlier in a dog than often observed, usually at about seven years of age. If we recall that each year of a dog's life roughly corresponds to about seven years in the life of a man, by the age of seven he is well into middle age. Your pet will become less active, will have a poorer appetite with increased thirst, there will be frequent periods of constipation and less than normal passage of urine. His skin and coat might become dull and dry and his hair will become thin and fall out. There is a tendency towards obesity in old age, which should be avoided by maintaining a regular exercise program. Remember, also, that your pet will be less able to cope

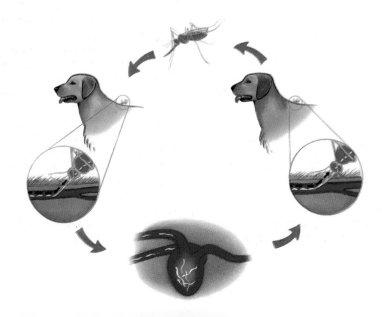

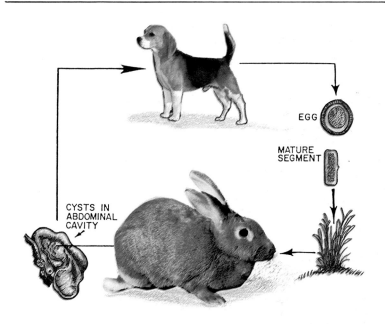

Tapeworms can be acquired in a number of ways; the infected dog must receive veterinary treatment.

with extreme heat, cold, fatigue, and change in routine.

There is the possibility of loss or impairment of hearing or eyesight. He may become bad-tempered more often than in the past. Other ailments such as rheumatism, arthritis, kidney infections, heart disease, male prostatism, and hip dysplasia may occur. Of course, all these require a veterinarian's examination and recommendation of suitable treatment. Care of the teeth is also important in the aging dog.

Indeed, the mouth can be a barometer of nutritional health. Degenerating gums, heavy tartar on the teeth, loose teeth, and sore lips are common. The worst of all diseases in old age, however, is neglect. Good care in early life will have its effect on your dog's later years; the nutrition and general health care of his first few years can determine his lifespan and the quality of his life. It is worth bearing in mind that the older, compared to the younger, animal needs more protein of good biological value, more vitamins A, B-complex, D and E, more calcium and iron, less fat and fewer carbohydrates.

Preventive Dental Care

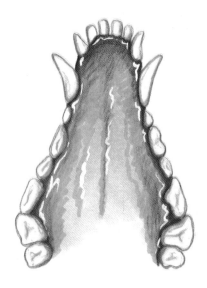 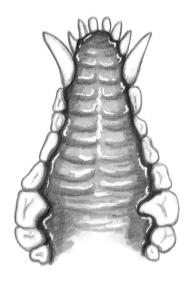

ALL DOGS NEED TO CHEW

Puppies and young dogs need something with resistance to chew on while their teeth and jaws are developing—to cut the puppy teeth, to induce growth of the permanent teeth under the puppy teeth, to assist in getting rid of the puppy teeth on time, to help the permanent teeth through the gums, to assure normal jaw development and to settle the permanent teeth solidly in the jaws.

The adult dog's desire to chew stems from the instinct for tooth cleaning, gum massage, and jaw exercise—plus the need to vent periodic doggie tensions. . . . A pacifier if you will!

Dental caries, as they affect the teeth of humans, are virtually

It is imperative that the owner take the necessary measures to ensure sound dental health. Ideal canine dentition illustrated: upper palate on right; lower palate on left.

unknown in dogs; but tartar (calculus) accumulates on the teeth of dogs, particularly at the gum line, more rapidly than on the teeth of humans. These accumulations, if not removed, bring irritation and then infection, which erode the tooth enamel and ultimately destroy the teeth at the roots. It is important that you take your dog to your local veterinarian for periodic dental examinations.

Tooth and jaw development will normally continue until the dog is more than a year old—but sometimes much longer, depending upon the dog, its chewing exercise, rate of calcium utilization and many other factors, known and unknown, which affect the development of individual dogs. Diseases, like distemper for example, may sometimes arrest development of the teeth and jaws, which may resume months or even years later.

This is why dogs, especially puppies and young dogs, will often destroy valuable property when their chewing instinct is not diverted from their owners'

his instinct tells him to chew. If your purposes, and those of your dog, are to be accomplished, what you provide for chewing must be desirable from the doggie viewpoint, have the necessary functional qualities, and, above all, be safe.

It is very important that dogs be prohibited from chewing on anything they can break or indigestible things from which they can bite sizeable chunks. Sharp pieces, such as those from a bone which can be broken by a dog, may pierce the intestinal wall and kill.

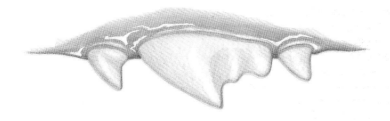

possessions, particularly during the widely varying critical period for young dogs. Saving your possessions from destruction, assuring proper development of teeth and jaws, providing for "interim" tooth cleaning and gum massage, and channeling doggie tensions into a non-destructive outlet are, therefore, all dependent upon the dog's having something suitable for chewing readily available when

A dog's teeth with little to no calculus build-up, a state achievable through consistent and appropriate care.

Indigestible things which can be bitten off in chunks, such as toys made of rubber compound or cheap plastic, may cause an intestinal stoppage; if not regurgitated, they are certain to bring painful death unless surgery is promptly performed.

NATURAL CHEW BONES

Strong natural bones, such as 4- to 8-inch lengths of round shin bone from mature beef—either the kind you can get from your butcher or one of the varieties available commercially in pet stores—may serve your dog's teething needs, if his mouth is large enough to handle them.

You may be tempted to give your puppy a smaller bone and he may not be able to break it when you do, but puppies grow rapidly and the power of their jaws constantly increases until maturity. This means that a growing dog may break one of the smaller bones at any time, swallow the pieces and die painfully before you realize what is wrong.

Many people have the mistaken notion that their dog's teeth are like those of wild carnivores or of dogs from antiquity. The teeth of wild carnivorous animals and those found in the fossils of the dog-like creatures of antiquity have far thicker and stronger enamel than those of our dogs today.

All hard natural bones are highly abrasive. If your dog is an avid chewer, natural bones may wear away his teeth prematurely; hence, they then should be taken away from your dog when the teething purposes have been served. The badly worn, and usually painful, teeth of many mature dogs can be traced to excessive chewing on animal bones. Contrary to popular belief, knuckle bones that can be chewed up and swallowed by the dog provide little, if any, useable calcium or other nutrient. They do, however, disturb the digestion of most dogs and might cause them to vomit the nourishing food they really need.

Never give a dog your old shoe to chew on, even if you have removed all the nails or metal parts, such as lace grommets, buckles, metal arches, and so on. Rubber heels are especially dangerous, as the dog can bite off chunks, swallow them, and suffer from intestinal blockage as a result. Additionally, if the rubber should happen to have a nail imbedded in it that you cannot detect, this could pierce or tear the intestinal wall. There is always the possibility, too, that your dog may fail to differentiate between his shoe and yours and chew up a good pair while you're not looking. It is strongly recommended that you refrain from offering old shoes as chew toys, since there are much safer products available.

RAWHIDE CHEWS

The most popular material from which dog chews are made is the hide from cows, horses, and other animals. Most of these chews are made in foreign countries where the quality of the hide is not good enough for

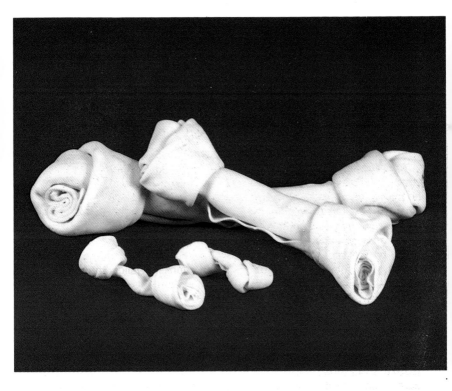

Many dogs love rawhide, and many stores carry a variety of rawhide chew products.

making leather. These foreign hides may contain lead, antibiotics, arsenic, or insecticides which might be detrimental to the health of your dog . . . or even your children. It is not impossible that a small child will start chewing on a piece of rawhide meant for the dog! Rawhide chews do not serve the primary chewing functions very well. They are also a bit messy when wet from mouthing, and most dogs chew them up rather rapidly. They have been considered safe for dogs until recently.

Rawhide is flavorful to dogs. They like it. Currently, some veterinarians have been attributing cases of acute constipation to large pieces of incompletely digested rawhide in ·the intestine. Basically it is good for them to chew on, but dogs think rawhide is food. They do not play with it nor do they use it as a pacifier to relieve doggie tension. They eat it as they would any other food. This is dangerous, for the hide is very difficult for dogs to digest and swallow, and many dogs choke on large particles of rawhide that become stuck in their throats. *Before you offer your dog rawhide chews, consult your veterinarian.* Vets have a lot of

Annealed nylon chews are recommended by veterinarians as proven-safe and effective canine chew devices.

experience with canine chewing devices; ask them what they recommend.

NYLON CHEW DEVICES

The nylon bones, especially those with natural meat and bone flavor added, are probably the most complete, safe, and economical answer to the chewing need. Dogs cannot break them nor bite off sizeable chunks; hence, they are completely safe. And being longer lasting than other things offered for the purpose, they are very economical.

Hard chewing raises little bristle-like projections on the surface of the nylon bones to provide effective interim tooth cleaning and vigorous gum massage, much in the same way your toothbrush does it for you. The little projections are raked off and swallowed in the form of thin shavings, but the chemistry of the nylon is such that they break down in the stomach fluids and pass through without effect.

The toughness of the nylon provides the strong chewing resistance needed for important jaw exercise and effective help for the teething functions; however, there is no tooth wear because nylon is non-abrasive. Being inert, nylon does not support the growth of microorganisms, and it can be washed in soap and water or sterilized by boiling or in an autoclave.

There are a great variety of Nylabone® products available that veterinarians recommend as safe and healthy for your dog or puppy to chew on. These Nylabone® Pooch Pacifiers® usually don't splinter, chip, or break off in large chunks; instead, they are frizzled by the

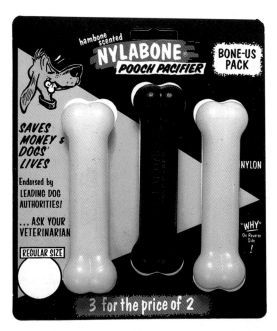

One of the many advantages of annealed nylon chew products is durability and long life. To keep your Nylabone® products sterile and to re-energize their flavor, these bones can be boiled in broth.

dog's chewing action, and this creates a toothbrush-like surface that cleanses the teeth and massages the gums. At the same time, these hard-nylon therapeutic devices channel doggie tension and chewing frustation into constructive rather than destructive behavior. The original nylon bone (Nylabone®) is not a toy and dogs use it only when in need of pacification. Keeping a bone in each of your dog's recreation rooms is the best method of providing the requisite pacification. Unfortunately, many nylon chew products have been copied. These inferior quality copies are sold in supermarkets and other chain stores. The really good products are sold only through veterinarians, pet shops, grooming salons and places where the sales people really know something about dogs. The good products have the flavor impregnated *into* the bone. This makes the taste last longer. The smell is undetectable

Preventive Dental Care

to humans. The artificial bones which have a strong odor are poor-quality bones with the odor sprayed on to impress the dog owner (not the dog)! These heavily scented dog toys may impart the odor to your carpets or furniture if an odor-sprayed bone lies there wet from a dog's chewing on it.

Food particles can be deposited between the teeth, where they are difficult to remove. Even the best chew products may not be able to free these decaying food pieces. For this reason, the Nylafloss® dental device is recommended. It is the only effective product to clean between the dog's teeth.

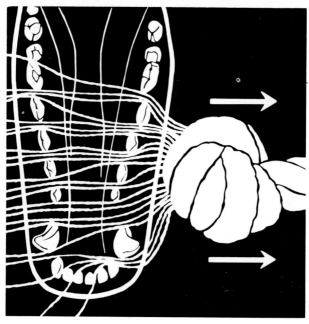

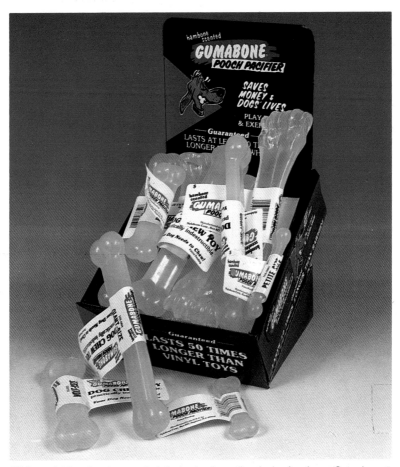

While satisfying the deep-rooted desire to chew, the dog's chewing a Gumabone® works to prevent tartar and plaque build-up. A dog should have access to an effective chew product at all times.

FLOSS OR LOSS!

Most dentists relay that brushing daily is just not enough. In order to prevent unnecessary tooth loss, flossing is essential. For dogs, human dental floss is not the answer—however,

canine dental devices are available. The Nylafloss® is a revolutionary product that is designed to save dogs teeth and keep them healthy. Even though your dogs won't believe you, Nylafloss® is not a toy but rather

Prevention is the key to good dental health. It makes little sense to ignore your dog's dental needs; tooth problems can be costly and detrimental to your dog's well being. Nylafloss® is one very important part of preventive dental care.

a most effective agent in removing destructive plaque between the teeth and *beneath* the gum line where gum disease begins. Gentle tugging is all that is necessary to activate the Nylafloss®. These 100% inert nylon products are guaranteed to outlast rawhide chews by ten times and are available for sale at all pet shops.

THE IMPORTANCE OF PREVENTION

In order to get to the root of canine dentistry problems, it is important for owners to realize that no less than 75% of all canine dental health problems serious enough to require a vet's assistance and nearly 98% of all canine teeth lost are attributable to periodontal disease. Periodontal disease not only mars the teeth but also the gums and other buccal tissue in the mouth. Severe cases of periodontal disease involve resultant bacterial toxins which are absorbed into the blood stream and cause permanent damage to the heart and kidneys. In the infected mouth, teeth are loosened; tartar, unsightly and bad smelling, accumulates heavily; and the dog experiences a complete loss of appetite. Long-standing periodontitis can also manifest itself in simple symptoms such as diarrhea and vomiting.

Periodontal disease deserves the attention of every dog owner—a dog's teeth are extremely important to his ongoing health. The accumulation of plaque, food matter mixed with saliva attaching itself to the tooth surface, is a sure sign of potential bacteria build-up. As toxic material gathers, the bone surrounding the teeth erodes. If plaque and calculus continue to reside without attention, bacteria-fighting cells will form residual pus at the root of the teeth, dividing the gum from the tooth. The debris is toxic and actually kills the buccal tissue. This is a most undesirable situation, as hardened dental calculus is one of the most direct causative agents of periodontitis.

In actuality, the disease is a result of a number of contributing factors. Old age, a diet comprised solely of soft or semi-soft foods, dental tartar, constant chewing of hair and even coprophagy (the eating of stool) are among the most common contributors.

Just as regular dental visits and brushing are necessary for humans, regular hygienic care and veterinary check-ups can help control tooth problems in canines. Involved and expensive routines can be performed on the affected, neglected mouth and teeth if decay has begun

eroding the enamel and infecting the gums. Cleaning, polishing, and scaling are routine to remove calculus build-up.

Owners must claim responsibility for their dog's health, and tooth care is no small aspect of the care required. Daily brushing with a salt/baking soda solution is the best answer, but many owners find this tedious or just too difficult to perform. The simpler and more proven effective way to avoid, reduce, and fight periodontal disease and calculus build-up is giving the dog regular access to a thermoplastic polymer chew device. The Gumabone® products are the only scientifically proven line that offers the desired protection from calculus and tartar build-up.

CANINE DENTAL BREAKTHROUGH

The independent research of Dr. Andrew Duke, D.V.M., reveals that 70% of the dogs that regularly use Gumabone® experience a reduction of calculus build-up. This find is a breakthrough for the dog world, since the Gumabone® has already resided in the toy boxes of many dogs as their favorite play item. Little did owners know previously that their dogs were gaining entertainment and unparalleled dental treatment at the same time. Dr. Duke writes: "There is little debate left that

THE CALCULUS INDEX

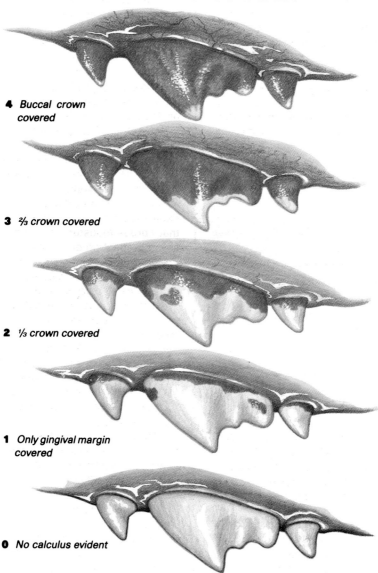

4 *Buccal crown covered*

3 *⅔ crown covered*

2 *⅓ crown covered*

1 *Only gingival margin covered*

0 *No calculus evident*

*An artist's representation of the calculus index, ranging from index rating **4** (topmost drawing) through index rating **0** (lowest drawing).*

dental calculus is an excellent indicator of periodontal health in the dog, just as it is in humans. "Calculus does not cause gingivitis and periodontitis, but the plaque and bacteria that cause periodontitis are responsible for the mineral precipitation we know as 'calculus.' All veterinarians who have made a study of dogs' oral

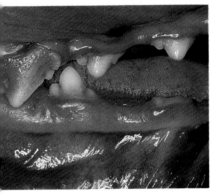

A dog's teeth showing a moderate calculus build-up.

health have noticed the middle aged dog who actively chews with excellent gingival health. Many of these dogs that chew hard substances regularly wear the cusps down and even may expose the pulp cavity faster than secondary dentin can be formed. Often these 'excellent chewers' are presented with slab fractures of the premolars or apical abcesses.

"The challenge then becomes to find a substance which is effective in removing calculus and plaque but does not wear the enamel excessively. In an attempt to duplicate the chewstuffs enjoyed by dogs in the wild, researchers have used bovine tracheas to demonstrate the inhibition of plaque and gingivitis. Very little else has been done in veterinary medicine to establish a scientific basis for evaluating chewstuffs.

"In the human field it is generally accepted (incorrectly) that fibrous foodstuffs and diet have no effect on oral health. This is a moot point since the practice of brushing is by far a more efficient technique of preventing plaque accumulation, calculus and periodontal disease. Studies in human subjects failed to find any benefits in eating apples, raw carrots, etc. If people are not allowed to brush, it is difficult to conduct clinical trials of more than one week.

"The increased awareness of animals' dental health of recent years has resulted in most veterinary practitioners' recommending some kind of chewstuff to their dog owners. To meet this market demand, there has been a stampede into the market by vendors ready to promote their products. The veterinarian is furnished no

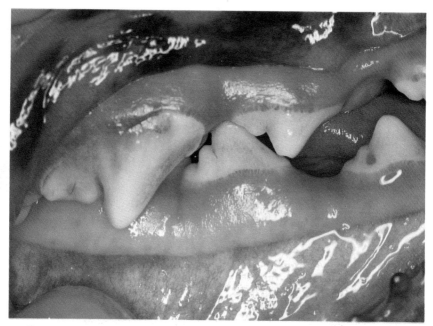

Plaque is formed by the food debris and bacterial deposits on the teeth. Due to the high carbon dioxide and pH level in the mouth, minerals precipitate on the plaque to form calculus.

scientific data, but is asked to promote rawhide, bounce, and squeaky toys. How would our human colleagues handle this situation? Can Listerine® say that it prevents colds, but not support the claim? Can Tartar Control Crest® or Colgate Tartar Control Formula® be sold if it is not proven that it does in fact reduce tartar? Of course not.

"To this end, the following study was made.

"*Method:* Twenty dogs of different breeds and age were selected from a veterinary practice's clientele. Although most were from multiple pet households, none were colony dogs. The owners were asked if they would allow their dogs to be anesthetized for two prophylactic cleanings which included root planing, polishing, and gingival debridement necessary to insure good oral hygiene.

"The dogs were divided into two groups of 10. Their teeth were cleaned and their calculus index converted to 0. One group was allowed only their normal dry commercial dog ration for 30 days. The other was allowed to have free choice access to Gumabone® products of the appropriate size.

"After 30 days, photoslides were made of the upper 3rd premolar, upper 4th premolar, and the lower 4th premolar on both sides of the dog's mouth. The dogs were again subjected to a prophylactic cleaning and the group reversed. After the second 30 days, photoslides were again made. A total of six teeth in each mouth were evaluated on each dog. This was 80 slides representing 240 teeth."

Fourteen out of 20 dogs (or 70%) experienced a reduction in calculus build-up by regularly

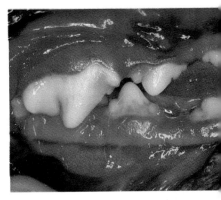

Regular use of the Gumabone® chew products can significantly reduce plaque build-up.

using the Gumabone® product. These products are available in a variety of sizes (for different size dogs) and designed in interesting shapes: bones, balls, knots and rings (and even a tug toy). The entertainment value of the Gumabone® products is but an added advantage to the fighting of tooth decay and periodontitis. The products are ham-flavored and made of a thermoplastic polymer that is designed to outlast by ten times any other rawhide, rubber or vinyl chew product, none of which can promise the proven benefit of the Gumabone®.

If your dog is able to chew apart a Gumabone®, it is probable that you provided him with a bone that is too small for him. Replace it with a larger one and the problem should not re-

Teeth of affected canine showing little to no plaque or calculus build-up after professional cleaning.

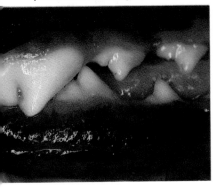

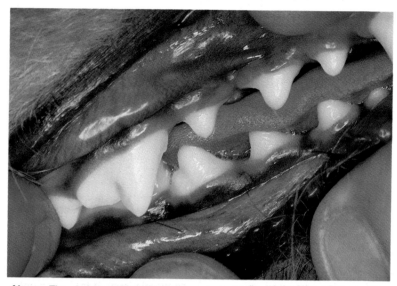

Above: The clean healthy teeth that are desired in dogs should inspire owners to work towards better dental hygiene. *Below:* The beginning of undesirable deposits forming on improperly maintained teeth.

materialize. Economically, the Gumabone® is a smart choice, even without comparing it to the cost of extensive dental care.

Of course, nothing can *substitute* for periodic professional attention to your dog's teeth and gums, no more than your toothbrush can replace your dentist. Have your dog's teeth cleaned by your veterinarian at least once a year—twice a year is better—and he will be healthier, happier, and a far more pleasant companion.

Gumabones® are available through veterinarians and pet shops.

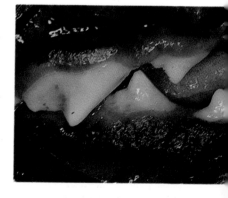

Breeding

If you own a bitch and you want to breed her, first make sure you can handle the responsibility of caring for her and her litter of pups. Consider the time and money involved just to get her into breeding condition and then to sustain her throughout pregnancy and afterwards while she tends her young. You will be obligated to house, feed, groom, and housebreak the puppies until good homes can be found for them; and, lest we forget, there will be periodic trips to the vet for check-ups, wormings, and inoculations. Common sense should tell you that it is indeed cruel to bring unwanted or unplanned puppies into an already crowded canine world; only negligent pet owners allow this to happen. With pet-quality purebred dogs, most breeders require prospective pet owners to sign a neuter/spay agreement when they purchase their dogs. In this way breeders can be assured that only their very best stock of show-quality and breeder-quality animals, i.e., those that match closely their individual standards of perfection and those that are free of genetic disorders or disease, will be used to propagate the breed.

Before you select a stud to mate with your bitch, think carefully about why you want her to give birth to a litter of puppies. If you feel she will be deprived in some way if she is not bred, if you think your children will learn from the experience, if you have the mistaken notion that you will make money from this great undertaking, think again. A dog can lead a perfectly happy, healthy, normal life without having been mated; in fact, spaying a female and neutering a male helps them become better pets, as they are not so anxious to search for a mate in an effort to relieve their sexual tensions. As for giving the children a lesson in sex education, this is hardly a valid reason for breeding your dog. And on an economic level, it takes not only years of hard work (researching pedigrees and bloodlines, studying genetics, among other things), but it takes plenty of capital (money, equipment, facilities) to make a decent profit from dog breeding. Why most dedicated breeders are lucky just to break even. If you have only a casual interest in dog breeding, it is best to leave this pastime to those who are more experienced in such matters, those who consider it a serious hobby or vocation. If you have bought a breeder– or show-quality canine, one that may be capable of producing champions, and if you are just starting out with this breeding venture, seek advice from the seller of your dog, from other veteran breeders, and from your vet before you begin.

Breeding

THE FEMALE "IN SEASON"

A bitch may come into season (also known as "heat" or estrus) once or several times a year, depending on the particular breed and the individual dog. Her first seasonal period, that is to say, the time when she is capable of being fertilized by a male dog, may occur as early as six months with some breeds. If you own a female and your portion of the female's reproductive tract; the soft, flabby vulva indicates her readiness to mate. Around this second week or so ovulation occurs, and this is the crucial period for her to be bred, if this is what you have in mind for her. It is during this middle phase of the heat cycle when conception can take place. Just remember that there is great variation from

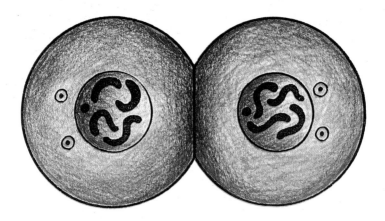

Cells reproduce by a process called mitosis, in which the cells divide, forming two identical cells.

intention is *not* to breed her, by all means discuss with the vet the possibility of having her spayed: this means before she reaches sexual maturity.

The first sign of the female's being in season is a thin red discharge, which may increase for about a week; it then changes color to a thin yellowish stain, which lasts about another week. Simultaneously, there is a swelling of the vulva, the exterior

bitch to bitch with regard to how often they come into heat, how long the heat cycles last, how long the period of ovulation lasts, and how much time elapses between heat cycles. Generally, after the third week of heat, the vulval swelling decreases and the estrus period

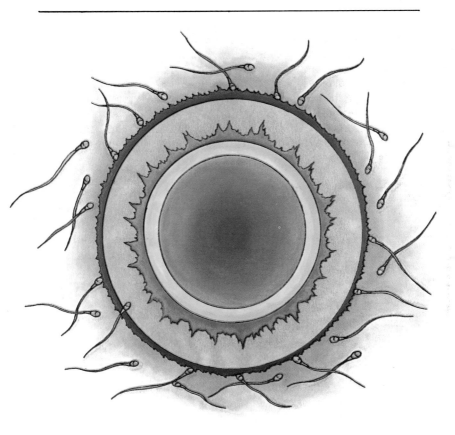

ceases for several months.

It should be mentioned that the female will probably lose her puppy coat, or at least shed part of it, about three months after she has come into season. This is the time when her puppies would have been weaned, had she been mated, and females generally drop coat at this time.

With female dogs, there are few, if any, behavioral changes during estrus. A bitch may dart out of an open door to greet all

The egg within the female is surrounded by a wall that normally takes many sperm to penetrate. In this way, only the strongest sperm will fertilize the egg. A fertile female in season usually has a number of eggs, known as gametes.

available male dogs that show an interest in her, and she may occasionally raise her tail and assume a mating stance, particularly if you pet her lower back; but these signs are not as dramatic as those of the sexually mature male. He himself does not experience heat cycles; rather, he is attracted to the female during all phases of her seasonal period. He usually becomes more aggressive and tends to fight with other males, especially over females in heat. He tends to mark his territory with urine to attract females and at the same time to warn other competitive males. It is not uncommon to see him mount various objects, and people, in an effort to satisfy his mature sexual urges.

If you are a homeowner and you have an absolutely climb-proof and dig-proof run within your yard, it may be safe to leave your bitch in season there. But then again it may not be a wise idea, as there have been cases of males mating with females right through chain-link fencing! Just to be on the safe side, shut her indoors during her heat periods and don't let her outdoors until you are certain the estrus period is over. Never leave a bitch in heat outdoors, unsupervised, even for a minute so that she can defecate or

A whelping box provides the female with a safe place to deliver her pups. Introduce the female to the box several days prior to delivery to get her adjusted to it. Later, when whelping is near, move her to the box so that she may prepare for delivery.

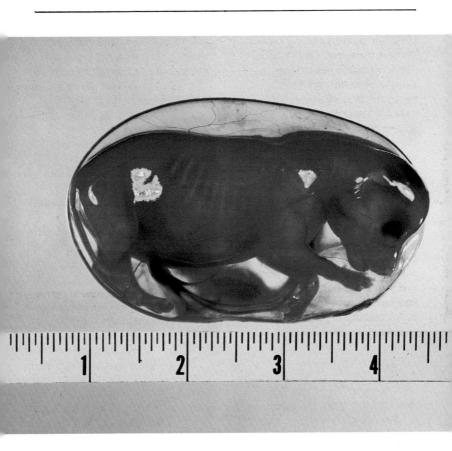

urinate. If you want to prevent the neighborhood dogs from hanging around your doorstep, as they inevitably will do when they discover your female is in season, take her some distance away from the house before you let her do her business. Otherwise, these canine suitors will be attracted to her by the arousing odor of her urine, and they will know instinctively that she isn't far from her scented

While in the womb, each pup is encased within a protective sac.

"calling card." If you need to walk your bitch, take her in the car to a nearby park or field for a chance to stretch her legs. Remember that after about three weeks, and this varies from dog to dog, you can let her outdoors again with no worry that she can have puppies until the next heat period.

Breeding

WHEN TO BREED

It is usually best to breed a bitch when she comes into her second or third season. Plan in advance the time of year which is best for you, taking into account your own schedule of activities (vacations, business trips, social engagements, and so on). Make sure you will be able to set aside plenty of time to assist with whelping of the newborn pups and caring for the dam and her litter for the next few weeks. At the very least, it probably will take an hour or so each day just to feed and clean up after the brood—but undoubtedly you will find it takes much longer if you stop to admire and play with the youngsters periodically! Refrain from selling the litter until it is at least six weeks old, keeping in mind that a litter of pups takes up a fair amount of space by then. It will be your responsibility to provide for them until they have been weaned from their mother, properly socialized, housebroken, and ready to go to new homes (unless you plan to keep them all). Hopefully, as strongly recommended, you will have already lined up buyers for the pups in advance of their arrival into this world.

CHOOSING THE STUD

You can plan to breed your female about six-and-one-half months after the start of her last season, although a variation of a month or two either way is not unusual. Do some research into the various bloodlines within your breed and then choose a stud dog and make arrangements well in advance. If you are breeding for show stock, which will command higher prices than pet-quality animals, a mate should be chosen very carefully. He should complement any deficiencies (bad traits) that your female may have, and he should have a good show record or be the sire of show winners, if he is old enough to have proven himself. If possible, the bitch and stud should have several ancestors in common within the last two or three generations, as such combinations have been known, generally, to "click" best.

The owner of a stud dog usually charges a stud fee for use of the animal's services. This does not always guarantee a litter, but if she fails to conceive, chances are you may be able to breed your female to that stud

Facing page: Dogs have an average gestation period of 63 to 65 days. This chart gives the expected delivery date according to the date on which the bitch was mated. The due date is an approximation only, and the owner should be prepared well in advance of the due date, especially with first-time mothers. If a bitch is mated more than once, the owner should use the date of the first mating but realize the possibility of a later delivery.

PERPETUAL WHELPING CHART

Bred → Due	1	2	3	4	5	6	7	8	9	10	11	12	13	14	15	16	17	18	19	20	21	22	23	24	25	26	27	28	29	30	31
Bred—Jan. / Due—March	5	6	7	8	9	10	11	12	13	14	15	16	17	18	19	20	21	22	23	24	25	26	27	28	29	30	31	Apr. 1	Apr. 2	Apr. 3	Apr. 4
Bred—Feb. / Due—April	5	6	7	8	9	10	11	12	13	14	15	16	17	18	19	20	21	22	23	24	25	26	27	28	29	30	May 1	May 2			
Bred—Mar. / Due—May	3	4	5	6	7	8	9	10	11	12	13	14	15	16	17	18	19	20	21	22	23	24	25	26	27	28	29	30	31	June 1	June 2
Bred—Apr. / Due—June	3	4	5	6	7	8	9	10	11	12	13	14	15	16	17	18	19	20	21	22	23	24	25	26	27	28	29	30	July 1	July 2	
Bred—May / Due—July	3	4	5	6	7	8	9	10	11	12	13	14	15	16	17	18	19	20	21	22	23	24	25	26	27	28	29	30	31	Aug. 1	Aug. 2
Bred—June / Due—August	3	4	5	6	7	8	9	10	11	12	13	14	15	16	17	18	19	20	21	22	23	24	25	26	27	28	29	30	31	Sept. 1	
Bred—July / Due—September	2	3	4	5	6	7	8	9	10	11	12	13	14	15	16	17	18	19	20	21	22	23	24	25	26	27	28	29	30	Oct. 1	Oct. 2
Bred—Aug. / Due—October	3	4	5	6	7	8	9	10	11	12	13	14	15	16	17	18	19	20	21	22	23	24	25	26	27	28	29	30	31	Nov. 1	Nov. 2
Bred—Sept. / Due—November	3	4	5	6	7	8	9	10	11	12	13	14	15	16	17	18	19	20	21	22	23	24	25	26	27	28	29	30	Dec. 1	Dec. 2	
Bred—Oct. / Due—December	3	4	5	6	7	8	9	10	11	12	13	14	15	16	17	18	19	20	21	22	23	24	25	26	27	28	29	30	31	Jan. 1	Jan. 2
Bred—Nov. / Due—January	3	4	5	6	7	8	9	10	11	12	13	14	15	16	17	18	19	20	21	22	23	24	25	26	27	28	29	30	31	Feb. 1	
Bred—Dec. / Due—February	2	3	4	5	6	7	8	9	10	11	12	13	14	15	16	17	18	19	20	21	22	23	24	25	26	27	28	March 1	March 2	March 3	March 4

Breeding

again. In some instances the owner of the stud will agree to take a "first pick of the litter" in place of a fee. You should, of course, settle all details beforehand, including the possibility of a single puppy surviving, deciding the age at which the pup is to be taken, and so forth.

If you plan to raise a litter that will be sold exclusively as pets,

and if you merely plan to make use of an available male (not a top stud dog), the most important selection point involves temperament. Make sure the dog is friendly, as well as healthy, because a bad disposition can be passed on to his puppies—and this is the worst of all traits in a dog destined to be a pet. If you are breeding pet-quality dogs, a "stud fee puppy," not necessarily the choice of the litter, is the usual payment. Don't

The reproductive system of the female dog consists of a highly specialized group of organs situated at the rear of the animal.

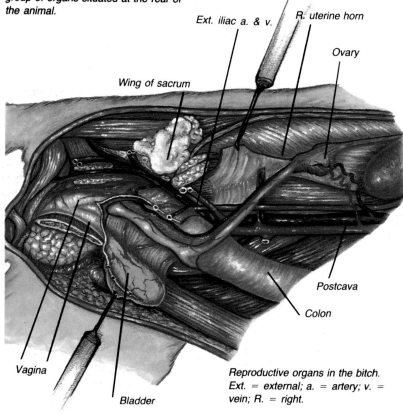

Reproductive organs in the bitch. *Ext. = external; a. = artery; v. = vein; R. = right.*

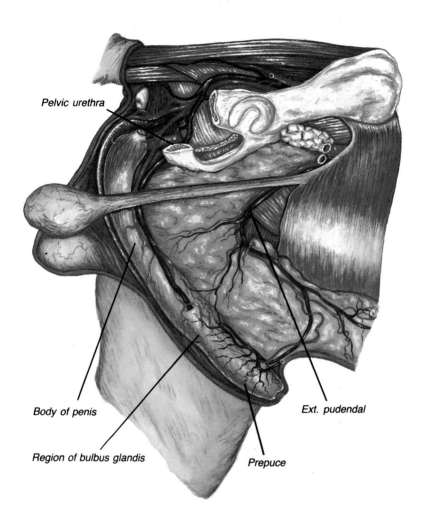

Pelvic urethra

Body of penis

Region of bulbus glandis

Ext. pudendal

Prepuce

The reproductive system of the male dog includes the penis and testicles. The sperm and testosterone producing testes are contained within the scrotal sac. When not excited, the penis is withdrawn into the dog. The dog's penis is unique in that the base of the shaft has a bulbous swelling that forbids retraction from the vagina until some time has passed after intercourse.

breed indiscriminately; be sure you will be able to find good homes for each of the pups, or be sure you have the facilities to keep them yourself, *before* you plan to mate your dog.

PREPARATION FOR BREEDING

Before you breed your female, make sure she is in good health.

She should be neither too thin nor too fat. Any skin disease *must* be cured first so that it is not passed on to the puppies. If she has worms, she should be wormed before being bred or within three weeks after the mating. It is generally considered a good idea to revaccinate her against distemper and hepatitis before the puppies are born. This will increase the immunity the puppies receive during their early, most vulnerable period.

The female will probably be ready to breed twelve days after the first colored discharge appears. You can usually make arrangements to board her with the owner of the stud for a few days, to insure her being there at the proper time; or you can take her to be mated and bring her home the same day if you live near enough to the stud's owner. If the bitch still appears receptive she may be bred again two days later, just to make certain the mating was successful.

However, some females never show signs of willingness, so it helps to have an experienced breeder on hand. In fact, you both may have to assist with the

The canine uterus is quite different from the human uterus. Besides the difference in shape, the canine uterus is designed to house an average of five to eight offspring.

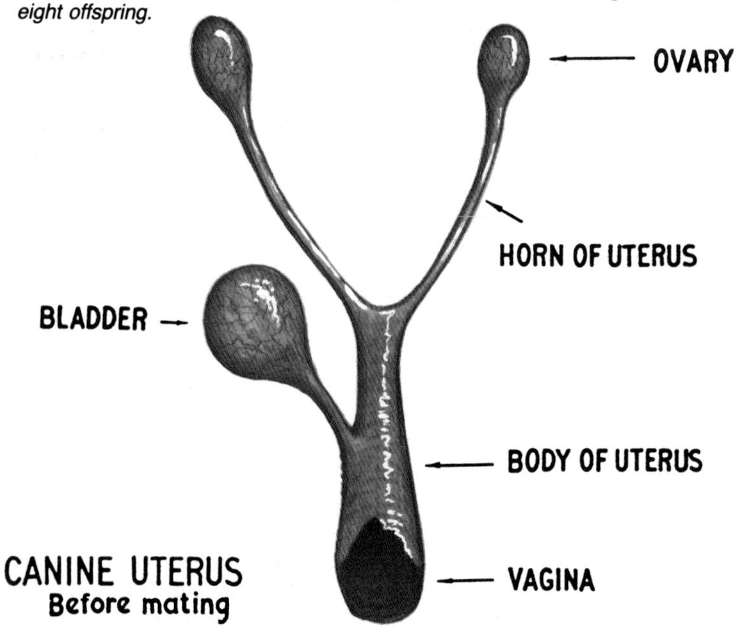

OVARY

HORN OF UTERUS

BLADDER —

BODY OF UTERUS

CANINE UTERUS
Before mating

VAGINA

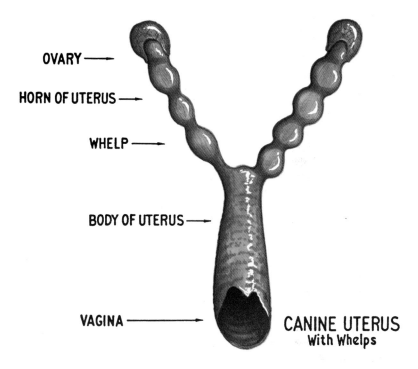

OVARY

HORN OF UTERUS

WHELP

BODY OF UTERUS

VAGINA

CANINE UTERUS
With Whelps

Prior to birth, the developing pups are housed in the horns of the uterus.

mating by holding the animals against each other to ensure the "tie" is not broken, that is, to make certain copulation takes place. Sometimes, too, you'll need to muzzle the bitch to keep her from biting you or the stud.

Usually the second day after the discharge changes color is the proper time to mate the bitch, and she may be bred for about three days following this time. For an additional week or so, she may have some discharge and attract other dogs by her odor; but she should not be bred. Once she has been bred, keep her far from all other male dogs, as they have the capacity to impregnate her again and sire some of her puppies. This could prove disastrous where purebred puppies—especially show-quality ones—are concerned.

THE FEMALE IN WHELP

You can expect the puppies nine weeks from the day of the mating, although sixty-one days is as common as sixty-three. Gestation, that period when the pups are developing inside their mother, varies among individual bitches. During this time the female should receive normal

Breeding

care and exercise. If she was overweight at the start, don't increase her food right away; excess weight at whelping time can be a problem with some dogs. If she is on the thin side, however, supplement her meal or meals with a portion of milk and biscuit at noontime. This will help build her up and put weight on her.

You may want to add a mineral and vitamin supplement to her diet, on the advice of your veterinarian, since she will need an extra supply not only for herself but for the puppies growing inside of her. As the mother's appetite increases, feed her more. During the last two weeks of pregnancy, the pups grow enormously and the mother will have little room for food and less of an appetite. She should be tempted with meat, liver, and milk, however.

As the female in whelp grows heavier, cut out violent exercise

Using simple genetic rules, an owner can predict to some degree the traits that the offspring of a given mating can exhibit. The six possible ways in which a pair of determiners can unite are illustrated on this Mendelian expectation chart. Ratios apply to expectancy over large numbers, except in lines 1, 2, and 6 where exact expectancy is realized in every litter.

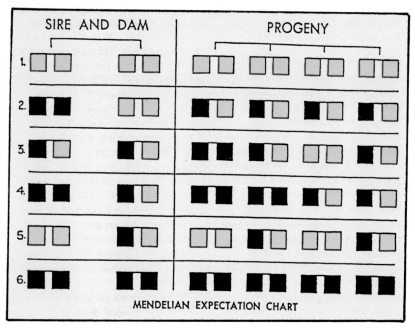

MENDELIAN EXPECTATION CHART

and jumping from her usual routine. Although a dog used to such activities will often play with the children or run around voluntarily, restrain her for her own sake.

A sign that whelping is imminent is the loss of hair around her breasts. This is nature's way of "clearing a path" so that the puppies will be able to find their source of nourishment. As parturition draws near, the breasts will have swelled with milk and the nipples will have enlarged and darkened to a rosy pink. If the hair in the breast region does not shed for some reason, you can easily cut it short with a pair of scissors or comb it out so that it does not mat and become a hindrance to the suckling pups later on.

PREPARING FOR THE PUPPIES

Prepare a whelping box a few days before the puppies are due, and allow the mother to sleep there overnight or to spend some time in it during the day to become accustomed to it. This way she is less likely to try to have her pups under the front porch or in the middle of your bed. A variety of places will serve, such as the corner of your cellar or garage (provided these places are warm and dry). An unused room, such as a dimly lit spare bedroom, can also serve as the place for delivery. If the weather is warm, a large outdoor dog house will do, as long as it is well protected from rain, drafts, and the cold—and enclosed by fencing or a run. A whelping box serves to separate mother and puppies from visitors and other distractions. The walls should be high enough to restrain the puppies yet low enough to allow the mother to take a short respite from her brood after she has fed them. Four feet square is minimum size (for most dogs) and six-to-eight-inch high walls will keep the pups in until they begin to climb; then side walls should be built up so that the young ones cannot wander away from their nest. As the puppies grow, they really need more room anyway, so double the space with a very low partition down the middle of the box, and soon you will find them naturally housebreaking themselves. Puppies rarely relieve themselves where they sleep. Layers of newspapers spread over the whole area will make excellent bedding and be absorbent enough to keep the surface warm and dry. These should be removed daily and replaced with another thick layer. An old quilt or washable blanket makes better footing for the nursing puppies than slippery newspaper during the first week; this is also softer for the mother to lie on.

Be prepared for the actual whelping several days in

Breeding

advance. Usually the mother will tear up papers, refuse food, and become restless. These may be false alarms; the real test is her temperature, which will drop to below 100°F (38°C) about twelve hours before whelping. Take her temperature with a rectal thermometer, morning and evening, and usher her to her whelping box when her temperature goes down. Keep a close watch on her and make sure she stays safely indoors (or outdoors in a safe enclosure); if she is let outside, unleashed, or allowed to roam freely, she could wander off and start to go into labor. It is possible that she could whelp anywhere, and this could be unfortunate if she needs your assistance.

WHELPING

Usually little help is needed from you, but it is wise to stay close to be sure that the mother's lack of experience (if this is her first time) does not cause an unnecessary complication. Be ready to help when the first puppy arrives, for it could smother if she does not break the amniotic membrane enclosing it. She should tear open the sac and start licking the puppy, drying and stimulating it. Check to see that all fluids have been cleared from the pup's nostrils and mouth after the mother has licked her youngster clean; otherwise the pup may

have difficulty breathing. If the mother fails to tear open the sac and stimulate the newborn's breathing, you can do this yourself by tearing the sack with your hands and then gently rubbing the infant with a soft, rough towel. The afterbirth attached to the puppy by the long umbilical cord should follow the birth of each puppy. Watch to be sure that each afterbirth is expelled, for the retention of this material can cause infection. In her instinct for cleanliness the mother will probably eat the afterbirth after severing the umbilical cord. One or two meals of this will not hurt her; they stimulate her milk supply, as well as labor, for remaining pups. However, eating too many afterbirths can make her lose appetite for the food she needs to feed her pups and regain her strength. So remove the rest of them, along with the wet newspapers, and keep the box dry and clean.

If the mother does not bite the cord or bites it too close to the puppy's body, take over the job to prevent an umbilical hernia. Tearing is recommended, but you can cut the cord, about two inches from the body, with a sawing motion with scissors that have been sterilized in alcohol. Then dip the end of the cut cord in a shallow dish of iodine; the cord will dry up and fall off in a few days.

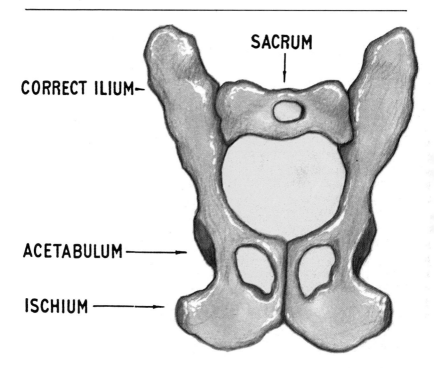

Shape of pelvic entrance in the average female dog, showing adequate aperture through which the whelps have to pass.

The puppies should follow each other at intervals of not more than half an hour. If more time goes past and you are sure there are still pups to come, taking the mother for a brisk walk outside may start labor again. If she is actively straining without producing a puppy, the youngster may be presented backward, a so-called "breech" birth. Careful assistance with a well-lubricated finger to feel for the puppy or to ease it back may help, but never attempt to pull it out by force. This could cause serious damage, so seek the services of an expert—your veterinarian or an experienced breeder.

Even the best planned breeding can bear unexpected problems and complications. Therefore, do not rely solely on textbook knowledge of breeding and genetics. Experienced breeders and veterinarians will generally lend their words of wisdom—take full advantage of their generosity. Mere trial and

Breeding

error is no basis for any responsible breeding program.

If *anything* seems wrong during labor or parturition, waste no time in calling your veterinarian, who will examine the bitch and, if necessary, give her hormones to stimulate the birth of the remaining puppies. You may want his experience in whelping the litter even if all goes well. He will probably prefer to have the puppies born at his hospital rather than getting up in the middle of the night to come

A puppy nurser kit is considered standard equipment by many breeders. These kits are available at your local pet shop.

to your home. The mother would, no doubt, prefer to stay at home; but you can be sure she will get the best of care in a veterinary hospital. If the puppies are born at home, and all goes as it should, watch the mother carefully afterward. Within a day or two of the birth, it is wise to have the veterinarian check her and the pups to ensure that all is well.

Be sure each puppy finds a teat and starts nursing right away, as these first few meals supply colostral antibodies to help him fight disease. As soon as he is dry, hold each puppy to a nipple for a good meal without competition. Then he may join his littermates in the whelping box, out of his mother's way while she continues giving birth. Keep a supply of puppy formula on hand for emergency feedings or later weaning. An alternative formula of evaporated milk, corn syrup, and a little water with egg yolk can be warmed and fed if necessary. A pet nurser kit is also a good thing to have on hand; these are available at local pet shops. A supplementary feeding often helps weak pups (those that may have difficulty nursing) over the hump. Keep track of birth weights and weekly readings thereafter; this will furnish an accurate record of the pups' growth and health, and the information will be valuable to your veterinarian.

RAISING THE PUPPIES

After all the puppies have been born, take the mother outside for a walk and drink of water, and then return her to take care of her brood. She will probably not want to stay away for more than a minute or two for the first few weeks. Be sure to keep water available at all times and feed her milk or broth frequently, as she needs nourishment to produce milk. Encourage her to eat, with her favorite foods, until she seeks them of her own accord. She will soon develop a ravenous appetite and should have at least two large meals a day, with dry food available in addition. Your veterinarian can guide you on the finer points of nutrition as they apply to nursing dams.

Prepare a warm place to put the puppies after they are born to keep them dry and to help them to a good start in life. An electric heating pad, heat lamp or hot water bottle covered with flannel can be placed in the bottom of a cardboard box and near the mother so that she can see her puppies. She will usually allow you to help her care for the youngsters, but don't take them out of her sight. Let her handle things if your interference seems to make her nervous.

Be sure that all the puppies are getting enough to eat. If the mother sits or stands instead of lying still to nurse, the probable cause is scratching from the puppies' nails. You can remedy this by clipping them, as you would the bitch's, with a pet nail clipper. Manicure scissors also do for these tiny claws. Some breeders advise disposing of the smaller or weaker pups in a large litter, as the mother has trouble handling more than six or seven. You can help her out by preparing an extra puppy box or basket furnished with a heating pad and/or heating lamp and some bedding material. Leave half the litter with the mother and the other half in the extra box, changing off at two-hour intervals at first. Later you may exchange them less frequently, leaving them all together except during the day. Try supplementary feedings, too. As soon as their eyes open, at about two weeks, they will lap from a small dish.

WEANING THE PUPPIES

Normally the puppies should be completely weaned at five weeks, although you can start to feed them at three weeks. They will find it easier to lap semi-solid food than to drink milk at first, so mix baby cereal with whole or evaporated milk, warmed to body temperature, and offer it to the puppies in a saucer. Until they learn to lap it, it is best to feed one or two at a time because they are more likely to walk into it than to eat it. Hold the saucer at their chin level, and let them gather around, keeping paws off

Breeding

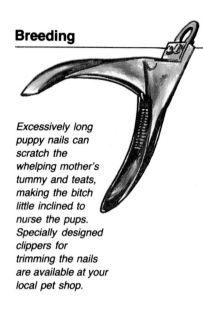

Excessively long puppy nails can scratch the whelping mother's tummy and teats, making the bitch little inclined to nurse the pups. Specially designed clippers for trimming the nails are available at your local pet shop.

the dish. Cleaning with a damp sponge afterward prevents most of the cereal from sticking to the pups if the mother doesn't clean them up. Once they have gotten the idea, broth or babies' meat soup may be alternated with milk, and you can start them on finely chopped meat. At about four weeks, they will eat four meals a day and soon do without their mother entirely. Start them on canned dog food, or leave dry puppy food with them in a dish for self-feeding. Don't leave the water dish with them all the time; at this age everything is a play toy and they will use it as a wading pool. They can drink all they need if it is offered several times a day, after meals. As the puppies grow up, the mother will go into their "pen" only to nurse them, first sitting up and then standing. To dry up her milk

supply completely, keep the mother away for longer periods; after a few days of part-time nursing she can stay away for even longer periods, and then permanently. The little milk left will be resorbed by her body.

The puppies may be put outside during the day, unless it is too cold or rainy, as soon as their eyes are open. They will benefit from the sunlight. A rubber mat or newspapers underneath will protect them from cold or dampness. As they mature, the pups can be let out for longer intervals, although you must provide them with a shelter at night or in bad weather. By now, cleaning up after the matured youngsters is a man-sized job, so put them out at least during the day and make your task easier. If you enclose them in a run or kennel, remember to clean it *daily*, as various parasites and other infectious organisms may be lurking if the quarters are kept dirty.

You can expect the pups to need at least one worming before they are ready to go to new homes. Before the pups are three weeks old, take a stool sample from each to your veterinarian. The vet can determine, by analyzing the stool, if any of the pups have worms—and if so, what kind of worms are present. If one puppy is infected, then all should be wormed as a preventive measure. Follow the veterinarian's advice; this also applies to vaccinations. You will want to vaccinate the pups at the earliest possible age. This way, the pups destined for new homes will be protected against some of the more debilitating canine diseases.

THE DECISION TO SPAY OR NEUTER

If you decide not to use your male or female for breeding, or if you are obligated to have the animal altered based on an agreement made between you and the seller, make the necessary arrangements with your veterinarian as soon as possible. The surgery involved for both males and females is relatively simple and painless: males will be castrated and females will have their ovaries and uterus removed. In both cases, the operation does not alter their personalities; you will, however, notice that males will be less likely to roam, to get into fights with other male dogs, and to mount objects and people.

Your veterinarian can best determine at what age neutering or spaying should be done. With a young female dog, the operation may be somewhat more involved, and as a result be more costly; however, in the long run you will be glad you made the decision to have this done for your pet. After a night or two at the veterinarian's or an animal hospital, your bitch can be safely returned to your home. Her stitches will heal in a short time, and when they are removed, you will hardly notice her souvenir scar of the routine operation. Once she has been spayed, she no longer will be capable of having a litter of puppies. Pet adoption agencies and other animal welfare organizations can house only so many animals at one time, given the money, space, and other resources they have available. This is why pet owners are urged to have their pets altered, so that puppies resulting from accidental breedings won't end up being put to sleep as so many others have that are lost, stray, unwanted, or abandoned.

Top view of a dog's skeletal structure. The dog is a highly specialized animal.

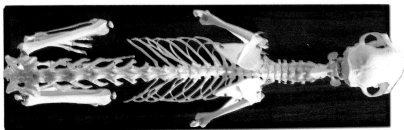

Dogs and the Law

By Anmarie Barrie, Esq.

This chapter is written merely as a general survey of the laws pertaining to dogs. The laws vary tremendously from jurisdiction to jurisdiction. They also change over time, and are subject to the interpretation of the controlling authorities.

Any reference to a resource material or facility is not an endorsement.

As civilization advances and living conditions become more crowded, laws are created to keep society functioning smoothly. Our lives become more regulated. This includes how we care for our dogs.

Laws dealing with dogs are in effect at all levels of government. Mostly, though, dog law is a local affair. There are many dog laws. They vary from country to country and from city to city. However, there are general rules and guidelines that are common to all dog laws.

BUYING AND SELLING

Most of the law regulating buyers, sellers, and breeders of dogs pertains to dealers. A dealer is a person who buys and sells dogs in the regular course of his business. Therefore, an owner who sells the family pet's puppies at a yard sale is not covered. However, some laws do encompass the occasional seller.

If you regularly sell, keep, or breed more than a certain number of dogs, you may need a kennel or breeder's license. Puppies may or may not be included in this number. Usually diseased dogs, and dogs under a specified age, are forbidden to be sold.

Whether you are the buyer or the seller, put the sales agreement in writing. Until you write it out, you may not realize that you and the other party have different understandings. The agreement should include, but is certainly not limited to, the following:

1. Breed, sex, age, color, quality, and birth date of the dog
2. Names and addresses of

the buyer and the seller

3. Name and address of the breeder

4. Names and registration numbers of the sire and dam (pedigree)

5. Date of the last veterinary exam, the name and address of the veterinarian, and any findings

6. Date and types of vaccinations

7. Behavior (viciousness) and propensities (training) of the dog

8. Any health problems the dog may have

9. Any warranties (guarantees) the seller is making

10. The name of the original owner (if the seller purchased the dog from someone else).

GENERAL GUIDELINES FOR DOG OWNERS

Licenses

Probably wherever you live, a dog needs a license. A license involves a fee and usually has to be renewed periodically. It should be worn by the dog at all times. Puppies under a certain age are exempt from the licensing requirements. A license may cost less for a spayed or neutered dog, an assistance dog, or a dog belonging to an old or disabled person. To find out where to get a license, talk to your pet shop owner, veterinarian, local officials, the animal control or health department, or look in the telephone book.

Licensed and unlicensed dogs may be accorded different treatment under the law. Any unlicensed dog, or a dog running at large without a license tag, may be impounded. Unlicensed dogs that are impounded are destroyed or sold sooner than licensed dogs, because local authorities are unable to trace ownership. Furthermore, some authorities permit the killing of an unlicensed dog, or a licensed dog not wearing its license, at any given time. Yet a dog wearing a license can be killed only if it is attacking a person or livestock.

Dogs and the Law

If your dog is lost or stolen, it will be harder to find if it does not have a license. An owner of an unlicensed dog may be subject to a fine or penalty.

Vaccinations

A current rabies vaccination is a common requirement. Other inoculations, such as a distemper shot, may be necessary as well. Proof of vaccination may be required in order to get a license. Puppies under a certain age are not required to be vaccinated.

Leash Laws

Many areas have leash laws. These laws require a dog to be under the control of its owner at all times. This may involve confinement, that the dog be on a leash, or even muzzled.

No dog should be allowed to roam free. A dog at large could be impounded and disposed of according to regulations. Its owner may be fined and have to pay for the cost of confining the dog. Some communities have special areas where dogs are allowed to run loose.

Other Restrictions

Muzzle laws are becoming more popular, as are laws requiring owners to clean up their dog's solid waste (pooper-scooper laws) if deposited anywhere off their own property. Many buildings, such as restaurants, apartments, and hotels, and other areas, such as beaches, are strictly off limits to dogs. Owners of assistance dogs are commonly excluded from these laws.

You should also be aware that some municipalities actually prohibit a dog from being left alone in a car. An owner may be violating anti-cruelty laws.

How Many Dogs Allowed?

Many animal lovers have more than one dog. However, some communities restrict the number of dogs allowed per household, and some residencies refuse to permit dogs at all.

These laws are taken quite seriously. If your condominium or apartment lease has a no-pets clause, you can be evicted for harboring a dog. If your residence limits the number of dogs you can keep, exceeding that number can subject you to a daily fine.

If you want to keep more dogs, you may need to apply for a city permit or a kennel license. This may entail extra fees, rules, and inspections.

An owner may be required to dispose of the number of dogs exceeding the allowable limit. Fines and jail sentences can be imposed as well. These enforcement measures can be imposed even if you are caring for someone else's dog only temporarily. Puppies less than a certain age may or may not be exempted.

Lost and Found

If your dog is lost, call any agency you think handles dogs. Include the police, health and animal control departments, and humane societies. Listen to local radio stations and read the local newspapers that list found animals. Visit the police station,

animal shelter, and government offices where lists may be posted. Leave a picture and an accurate description of the dog every place you visit. If at first you are not successful, keep asking around. The dog may show up later.

If you find a dog, attempt to find its owner, or give the dog to the local authorities. If you do not make an effort to return the dog to its owner, you may be liable to the owner for the value of the dog. The law may require you to notify the animal control authorities.

If the dog remains in your possession, check for

identification. The dog may have the name and address of its owner on a tag. Call the owner. If the dog has a license tag, call the agency that issued the tag to get the name of the owner.

Ask local residents if they recognize the dog. Post signs around the area where the dog was found. Put a notice in the paper and notify the local radio station.

Impoundment laws often give animal control officials the authority to pick up, impound, sell, and/or destroy dogs. However, since a dog is considered the personal property of its owner, a dog cannot be confiscated without notice, and possibly a hearing.

An owner's property rights may be lost, though, under certain conditions. Any unlicensed dog, or a dog running at large without a vaccination tag, or running at large without a license tag may be impounded without first notifying its owner.

Dogs running around loose are

typical pound inhabitants. Injured, abandoned, and vicious dogs also end up at the pound. A dog that has bitten a person, caused damage, or been declared a nuisance can be taken from its owner and impounded. An owner who has his dog in his possession, though, is entitled to be notified before the dog is seized. An owner must usually be notified again before the dog is destroyed.

A pound is required to keep the dog for a prescribed period of time before it can take action. If the owner can be identified, he must be notified. To reclaim the dog, an owner may have to have the dog licensed, vaccinated, pay a fine, and pay a charge for every day that the dog is kept. If the owner does not claim the dog, it can be sold, offered for adoption, or killed in a humane manner. The law may allow a dog to be given to an assistance dog agency or a research facility.

Dog laws may be enforced by any number of agencies. These include the police, a humane society, an animal control center, or a health department. No matter which organization is responsible for enforcing the law, all of them must respect the legal rights of an owner.

Burial

Contact your local animal control authority for information on how to dispose of your dog's remains. You may not be permitted to bury the dog on your own property. You may have to bring the dog's body to a pet cemetery. The wisest thing to do is to have your vet handle the burial. Some towns will dispose of the dog for a fee.

DOGS AS PROPERTY

A dog is personal property. This fact has a lot of legal implications, because an owner of property has legally enforceable rights. The law prohibits a person from injuring, taking, or destroying the property of another. So an owner who has a property interest in

his dog is entitled to compensation if his dog is killed, stolen, or injured.

Damages typically include actual out-of-pocket expenses. But other criteria may have some bearing as well. For example, consider the market value and age of the dog. Its type, traits, pedigree, and purchase price are all legitimate concerns. The feelings of the owner will probably not be considered in a damage award. Other considerations include registration, breeding value, value as a watchdog, and if the dog is expecting a litter.

For an owner to enforce his rights as an owner of property, the dog may need to be licensed. An owner of an unlicensed dog may not be afforded any protection under the law. An owner of a puppy that does not yet require a license should still benefit from the property laws concerning dogs.

Since a dog is not a person, it cannot be a beneficiary of a will. It cannot inherit money or other property. If you want your dog to be cared for after your death, you must designate a new owner for the dog in your will. It is wise to leave money to the new owner to care for your dog. Be sure to consider medical expenses—as your dog gets older, its veterinary bills will increase.

A dog may be contested property in a divorce proceeding. A court will determine custody and visitation rights.

Property cannot be taken from an owner without due process of the law. This means that the dog owner must have notice, and possibly be given a hearing before his property is taken or destroyed. Therefore, before a dog can be impounded, killed, or offered for adoption, its owner must be given adequate notice. The amount of time considered "adequate notice" varies from place to place and may depend on whether or not the dog is licensed.

Who is Responsible for the Dog?

An owner is legally responsible for controlling his dog. However, the definition of an owner may be broad enough to include the legal owner, as well as anyone who cares for, harbors, or has custody of the dog. So someone besides the owner, or more than one person, may be liable for the actions of the dog.

A dog owner may be a minor. In such a situation, the youngster's parents or legal guardian may be responsible for any injury or damage caused by the dog. Under certain circumstances, a landlord may be responsible. The landlord must have known that a tenant's dog was dangerous, have had

Dogs and the Law

the power to remove the dog, but did nothing about it.

A veterinarian and his staff members may be injured by a dog during the course of its treatment. The dog owner is probably not responsible because these people know and accept the risk of injury. Of course, an owner cannot conceal the fact that his dog is dangerous. A doctor has insurance to cover these mishaps.

Liability for Damage and Injury

Typically, an owner is legally liable for any personal injury or property damage (including killing livestock) caused by his pet. Depending upon the circumstances, an owner may be fined or jailed as well.

An owner may have to pay medical expenses. This can include costs for doctors, hospitals, medications, physical therapy, and counselling. A victim may also be entitled to compensation for loss of earnings if he was out of work due to his injury. The time off may involve both treatment and recuperation.

Some victims of dog attacks are awarded compensation for pain and suffering. The amount

of the award can vary tremendously depending on the circumstances because it is difficult to calculate the cost specifically. Sometimes a spouse or close relative can receive compensation as well. The theory is loss of service of the injured person. Loss of service is not limited to economics; it may also include loss of companionship.

If the fault on the part of the owner is particularly shocking or reckless, an award may be doubled or even tripled. Additionally, the victim may be entitled to punitive damages. This recovery punishes the owner's poor conduct by making him pay even more than the amount considered adequate compensation to the victim. The financial status of the owner can be taken into account when establishing a punitive damage award.

Also, the owner will have to take measures designed to prevent further detriment. In serious cases, this could mean destruction of the dog. Since any dog can cause injury or damage under the right circumstances, a prudent owner will take precautionary measures designed to prevent his dog from causing harm.

There are several legal theories under which dog owners may be found liable for their dog's acts. Some of the theories are strict liability, common law rules, negligence, and nuisance. Strict liability means that the owner is responsible for the dog's actions even though the owner is not at fault in any way. Common law doctrines are defined in court decisions. They are not codified in statutes. An owner is negligent if he does not exercise reasonable and ordinary care in controlling his dog. A dog is a nuisance if it unreasonably and substantially offends or inconveniences a person.

Often there is an on-duty exemption for trained police or military dogs. The police or government may be immune from liability if the injury occurred because the dog was

Dogs and the Law

provoked or while it was working.

Vicious Dogs

Once a dog has bitten or exhibited menacing behavior, it may be officially declared a vicious dog. Dogs that have been trained to attack or fight may also be considered vicious. A few dog breeds are believed to be inherently dangerous.

Owners of such vicious dogs may be required to take further measures to control their dogs. The dogs may have to be securely confined at all times, on a leash and muzzled when in public, and have a special vicious dog license. The dog may have to be tattooed. The owner may be required to have liability insurance for the dog. Signs may be necessary to warn the public that a vicious dog is in residence. A bond may have to be posted with the municipality to cover any potential injury or damage. Some cities ban vicious dogs.

An owner who fails to comply with the law may be fined or jailed. He may also be liable for double or triple the amount of damage caused by the dog. The dog may be impounded and killed.

Preventing Injury

If you are a dog owner or keeper, the best way to avoid liability is to prevent injury. Adhere to a few common sense rules to keep risk of harm to a minimum.

No matter how small, old or timid the dog is, it can hurt someone, damage property, or be a nuisance. Any dog may bite or scratch if it is threatened, or if it is protecting its owner, its puppies, or its food. A dog racing around a corner or barking unexpectedly may startle an unsuspecting person and result in injury.

Therefore, keep your dog securely contained in the house or yard. Be sure it cannot escape to scare or otherwise get in the way of strangers. Post warning signs that alert passers-by that a dog is present. Never let your dog off its leash to run at large. The owner must be in control at all times.

Lastly, keep the dog's license and vaccinations up-to-date. If your dog does manage to get free, its return will be more expedient if it is properly identified. The less time out of your care, the less time the dog has to cause trouble. Should the dog bite someone, the dog will not need to be quarantined if its rabies vaccine is current.

Dogs and the Law

Insurance

The cost of the potential damage and injury inflicted by a dog can be enormous. A wise owner will check to see that his homeowner's or renter's policy covers his dog. A dog that has a menacing behavior should have its own insurance coverage. Dangerous and vicious dogs may be obligated by law to have liability insurance.

A typical homeowner's or renter's insurance plan covers any damage caused by the policy holder's negligence. This coverage often extends to incidents that take place away from the owner's property, even if a vehicle is involved. If policy does not extend to vehicular events, look to your auto insurance plan. Some insurance companies refuse to issue a policy altogether if a vicious dog lives in the home.

Often a plan limits its coverage to the first instance of harm caused by a dog. After that, the owner must pay out of his own pocket. Other companies exclude certain types of dog-related harm from their coverage. This is why it is important to read your policy carefully. If you do not understand the terms, call your agent for an explanation. It is important to know your liability before an accident occurs.

If your home and auto insurance do not extend to dog-related injuries, or you think the coverage is not broad enough, buy insurance for your pet. Take out insurance that will protect you and the dog while at home and/or away.

Your dog may become ill or injured. Get coverage that will pay for its medical expenses. Some insurance firms offer pet health insurance. These policies may pay for medications, doctors' bills, and hospital fees.

Handling a Controversy

A dog can be dangerous, or it can be just a nuisance. Either way, if you have a dog like this in your neighborhood, or if it is your dog, you may be involved in a dispute. Your dog may have caused injury or damage, or your dog may have been the victim. Either way, you should be prepared to handle the controversy in a responsible and legally acceptable manner.

A dog may not be dangerous, but it can be a nuisance. Some irksome antics include digging up a yard, chasing a car, scattering garbage across the lawn, ravaging a prized garden, barking incessantly, roaming the neighborhood, and frightening people.

If you are the property owner, the first thing to do is to talk to the owner of the dog. Use a reasonable and friendly approach—*avoid animosity*. Offer your neighbor some advice

as to how to stop the dog's bad habits. Suggest obedience school or calling the local humane society for some tips. If the dog's poor behavior stops, call on your neighbor again to thank him for taking the necessary measures.

If you happen to be the owner of the dog wreaking havoc, be understanding, not hostile. After all, you are responsible for keeping your dog from annoying your neighbors. Your neighbor has probably had several encounters with your dog before he came to talk to you. Take the proper measures to stop the dog's poor behavior. After a few days, visit your neighbor to be sure the problem has been solved.

If talking to your neighbor is a dead-end, try mediation. This method of settling disputes outside of a courtroom involves the imposition of a neutral third party. This individual acts as a link between the disputing parties to keep the lines of communication open. A mediator does not choose sides, he merely identifies problems and suggests compromises. Once the differences are settled, define the terms in a writing

Dogs and the Law

signed by both parties.

There may be a reason that you do not want to talk to your neighbor, or talking to him proves disastrous, or maybe you just do not know who owns the troublesome dog. Call your police, animal control department, health or public safety authorities. The people responsible for controlling dogs can call or visit the dog owner, or even issue a citation.

Look up all the pertinent local law, such as ordinances dealing with noise, vicious dogs, leash laws, nuisances, dogs running at large, personal injury, property damage, or the number of dogs allowed per household, and have it enforced. Enlist the aid of other neighbors who are annoyed. And, most importantly, be persistent.

You may be compelled to go to court. If so, familiarize yourself with the law so that you can make sure your complaint meets all the required elements. Good preparation is vital to presenting a sound argument. Be brief and articulate, not boring. Present your case in an organized manner. You may be allowed to present witnesses, and to utilize documents, police reports, hospital records, medical bills, and photographs. Avoid

confusion or repetition. But most importantly, always be respectful to both the judge and your adversary.

CRUELTY

In most modern societies, cruelty against dogs is forbidden. Inhumane treatment may include intentional abuse, neglect, theft, abandonment, and dog fighting. Cropping ears and tails without using anesthesia, leaving a dog which was hit by your car, confining a dog in a parked car, and poor conditions in a shelter may all be considered cruelty. In Great Britain, ear cropping is expressly prohibited. It is lawful, though, to kill a dog in the act of injuring a person or damaging property. Using dogs for scientific research is usually not punishable by law, even though it is distasteful.

If you suspect improper behavior, first talk to the owner. If the maltreatment does not cease, report the abuse to the humane society, the police, a local dog society, or anyone else you think has the right to take action. It is best to have the complaint in writing. Keep a copy for yourself.

Except in the case of an emergency, the dog owner is entitled to notice before his dog can be taken away. A mistreated dog is seized by the authorities and impounded. If the cruelty is particularly outrageous, the abuser may be subject to a fine or a jail sentence.

TRAVEL

It is a common sight to see a

tagged on the outside with the names and addresses of the shipper and the consignee. An accurate invoice statement specifying the number of each species contained in the shipment must also be included.

Since the hours of service and the availability of inspectors vary from port to port, check with your anticipated port of arrival prior to importation. This will reduce the possibility of unnecessary delay.

An airline may refuse to transport an animal unless specific criteria are met. Common restrictions include that the dog must be at least eight weeks old; certified as

dog owner traveling with his pet. In fact, many owners refuse to go anywhere without their dog. However, most owners do not realize that traveling is stressful for their pet. So if you are not going to leave your dog at home, at least make the trip as comfortable as possible.

Restrictions regarding pet travel are constantly changing due to health and international situations. Therefore, call the appropriate agricultural department, embassy, or consulate before departing. Most countries require a recent certificate of health. Vaccinations may be necessary.

Of course, your dog should be properly identified. A tag with the dog's name, and your name, address, and phone number should be attached to the dog at all times.

Each container should be plainly marked, labeled, or

healthy; secured in a carrier; and adequately identified.

A dog traveling on an airline must be contained in a shipping crate. The crate should be sturdy and well ventilated. It should be large enough to allow your pet to stand, turn around, and lie down comfortably. The carrier should be marked "*Live Animals*" and "*This End Up.*" Your name, address, and phone number, the dog's name, and the destination should be on the crate.

LANDLORDS AND DOGS

Many landlords prefer not to rent to dog owners. A dog can disturb other tenants if it is noisy, messy, or smelly. Under the right circumstances, any dog can destroy property or injure a person. A landlord can experience a lot of aggravation and expense. Violation of an existing no-pets clause may be a sufficient cause for eviction or a penalty.

A no-dogs policy may be negotiable. An exception may be made if the prospective tenant can assure the landlord that the dog will not be a problem. But how do you convince the landlord?

There are several things that can be done. Introduce the dog to the landlord. The landlord can see for himself that the dog is well groomed and well mannered. An untrained puppy is not as desirable as a mature, adult dog. A spayed or neutered dog will probably get bonus points. Bring along written references from previous landlords and neighbors saying that the dog has not been a problem and is well liked.

Special provisions can be negotiated in private leases that are fair to both sides. Dog owners are still responsible for damage and injury caused by their dogs.

Index

Required Reading

The Atlas of Dog Breeds of the World By Bonnie Wilcox, DVM, & Chris Walkowicz (H-1091)
Traces the history and highlights the characteristics, appearance and function of every recognized dog breed in the world. 409 different breeds receive full-color treatment and individual study. Hundreds of breeds in addition to those recognized by the American Kennel Club and the Kennel Club of Great Britain are included—the dogs of the world complete! The ultimate reference work, comprehensive coverage, intelligent and delightful discussions. The perfect gift book. *Hard cover, 9″ × 12″, 912 pages, 1,106 color photos. ISBN 0-86622-930-2*

Dog Training By Lew Burke (H-962)
The elements of dog training are easy to grasp and apply. The author uses the psychological makeup of dogs to his advantage by making them want to be what they should be—substituting the family for the pack. *Hard cover, 5½″ × 8″, 255 pages, 64 black and white photos, 23 color photos. ISBN 0-87666-656-X*

The Complete Dog Buyer's Guide By Dr. William Bruette & Kerry V. Donnelly (H-989)
Plots the advances in veterinary care and genetics of the last fifty years by incorporating descriptions of the breeds as they are today. Many of the photos illustrate Best In Show winners and top and historical dogs. Individual complete sections on breeding, selection, caring, etc. *Hard cover, 5½″ × 8″, 608 pages. Illustrated. ISBN 0-86622-026-7*

The Mini Atlas of Dog Breeds By Andrew De Prisco & James B. Johnson (H-1106)
An identification handbook giving a concise and thorough look at over 400 of the world's dog breeds. The authors' enthusiastic and knowledgeable approach brings to life instantly man's oldest friend and companion. A flowing and witty text, further enlivened by 500 full-color photos, successfully maps out the world of dogs; an easy-reference format pinpoints each breed's development, portrait, registry, and pet attributes. The volume is captioned with specially designed symbols. *Hard cover, 5½″ × 8½″, 544 pages, nearly 700 color photos. ISBN 0-86622-091-7*

Dog Owner's Encyclopedia of Veterinary Medicine By Allan H. Hart, B.V.Sc. (H-934)
Written by a vet who feels that most dog owners should recognize the symptoms and understand the cures of most diseases of dogs so they can properly communicate with their veterinarian. This book is a necessity for every dog owner, especially those who have more than one dog. *Hard cover, 5½″ × 8″, 186 pages, 86 black and white photos. ISBN 0-87666-287-4*

Dog Breeding for Professionals By Dr. Herbert Richards (H-969)
For dog owners who need and actively seek good advice about how to go about breeding their dogs whether for profit or purely because of their attachment to animals. *Please note* that the breeding photography is sexually explicit and some readers may find it offensive. *Hard cover, 5½″ × 8″, 224 pages, 105 black and white photos, 62 color photos. ISBN 0-87666-659-4*

Dogs and the Law By Anmarie Barrie, Esq. (DS-130)
A practical and reliable survey of laws pertaining to our dogs. Advice concerning liability, licenses, impoundment, vehicles, insurance, wills, vaccinations and many other useful and often entertaining topics. Full color cartoon illustrations add a delightful twist. *Hard cover, 6″ × 9″, 160 pages, over 55 color illustrations, appendices, charts. ISBN 0-86622-088-7*

Flames
of
Glory

Flames of Glory

by Patricia Matthews

BANTAM BOOKS
Toronto / New York / London / Sydney

For my sister,
Nancy,
who also likes the old places.

Prologue
Tampa, 1891

IT was, at last, eight o'clock, and Jessica Manning was sitting beside her mother and father in the carriage. Her body was rigid with suppressed excitement and the desire not to wrinkle her new gown. It was a beautiful dress, and the wonder of it, the wonder of the whole evening ahead, loomed large in Jessica's mind.

The fact that she, Jessica, just fourteen years old that day, was being allowed to attend the grand opening ball of the new Tampa Bay Hotel, was the fulfillment of her greatest dream; and she felt that she could literally not bear it if even the least thing went awry.

She sat decorously, ankles crossed, feet in white kid slippers, one hand holding her small, white lace fan, the other touching one of the tiny, white silk rosebuds that gathered and adorned the full skirt of her gown. She hoped that she presented a picture of grace and poise, but inside she bubbled and tingled with delight and anticipation.

Her mother, sitting on her left, was splendidly beautiful in rose silk, the waist of her corset drawn in so tightly that Jessica wondered how she could even breathe; the corset made her waist so small that Jessica's father could span it easily with both his hands. Her father, sitting on Jessica's right, looked dignified and rather formidable, she thought, in his dress suit and the long tails, even though his face, beneath the tall, shiny top hat, was smiling.

There was a regular parade of vehicles of every sort upon the road. Mr. Henry B. Plant, the builder of the Tampa Bay Hotel, had invited everyone who was anyone in the whole of the United States, or so her father had told Jessica. It was going to be the largest social event in the history of Florida, on this night of February 5, 1891.

The stream of vehicles winding toward the hotel was so thick that occasionally one carriage crowded another, sometimes colliding, but even the rudeness of a few could not disturb the good mood of the party-goers on this night, for they all knew that they were special. If they were not, they would not have received invitations to this lavish and prestigious ball.

As the Manning carriage approached the hotel, Jessica could see hundreds of electric lights, like stationary fireflies, outlining the towers; and as they moved nearer still, she drew in her breath with awe at the sight of the verandas and gardens hung with thousands of Chinese lanterns and fairy lights in shades of green, opal, topaz, and ruby.

Jessica had watched the hotel being built, and so she was familiar with the sight of the huge building, but to see it now, with its thirteen silver minarets ablaze with light, was like seeing a fairy-tale palace come to life, right before her eyes.

She must have sighed aloud, for Anne Manning turned to her, smiled, and patted her hand. "It is beautiful, isn't it, dear? The original cannot be more so, I'm sure."

Jessica nodded, not trusting herself to speak. She, like most residents of Tampa, knew the story behind the construction of the new hotel.

Mr. Plant, a wealthy businessman, had brought the railroad to Tampa in 1884; only seven hundred people lived in the white-sand city at the time.

Plant was an ambitious and competitive man; and when he heard that Henry M. Flagler, the multimillionaire railroad man, had finished his Hotel Ponce de Léon in St. Augustine and then built the Spanish/Moorish Alcazar, Henry Plant was goaded into announcing that he would construct "the greatest hotel in the world" in Tampa, using the Moorish/Turkish Alhambra, in Granada, Spain, as his model.

And Plant was as good as his word. He bought sixty acres of land from Jesse Hayden, who had purchased the acreage twenty years earlier by swapping a white horse and a wagon for it. Plant talked the city and county into building a bridge across the river at Lafayette Street, at the cost of eighteen thousand dollars, and extracted a promise from the local officials that his taxes would not exceed two hundred dollars a year.

This done, he began construction of his grand hotel. It cost over two million to build and about five hundred thousand to furnish, and those who had seen it inside and out declared it at least the eighth wonder of the world. The building was approximately twelve hundred feet long, and people said that a walk around the exterior equaled nearly a mile. The citizens of Tampa—now numbering six thousand—were justly proud of the beautiful edifice and looked forward to the fact that the hotel was certain to lure flocks of tourists and visitors to their city.

Now the Manning carriage was turning into the hotel's west entrance, and then they were pulling up in front of the steps, and Jackson, their driver, was helping Jessica's mother down from the carriage. Jessica could hardly breathe, such was her excitement.

Wyngate Manning escorted his wife and daughter through the throng of arriving guests to the wide front doors, and Jessica stepped into fairyland. Inside, all was one white blaze of light. Jessica's head swiveled constantly as she attempted to see everything at once, an impossibility that would leave her neck stiff for days after the ball.

She saw potted palms rustling in the winds moving through the great lobby that rose two stories high through balustraded open floors to the roof. Great masses of flowers were banked everywhere, and music seemed to come from all directions.

Jessica gaped in speechless awe as a handsome young page trotted past pulling a strange, high, two-wheeled vehicle. Riding in the vehicle was a regal young woman, dressed in pale blue, with diamonds flashing at her throat, wrists, and ears.

Jessica tugged at her mother's arm. "What was that, Mother? That strange cart?"

Her mother laughed and leaned down toward her so that her voice could be heard above the babble. "It's a jinrikisha, darling. They use them in the Orient. Mr. Plant imported them so his guests would not tire themselves walking down these long corridors."

Jessica wanted to ask if they might ride in one; but at that moment she was bumped by a large lady in red velvet and had to concentrate on clinging to her mother's hand and then on following in her parents' wake as they made their way through the crowd, toward one of the long corridors.

As they progressed, Jessica caught glimpses of the much talked about furnishings. She had heard that Mr. Plant had furnished the hotel with priceless antiques from Europe, but she was not prepared for the splendor that met her gaze.

Beneath their feet was the most beautiful carpet she had ever seen, a glowing red color with blue dragons woven into it. Along the walls and up the stairways were magnificent marble statues; and the rooms and hallways were filled with satin and brocaded sofas, inlaid and gilt chairs, onyx and marble tables decorated with gold leaf, hundreds of gilt-framed ornamental mirrors, and glowing bronze and porcelain lamps.

Never had she beheld such richness and beauty, and it seemed that she was not alone in her awe and wonder, for the adults, too, were exclaiming and sighing over the priceless items, the likes of which were not usually seen on this coast of simple, even primitive, board houses.

Jessica, following her parents down the seemingly endless corridor toward the dining rotunda, thought that this was easily the most wonderful and happiest day of her life. She knew that she would never forget it as long as she lived; and some day, when she was a woman grown, she would stay in this hotel, in one of the beautiful rooms she had heard so much about; for in her experience, this was absolutely the most beautiful and perfect place in the whole world!

It was hot behind the heavy drapery, but by moving her head to the left, Maria Mendes had an excellent view of the lobby and the arriving guests.

There was a large palm tree directly in front of the drapes, which concealed her presence, and through its green, gently moving fronds, she watched in awe as the richest and most famous people in the country streamed in.

How beautiful and elegant they looked in their silks, satins, and jewels! The wasp-waisted women, in their long gowns, with their hair elaborately coiffed; the men looking very tall and very elegant in their black dress suits. The lobby itself, with its statues, mirrors, palms, and flowers, looked like something from a dream of another world, a world that Maria did not yet fully understand.

She knew that there was a vast chasm between her people and these others, these North Americans in their expensive clothes and jewels, but she did not question this. It was simply a fact. She felt no jealousy, she merely watched, in awe and amazement, as they paraded past, laughing and chatting, nodding and smiling, like gods out of the old tales.

Her black eyes bright with excitement, Maria leaned farther to the left to get a better look at three people just entering the lobby—a tall, handsome man; a slender, beautiful woman in a rose gown; and a lovely blond girl, about Maria's own age.

The presence of the girl aroused Maria's curiosity. She was the first person that Maria, just fourteen, had seen at the ball who looked as young as herself. The girl was very pretty, dressed all in white, her long skirt caught in gathers and covered with white silk roses. She had a lovely silk shawl on as well, for which Maria felt a pang of envy; long, white gloves, and little, white kid slippers. Maria wondered who she was. She must be the daughter of someone very important to have been invited to the ball.

As the trio moved out of her view, Maria shifted her weight on the small stool upon which she sat. She was beginning to get hungry, but she did not want to leave her vantage point just yet. There was so much to see!

Down below, in the kitchen, she knew that her father and the other chefs were scurrying to and fro, stirring pots, making salads and sauces. As daughter of the head sauce chef, she could enter into that inner sanctum with impunity—so long as she had her father's permission—and be certain of being well fed. In that respect at least, they were better off than many Cubans in the area; most of them had to struggle to get enough to survive.

Another group of people passed, and two men stopped, right in front of her hiding place, and began to talk as they lit up cigars. Maria knew that it was impolite to listen to other people's conversations, yet she could not escape without being observed. She drew back from the opening in the drapes.

"Well, old Henry has done himself proud, hasn't he?" said a deep voice.

"I should say so," the second man replied. "The furnishings alone must have cost a small fortune, and everybody in the whole world is here tonight. I heard that fifteen thousand invitations were sent out."

"And they must all be here. By the way, did you hear the story about Henry Flagler?"

The other man laughed. "*Which* story? There are dozens going around."

"Well, the way I heard it, Plant sent Flagler an invitation to the ball tonight, and Flagler wired back: 'Where is Tampa?' "

Both men laughed.

"But that's not the end of it. I understand that Plant wired back to Flagler: 'Just follow the crowd, Henry!' "

The men laughed again and began to move away, and Maria gave a sigh of relief. She did not know who Mr. Flagler was, and she did not care, although she knew he must be somebody rich and famous. She felt a glow of pride that none of these beautiful people, rich and famous though they might be, knew the hotel as she did.

Maria had watched it being built, watched as the silver towers were made to reach into the sky. And when it was finished and her father had been hired as the sauce chef, she had persuaded him to bring her with him to the hotel, and once there, she had made herself intimately familiar with its whole majestic length and breadth—the endless corridors; the huge lobby with its wonderful bronze statue of the lady and the goat; the beautiful, beautiful furnishings; the subterranean rooms under the lobby, which included rooms for billiards and shuffleboard, as well as mineral water baths, massage rooms, and café facilities; and even a hotel casino.

The room she liked best was the Grand Salon, with its priceless art objects and antique furniture. Her father had told her that the cabinets she so much admired had once belonged to Queen Isabella and King Ferdinand of Spain, and Mary, Queen of Scots. Maria thought the room looked like a great museum.

She also particularly liked the statues on the main stairway of the hotel—two African girls, who had beautiful, shiny black skin that gleamed in the light.

Maria felt privileged and rather smug in her private knowledge of the place. She loved the huge building and felt at home there, much more so than in her family's small cottage on the outskirts of Ybor City. Her father knew of her love for the hotel, and since she was his only daughter he indulged her in letting her come with him to his work now and again. It was he who had arranged for her to be present on this wonderful night, despite her mother's strong objections, and Maria was grateful to him.

She smoothed the skirt of her blue cotton dress and pushed aside one long, shiny, black braid of hair that had fallen forward over one shoulder. She might not have wonderful clothes, like the beautiful people out there, but she had something else just as good—she *knew* the hotel intimately. They did not.

Maria smiled softly to herself, vowing that she would always remember this night of nights.

Tampa 1898

Chapter One

JESSICA Manning sat on the glider on the front porch of the Manning home, fanning herself with a Japanese fan, trying to agitate the humid air enough to gain some relief from the sticky heat of April.

Inside the house the air was redolent with the sweet scent of apricots and sugar, for her mother and Ruby, the housekeeper, were in the kitchen making preserves out of the crate of apricots that one of Mr. Manning's business acquaintances had given them.

How her mother and Ruby could bear to stand over a hot stove on a day like this, Jessica could not imagine; she was only grateful that her offer of help had been refused. She felt as limp and exhausted as if she had been at hard labor since early morning; and bored, she was bored to near distraction.

Making a great effort, she touched the porch floor with one foot and set the glider into lazy motion.

Her white lawn dress, crisp and fresh when she had put it on that morning, was already wilted and damp under the arms and along the back, although it was only ten in the morning. She thought again of her mother, in the kitchen with Ruby, and she gave a guilty sigh. Well, Mother did not *have* to help Ruby, she thought. Ruby was a real wonder, and capable of canning dozens of crates of fruit by herself. It was just that her mother liked working in the kitchen, liked cooking, even though she did not have to. No matter what she was doing, Anne Manning always managed to look fresh. If her mother came out of the steaming kitchen right now, Jessica thought, she would surely look neater and fresher than her daughter, who had not done a thing since getting up, save look at a few dress patterns and practice a bit on the piano.

Jessica sighed again. Sometimes it was difficult having a perfect and beautiful mother. Of course, she loved and admired her mother very much, that was understood, but she could not help but make comparisons.

Not that she herself was ugly, it was just that her pale, fine hair never seemed to stay completely under control, always escaping into

wispy tendrils around her face and neck, and it was a constant struggle to stay neat and wrinkle-free. Her mother, on the other hand, always looked as if she had stepped out of the proverbial bandbox, no
matter what activity she might be engaged in. Not a hair ever seemed
to escape from its allotted place, and Jessica envied Anne Manning her
heavy, rather coarse but glowing auburn hair and her serene, even-
featured face and blue eyes.

Jessica had her father's hair—although she had a good deal more
than he had, for he was rapidly becoming bald—and his flecked,
greenish eyes. People said that she was pretty. She once heard one of
her mother's friends refer to her as "delicate as a Dresden figurine,
and just as lovely." Jessica knew that many of her girl friends envied
her her fashionably pale complexion and tiny waist; but if she could
have had her choice, Jessica would have looked like her mother—
shorter, more rounded in the bosom and hips, and more vivid in coloring. Still she supposed that she should be glad she was not really ugly,
like poor Sally McGill, who had her father's long, beaky nose and her
mother's pale eyes set too close together.

Jessica gave the glider another nudge and dropped the fan into her
lap—it was not doing the least bit of good.

She thought about the afternoon ahead and wondered how she was
going to fill it. There was absolutely nothing of interest going on until
the next evening, when Dulcy Thomas's party was set for six o'clock;
and that was the only thing to look forward to throughout the whole
week. This really was the dullest year that Jessica could remember.
Sometimes she wished that her parents would move to some larger,
more exciting city, someplace like New York or Boston, where there
were plays to see and concerts to attend and museums to visit; and
parties, lots of parties.

Of course, there were parties in Tampa, too, but not that often, and
they were always attended by the same old circle of friends, known
too well, for too long, to be really exciting. There were never enough
young men, and what men there were seemed a dismal lot to Jessica.
She had known most of them since grammar school and thus knew too
well all their faults and weaknesses.

She picked up the fan and began moving it back and forth again. If
only there was something to *do!* If only something exciting would
happen!

There had been some promise of excitement when the battleship
Maine was blown up in Havana harbor, and there had been some talk

of a possible war with Spain; but here it was April, and nothing had really come of it. Oh, her parents talked about it; her father in particular seemed to think that war was inevitable, but so far nothing had really happened, although her father had said that the Cubans were hoping for war.

Inside a modest frame bungalow in Ybor City, Maria Mendes was setting the table for the noonday meal, which her mother, Ynez, was preparing in the kitchen.

Despite the heat, it would be a robust meal of black beans, rice, and pork, a meal to fill the stomachs of Maria's two older brothers, Ramon and Eduardo, and her younger brother, Paulo.

Ramon and Eduardo would be home from the cigar factory where they worked, for their midday meal and a short siesta before returning to work for the rest of the afternoon. Their father, Felix, would not be home, as he took his noon meal at the hotel.

Maria set the flowered plates at each place and arranged the napkins and silver carefully. Her mother liked the table to look attractive at all meals. "It makes the food taste all the better," she was fond of saying; and it was also, Maria knew, her mother's way of reminding them all that they came from a good family, a family who knew about such things as proper table settings and good, solid silver, such as the set that Maria was now arranging—one of the few things of value her mother had managed to bring with her from Cuba.

It was stiflingly hot in the small dining room, and Maria felt the weight of her long, shining braids pull at her skull. Sometimes, like today, she would have liked to cut all her hair off, let the ripe, black weight of it fall to the floor, and then sweep it away. Other times, she was proud of it, of the sheer mass, the shine, and beauty of it.

She sighed, knowing that her mother, busy in the kitchen, could not hear her. Her mother would not approve of the fact that she was bored. For some women, like Ynez Mendes, the house was enough—the cleaning, the washing, the cooking, the caring for family.

But there were other women, like herself, who wanted more from life. Women who wanted work outside the house, who wanted to make their way in the world. Foolish, and too lofty ambitions, her mother would say, Maria well knew. But her father understood and, she felt, sympathized with her longings.

Maria paused in her work, and a smile brightened her rather somber features as she recalled that day seven years before when her fa-

ther had smuggled her into the Tampa Bay Hotel to watch the opening night's festivities. She had long hoped for a job in the hotel, but so
far there had always been more applicants than jobs. She had become
acquainted with one of the girls who worked there, Theresa, who
made a great deal of money in gratuities during the winter, when the
wealthy came down from the chilly northern states to enjoy the warm
winters of Tampa Bay. Felix Mendes had promised her, now that she
was twenty-one, that she could go to work there as soon as there was
an opening.

Of course, she could go to work in one of the cigar factories, but her
mother was adamant about that. She would not have her daughter
doing factory work, although the pay was good and the work steady.
Even her father did not approve of factory work for girls.

Maria sighed. Well, she would keep trying for something, and until
then there was enough to keep her busy here. She was only afraid that
her mother would begin to find her help at home invaluable and
would fight all the harder to keep her there.

There! The table was set, and her brothers would soon be home.
She thought back to the argument at breakfast. The table talk had
been the same as it had been for months—talk about the hoped-for
war with Spain over Cuban independence. Both her brothers
belonged to a so-called "Cuban club," the LFC (Liberty For Cuba),
and both of them, Maria knew, gave ten percent of their wages to the
"fund," money that went mainly to buy arms for the Cuban rebels.

Felix Mendes disapproved of this. It was not that he was unsym-
pathetic to Cuba's plight, but he was now a citizen of the United
States and considered himself an American first. As such, he believed
that he should spend his money, and his interest, in ways that would
help him and his family to become integrated into the American way
of life. The breakfast-time discussions sometimes became rather
heated with both Felix and his sons pounding on the table to drive
home points and raising their voices to be heard above the opposing
viewpoints.

Ynez, Maria, and Paulo did not participate in these discussions;
Paulo was too young; Maria because she recognized the futility of
such arguments; and Ynez because she was torn between loyalty to
her husband and agreement with the views of her sons.

At any rate, it did not make for a peaceful table, and Maria had
begun to dread the mornings, one of the few times all the members of
the family were together.

And now there was another meal to prepare for, and when it was over, there would be the cleaning up to do and perhaps some mending; and then, later, the evening meal, then nothing really to do until bedtime. Another normal day. Another dull day. It seemed to Maria that this was the longest, dullest spring that she could remember.

Jessica was in her room, changing into a fresh dress for supper, when she heard the front door slam with unaccustomed loudness.

She wondered briefly who had slammed it, but it was not until she heard the sound of her father's usually quiet voice raised in excitement that she really became curious. What on earth was going on?

Quickly she buttoned her dress and straightened her hair, then hurried to the stairs, which she descended with unladylike haste.

Her father was in the dining room with her mother, and Jessica was surprised to see his usually calm face flushed with some strong emotion. He had a sheet of yellow paper in his hand, which he had evidently been showing to her mother.

Alarmed, Jessica stopped short in the doorway, staring at them both. "What is it, Daddy? What's wrong?" she cried.

Anne Manning, seeing that Jessica was upset, made haste to soothe her. "It's nothing to worry about, darling. Nothing to be frightened of."

Wyngate Manning had himself under more control when he spoke again. "I'm sorry if I startled you, Jessica, but I was just telling your mother that we received word today that three thousand government troops are on their way to Tampa. They are sending a man, Major J.W. Pope, to arrange for their arrival. Do you know what this means?"

"I suppose it means war," Anne Manning said disapprovingly.

Wyngate Manning looked at her and frowned. "It also means business," he said emphatically. "Big business, for all of us."

Jessica felt anticipation rise in her. This news might mean war with Spain, and it might mean big business for her father, but it also meant something else. It meant that at long last something really exciting was going to happen to Tampa!

Chapter Two

In the seat in front of the railroad car, Lieutenants Price and Fisher were engaged in a raucous game of two-handed poker. Despite Lieutenant Colonel Roosevelt's edict concerning drunkenness, and the severe punishment involved, both men were well on their way to becoming intoxicated, and the game was quickly degenerating into a shouting match. Lieutenant Neil Dancer, seated three rows back, thought of remonstrating with the two officers, but he was sure that would only succeed in irritating them.

In the seat next to Neil, Lieutenant John Gage was snoring, his plump face nestled down into the support of his several chins, his stubby fingers laced together across his hard, but ample stomach.

Neil sighed in disgust. As if the heat, the cinders, and the stench of vomit weren't enough! Lord, what he would not give for a good, hot soak in a tub. Four days confined in this hellhole of a railroad car seemed like forty. Thank God, they should be arriving in Tampa this evening.

Getting to his feet, Neil, a tall young man of twenty-five, with short, ginger hair and long, bright blue eyes, pushed past Gage's outstretched legs and stepped into the aisle. The train, traveling at top speed, rocketed along, swaying and rattling, and Neil had to hold onto the seat backs to keep from falling.

The outside platform was already crowded, but he managed to squeeze out into the open air, where he found himself standing close to one of the enlisted men, a bandy-legged, little cowboy who had a tough, leathery face and bright, intelligent eyes. The man grinned at Neil and winked.

"We're packed in too close to salute, sir. And besides, it's too damned hot."

Neil nodded. "Forget it, soldier. Crowded into the cars the way we are, I figure we're none of us more than a bunch of cattle, anyway. At least for the time being."

The little man's grin widened. "Don't let Terrible Teddy hear you say that. He thinks his Rough Riders are the finest fighting outfit in the U.S. Army, bar none."

Neil chuckled and relaxed. He produced a pack of cigarettes, which he offered to the smaller man. "Well, he's right about that. We are, but right now we're just one sorry band of hot, tired, irritable men. When we get to Tampa, it'll be different—I hope. Then we'll turn back into Teddy's Rough Riders, the scourge of the battlefield. Say, what's your name, soldier?"

The little man pushed his broad-brimmed hat back on his head, showing a white band of skin above his weathered forehead. "Trooper Billy McGinty, sir, from Oklahoma."

Neil smiled and offered his hand. "Lieutenant Neil Dancer from New York."

McGinty nodded. "I thought so. You're one of them Knicks." He shook his head dolefully. "You know, sir, this is sure one strange mixture of soldiers we got here. You'll have to own up to that."

Neil drew deeply on his cigarette. "I certainly can't deny it, McGinty."

"We got the gents, like you, from New York and Boston. Then we've got the cowpokes and Injuns from out West. I mean, it's passing strange for a cowhand like me to be soldiering alongside the likes of the United States tennis champion. Why, hell, I didn't even know what tennis was until I met Wrenn."

Neil found himself experiencing a strong liking for this tough little rooster of a man. "Yes, we are a mixed lot, no doubt about that. But we're in this together now, and no one man is better than another, except by the manner in which he conducts himself with the other men, and on the battlefield."

The words sounded pompous to Neil, even as he voiced them. Yet, they did express pretty much what he felt.

McGinty did not seem to find the statement pompous in the least. His small face turned solemn. "You're damned right, sir. And that's what makes the First U.S. Volunteer Cavalry the grand group that it is. Mark my word, Lieutenant, people will always remember Teddy's Rough Riders. You see if they don't—hey!"

Both Neil and McGinty were forced hard against the railing of the platform as the train slowed without warning, metal squealing as the brakes were applied.

"Must be a water stop." McGinty swiped at his mouth with the back of his hand. "Me, I'm dryer than sand. Sure hope the townsfolk are thinking of us."

Neil felt his own mouth fill with saliva at the thought of water. So far, no village or train depot along their route had been so remote that the people there had not heard of the Rough Riders; and the townspeople, alerted by all the newspaper publicity, would flock down to meet the train, calling out the names of such celebrities as Woodbury Kane, Hamilton Fish, and of course, Theodore Roosevelt.

But it was not because of this that Neil and McGinty were excited; it was the hoped-for watermelon and cold beer that the ladies of the town, attired in neatly ironed dresses and straw hats, usually passed out to the parched and weary soldiers. It had happened at almost every stop that the troop train had made.

Neil felt McGinty's elbow in his ribs. "Here they come, bless them one and all!"

Neil, looking over McGinty's head, saw and heard the crowd of townspeople coming toward the now stilled train; and sure enough, they were toting watermelons and beer.

The laughing, chattering crowd surged around the platform and alongside the train. Soldiers reached out the open windows, eagerly accepting what was offered. Neil took a cold, striped watermelon from the arms of a pretty woman in blue, while McGinty neatly hoisted a heavy pail of cold beer from a tall man in overalls. The excitement of the crowd, their obvious pleasure in offering refreshments to the soldiers, raised Neil's spirits as much as the anticipated enjoyment of the beer and melon. Clutching the melon under one arm, he waved to the crowd, sharing their excitement and pleasure. As the train began to move again, Neil and the other men continued to wave until the town was out of sight. Neil realized that he did not even know the name of it.

"Now, lads, let's have at that watermelon," said McGinty, who had already sampled the beer, tipping it up and drinking right from the pail. Foam formed a mustache around his upper lip.

Neil took out his pocket knife, and right there, on the crowded platform, he sliced the ripe, juicy melon and handed pieces to the others. It was better than anything he had ever before tasted.

The seven trains bearing the First U.S. Volunteer Cavalry pulled into the pine flats of western Florida that evening, six miles short of Tampa.

Whooping with delight, Neil and the other men got down from the train but were soon silenced when they gradually realized that they had not yet reached their destination.

There was a good deal of confusion and milling about, and no one, not even Colonel Roosevelt, was able to get a satisfactory explanation as to why the railroad employees would not haul the regiment any farther.

Finally, after some hours of frustration, the regiment set out for Tampa on horseback, dragging their equipment behind them in wagons that they had hastily commandeered.

Neil, tired from the four-day train ride, rode slumped in the saddle, dozing as his horse, Excalibur, followed the other horses, occasionally prancing or shaking his head to show his delight at being finally freed from the confines of the boxcar.

When they finally reached the Fifth Corps encampment, they found it shrouded in sleep. There was no official welcome, and the men waited resignedly in the dark while Colonel Roosevelt and Colonel Wood rode through the acres of tents until they located the regiment's allotted space.

By the time the tents were pitched, Neil was almost comatose with fatigue. Fully dressed, he fell onto his hastily assembled cot, too weary to notice that he had drawn Lieutenants John Gage and Roger Price as his tentmates.

The bright, clear tones of reveille sounded, to Neil, as an obscenity in the early morning air, but habit forced him to struggle toward consciousness; and in a few moments he was sitting on the edge of his cot, his head in his hands.

His mouth tasted foul, and his eyes felt gritty from too little sleep, but he managed to get to his feet, for a moment not realizing exactly where he was.

When the knowledge finally dawned on him, excitement washed away his discomfort. They were in Tampa, at last!

He quickly pulled his toilet kit out from under the cot and examined his face in the mirror. He looked, he thought, surprisingly well, except for the ginger-colored stubble on his cheeks and chin; and of course his clothes looked as if he had slept in them, which he had.

At that moment Neil caught sight of his two tentmates, also struggling up from sleep. Good Lord, Price and Gage! he thought. What foul luck! He would have to draw as tentmates the two men in the outfit he most actively disliked. Oh, well, what the hell. He might have to share the same tent, but that was as far as he would go.

He picked up his canteen and kit and went outside, in search of water in which to shave.

For a few seconds after emerging from the tent, Neil stood transfixed. Around him, to the right, left, in front and behind, were hundreds of tents, stretching out in all directions in a seemingly endless array.

"My God!" he whispered to himself, awed by the sheer size of the camp and the implied numbers of men. He wondered just how many there actually were. Later, he would learn that there were twenty-five thousand troops camped beneath the moss-hung pines, the largest gathering of the U.S. Army in four decades.

He finally found the water barrels, which were on a slight rise, and as he bent to dip his canteen, Neil caught sight of the city of Tampa in the distance. One building struck him as strangely exotic, like a Middle Eastern mirage, its silver domes and minarets floating on the coastal haze. He shook his head in wonder. *Was* it a mirage? Or was it a real building?

He returned to the tent to find Price and Gage finally awake and rummaging in their kits.

"The water barrels are about six tents away, on the right," he told them brusquely.

"Oh, Lord!" moaned Price. "I feel like a whole herd of prairie buffalo has been tromping across my skull, and my belly feels emptier than a fox-raped henhouse!"

Gage laughed, a rather snorting, high-pitched sound that grated on Neil's nerves. And Neil groaned inwardly at Price's remark. Roger Price, besides his other unpleasant habits, had taken an inordinate fancy to the colorful language employed by the cowboys; and although he was a Bostonian, of impeccable background, or so he claimed, he went about talking like a character out of a Buntline dime novel.

It annoyed Neil for some reason. Perhaps because it seemed so phony and seemed to mock the regional language of the legitimate southwesterners in the Rough Riders. He reflected that little Trooper McGinty had been right—they were an odd lot altogether.

When Colonel Roosevelt and Colonel Wood had put together the regiment, Roosevelt had enlisted fifty of what he referred to as "gentlemen rankers," to give the outfit its necessary tone. He had chosen these men from the best schools and clubs of Manhattan and Boston. He had made it clear, however, that no man would earn a commission except by exhibiting bravery and merit, and that once they were in Texas, where they were to train, they would be considered no better or worse than the cowboys, Indians, and assorted southwesterners with whom they would go into battle, when and if it came down to that. As Roosevelt once put it in Texas, "The cowboys and the Knickerbockers ride side by side."

And so it had been. In San Antonio, they had all worked hard, thinking of the battle ahead and wanting to be the best damned unit in the U.S. Army, and it was possible that they now were just that.

Neil smiled at the thought of Woodbury Kane, a yachting dandy, who fought with the same natural ease as he dressed, cooking and washing dishes for a troop of New Mexicans.

There were also Joe Sampson Stevens, the world's greatest polo player; Dudley Dean, the legendary Harvard football quarterback; Hamilton Fish, ex-captain of the Columbia rowing crew; and Bob Wrenn, tennis champion of the United States. There were the high jumpers from Yale, as well as football players from Princeton, of which Neil was one, and huntsmen with such names as Tiffany and Wadsworth. In addition to these, the gentlemen rankers included two English bluebloods and one Scot. The remaining men were rough and ready southwesterners—cowboys, Indians, and descendents of the Crocketts, Adamses, Hamiltons, and Jacksons. Good men all; at least twenty men had been turned down for every one chosen.

Neil felt a strong sense of pride, for he was one of the "rankers," and he was certain that Trooper McGinty was right in another respect. The world would long remember Teddy Roosevelt's Rough Riders; their fame was already growing. He grinned to himself. Now all they had to do was live up to that fame. It *would* be embarrassing if they accomplished nothing noteworthy once they were in Cuba. In Neil's opinion, that was unlikely. They were a fine group of fighting men, with very few exceptions, no matter their backgrounds, and they would come through. It was unthinkable that they would not.

The afternoon was hot, but as the horses picked their way daintily through the mosquito-ridden swamps and ankle-deep drifts of sand toward the sea, the air began to freshen.

Neil, riding alongside Price, Gage, and another lieutenant, Tom Farrel, was beginning to feel good, as the electricity of anticipation began to fill him. Price and Gage even seemed less objectionable than usual—mainly because of the presence of Tom Farrel, whom Neil genuinely liked. Of course, his improved spirits could also be attributed to the fact that they were on leave and were on their way to attend a dance at the famous Tampa Bay Hotel.

"The damned thing looks like some kind of a Turkish palace," Price drawled. "Look at them minarets!"

"It's Moorish, stupid," Gage snapped in an uncharacteristically waspish tone. "Don't you ever read, Price? Or has pretending to be one of the 'fellers' jellied your brains? I think it's beautiful."

Neil looked at the stubby Gage in some astonishment and with a new respect. Evidently the butterball was not all bad.

"It *is* beautiful," he agreed, grinning at Gage. "And it will be even more beautiful this evening, when it is filled with lovely young ladies just waiting to dance with us."

"I hear that Florida girls are pretty," Farrel said dreamily.

"Hell, it's been so long since I've been close to a girl that *any* woman would look pretty to me," Price said. "I do hope that at least some of them are more than pretty, if you get my meaning."

"No, what do you mean?" Gage looked at Price curiously.

"Why, I mean that I hope they are obliging, so to speak." Price leered. "If you know what I mean."

"Oh, I think we know what you mean," Farrel said disgustedly. "But these are nice girls, Price, don't forget that. The daughters of the finest families in Tampa. I don't know how the hell they came to invite a clod like you."

Price snickered. "I happen to come from a fine family myself, lads, in case you didn't know. And I'll tell you another thing I know for sure. The girls from the finest families lay down for men, just like the girls from the lower classes. They just don't let the whole world know about it, is all."

Gage giggled nervously, and Neil felt a strong surge of dislike for Price. It was not because Price talked about sex, hell, they all talked about sex—talked a lot more about it than they did it, in fact—but it was the *way* in which he talked about it, like it was something dark and secret, dirty and somehow shameful.

"That'll be enough of that kind of talk, Price," he said curtly.

The smaller man grinned lazily. "What's the matter, Dancer? You a virgin or something? You saving yourself for the marriage bed?"

He snickered again, and Gage followed suit, as if on cue.

Neil felt his face grow hot. "You know better than that, filth mouth. It's just your idea of sex that I can't abide. You've got the attitude of an adolescent peeking through a knothole in a ladies outhouse."

Price's face grew pink, and he aimed a venomous glance at Neil. "Well, tonight we'll just see who does better: Mr. Pureheart or the adolescent. I don't give a damn what you three do, I intend to get into some lady's drawers."

"Look!" Farrel said suddenly, pointing. "You can see the hotel plainly now."

Neil found himself impressed anew, as they reined in their mounts for a better look at the towered and minareted wonder that soared up before them, white and shining in the late afternoon air.

"I hear it's got five hundred rooms," Farrel said in an awed voice.

"And a swimming pool, a huge ballroom, and even a casino," Gage said wistfully. "I could use a swim in that pool right about now."

"Well," Farrel said, reaching over to clap him on the shoulder, "there's no reason you can't have it. The major said that 'all the amenities of the hotel' would be made available to us."

"Gee, that's right, he did!" Gage's slightly pink face brightened. "Come on, let's get moving!"

The men urged their horses on, and the animals reluctantly increased their pace.

Soon they were approaching the drive and in another five minutes were giving their horses over to the handlers provided by the hotel.

As they mounted the wooden steps to the long, ornately ornamented veranda, Neil could see that the area was packed with elegant bentwood rocking chairs. The comfortable rockers held high-ranking army and navy officers, newspaper correspondents, foreign attachés, and, best of all, pretty women, gracefully sipping iced tea and champagne.

Neil's gaze was drawn to a huge, middle-aged man, mountainous in his army blue, wearing the insignia of a brigadier general. Neil touched Farrel's arm. "Isn't that General Shafter?"

Farrel peered and then nodded. "Yep, it must be. Nobody else could be that big. I wonder where they found a rocker that size?"

Neil put a hand to his mouth to hide a grin, for the general was staring their way.

Price, close behind them, snorted. "And *that's* what's supposed to lead us into battle in Cuba? Fat chance. And I use the term advisedly!"

Despite the fact that it was Price who said it, Neil had to smile in agreement, for the very thought of this three-hundred-pound, drop-sical general, who reportedly could barely heave his great bulk up the grand stairway of the hotel, leading them into battle was amusing. Price, when he was not putting on his cowpoke act, was bright enough.

On second thought, it was not so humorous. Neil had heard Roosevelt's blunt-spoken views on the subject of General Shafter, whom he considered woefully incompetent.

They were across the veranda now and into the coolness of the lofty-ceilinged lobby. Neil drew in his breath sharply. He was accustomed to fine hotels, but nothing he had ever seen could approach this.

"Where to first, fellows?" Farrel demanded. "I, for one, intend to have several long, cold beers."

"I'm for that," Price said. "How about you two?" He turned to Neil and Gage. "Or is Mr. Pureheart too noble to indulge in alcoholic beverages?"

"I'm heading for the pool first," Gage said. He glanced at Neil expectantly, but Neil looked away. The thought of a swim was attractive, yet the prospect of Gage's company was not, particularly, and he *was* thirsty.

"I think I'll settle for the beer," he said, smiling amiably at Price. "I don't think it'll damage me greatly. After all, pure heart overcomes all. At least that's what I've been told."

Price laughed heartily. "Sometimes I have hopes for you, Dancer, I purely do."

The large saloon was crowded with officers, enlisted men, and civilians, the sound of their voices an oceanic murmur under the high roof. The three young officers managed to finally push their way up to the long mahogany bar and place their orders.

Once the orders were given, Neil faced about to gaze around the crowded saloon. An almost visible feeling of excitement pervaded the barroom—a feeling of great purpose and expectant adventure. This, he thought contentedly, is where things are happening, and I'm right here in the middle of it.

His mug of beer was placed on the bar, and he reached for it thirstily, not noticing until he had the mug to his mouth that the officer on his right, whose back had been to him, was turning toward him. He almost choked as he recognized the slightly bucked teeth and eyeglasses of his commanding officer, Lieutenant Colonel Theodore Roosevelt.

Neil coughed embarrassedly as he took the mug from his mouth. "Sorry, sir," he stammered, attempting to salute and replace the mug on the bar at the same time. "I didn't see you, sir!"

Roosevelt, his intelligent beaver face creased in a wide grin, laughed, a sharp bark that Neil knew was meant to be friendly.

"At ease, Lieutenant," Roosevelt said briskly. "We don't need to be formal here."

As Neil tried to regain his poise, he noticed, over Roosevelt's shoulder, the face of a civilian—a small, boyishly handsome, brown-haired man with a full mustache. He appeared to be about Neil's own age. Neil wondered who he was. His question was quickly answered.

"There's someone here I'd like you to meet, Dancer," said Roosevelt in his usual brisk manner, as he motioned to the man slightly behind him. "Lieutenant Dancer, this is Stephen Crane, the well-known writer. Mr. Crane is here as a war correspondent for the *New York World*. Mr. Crane, this is Lieutenant Neil Dancer, one of my boys and a fine officer."

Stephen Crane nodded and smiled, showing, briefly, very bad teeth. His eyes, Neil noted, were bright with intelligence and were of an unusual size and shape.

Roosevelt turned back to Neil. "Mr. Crane wants to interview some of the men, both officers and enlisted, to get their feelings about the war."

Stephen Crane nodded. "How do you do, Lieutenant Dancer? What I'm doing, really, is looking for some human interest. You know, how you men feel about being so far from home, and so forth. Would you mind answering a few questions of that nature for me?"

Neil, flattered that such a famous author should seek his opinions, shook his head. "Not at all, Mr. Crane. I would be pleased to do so. I've read your book, *The Red Badge of Courage*, the serialized version, that is, in the *Philadelphia Press*. I must tell you that I was very moved by the story."

Stephen Crane smiled again, partially covering his bad teeth with his hand. He seemed pleased. "Thank you, Lieutenant. A writer always likes to hear that. Now, shall we find ourselves a quiet corner some place? It's like a zoo at feeding time in here."

Neil nodded, and Stephen Crane slipped from his stool. Standing, the writer was even smaller than Neil had thought, surely not over five-foot-four, and very slight. Still, he seemed sure enough of himself and did not seem put off in the least that Neil towered almost a foot over him.

"Bully, Lieutenant," Teddy Roosevelt said. He smiled slyly. "Tell the truth now, but paint the Rough Riders in a good light."

Stephen Crane led the way to an almost empty corner of the veranda and seated himself in one of the ubiquitous rockers. Taking a note pad and pen from one of his coat pockets, he looked at Neil expectantly. "Shall we begin then?"

After the interview with Stephen Crane, Neil felt faintly embarrassed. It seemed to him that, once he had started talking, he had told the writer his whole life story; and it was not like him to talk about himself so freely, yet Stephen Crane had a way about him, an interest in his subject that was difficult to resist. Or perhaps, Neil thought, the urge to have something put down, something that would define his life, in the event that he did not make it back from Cuba, had something to do with his talking so much. A depressing thought, that, but a valid one. If he did not come back, would it make a great deal of difference to the world? Not a lot, he concluded, except for his father and mother, and his elder sister, Katie. It would be a shame for him to die without ever having left any memorial to himself, some kind of mark on the world to show that he had been here.

Of course, it was not as if his had not been a pleasant enough life, a good life actually, up until now.

Second child and only son of a wealthy industrialist and New York socialite, Neil had been raised with every privilege—the best nursemaids, the best schools, the best environment. His parents had been affectionate and fair—no complaints there—and his sister had been fond of him and less bossy than most of the older sisters he knew.

When the time came for him to go to college, Neil had gone to Princeton, like his father before him, and had done well both academically and athletically; and then this had come along, the threat of war with Spain. When he had heard about Theodore Roosevelt forming his regiment, Neil had been fired with purpose. Like most young men of his age and time, he felt strongly the call of patriotism, and his father, who knew Roosevelt well, had encouraged him.

There was more to it than that, of course. Intelligent, with an uncanny ability to read his own character, Neil was very dissatisfied with his life. He had always had it easy, with few obstacles to overcome;

his family's wealth and prestige had always paved the way for him. He easily could have gone into the business world, starting far from the bottom, and his success would have been assured. Yet by nature Neil was competitive, yearning for challenges, and the only challenges he had been confronted with were athletic and scholastic; and he was such a natural athlete and fine scholar that he had had to exert himself very little to meet those challenges. He wanted challenges in which he would have to extend himself; at the least, he wished to see how he would rise to trials and hardships.

Thus, on graduation from Princeton, he had joined with Roosevelt. If ever a man had been faced with hard challenges, it was Theodore Roosevelt. Perhaps the military, and war, was not what Neil sought, but certainly no man could do better than to emulate Teddy Roosevelt.

And so here he was, half anxious to plunge into the heat of battle and half reluctant, thinking thoughts of mortality.

Neil shook his head and grinned wryly. Lord, wasn't he getting philosophical! And all because a newspaper correspondent had asked him a few questions. Well, he had better get his wits together and return to the saloon, if he wanted to quench his thirst.

Tonight there would be laughter and merriment and dancing aplenty. He would find himself the prettiest girl at the dance—he was not unaware of his charm with women—and dance with her until her slippers were worn out; and then, if he was fortunate, he would take her outside onto the veranda, and if she was friendly. . . .

Suddenly he thought of Price and grimaced. Sure, every man occasionally thought of what he would *like* to do to a beautiful woman; but if she was a girl from a good family, the chances were that all he would get were a quick hug and a chaste kiss. A man had to face up to that. Of course, a man still *tried,* and sometimes even succeeded in getting further, but he did not think about it, or talk about it in the terms that Price did. Such thoughts, and talk, somehow diminished a man.

Still, thoughts of love, of sex, would not leave Neil's mind. It was his rather gloomy reflections that had brought it on, he realized—at least in part. When a man thought of his possible death, the next thought was of an affirmation of life, and what was more affirmative than love and sex? Besides, it had been a long time since he had been in the intimate company of a woman. The idea of a brothel intruded briefly into his mind and was as quickly dismissed. He did not want that kind of a woman. He wanted a woman, but he wanted it to *mean* something.

Neil shook his head ruefully. Lord, he was getting maudlin now! He had better get on along to the barroom and have another beer, so that he would have something to cry into.

Laughing at himself, he went inside the hotel.

Chapter Three

JESSICA took one last look at herself in the gilt-edged mirror before she left the powder room. She carefully smoothed down the soft, peach fabric of her party gown, noting with approval how the warm color set off the skin of her shoulders and arms. She rearranged a ringlet of her soft, pale hair. Her eyes glowed with excitement, and her cheeks were pink.

More or less satisfied, she picked up her fan and turned to leave, just as the door burst open and two of her friends swept in.

Chattering and giggling, the two young women faced her, their faces as flushed and eyes as bright as her own.

"Oh, Jess!" gasped Mary Winston, the smaller of the pair. "You should see all the soldiers! There are dozens and dozens of them, and they are all so handsome in their uniforms. I think I may just die!"

The other young woman, Dulcy Thomas, smiled smugly. "I've already been asked to dance by at *least* a dozen, myself. Not to mention being propositioned."

"Oh, Dulcy, you're terrible!" Mary shrieked, opening her fan and waving it rapidly back and forth before her pink face. "How can you talk like that, you naughty thing!"

Dulcy shook her head, causing her blond curls to tremble. "Mary, Mary." She sighed. "You're *so* provincial. Don't you know that such things happen all the time to pretty girls? You just have to learn to ignore it." Her expression turned sly. "Or to accept it!"

"Oh, Dulcy!" Mary began to fan faster, as Jessica turned away.

Mary was a sweet girl, if a little young for her age. Jessica did not really care much for Dulcy Thomas, although they were a part of the same social set and saw one another quite often. Dulcy had a reputation for being somewhat fast, and Jessica thought her affected and shallow.

"I'll see you two later," she said, as she opened the powder room door, wanting, for some reason, to get away from both of them.

Ever since the war with Spain had begun, her wish for something exciting to happen had certainly been granted. Almost immediately after her father had come home with his announcement that a large number of troops were being sent to Tampa, the town started to fill up with people—troops, military advisers, and newspapermen began to arrive in droves. Most of the new arrivals, other than the military, were putting up at the Tampa Bay Hotel. The shops were busy, business was booming, and Tampa had taken on a sort of carnival atmosphere of action and anticipation that it had never experienced before. Infused by patriotic fervor, the young men all rushed to enlist, and the young women, Jessica included, all looked for something they might do to aid the war effort.

Jessica had volunteered to work for the Red Cross, which had set up headquarters in the Tampa Bay Hotel casino.

Jessica, her hair tied back with a white scarf and wearing a white apron over her dress, felt like an integral part of the cause as she rolled bandages and served refreshments to the servicemen, who continued to arrive almost daily. She basked in the attention she received from the men, who, far from home and lonely, paid extravagant compliments to the girls and women. It was thrilling to have so many attractive men and boys paying such homage, and Jessica sometimes felt like a child in a candy shop, not knowing which way to turn or which sweets to choose first.

Suddenly recognizing the direction of her thoughts, Jessica blushed and glanced around furtively to see if she was observed. Oh, well, there was no real harm in wanting to be admired, was there? And it just might lead to something. She might fall in love and get married! Her blush deepened.

And tonight was the most exciting event of all, she reflected—a ball given by the hotel for the army officers and the local gentry. Jessica had heard that a number of Roosevelt's Rough Riders would be there, and she wondered if any of the famous ones would appear, the men she had read about in the newspapers.

Well, she had better stop dallying about and hie herself to the ballroom, or Mary and Dulcy would be returning shortly, and she would be forced to join them.

The dance was being held in the ballroom, or small saloon, just off the hotel lobby.

Under the high, domed ceiling, crystal chandeliers poured light down upon the creamy shoulders of the beautifully gowned young women and neatly uniformed officers. The orchestra was playing a fast waltz, and the sound of the lively music almost, but not quite, drowned out the chatter and rumble of voices.

As Jessica made her way into the crowded ballroom, she was swept by a feeling of excitement so intense that it made her catch her breath sharply. *This* was the way life should be, she thought, full of color and enchantment. Of course, she was not glad that her country was at war; but she had to admit to herself that life had certainly taken on new meaning for her since the military had arrived.

Dulcy was right in one respect—there certainly *were* a great many handsome young men present, all brushed and polished, resplendent in their blue army uniforms, save for a few who were in brown, a distinction that puzzled Jessica.

As she eagerly scanned the room, one of the young officers in brown approached her. He was rather short, not much taller than she, and very stocky, with a protruding stomach.

When Jessica had been dreaming of the dance, earlier, this was certainly not the dance partner she had envisioned; yet being well schooled in the social amenities, she could not refuse him when he hesitantly asked her to dance.

They made their way, with some difficulty, onto the dance floor, and he, handkerchief in hand, put his right hand on her back and took her right hand in his left. As the other dancers swirled about them, Jessica was happy to discover that, despite his ungainly appearance, her partner was a skillful dancer, leading her firmly but gently through the steps and keeping excellent time. Relaxing a bit, she let herself be carried away by the enjoyment of the moment.

"I'm Lieutenant Gage. John Gage, that is," the young soldier managed to get out between dips and sways.

"How do you do?" Jessica said primly. "I'm Jessica Manning."

John Gage smiled. "I'm delighted to make your acquaintance, Miss Manning, and I must say that you are the prettiest girl here tonight."

Jessica said nothing for a moment, creating an awkward pause. She was growing accustomed to the outrageous compliments paid her by these young soldiers, but it still unsettled her, as she was never certain how to respond to them.

Instead of replying directly to his remark, she made one of her own. "Lieutenant, I'm curious. Why do you wear a brown uniform, instead of blue, like most of the others?"

Gage dipped her gracefully toward the floor, his rather ruddy face reddening further with the effort, and did not reply until he had raised her again to the perpendicular. Then he said simply, "That's because I'm with Roosevelt's Rough Riders," as if the statement alone was sufficient explanation.

And to Jessica, it was. Everyone had read about this special regiment of cavalry, led by the ex-assistant secretary of the navy, Theodore Roosevelt; and Jessica was thrilled to be dancing with one of their ranks, even though he was not physically as handsome as many of the other officers present.

When the dance ended, Gage bowed low over her hand, but before he could escort her off the floor, they were joined by another young lieutenant in brown.

"Why, hello there, Gage, you sly rascal. I do believe you've captured the prettiest girl here."

The newcomer was taller than Gage, and much slimmer, with thick, ginger-colored hair, cut short in the military fashion, and long, blue mischievous eyes. "Come on, Gage, remember that you are a gentleman and an officer, and introduce me."

Gage, reluctantly letting go of Jessica's hand, sighed, as if resigning himself to the inevitable. "Miss Jessica Manning," he said formally, "I would like you to meet Lieutenant Neil Dancer, also of the Rough Riders, and like myself an officer and a gentleman, although not nearly as good a dancer, despite his name."

Neil Dancer laughed and bowed low over Jessica's hand. "You must not listen to the calumnies spread by the good lieutenant, Miss Manning, for he labors under the delusion that the grotesque movements he makes on the dance floor pass for the act of dancing. I, on the other hand, am an expert at the art, which I would very much like to demonstrate to you."

Jessica was quite captivated. This was more as she had imagined it would be. Lieutenant Gage was rather sweet, but surely no match for his handsome friend, who authoritatively swept her onto the floor. She had one last glimpse of Gage's woebegone face; and then they were surrounded by the other dancers, and she forgot everything else and gave herself up to the sheer pleasure of dancing and the not-quite-suppressed inner excitement of being in the arms of this self-assured young officer.

Neil Dancer wasted no time in idle conversation but devoted all his energies to the act of dancing. When the music finally stopped, he took her arm under his and began to lead her off the floor, turning to gaze down into her face.

"Would you care for a glass of punch?" he asked. He was already guiding her toward the buffet table, where huge silver bowls held a rosy pink liquid in which flowers and cakes of ice floated.

Jessica nodded, feeling a bit unsure of herself in the company of this authoritative young man. She was quite used to male attention, but most of the young men she knew were old acquaintances, whom she knew all too well, and generally she could handle them with ease and aplomb. This young man was a different cup of tea entirely— much more sophisticated, more forceful, and somewhat older than the boys and young men of her circle.

Normally, Jessica was quite at ease in the company of men, accustomed to flirting and teasing them; however, in this instance something warned her that her usual tactics might, in some way, backfire, so that although she was flattered and pleased by his ardent attention, she felt ill at ease, off-balance, a feeling that she did not particularly care for, and one that belied her own image of herself as a sophisticated and modern young woman.

Neil Dancer kept her arm entwined with his as he approached the buffet, and she was both flattered and uneasy by his refusal to leave her while he fetched their cups of punch. His actions were not exactly improper, she thought in distress; it was just that it seemed to her that things were proceeding somewhat faster than she liked. His attitude, if not calculated, struck her as being so, and that was unsettling.

As Neil handed her a cup of the punch, Jessica became conscious of just how thirsty she was, and she accepted the cup eagerly. She had the cup to her mouth when Mary and Dulcy, squired by two young officers in blue, came up beside her and Neil Dancer. Both girls' faces were flushed and their hair damp with perspiration.

Hastily lowering her punch cup, Jessica noticed that Dulcy was frankly appraising Neil, and her expression seemed to indicate that she approved of what she saw.

"Why, hello, Jess," Dulcy said, although her gaze never left Neil's face. "Aren't you going to introduce us to your friend?"

Noting wryly that Dulcy's phrase was almost the same that Neil had used on Lieutenant Gage, Jessica felt a sudden prod of jealousy, which was silly, she thought. She had just met the man, for heaven's sake!

But her feeling did not abate when she looked at Neil and found that he was staring back at Dulcy with what seemed as much interest as Dulcy was showing in him. The *nerve* of Dulcy Thomas! How

could she be so brazen? How dare she be so bold? Why, the lieutenant might think—

Jessica could not quite articulate to herself what it was that the lieutenant might think, but it had something to do with his assuming that
Dulcy might be available to do those secret things that men wanted to
do with women, starting with kissing and ending with. . . . She refused to finish the thought.

Mary had spoken not a word so far, merely standing there simper-
ing up at the young man by her side and giggling now and then,
rather foolishly, Jessica thought.

Looking at the two young women, Jessica felt annoyed. Mary was
so empty-headed and silly, and Dulcy so . . . so predatory. If Dulcy
was interested in Lieutenant Dancer, well then, let her have him! He
made her uncomfortable, anyway. But how to escape the present, uneasy moment?

The solution came about without her having to do anything. Dulcy,
with a look at Jessica that managed to be both crafty and triumphant,
smiled coyly, and said, "I have a marvelous idea. Let's all change
partners for the next dance!"

If those two wanted to be together, Jessica had no intention of
standing in their way. She did not even glance at the man by her side
as she said with forced gaiety, "That's a fine idea, Dulcy. That is, if
our partners don't mind."

The next few moments were a little confusing, as they all switched
partners and the music began; and Jessica still did not meet the gaze
of Neil Dancer as she was swept away by the young officer who had
been Mary's partner.

Feeling an anger she could not define, Jessica determinedly gazed
up into the open face of her partner and smiled and smiled. He was
not the dancer her two prior partners had been, and she was forced to
concentrate on following him. She barely heard his halting small talk
and was not even really aware of what she said in reply; she was
upset by the fact that she was having less than a wonderful time. This
evening was one she had been looking forward to for days, and it was
supposed to have been perfect; now it had turned sour.

But then another officer asked her to dance, then another, and their
compliments and flattery, coupled with the magic of the music, began
to do their work, and soon she had forgotten, or nearly forgotten, Neil
Dancer and the unpleasantness of Dulcy's manipulative behavior. The
evening was again wonderful and shining, as Jessica had anticipated it
would be.

Chapter Four

NEIL Dancer, holding Dulcy Thomas in his arms, looked over her head at the other dancers. He was looking for Jessica Manning's fair hair and peach gown, although he did not really know why. Dulcy was just as pretty and a great deal more friendly; but somehow the slender, delicate-looking Jessica was the one who lingered stubbornly in his thoughts. He was astute enough to realize that he had, in some way, offended her, and he knew enough about women to also realize that he might never learn the true reason. Still, he wanted to dance with her again and perhaps try a different approach. She struck him as rather shy; perhaps he had been too forward. Whatever the reason for her quick agreement to changing partners, Neil wanted another chance with her, and he was confident that with a little effort he could bring her around.

Just as the dance was ending, he saw her, quite nearby, dancing with a stocky, dark-haired naval officer. Quickly, keeping an eye on Jessica all the while, Neil escorted Dulcy to a chair, despite her obvious reluctance to see him go. Leaving the disgruntled Dulcy on the sidelines, Neil hastily made his way in the direction where he had seen Jessica and the officer. He finally found them at the buffet table, filling their plates with the delicacies on display there. Abruptly realizing that he was hungry, Neil stepped into line directly behind Jessica, pushing in front of another officer to do so.

"What the devil!" said the officer. "Just what do you think you're doing, shoving in front of me?"

Neil turned and gave his most engaging smile. "It's a matter of life and love, Ensign. Surely you wouldn't want to stand in the way of romance?" He indicated Jessica and sighed tragically.

The ensign shrugged good-naturedly. "Well, when you put it like that."

"Thanks, old fellow," Neil said, giving him a clap on the shoulder. "I'll do the same for you some time."

"Well, I should certainly hope so," the ensign said, grinning. "I sure as hell wouldn't mind finding a girl as pretty as that one."

Neil switched his attention back to the buffet, occasionally stealing a glance at Jessica, who so far seemed unaware of his proximity.

When they were almost at the end of the table, he spoke to her. "Lovely buffet, don't you agree?"

She turned with a start of surprise and frowned when she recognized him. He could tell by her set expression that this was going to be more difficult than he had thought. He turned on his smile—women had told him that it was very winning. "I hope that I didn't do or say anything to displease you, Miss Manning, but you did seem in a great hurry to get away from me."

Jessica's pale face flushed a rosy pink, and Neil knew that he had struck home. "I thought it was the other way around, Lieutenant," she said in a cool voice. "You seemed only too anxious to make the acquaintance of Miss Thomas, and I certainly had no wish to stand in your way."

Neil's smile widened. She was jealous! Now all he had to do was apologize properly and deny that he had any interest in Dulcy Thomas, and matters between them should proceed smoothly.

"I'm afraid that presumption was incorrect, Miss Manning. After dancing with you, how could a fellow even look at another woman?"

They were at the end of the table now, and Neil knew that he had to make his move, or he would lose her again to the young ensign.

"Look," he said, "will you have supper with me? We'll find a nice, quiet place and get to know one another better. I'm sure we have a lot in common."

He watched Jessica raise her chin, and the cold look in her eyes filled him with dismay.

"Thank you, Lieutenant," she said politely, "but as you can plainly see, I already have an escort for supper, and it would be ungracious of me to go back on my promise to him. Good evening, sir!"

Her tone told Neil that it had been rude of *him* to even make such a suggestion, and the implied rebuke made his own face begin to burn.

Well, to hell with her! Snippety little wench!

Taking a cup of punch to go with his food, he stalked away from the table toward the veranda, where the windows stood open to accommodate the overflow of guests from the ballroom.

He found a place to sit and ate quickly, scarcely savoring the food, so preoccupied was he with his embarrassment and displeasure. He barely looked up when someone sat down next to him, only taking notice when that someone waved a silver flask under his nose.

He glanced up to see Farrel grinning at him, offering the flask. "Here, friend, have a drink. You look like you sure as hell could use one, with that black scowl on your face."

Neil grunted and accepted the flask. Tilting it to his lips, he took a long, satisfying pull.

"Hey!" Farrel reached for the flask. "I didn't say to drink it all. And why are you out here all by yourself, anyway? Don't tell me that with all those little beauties inside, you haven't found one for yourself?"

Neil gave him a weak smile and relinquished the flask. "Of course not. How could you even think such a thing? No, it's just that I had an argument with some troublemaker and came out here to calm down. Now that I've done so, I shall return to the fray."

Getting up, he gave Farrel a mock salute and strode back into the ballroom, determined to make up for lost time. He almost ran into Dulcy Thomas, who was just coming toward the veranda.

"Where have you been, you handsome devil?" She caught him by the arm. "You're terrible, you know, leaving me for that Jessica. Oh, I saw you talking with her! I should never speak to you again."

She pouted and looked at him with teasing eyes. By Lord, she was a pretty creature and, as Neil had thought to himself earlier, a hell of a lot more friendly than Jessica Manning. Why should he waste his time on someone who did not appreciate him when this girl so obviously did?

Feeling immensely better all at once, he took her into his arms and swung her onto the dance floor. They were playing a slow waltz, and instead of holding her at arm's length, as was proper, Neil pulled her close until he could feel the warm weight of her breasts against his chest. She laughed softly but did not protest, and the warm womanly smell of her so close to him began to have an arousing effect on Neil. He felt himself getting an erection and started to pull back, but Dulcy tugged him back to her, pushing her lower body hard against his, and then away; and suddenly he was weak with desire. My God, he thought, did she know what she was doing to him? Evidently she did, for she was now moving against him even more provocatively, staring up at him with smoldering eyes that erased any doubt in his mind as to her awareness of his aroused condition.

Neil was suffering from a mixture of feelings. Was she leading him on purposely, or was she just a tease, one of those women who liked to get a man aroused and then leave him in an embarrassing condition? Then she did something that answered his question. Raising herself up on her toes, she whispered into his ear, her breath hot and tickling against his skin. "Do you want to go outside? To the garden? It's private out there."

Neil could only nod breathlessly. Quickly he began to maneuver her toward the veranda doorway. He could not quite believe his sudden good fortune; he had never known a girl from a good family to be this brazen. Yet he would be an idiot not to take advantage of the opportunity—truly Price's "Mr. Pureheart."

In a few moments they were out on the hotel veranda, where the lights were dim. Neil hurried her down the steps, Dulcy giggling.

Once they were down the steps, she took charge, guiding him along a pathway between a heavy stand of ornamental shrubs, as if she was quite familiar with the route. "Over here," she whispered urgently, as if she, not Neil, was in the grip of passion.

He followed her into the seclusion of the shrubbery, and they were scarcely out of sight of the hotel before she seized his face in both hands and pushed herself wantonly against him, her mouth searching for his in the dark.

Too excited to be gentle, Neil grabbed her waist with his hands and pressed his mouth to hers. Her lips were warm and yielding, and her breath smelled of violets.

He could feel the full contours of her breasts through the thin material of her dress, but his efforts were frustrated as his hands moved lower, trying to cup the ripeness of her buttocks.

Groaning, he tore his mouth from hers and bent to hoist her skirts, then slid his hands upward over her silken calves and thighs. To his vast astonishment, he discovered that she was naked beneath the full skirt of her gown. Dulcy exhaled softly against his cheek as he again sought her mouth, his hands kneading and stroking the smooth mounds of flesh. Mindless in his desire, he tried to lower her to the grass, but she resisted with surprising strength.

"No, no, you silly man! We can't ruin my dress with grass stains. We'll have to do it standing up."

"What—what?" he stammered. "How can we—?"

The solution to the problem came to him. He fumbled his trousers open, then lifted her, skirts rucked up around her waist, and felt her legs lock around him. Almost sobbing aloud with need, he lowered her carefully upon his upright organ and felt her hot breath almost scorching his throat as she gasped at his entry into her. It took only a few, awkward, lunging thrusts before Neil felt himself burst inside her. He groaned aloud, and Dulcy, giggling, shushed him.

Passion spent, legs weak as water, he lowered her to the ground. "Your handkerchief, please, sir," Dulcy whispered.

"What?" he said stupidly, chest heaving, heart thudding.

He fumbled out the square of white linen, and she took it, turning her back on him. Dimly, Neil wondered what pleasure she had received from the coupling—he had ended far too soon—yet she did not seem the least disappointed or angry. He had heard that some women received their pleasure not from the sexual act itself, but from the momentary power it gave them over men; perhaps she was one of those. He dismissed it from his mind and busied himself arranging his clothes.

"There now, I'm ready," she said, taking his hand. "We can go back now."

Trailing behind her like some idiot child, Neil let her lead him back to the veranda and the lights. Evidently Price had been correct about one thing—*some* girls from good families were as easy to seduce as their more lowly sisters. The possible repercussion of their hasty coupling was troubling Neil. What if she became pregnant? In his heedless passion he had taken no precautions whatsoever. Should he question her about it? And if he did, would he appear foolish? Well, she seemed to have been well aware of what she was doing, and her eagerness belied virginity.

They were at the veranda steps now, and Neil decided to say nothing. Women like Dulcy, he had been told, had ways of taking care of such things. Giving a mental shrug, he stepped up onto the veranda beside her, and she darted a mischievous glance at him.

"Goodness me, all that walking surely did give me a thirst! Do you suppose we might have a cup or two of that punch?"

Neil, feeling more ill at ease than she appeared to be, managed a smile. "Certainly. You wait here, and I'll bring some out to you."

Making his way across the crowded room, seeing the eager, yearning faces of his fellow officers, a certain satisfaction began to fill Neil, despite his misgivings. He knew that any man there would give anything to have been in his boots a few moments ago. Most of them would go back to their tents tonight frustrated. So, the least he could do for Dulcy was fetch her a good supply of punch.

The small crystal cups only held a small amount, scarcely enough to quench anyone's thirst. Neil looked along the table for a larger con-

tainer and caught the eye of a pretty, dark-skinned waitress standing
behind the table at the punch bowl.

"Miss," he said, giving her a winning smile, "do you suppose it
would be possible to get a couple of glasses for me? My partner's
quite thirsty, and these cups don't hold much more than a thimbleful."

The young woman, slender and graceful in her black dress and
white, starched apron and cap, smiled and nodded. "I think I might
manage that, sir, if you don't tell anyone else, so that they demand
glasses, too."

"I promise that it will always be our secret," he said, holding his
hand over his heart. He was charmed by the young woman's obvious
intelligence and warmth.

Turning away, the waitress went to a nearby cabinet, set against the
wall, and opened it. In a moment she returned with two tall glasses,
which she proceeded to fill from the punch bowl.

"Here you are, sir," she said, extending the glasses toward him. At
that moment a couple crowding up to the table bumped into her outstretched arm, causing the red punch to spill over the skirt of the
young lady.

Neil heard the waitress gasp and then saw with surprise that the
young woman was Jessica Manning. She noticed him looking at her,
and she frowned, trying futilely to brush the punch from her skirt. "I
might have guessed it would have something to do with you, Lieutenant!" Jessica whirled on the waitress. "My dress is ruined, you clumsy
oaf!"

Neil, startled by her outburst, felt his own temper rising. After all,
he had observed the whole incident, and it was not the fault of the
waitress. The young naval officer with Jessica had bumped into the
waitress, not the other way around.

Neil felt that he had to intervene on the behalf of the beleaguered
waitress. "It was not her fault, Miss Manning. Your friend there is to
blame, if anyone is. He bumped into her arm."

Upon hearing this, Jessica stopped rubbing at her skirt and flushed
even more. She turned to the young woman behind the table. "I'm
sorry, miss," she said, biting her lip. "I really didn't mean to shout at
you. I was just upset about my dress. I hope you will forgive my bad
manners."

Without waiting for a response, not even looking to see if her escort
was accompanying her, Jessica fled into the crowd. Neil was left

standing there, staring after her, as the naval officer quickly followed
her, after making his own quick apology to the waitress.

Neil, somewhat at a loss, could only glance at the waitress and
shrug ruefully. She smiled at him with knowledgeable eyes and after
refilling the spilled one, again extended the glasses of punch. Although she did not speak, Neil was left with the feeling that she had
understood far more about the circumstances of what had just happened than he did.

Carrying the glasses, he returned to Dulcy. She smiled smugly at
him as he approached, and made a sound of delight when she saw the
large glasses. Neil bowed and gave her one, scarcely aware of what he
was doing. His mind was on Jessica and the annoying ability that she
had to make him feel uncomfortable. He had come here tonight expecting only to have a good time—some dances with pretty girls,
maybe a drink or two; and if he was fortunate, perhaps a few stolen
kisses, or maybe even a bit of a fondle. Well, in the last respect he had
gotten much more than he had expected. Still, he felt restless and dis-
contented, and he could not help but feel that it was all Jessica's fault.

Maria Mendes, standing behind the punch bowl at the buffet,
watched the young lieutenant stride away with his two glasses of
punch, and she smiled to herself. It was obvious that there was something, some kind of strong feeling, between the lieutenant and the
pretty blond woman; but neither of them seemed to realize it, or
admit it to themselves. They were a strange breed, these well-to-do
Americans, with peculiar rituals. Oh, her own people had their rituals,
of course; but to Maria, at least, they seemed more direct, less hypo-
critical. When a Cuban man was interested in a Cuban woman, he
usually made no pretense that it was otherwise. He might have to
suffer a chaperon when he came to call on the young woman, but his
interest was no secret, least of all to himself!

But this thing between the lieutenant and the blond girl was none
of her affair, she thought. She had work to do, and she had best get to
it and not idle about. A large bowl, which had been filled to the brim
with chocolate mousse, was empty save for a few spoonfuls of creamy
liquid in the bottom. The head chef was right, it was always the des-
serts that needed to be refilled. No matter what was on the table—
shrimp, lobster, beef, salads—people still liked sweets the best.

As she lifted the heavy bowl, Maria saw again the tall, dark-haired
man with the pale skin, whom she had noticed earlier in the evening.

Dressed in fine clothing, a dandy, in fact, he stood in the doorway, smoking a long, thin cigar, and he was very obviously staring at her, as she had caught him doing earlier.

Maria tightened her lips and turned away, but she could still feel his burning gaze on her back, like an unwelcome touch. It was not that she was unaccustomed to the lewd stares of men, but there was something in the eyes of this one that disturbed her deeply. Some women might find him handsome, she supposed, with his fine clothes; but she did not care for his looks—that unnaturally pale skin and those very large and moist-looking eyes, like a spaniel's. She smiled at that thought. However, there was nothing spaniellike in his appraising look.

Maria wondered, briefly, who he was. Obviously he was not of the military, since he was not in uniform, and he did not have the look of a newspaper correspondent. Whatever or whomever he was, he had nothing to do with her; and so far as she was concerned, he never would.

She was almost to the kitchen, when she heard someone calling her name. She faced around to see one of her older brothers, Ramon, hurrying toward her down the long corridor.

Seeing Ramon always filled Maria with a sense of great pride. He was so handsome, so straight and tall. They had always been very close, for he had been her adviser and protector since she could remember. Nowadays she often wished that Ramon had not turned so serious, become so preoccupied with the Cuban clubs and their political involvements; for she remembered him as a happy youth, full of laughter and pranks. Now he seldom joked, and his thoughts always seemed so far away, on weighty and serious matters. Withal, she loved and admired him and enjoyed his company on those occasions when he would put aside his political concerns and relax, although it seemed that those times were growing fewer and fewer.

"Ramon!" she exclaimed. "What are you doing here?"

He smiled gently. "Mama sent me. Why else would I be here? She ordered me to come and see you home. Are you about finished?"

Maria sighed, running a hand distractedly through her long, dark hair. "I'm sorry, Ramon, but no. Isn't tonight your club meeting?"

He nodded. "That is why I want to see you home as quickly as possible. They are expecting me at the club. Here, let me take that."

Maria surrendered the bowl and sighed again. "When will Mama ever realize that I am a woman grown? I can get home by myself, Ramon. She didn't need to hold you from your meeting!"

He shrugged. "That is as may be, little sister, but she *is* worried, what with all the soldiers in town, that you might be molested. And I happen to agree with her. When there are a great number of hungry men about, you do not show them a lovely Cuban pastry. It is simply logic, Maria."

He smiled broadly, and in his face Maria could see the shadow of the boy he had once been. Laughing at his remark, she nodded toward the kitchen. "I still have to work a bit longer. I must get this"— she indicated the bowl in his arms—"to the kitchen and bring a replacement to the buffet. I will check with the supervisor to see if I may leave then. All right?"

"Fine." He returned the bowl to her, and Maria started again toward the kitchen.

"Oh, miss! Waitress!"

The voice came from the hallway behind them, and Maria faced around to see the slender blond woman, on whom she had spilled the punch, hurrying toward them.

The woman stopped a few feet in front of Maria and Ramon, apparently a bit discomfited by the presence of another person. She said, "Oh! I'm sorry, I didn't know you were talking to someone."

Maria smiled. "It's all right, miss. This is my brother, come to see me home."

Jessica nodded. "I see. I was just returning from the powder room and chanced to see you, and I, well, I wanted to apologize again for my rude behavior. It wasn't you I was angry at."

"I know," Maria said, smiling. "And it's quite all right. Did you get the stain out of the dress?"

Jessica did not seem to hear; she was staring at Ramon. She said, "I should introduce myself. I am Jessica Manning."

Maria said, "I am Maria Mendes, and this is my older brother, Ramon."

Ramon bowed slightly, without speaking, his face guarded. Maria knew that he viewed all Americans somewhat warily, and he was clearly both intrigued by and defensive toward this pretty *gringa*.

"Well, I have to get this back to the kitchen," Maria said into the sudden silence.

Jessica gave a start and smiled at Maria, somewhat nervously, Maria thought.

"And I must be going," Jessica said in a rush. "It was awfully nice to meet you, both of you. And I do hope, Maria, that you will forgive me for my behavior." With a slight wave of her gloved hand, she whirled and hastened away toward the ballroom.

Maria turned to Ramon and began to laugh. "Did you see her staring at you, Ramon? I do believe she fancies you!"

Ramon flushed. "Don't be silly, Maria. She is a *gringa*, and *gringas* seldom lower themselves to even look at Latin men. She is a butterfly, a pretty parasite, who no doubt has never known an honest day's work in her life, and as such she is of no interest to me. Now, get your work done so that we may leave. I do not want to be any later than need be."

Aware that she had ruffled her brother's composure, Maria smiled secretly to herself as she pushed open the kitchen door. Despite what Ramon had said, Maria knew that he had found the blond woman attractive. First the brown-uniformed lieutenant, then her brother. What was it she had? Something, obviously. The ways of a man and a woman were very strange, Maria reflected; there was no doubt about that. Still smiling, she went on into the kitchen.

She felt badly that Ramon had to delay attending his meeting because of her, but it was her mother's fault, really. Usually Maria was finished with her work fairly early, about the same time that her father's shift was over, and the two of them went home together, but tonight was a different matter because of the ball.

This was the first time that Maria had been asked to work at one of these special affairs, and she had been flattered, as only the most efficient and attractive dining room waitresses were asked to work such events. She knew that her mother disapproved, but it meant extra money, which the family could always use. Maria herself had no fears about going home alone this late. She had her horse, old Miguelito, who knew his way to and from the hotel as well as he knew his own stall; and she was confident of her own ability to deal with any randy soldiers she might encounter.

It was the old way, the Latin protectiveness toward their women; yet it was done out of love, because her family cared deeply for her. Of course, if she had an admirer of her own, someone who was paying court to her, *he* would be seeing her home. But there was no one—a fact that Maria knew caused her mother much unhappiness.

As to why there was no one, even Maria was not sure. She was pretty enough—very pretty, some said—and she was intelligent; but then perhaps it was true, as her mother said, that Cuban men did not want an intelligent woman, they wanted a woman who was good to look at, a good housekeeper, potentially a good mother, and one who always said "yes" to whatever her husband decreed. How many times had her mother scolded her for being too outspoken, too free in her ways? Well, somewhere there *must* be a man who wanted more than a docile servant for a wife. Somewhere there had to be a man who could accept her as an equal, a partner.

But thinking about such things did not get her work done, she scolded herself. Quickly she picked up a fresh bowl of mousse and carried it out to the buffet table.

She could see that the crowd was thinning now, and she went back to the kitchen to check with Mrs. Nelson, her supervisor, about leaving. Mrs. Nelson was understanding but firm. "I'll need you for another hour, Maria. Then you may go."

Maria did not argue. Ramon would miss his meeting if he waited for her. She must persuade him to go on without her. She could get home by herself, despite her mother's worries.

When she told Ramon that she could not yet leave, and urged him to go to his meeting, he reacted in anger. However, this did not disturb Maria unduly, for she realized that he was torn between what he saw as two duties—one to her, the other to his comrades at the club.

Finally Ramon decided to go along to the club, but he was not happy about leaving her to get home by herself, despite her reassurances that she would be fine.

Shaking her head, Maria stared after him through the back door of the kitchen. Ramon blamed her, she knew, for putting him in such an awkward position, forcing him to choose between her safety and his duty to the sacred cause. Men were strange, she thought; always going on about their "honor," setting such impossible goals for themselves, so many things to live up to, so many things to achieve.

Sighing, she went back to work, removing empty dishes from the buffet table, helping the other women clean up in the kitchen; and then at last, the ball was officially over, the guests gone, and Maria and the others were finished. She prepared to leave.

As she approached the spot where she had tethered Miguelito, he whinnied an affectionate greeting. Now in her cloak, and carrying a large basket of leftover food from the buffet, she walked up to him, hand outstretched to offer him the sugar cubes she had brought for him.

"Good old horse," she murmured fondly. "Faithful old Miguelito. It is time to go home now."

As Miguelito's velvet muzzle rooted in her hand for the sugar, a man's voice spoke behind her. "Surely, he is a very fortunate horse, to have such a lovely mistress."

Maria jumped and drew in her breath sharply, which startled the horse, causing him to rear. Maria whirled around.

A tall figure stepped out of the shadows into the light from the kitchen windows, and Maria saw, with displeasure, that it was the tall, pale-skinned man she had noticed watching her during the evening. She experienced some unease, but no real fear; the cleaning staff was busy in the kitchen, and if the man made any untoward advances, all she had to do was call out.

"You startled me, sir," she said coldly.

He had removed his tall hat and now bowed to her. "I beg your pardon for that, my dear lady. It was not my intention to frighten you."

Maria stared at him in dislike. His words were flowery and blatantly insincere. His manner was as florid as his dandified appearance. What did he want with her?

He had straightened up now and was staring boldly at her with those strange, luminous eyes. "I see that you are alone. I should indeed be honored if you would allow me to escort you home. A beautiful young woman like yourself should not be abroad unattended when there are so many young soldiers about. They are a rough and rowdy lot."

As he spoke, he moved toward her, and Maria involuntarily took a step backward.

"Yes, indeed," he went on. "A lovely young woman like yourself should be protected and cherished." His voice had grown soft and musing, and before she could move, he had reached out to stroke her hair.

Her anger flared. How dare he touch her! Did he think that just because she was Cuban, not a "white" woman, that he could make advances to her?

"I am meeting my brother, señor," she lied. "*He* is seeing me home, and I think that I should warn you that we are Cubans, and Cuban men are very protective of their women. If he should come now, and see you talking to me this way, he would likely get the idea that you are accosting me, then act accordingly. Do I make myself clear, señor?"

"Oh, yes, yes, indeed, señorita." The man seemed amused instead of alarmed. His teeth gleamed in the semi-darkness as he smiled. "You make yourself quite clear. I can only hope that in the future we may meet again, when your brother is not expected. My name is Brill Kroger, and we shall meet again. Indeed, I shall make a point of it."

Bowing again, Kroger put on his hat and moved back into the darkness, leaving Maria alone with Miguelito and her thoughts, which were not altogether pleasant. There was something about this man, something that she felt was dangerous, despite his suave demeanor. But the question was, why had he focused on her? She had no idea, but she vowed to stay out of his way in the future. Why she felt that he represented a threat to her, she did not know, either. His words had been harmless enough, but something in the way he spoke them seemed to say more, to have a hidden, even sinister meaning.

Shivering slightly, Maria mounted Miguelito and headed for home. She made up her mind that she definitely would not mention the incident to her mother or Ramon, for it would only give emphasis to their notion that she was in jeopardy any time she was not accompanied by a member of the family.

Nonetheless, she determined to be on her guard, for the remark that Brill Kroger had made—that he intended to seek her out again—rang in her mind, and she had an intuitive feeling that Kroger meant trouble for her, and perhaps for others as well.

Chapter Five

BRILL Kroger stood in the shadows of the hotel wall, watching the Cuban woman as she mounted her horse and rode off. Perhaps her brother really was meeting her, perhaps not; but he would not press the matter at present. He wanted no scenes, no outraged brothers or parents just now to threaten his "operation," as he thought of it. All was just about arranged, all was ready for the big score. It had taken him several weeks to get the whole affair set up properly and to establish his credibility with the influential citizens of Ybor City and Tampa proper.

Kroger removed a thin, twisted cigar from a silver case, put it between his lips, and lit it. The girl *was* lovely, he thought, strong-bodied and rounded; and spirited, too. He had noticed that even before he spoke to her. It had been obvious in her gestures and in the intelligence of her dark eyes. She had seen him watching her, he knew, and it had bothered her.

He smiled, examining the glowing end of his cigar. It often bothered them, in one way or another; but that was a part of his technique, and it always worked, or almost always. He could wait, he was a patient man, patient in all things. Patience was a desired virtue for any good confidence man like himself, as well as in the pursuit of any woman catching his fancy. He knew where she worked, and he spent a great deal of time at the hotel, since he had a room there and most of his important contacts were made in the hotel's various public rooms. Yes, he could wait, and his pleausre, when he finally attained it, would be the greater for the waiting.

When Maria had ridden out of sight, Kroger turned and strolled around toward the front entrance of the hotel, his thoughts moving to the details of his plan. He had already convinced several of the Cuban clubs that they should sponsor a benefit ball to raise money for the war effort; and now he was working on the prominent businessmen of Tampa. Kroger was certain that he had just about convinced Wyngate Manning, one of the most influential bankers in Tampa; and if Manning went along, so would others. Kroger planned to have both balls on the same evening, one at the Tampa Bay Hotel, the other at the Cuban Lyceum in Ybor City. Both balls would be elegant, and all concerned would have a fine time. Afterward, however, when they came looking for Brill Kroger to see how much money they had taken in, they would find only that they had been taken.

His smile spread into a wolfish, self-satisfied grin. Yes, Brill Kroger would be long gone to somewhere where the air was dry and balmy; some place where fungi did not grow in one's shoes if they were left empty for too long; maybe the East, Long Island perhaps; some location where summer heat did not sap the strength and cloud the mind; maybe even California, he had heard that it was nice there. But wherever he went, he would go carrying a satchel packed with money, able to buy the best and to live in comfortable luxury until the next scam. Indeed he would!

He exhaled a puff of cigar smoke, the smoke forming a perfect ring. Yes, Lacey Kroger's son was doing all right for himself. All right, indeed!

At the thought of his mother, Kroger's face saddened, as always. His sweet mother, if only she had lived. If she were alive, he would shower her with expensive gifts, dinners at fine restaurants, and the best clothes.

He sighed dolefully. She had always loved pretty things and had had impeccable taste, even when matters were bad for them, even when there was little or no money coming in and they had been forced to live in that horrible, little, drab apartment, with the dreadful furniture. Moisture came to his eyes as he thought of his mother in her somewhat threadbare peignoir, her golden curls atumble around her shoulders, holding him when he was little, in her lap and speaking the words she had spoken to him so many times before: "Just remember, darling, what you see here isn't real. This is just a bad dream and soon we'll wake up and see the real world, the one we were born for, and we'll both have everything we want, and we'll be important and popular and very, very rich!"

And somehow, even when his belly was empty and it seemed that there was no chance of things ever changing, her words could always make it better, easing the present and giving promise to the future, and somehow they always came through—a new gentleman friend would turn up, a little money would come into the house, and for a while things would improve.

Kroger, unashamed, wiped the tears from his eyes. He had worshipped his pretty, yellow-haired mother. To his eyes, she had been the most beautiful, the most desirable woman in the world, and she, in turn, had pampered and fussed over him, making him her confidant and friend.

Kroger did not remember his father. He had been five when his father left; and although others had assured him that five was certainly old enough to retain memory of the man who had sired him, Kroger could not recall a thing about him. In the past he had tried, repeatedly, and come up with a blank every time. He could recall no face, no voice, no gestures of the man—nothing of his father lived in his memory. All he could remember was his mother.

In fact, Kroger could not even recall his ever experiencing any real curiosity about the man, and the only time his mother had ever discussed the matter of his father's leaving was when the questions of his playmates had driven Kroger to inquire of her as to the reason his father had left them.

Large tears had filled her blue eyes, and she had looked at him sorrowfully. "Oh, my poor, fatherless baby! You are too young to have to know the sadness the cold, cruel world can bring upon us. Your father was a wonderful man, my darling, a fine man, and he didn't leave us willingly, you can be sure. How could he? He loved us both dearly. He was given the chance to make a great deal of money, going into business in South America. He didn't want to leave us, but he did so, thinking that it would only be for a few months, and when he returned, we would be rich. But the ship sank, and all aboard it were lost at sea. Since your dear father had mortgaged everything to make this investment, our monies were also lost, and we, you and I, were left destitute!"

Little Brill had accepted the story, as he accepted everything his mother told him. Strangely, for he was an intelligent though overly volatile child, he never wondered why there were no photographs of this noble father—no letters, no memorabilia.

Later, when Kroger was in his teens, an acquaintance, a boy who had been brought up in the same neighborhood, told him that his father had been a bank clerk who had left his mother because he could no longer countenance her infidelities—and because he was certain that Brill was not his son. Brill had flown into a great rage, blacked both the boy's eyes, broken his nose, and was well on his way to killing him when one of the teachers pulled Brill off the boy's battered form. As soon as the fight was over, Brill put the whole incident out of his mind. As far as he was concerned, it had never happened. Obviously, it was a lie, anyway, for what his mother had told him must assuredly be the truth.

And so the years had gone by, not unhappily for Kroger; although he sadly decried the lack of money with which to buy the finer things of life that his mother had taught him to covet, and even though his mother's prophecy did not come true—they did not waken from the dream—Kroger still believed her and still waited for the good life that she had promised him would come, in spite of the fact that the gentlemen "friends" grew shabbier and poorer as the years passed and the funds they contributed to the Kroger household grew less and less.

In Kroger's eyes his mother remained the same—young, blond, and beautiful. He did not see the lines that began to mar her fine, white skin, nor the gray that crept into her hair, nor the sagging body that finally, despite all her efforts, could no longer attract even the most desperate "friend."

It was then that Kroger took to the streets. Young, good-looking in a rather flashy way, he had made his first money as a gigolo, taking older women to the theater, restaurants, and then to bed.

Since he was handsome, cooperative, and bright, these women—like his mother—doted on him, lavishing money, fine clothes, and other gifts on him. For the first time Kroger was able to give things to his mother and was rewarded by seeing her wearing nice clothing, eating good food, and living in decent quarters. But as Kroger prospered, she had faded, as if the lack of male companionship she had always thrived on was drawing the strength from her; and one evening Kroger came home to find her, seemingly peacefully asleep in her chair, looking, he thought, just as she always had—young, beautiful, and very desirable.

He cried for a week, was inconsolable for months, and never, even to this day, forgot her.

When Kroger finally recovered enough from his grief to function again, he left the apartment and moved in with one of his lady "clients," a middle-aged widow who furnished him with enough money to enjoy himself but not enough to allow him to escape her domination.

This situation remained for a year, while Kroger, still brooding over his mother's death, tried to decide what to do with his life. His existence was pleasant enough, but these women, his clients, had a tendency to want to keep him under their thumbs; they allowed money and privilege in dribbles and drabs, and Kroger, now twenty, was growing impatient to live his own life, to be in control of his own destiny; in short, to live the kind of life he was intended for. How to manage it, was the question.

Untrained in any respect—he had been only an average student—and unwilling to invest many years of drudgery in an office job struggling to make his way to the top, Kroger pondered his options.

As he became more acquainted with the world, he met a smooth, dapper gentleman by the name of Randy Squires, a.k.a. Squires Dangerfield, a.k.a. Dan Resnick; a highly successful confidence man, who always seemed to have money to spend and a beautiful woman on his arm.

Kroger, intuitively feeling that Squires might be the solution to his problem, actively cultivated the man; and Squires, flattered by the younger man's interest and sensing that Kroger was a natural confidence man, introduced him to the business, so to speak, teaching him about human nature, its frailty and its gullibility.

Kroger was an apt pupil, and so the first con game that he and Squires worked together was an elaborate hoax upon Mrs. Haskins, the comely, rich widow whom Kroger had been keeping happy for the past year. The scheme involved purportedly stolen diamonds, actually paste imitations, which they conned Mrs. Haskins into buying. The successful operation netted them several thousand dollars each and required that both Kroger and Squires leave town immediately after its consummation.

They went to Chicago, where they proceeded to concoct another, even more successful, scheme, and Kroger was convinced that he had finally found his niche in life—a profession that peculiarly fitted his talents.

He loved his work, for it combined all that his mother had taught him—ignoring reality in favor of fantasy, enjoying the finer things of life—with the fact that he was now in control of his life. *He* was pulling the strings, making everything happen; and he was striking back at the world that had so grievously hurt his mother by failing to recognize her special qualities. It was an ideal life.

Kroger worked with Squires for five years. Five grand years filled with flash and dazzle, money, women, and success. And then, one dark night in December, Squires miscalculated and was caught in a compromising position with the wife of the intended victim of their current con game. The intended victim proved to be an excellent shot, and Squires's lifeblood spilled out all over the satin nightgown of the hysterical wife. Kroger, much shaken, fled the city of Chicago immediately.

However, it proved only a minor setback. Kroger missed Squires, yet he felt that he had served his apprenticeship and was now ready to make it on his own. Hesitant to take on a new partner, Kroger concocted schemes that he could handle by himself, and soon he was doing far better than he had with Squires.

And so it had been for several years, until he learned about the declaration of war with Spain and the influx of troops into the Tampa area. Then he knew that all that had come before had been little more than a prologue. He felt the familiar thrill that he always experienced when he devised a new scheme. The arrival of the military would bring much business activity and money into Tampa—and a great deal of confusion. A perfect situation for an enterprising man interested in turning a quick dollar.

Since Kroger was "between jobs," he got on a train and arrived in Tampa one day after the first troops appeared.

Settling himself into the posh and comfortable Tampa Bay Hotel, he immediately set about making the acquaintance of the town's most influential businessmen; and then, as he had become aware of the existence of Ybor City, a city within a city, he expanded on his idea to encompass the Cuban community as well.

His plan was simple, as the best plans usually were—he would organize a charity ball, or rather two charity balls, one in Tampa proper, the other in Ybor City, the express purpose being to raise funds for the war effort; funds to aid the soldiers, help the Red Cross, and to purchase medical supplies. A worthy cause that he was certain few would refuse. The ball would be arranged on credit, of course, with all expenses to be paid out of the proceeds on the day following the event. On the day after the balls, however, the townspeople would discover that he, and the money, had vanished.

So far things had gone according to plan. He had arranged his contacts, talked local businessmen and shopkeepers into donating goods and services; and now all that remained was to set the night for the balls and charm some lovely ladies into serving as official hostesses and others into taking care of the drudge work, such as lettering and mailing the invitations.

Most of the ladies for the Ybor City ball, Kroger had already recruited, for the Cubans were fiercely patriotic and could be counted upon to cooperate in any way that might contribute to the freeing of their homeland from Spain. They were constantly holding charity raffles, fiestas, and parties of their own to raise money for the cause, and it had been easy to convince them that a grand affair, inviting all the cream of Cuban society, would raise enough money so that they might pay for the transportation and arms for their own volunteer forces to get to Cuba.

In fact, Kroger had been amazed at the generosity of the Cubans, many of whom already contributed one day's wages a week to the cause. He did not find this particularly admirable, but rather evidence of their gullibility. To him, they were only "easy marks," and he wished that the non-Cuban population was as easy to deceive.

He had already decided that he was going to ask the banker, Wyngate Manning, if his daughter Jessica would like to be on the hospitality committee. It would flatter the man, and it should please the young woman, whom he had met briefly in the Manning home.

She was a pretty little thing, he reflected. In fact, she reminded Kroger of his mother, as did most slight, pretty, blond women, although he did not realize this.

It was one of Kroger's strange traits that he unconsciously divided women into two classes, ladies and whores, and although he had been known to seduce women of both classes, his attitude toward them was markedly different. Blond women were "good," like his mother, and despite their predilections, were viewed by him as true ladies. Dark women, on the other hand, seemed to him sensual and wanton, no matter what their true character might be. Kroger was totally unaware of this trait in himself and would not have admitted it or recognized it if it had been brought to his attention; nor would he have thought it strange that he classified his mother, who had literally supported both of them for years, through the contributions of the men with whom she bedded, as a "good" woman.

Finished with the cigar now, Kroger threw the butt aside and entered the hotel. Yes, he would contact Wyngate Manning the next day and inquire if his daughter would like to serve on the committee. Four weeks should be time enough to make all the arrangements. Ideally, it would be better to take a bit more time, yet Kroger had the uneasy feeling that this war, so abruptly declared and so haphazardly organized, might be over at any time, and it would not do for the fighting to cease before the balls were held.

So, four weeks it would be. He would impress upon the various participants that time was of the essence, for the money was needed *now*

—which was true enough—and their patriotic fervor should make the time limit possible.

Four weeks should also give him time to get acquainted with the Cuban girl, perhaps more than acquainted. He smiled, supremely confident of his skill as both a confidence man and a ladies' man, and he was inordinately pleased that he had found two women worthy of his attentions and his skill as a seducer, Jessica Manning and the dark-eyed Cuban.

Smugly Kroger wondered which of them he would enjoy the most, and for a moment he entertained the further question of which sort of plundering gave him the most satisfaction—the pillaging of a cash box or that hidden place of pleasure between a lovely woman's thighs?

Chapter Six

FROM the stairway, Jessica could catch only a glimpse of the profile of the guest whom her father was entertaining in the parlor, but it was enough for her to recognize the man as Brill Kroger. She remembered him from his previous visit and because he was someone new to her father's circle of acquaintances. Also, she thought him quite handsome, in a rather sinister way. He looked, she thought, like an actor, one of those matinee idols whom she saw pictured now and then in the newspapers. When they had met on his earlier visit, he had looked at her with what she had interpreted as a rather frightening intensity, not at all like the attention she received from her father's usual friends and acquaintances; but then of course Mr. Kroger was not old like her father. In fact, he was quite a youngish man.

Jessica wondered briefly what it was they were discussing, then continued on her way up the stairs. She was due at the Red Cross center at two, and it was now one o'clock. She would have to hurry. She hoped that her mother had laid out her uniform, for that would save her some time; and since her father was home, surely he would not mind driving her to the hotel in his buggy on the way back to the bank.

Entering her room, Jessica began unbuttoning her dress. She should not have stayed so long at Jenny's, she thought, but they had been having such a good time talking about the ball and discussing the young men they had met. . . .

As she stepped out of the dress, she thought of the young men—the stocky but nice Lieutenant Gage; the naval ensign; and the dashing but impossible Lieutenant Neil Dancer. For some reason he was the one her thoughts kept returning to time after time, and she had finally decided that it was simply because he had annoyed her so and because he had been the cause of her behaving in what she considered, after the fact, such an unladylike fashion.

Angered anew by thoughts of Neil Dancer, she kicked her dress aside and turned so that she was facing the tall pier glass in its mahogany frame. Staring at herself intently, Jessica wondered how she had looked to him that night. Had he found her pretty? As pretty as Dulcy?

At the memory of Dulcy and her flirtatious behavior, Jessica flushed and spun away from the mirror. What on earth was she doing lollygagging here, thinking of such unimportant matters, when she should be getting dressed?

Quickly she pulled on the brown skirt, white blouse, and white apron that made up her Red Cross uniform, then tied the large, white square of cloth over her pale curls. She rather admired the effect of the headdress as it accentuated the bone structure of her face, and she was also pleased by the fact that it made her look like a real nurse. Of course, she was, in a way. They all were, all the women and girls at the Red Cross. They had all been studying first aid; and even if they had as yet had no real chance to practice what they had learned, they might at any time.

Giving a final tug to the headdress, Jessica left her room and hurried down the stairs to catch her father before he left.

As she started toward the parlor, the curtains parted, and her father and Brill Kroger came toward her.

"Ah, there you are, Jessica!" Wyngate Manning said, smiling. "I was just coming to look for you. You remember Mr. Kroger?"

Jessica gave a demure nod. "Yes, of course. Mr. Kroger, it's nice to see you again."

Kroger bowed, then looked her full in the eyes and smiled. "Miss Manning, how delighted I am to see you. Yes, indeed! You are looking lovely, as always."

Jessica felt herself flush under his gaze, for his look struck her as unduly bold. She darted a glance at her father, to see if he had noticed, but it seemed not.

Wyngate Manning said, "Jessica, Mr. Kroger has just asked me if you would be interested in helping with the Cuban Fund Drive Ball. I told him that I couldn't be certain, but that I thought you might. What do you say? Would you like to participate? You would be in charge of the committee to send out the invitations, and you would be expected to serve as hostess at the ball itself."

"I would be highly honored if you would accept, Miss Manning," Kroger said smoothly. "I feel that it is important for the details to be in the hands of persons of good character, who are both conscientious and dependable, for a ball of this nature requires considerable effort to arrange."

Jessica momentarily forgot her haste to get to the hotel, caught off-balance by the proposal. "But I never even heard of this ball." She looked questioningly at her father. "What is it all about?"

"Oh, my dear young lady, I am indeed sorry," said Kroger, striking his brow in a rather theatrical fashion. "Forgive me. Of course you didn't know. No one really does as yet. We, your father and I, just made the final decision this very day. The ball is a fund-raising affair for the Cuban war effort. You know, of course, that the army still needs supplies, weapons, and uniforms. There is a tremendous expense involved, yes, indeed. Of course, many of your good citizens, your own father included, have contributed funds, but no one has, so far, mounted a large scale, concentrated effort. The ball is to be just such an effort, in conjunction with another, held on the same evening, in Ybor City, for the participation of the Cuban population. Together, the two affairs should net a tidy sum to help our brave soldiers and our country."

Something in Kroger's tone caused Jessica to look at him sharply, something theatrical and perhaps insincere, but under her scrutiny, his expression remained serious and intent, and she put it down to her imagination.

She considered his request carefully. Would she be interested? Of course she would! Partly because she would be aiding the war effort and partly because it would be exciting. She could see herself now at the ball. She would have to get a new dress, of course, and shoes. . . .

What *was* she thinking of? She was almost late now for her stint at the Red Cross center.

"I would be delighted to serve, Mr. Kroger," she said hurriedly, "but I really don't have time to discuss it just now. I am due at the Red Cross. Father, could you drive me, on your way back to the bank?"

Before her father could reply, Kroger broke in. "Please, Miss Manning, it would be my pleasure. I am returning to the hotel straightaway. My buggy is just outside." He turned to Wyngate Manning. "If that would be all right with you, sir?"

Wyngate Manning nodded, beaming. "Of course. You two can discuss the details of the benefit ball on the way. An ideal situation." He pulled his watch out of his waistcoat pocket and frowned at it. "And I must be going, also. I have a two-thirty meeting. You two have a nice talk, and you can tell me all about it at supper, Jessica."

Jessica was pleased to be riding in the buggy with Brill Kroger, and she secretly hoped that some of her friends would see her; or failing that, that the *parents* of some of her friends might see her and report it.

"I am indeed glad that you will be a part of this endeavor, Miss Manning," Kroger was saying, as he drove the buggy away from the Manning residence. "I must confess that you have been much in my thoughts since the day we first met, and I have been hoping to see you again."

Kroger stared at her now with the same, somewhat frightening, intensity that he had regarded her before, and Jessica, made a bit uneasy, did not know what to do other than smile.

"Yes, indeed," he said, shifting the reins to his left hand and taking her hand in his right. "I have been seeking a means to see more of you, Miss Manning. And if you do not object, the benefit ball may just be a means of doing so."

He smiled broadly, and his teeth, Jessica noted, were unusually white and large, making his smile very compelling. In a confusion of feelings, she pulled her hand quickly from his grasp. She did not know how it was in New York, where Kroger had informed them, he came from; but in Tampa, Florida, a man did not take a woman's hand like that unless they were very well acquainted, and she had only met Kroger twice. Still, she *was* flattered, and she did find him fascinating. She did not know whether she wanted him to continue in this fashion or whether she should demand that he stop. Not for the first time, Jessica wished that she were older, more sophisticated; then she would know what to do, how to act.

Kroger made no move to recapture her hand, but his smile remained intact. "*Do* you object, my dear? May I see more of you? May we become friends?"

"No, I—yes—" Jessica stammered, hating herself for her confusion. "I mean, of course I should like to be friends, Mr. Kroger, and if I am to consult with you on the details of the benefit, we shall doubtless see more of each other."

She felt herself blushing. She did sound like a prig! But Kroger leaned back in the buggy seat, apparently content with her answer, and for the rest of the trip, they talked only of the ball and what her duties would be.

When they arrived at the hotel, Jessica's wish was granted—Dulcy and Mary were just on their way up the drive as Kroger's buggy swept up. They watched with curiosity and envy as Kroger handed Jessica down; and Jessica made the most of it, curtsying to Kroger in a most ladylike manner and thanking him profusely for the ride and for appointing her to head the hospitality committee for the planned benefit ball. With some satisfaction she saw the look of outright envy on Dulcy's face.

"Who was that?" Dulcy whispered, as Kroger strode on into the hotel and Jessica paused.

"Well, who is he?" Dulcy repeated. She looked at Jessica with a new respect. "I didn't think you had it in you. He's gorgeous, and a real man, too, not a boy. What have you been up to, pray tell?"

Jessica tried to control the color she felt rising to her cheeks. "Why, that's Mr. Kroger," she said casually. "Mr. Brill Kroger, he's a businessman from New York. He's arranging a benefit ball at the hotel to raise money for the war. I'm going to be working with him. In fact, he asked me to be the chairwoman of the hospitality committee."

Mary gasped. "How exciting! Can I help? I mean, if you are having a committee, you'll have to have others to work with you on it, won't you?"

Jessica, delighted with this opportunity to dispense favors, said rather grandly, "Why, of course, Mary. And you, too, Dulcy, if you wish."

Dulcy shrugged. "Why not? I wouldn't mind working with Mr. Brill Kroger." She smiled secretively. "I might even enjoy it, who knows?"

Mary shrieked, "Oh, you awful thing!"

Now why on earth had she behaved that way? Jessica asked herself as she sat at a large table forming a long strip of white linen into a compact roll. Those two, Dulcy and Mary, always seemed to bring out the worst in her. She often found herself acting just like they did—petty and silly. And now they would be pestering her to work on the committee. Well, she had no one to blame but herself, since she had agreed to their request; out of pure vanity, she realized.

Angrily she rolled the linen and fastened the final roll by tucking the free end under the side. She was just reaching for another strip when a young soldier, hatless and disheveled, rushed into the room.

"Ma'am!" he shouted at Mrs. Bussy, the woman in charge. "Ma'am, there's been a terrible accident! A bunch of our boys has been all shot up, and we don't have enough doctors. They want you ladies to come help. I brought the wagon to fetch you."

Mrs. Bussy, a stout, friendly-faced woman, put her hand over her heart and gazed around the room at the young women volunteers.

Jessica knew that the same thought was in all their minds—would they be able to cope, now that a real emergency had arisen?

Then Mrs. Bussy became brisk. "Rest for a moment, young man," she said kindly. "Sit down and tell us what happened. Jessica, bring the lad some punch, he looks parched."

As Jessica hurried to the huge bowl of cold punch always kept ready for the soldiers, Mrs. Bussy guided the soldier to a chair. "Now, tell us what happened."

" 'Twas one of the cannons," the young soldier gasped out. To Jessica, he seemed little more than a boy.

"The cannon, it blew up on us whilst we were doing some maneuvers. All the men in the gun emplacement was hit." He shuddered and accepted the glass of punch Jessica offered him.

"It was horrible! They're all a-bleeding and a-moaning, and some are crying for their mothers." He looked up at Mrs. Bussy and Jessica with pleading eyes. "Is that how it's going to be when we get to where the real fighting is, all blood and screaming?"

"I expect so, lad." Mrs. Bussy, her face pale, smoothed his tousled hair away from his brow. "Shhh, now. War is a terrible thing, but sometimes it has to be. You drink that down, you'll feel a mite better."

Jessica, staring numbly at the youth, felt suddenly ill. The young soldier's words had affected her powerfully, and for the first time she realized that there would be more to this war than balls, parades, and rolling bandages. But then Mrs. Bussy brusquely ordered them to collect boxes of bandages and get into the wagon, and in the flurry of activity, Jessica had no time for further thought.

The worst thing was the blood. As the wounded were brought in, some on stretchers, some carried by their comrades, Jessica found herself amazed and sickened by the amount of blood, both on the men and seeping from them.

Some of the soldiers were only slightly wounded, but others had gaping wounds, and several had lost arms or legs. One boy had lost the lower part of his leg, and his screams and moans were horrible and heartbreaking to hear.

Trying to maintain her composure, Jessica strove to remember what she had been taught. Where should she start? What should she do first? These questions were soon resolved by the army doctors in charge; they began issuing orders, examining each soldier as he came into the medical tent and directing the orderlies and volunteers as to what measures to take, while the doctors themselves concentrated their attention on the more seriously wounded.

Jessica was directed to clean and bandage the leg of a soldier who had taken a piece of metal in the upper thigh. She was grateful that it was not one of the really bad wounds, although it was bleeding heavily. The wounded man was supported into the tent by an officer, who gently placed him on one of the mats on the floor of the tent. The soldier moaned as the officer lowered him to the mat, and Jessica winced at the animal sounds of his agony.

Confronted with an actual wound, she hesitated for a long moment, seized by panic. It was so different from the sessions during which the girls and women had practiced on one another. Here, she was faced with real pain, real blood; it could be a life or death situation.

Swallowing, she looked directly at the officer for the first time and was startled to meet the gaze of Neil Dancer, his face pale and grim. He looked quite different from the self-assured, smiling young man she had met at the ball.

"He's bleeding badly." Neil's voice was soft. "You'd best get him cleaned up and bandaged, Miss Manning."

Jessica, somehow drawing strength from his calm voice and manner, switched her attention back to the wounded man. He was very young —as most of them seemed to be—with a still undefined face that, contorted as it was with pain, looked vulnerable. He was trying to be brave, she could see, but he looked close to tears, and panic made his eyes wild.

"There now," she said maternally, smoothing the matted hair back from his brow. "You'll be all right. The wound's not that bad. We'll have you fixed up in a jiffy."

And then, miraculously, what she had been taught came back to her. She said to Neil, "Please rip away his trouser leg."

Neil did her bidding, and when the boy's leg was exposed, Jessica was not shocked by the sight, as she had feared she might be, but began to look upon the wound as a problem to be handled.

Quickly, with deft hands, she washed the area around the wound with hot water and soap, then applied a thick pad and pressed upon the wound to stop the bleeding. Fortunately the metal shard had missed the artery, and a few minutes of pressure stopped the bleeding. When it was clear that the bleeding had stopped, Jessica bound the pad in place with one of the linen bandages she had recently helped to roll.

As Jessica worked over the lad, she was moved by a profound sorrow and shame. She, all of the young women, had been viewing the war as something of a lark, a happy change, something exciting in their ordinarily mundane lives. The men, as well, looked upon the war as an adventure, an opportunity to exhibit their manliness, a chance to do something daring. Now she could see that they had all been foolish —childish, really. War meant blood and killing, pain and suffering. All this damage had come about through a mere accident on the training ground. How much worse would be an actual battle?

She sighed as she tied the bandage in place. The young soldier looked somewhat better now. Some color was seepng back into his face, although his teeth were still clenched against the pain.

Straightening, she turned to Neil. "Lieutenant, can you help me move him to one of the cots?"

Neil nodded without speaking, and together he and Jessica lifted the soldier, who groaned all the while, and helped him to one of the army cots set up along two sides of the hospital tent. They covered him with a blanket and left him resting as comfortably as could be expected under the circumstances.

As they moved away, Jessica smiled wanly at Neil. "Thank you for your help," she said sincerely. "I . . . it was my first experience at treating a real wound, and I was afraid that I would. . . ."

Returning her smile, he lightly touched her hand. "You did just fine, Miss Manning, and from now on it will be much easier."

One of the doctors, seeing that Jessica was finished with the soldier, directed her to another, and after that the afternoon became one long blur of wounded young men, blood, and bandages.

When, after an interminable time, all the wounded had been tended to, Jessica made her way outside the hospital tent. She had never been so weary in her life. She inhaled the tepid evening air gratefully; the stench of human blood was not pleasant. She felt drained, heavy with fatigue, and very depressed. Always empathetic, she had felt, with each of the wounded, their pain and despair. How, she wondered, did professional nurses endure it? How could they bear all the suffering and horror, day after day?

Sighing, she wiped her damp forehead with her hand. As she did, she sensed someone behind her and turned to see Neil Dancer, his face showing lines of fatigue as deep as her own.

"Well, it's over for now," he said. "We've done all we can for the moment."

"I reckon so." Jessica shook her head. "It was awful, absolutely awful. I can't get it out of my mind that this was just a training maneuver. I keep thinking of what it must be like on a real battlefield. How can the men stand it?"

Neil looked down at his feet and then raised his gaze to meet hers. "I don't know," he said slowly. "I guess most of us don't know, because most of us haven't been in battle before. I know I certainly haven't."

He looked at her intently. "You look all done in, Miss Manning. May I see you home? I'd feel better if I knew you got there safely."

She nodded, too exhausted to have feelings one way or another. Why had she been so upset with him at the ball? At the moment she could not remember, not really.

"I don't have a carriage," Neil said, "but you can ride behind me on my horse. That is, if you don't mind traveling that way?"

"Anything sounds better than walking." As tired as she was, Jessica would never be able to walk all the way home, she knew.

Mounted behind Neil, her arms locked around his waist, she felt, through a haze of fatigue, a confusion of feelings. Clasping him like this seemed too intimate, yet was so comforting. The warmth of his body came through his tunic, and the scratchy wool smelled of tobacco and bay rum.

She rested her head against his back as the horse proceeded at a gentle pace, the clip-clop of hooves a restful sound. Neil did not attempt to make conversation, for which she was grateful. Somehow their being so close together was a form of communication, and from it she took comfort and ease.

And then they were at her house, and he was helping her down from the horse, and her mother was opening the door as they went up the porch steps, her face pale and worried.

"I heard about the accident," she said, taking her daughter's hands in both of hers. "They said all the Red Cross women were called in to help. Are you all right, dear? Was it awful for you?"

Jessica nodded. "Yes, to both questions. Mother, this is Lieutenant Neil Dancer. He was kind enough to see me home."

Anne Manning looked up at Neil. "Thank you, sir. I do appreciate your seeing Jessica home."

"It was my pleasure, ma'am. And may I say that your daughter did splendidly today. Mrs. Manning"—he hesitated—"would it be all right if I called on your daughter tomorrow? I mean, if it is all right with you, Miss Manning?"

Anne Manning said, "Jessica?"

There was no trace of the insufferable self-assurance and boldness that he had shown the night of the ball, and Jessica answered, "I should like that, Lieutenant. Perhaps we could invite him to supper, Mother?"

"We would be pleased to have you," Anne Manning said. "Six o'clock, Lieutenant, if that time is convenient for you?"

"Six o'clock will be fine, Mrs. Manning. I will be looking forward to it." He bowed. "I will take my leave now." Yet he lingered for a moment, his gaze on Jessica.

"Come along, dear," Anne Manning said, leading Jessica inside. "You look pale as milk. You'd better lie down, or you will be as bad off as one of your patients."

Jessica allowed her mother to lead her across the porch, but at the last moment she turned her head. "Thank you again, Lieutenant Dancer, for your help and for the ride. You were very kind."

As her mother helped her upstairs toward her room, Jessica barely heard what she was saying, for her thoughts were on the way she had felt on the horseback ride home, on the warmth and comfort she had experienced being so close to Neil. It was a feeling she had never known before, but one that she was anxious to experience again.

All at once, it seemed a long time until the next evening.

Chapter Seven

Maria Mendes studied the piece of paper in her hand and frowned. Somehow she did not feel right about this whole idea, although she could find nothing wrong with it on the surface.

She turned to look at Ramon, standing on the other side of the Mendes parlor, talking to Brill Kroger. Was it really the idea of the Ybor City Benefit Ball that bothered her, or was she being influenced by her distrust of the man who had originated the idea? The others seemed to embrace it readily enough; in fact, they were highly enthused, including Ramon, for the ball seemed to them an ideal way in which to raise a great deal of money quickly, money that could be used to supply arms and supplies and to obtain a ship so that Cuban patriots could go to Cuba to fight for the fredeom of their mother country.

She sighed. Still, the idea *had* come from Kroger, and she instinctively did not trust the man or anything that he might be involved in. Yet, how could she say no in the face of Ramon's enthusiasm? She looked at her brother again. His eyes were bright and his gestures alive with his emotions as he talked animatedly with Kroger. Well, Maria decided, she would say yes. She would work with the other women on the arrangements for the ball, but she vowed to keep her eyes open, always fixed upon Mr. Brill Kroger. She wondered what Ramon would say if she were to tell him about Kroger approaching her outside the hotel the night of the dance.

Oh, Kroger was treating her in a different manner now, all politeness, the proper gentleman, but when Ramon was not looking, he smiled at her knowingly, raising his eyebrows, as if they shared a secret, as if there were something between them. Something between them—Maria's flesh crawled at the very thought. Still, he is a dangerous man, she thought, and I must always remember not to treat him lightly; I must be very careful how I handle him.

When Ramon turned toward her again, she smiled at him, carefully avoiding looking at Kroger. "Have you decided?" Ramon asked.

"Of course, I will be happy to help, my brother," she said in

Spanish. "If you are certain this is what you want. Can you trust this man?"

Ramon's face tightened with annoyance. "You must speak in English, Maria. Mr. Kroger does not understand our language."

Maria pretended embarrassment and looked at Kroger blandly. "Oh, I am sorry, Señor Kroger. It was habit only. I did not mean to exclude you from the conversation. I said that I would be pleased to lend my efforts to the committee to arrange the ball."

Kroger's eyes were wary, but he bowed slightly, as if he believed what she said. "I am delighted, Miss Mendes, yes, indeed. You will be a welcome addition to the group. I shall look forward to working closely with you."

His expression was subtly mocking, and Maria knew that he was aware of how she felt about him, and somehow found it amusing. She viewed that fact as profoundly disturbing.

"Well," Kroger went on, "it has been a pleasure, but I must leave now, as I have an appointment at Banker Manning's house to discuss the details of the Tampa Bay Hotel ball with his daughter and her friends." He made a small bow. "Until we meet again, Miss Mendes."

When he was gone, Ramon said, "What did you mean, Maria, when you asked if I trusted Señor Kroger? Do you know something about him that I do not?"

Maria shook her head. "No. It's just that I *feel* something about him. Something wrong. Something evil. I do not think that he is a man to be trusted."

Ramon gave vent to an exasperated sigh. "Ah, you thought, you felt! The famous woman's intuition at work! If you have nothing more than that, my sister. . . ." He shrugged. "This is a great opportunity he offers us. We have had our own fund-raising parties and socials, our benefits, but this will be a grand ball, attracting all the wealthy Cubans and their fat checkbooks and purses. This time, we can take in enough money to really do something, enough to get my compadres and me to Cuba so that we can truly aid in her liberation."

Maria glanced away. "Yes, perhaps enough money so that you can go to your death, Ramon," she said bitterly. "And as for my womanly intuition, as you call it, it has proved reliable in the past, and you would do well to heed it. But enough. I have told you what I feel, and you disagree with me. I am prepared to do what I can to help you with Kroger's benefit ball, but I will never trust him completely."

Ramon shrugged again and threw up his hands. "You women!" he said in a tone of frustration. "Who can ever understand you?"

Obviously not most men, Maria thought to herself, turning away. I hope, she thought further, that this time my feelings are wrong, for they tell me that this ball and Brill Kroger are going to bring trouble down on us.

The brisk sound of a knock interrupted her thoughts, and she turned to see a wide-shouldered male figure standing just outside the closed screen door. In the growing dusk, she was unable to make out the face of the caller.

Ramon had gone into the back of the house, so Maria went to the door, still not recognizing the caller. She wondered vaguely who he was and what he wanted. "Yes?" she said in Spanish. "What is it you wish?"

"Does Ramon Mendes still live here?" a deep voice asked. "I am Carlos Chavez. I would like to see him, if possible."

Carlos Chavez? The name rang a faint bell in Maria's mind. "Carlos Chavez?" she said slowly, staring at the face, which she could now see, behind the screen.

"Maria?" Carlos Chavez said questioningly. "Maria, is that you? Do you remember me at all? My heavens, you were so small, just a little girl, all dark eyes and hair. Can it be you, all grown up and so beautiful?"

Suddenly Maria remembered—Carlos Chavez, of course! "You lived next door," she said in astonishment. "You were Ramon's friend. But it has been so long since you moved away."

"In 1886, yes," he said, laughing. "All of twelve years ago."

"Well, come in, come in! Ramon is here, and I know he will be happy to see you."

She unlatched the screen door and pushed it open. "Mama will be happy to see you, too," she said as Carlos entered. "I remember that she always used to say that she thought you were a good influence on Ramon."

Now that she could see him clearly, Maria saw that the twelve years' absence had changed Carlos. She remembered him as a rather stocky, serious boy, with an as yet unformed face, the only distinguishing feature his large, highly intelligent dark eyes. He had seemed taller to her when she was a child, but she could see that he was only of average height, with a powerful build that bespoke great strength, carefully controlled.

His face had matured, naturally, and he had become a handsome man, with strong, bold features set off by the same dark eyes with the same probing glance.

When they were inside, he took her hands, leaning away from her and staring at her in admiration. "Little Maria! I cannot believe it! You were a charming child, but who would have thought that you would have turned out like this? You are a real beauty."

Maria, aware of the warmth of his hands holding hers, felt herself flush with embarrassment. He had always been like this, she remembered, outspoken and direct, but his words caused her a rather pleasant discomfort.

"If you weren't so grown up, I would kiss you," he said, his eyes sparkling. "I am so glad to see you again, Maria. So glad to *be* here again."

Still flustered, she led him to the sofa. "Sit down, Carlos. I'll get Mama and Ramon.

"Mama! Mama! Guess who is here," she called as she hastened into the kitchen.

Ynez Mendes turned away from the kettle of shrimp and rice she had been stirring, her broad-cheeked face shining with the heat from the stove.

"We have company? How nice." She put down the wooden spoon and brushed a tendril of straight, black hair back from her forehead. "You can invite them to stay for the evening meal. It is almost ready. Who is our visitor?"

Maria said, "You will never guess, Mama."

Her mother laughed, her generous bosom dancing with the effort. "If I would never guess, what is the use of trying, my daughter? Come now, it is not like you to play games with Mama, Maria."

Maria's smile widened. "I know, Mama, but this is *such* a surprise. It is Carlos, Carlos Chavez, who used to live next door!"

Her mother's expression showed her delight. "Little Carlos, Ramon's good friend, he's come back. Now that is a surprise, and a pleasant one. Where is he?"

"In the parlor."

Mrs. Mendes patted her hair. "You must take him some refreshment, something to drink, a little wine perhaps, while I change my apron and freshen myself. Little Carlos. I cannot believe it!"

"Not so little anymore, Mama. He is a grown man, and very handsome."

Her mother looked at her quickly, shrewdly, and for the second time that day, Maria found herself blushing. "Well, it is true, Mama. I am only making an observation."

"I wonder what brings him back to Ybor City?" her mother asked, untying her apron.

"We'll soon find out. Now, I must find Ramon. He hasn't gone out, has he?"

Mrs. Mendes shook her head. "No, no, he is in his room, working on some details for the ball. Oh, he will be *so* pleased to see Carlos!"

And indeed he was. Over wine in the parlor, the Mendes family and Carlos reaffirmed their affection for each other and exchanged information.

"You have come back to participate in the struggle to free our country?" Ramon asked, as they were finishing their wine.

Carlos put down his glass. "Yes, my friend. Estrada Palma, of the New York junta, has asked all young and unmarried Cubans disposed to go to Cuba and aid the rebel cause to come to Tampa. Also, I have never forgotten Ybor City and my friends here. When I was a boy, I had nothing to say concerning where I lived. My father's wishes, of necessity, had to be mine. But now that he and my mother are gone, God rest their souls, there is nothing to bind me to New York." He paused, sighing. "I never felt at home there, never at ease."

"Your parents," said Ynez Mendes, her eyes soft with sympathy. "What did they die of?"

Carlos looked down at his strong hands clasped together in his lap. "The smallpox," he said soberly. "It took my youngest sister, Dolores, also."

Mrs. Mendes shook her head. "A terrible disease. We lost many people here, several years ago, from the same thing."

Maria, wishing to change the subject to something more cheerful, asked, "And what have you been doing, Carlos? What have you been working at since you became a man?"

Carlos looked at her, and a slight smile touched his lips. "You may think it an odd profession, perhaps, Maria, but in New York I had a large band, an orchestra that played at one of the big hotels."

Ynez Mendes clapped her hands. "Ah, yes! I remember. You were always picking at that guitar of yours, making up songs."

Carlos's smile widened. "You remember well, Mrs. Mendes, and I must confess that I do it still."

"Did you bring your musicians along with you?" Maria asked.

He shook his head. "Not all of them, only those who are Cubans and who wished to come, or could come, to Tampa. I will find other musicians here, I'm sure. Ybor City has grown so, that I am sure we can all find work. We are very good," he added with mock pride.

They all laughed, and Maria could not remember a time recently when she had so thoroughly enjoyed herself.

"It is good you have come back, Carlos," Ramon said seriously, changing the festive mood. "We need all the men we can get. My club, the Liberty for Cuba Club, and the other Cuban clubs are arranging for a ship to take us to Cuba to fight. We have amassed considerable guns and other supplies, and after the Cuban ball, there will be enough money to buy more. Will you go with us?"

Carlos hesitated, looking for a moment at Maria, and then he nodded. "I am with you, brother, and with all Cubans who want to fight for the freedom of their mother country."

Maria listened with growing concern. She too wanted Cuba to be free, but she did not want to pay for that freedom with the lives of her brothers and friends.

"By the way," Carlos said, looking around, "where are Mr. Mendes and Eduardo?"

Ramon said, "Papa is working late at the hotel tonight, and Eduardo and little Paulo are visiting a friend who is ill. They shall be back soon."

Carlos's expression was a question. "Little Paulo?"

Ynez Mendes began to laugh. "He does not know."

"You've been away for twelve years, Carlos," Maria said, smiling. "Papa and Mama have added to the family since then. Paulo is nine years old, a fine boy. You will like him."

Carlos shook his head. "I cannot believe it!"

"We are not so old," Mrs. Mendes said slyly. "We may have more yet."

Maria said eagerly, "You must stay and see them."

"I shall be pleased and happy to."

Eduardo and Paulo arrived a short time later, followed soon after by Felix Mendes. There was much backslapping and much noisy conversation, and then the women went into the kitchen to finish preparing the evening meal. Maria went reluctantly, hating to leave the camaraderie of the parlor, and Carlos's company.

As she and her mother worked in the small kitchen, she strained to hear what the men were talking about in the other room, but could not. She fervently hoped that her father and her brothers would not get into one of their arguments in front of Carlos, but she had the feeling that it was a vain hope.

And indeed it was, for soon the voices in the parlor began to rise, and Maria looked at her mother, to see how she was reacting to the argument. Her mother returned her look with a shrug of resignation.

In the parlor, Carlos watched as Felix Mendes strode back and forth in front of his two sons, his gray hair ruffled and his face agitated and red.

"You know that I do not wish you to go!" he exclaimed. "I love Cuba, too, she is my mother country, but we are Americans now. We are safe here, and I have no wish for your blood to be spilled on foreign soil. And it is not enough that you both are determined to risk your own lives, now you have to try and persuade Carlos to join you in your foolishness! Fah! I wash my hands of you."

"They did not persuade me, Mr. Mendes. I made the decision on my own. This is what I came back to Tampa for."

Mendes shook his head. "It is a great risk you take, a stupid risk. You have so much to live for, all of you, and you are willing to throw it all away!"

"It is our country, Papa," Eduardo said pleadingly. "We want to see it free!"

"*This* is our country!" Mendes thundered, striking his open palm with a fist. "You know you will never go back to Cuba to live."

"That's not important," Ramon said. "What's important is that Cuba be free. The Spanish have dominated us long enough, Papa. We are going, and there is nothing you can do about it."

His father, his face closed and white with anger, bowed stiffly to Carlos. "I apologize, Carlos, for the ill manners of my sons. Here you are, the first day back among us, and they start up with this again."

Carlos shook his head. "There is no need for apologies, sir. These are painful times, and men's passions run strong."

"How are things going between the Cubans and the Spaniards here in Ybor City?" Carlos asked Ramon.

"Both good and bad," Ramon responded. "Some of the Spaniards have made it clear that they are staying out of it, that they will not interfere with our efforts. They are sympathetic, but the others—"

"Others are very militant," Eduardo interjected. "There have been some harassments, some bad incidents. You remember Pedro Hernandez? We went to school with him. He was discharged last week for trying to recruit his fellow workers into our movement. The factory he worked in is owned by Spaniards and employs only Spaniards. Months ago, almost all the Cubans left. They refused to work under the *Peninsulares*. Yes, there is bad feeling, but so far no violence."

The kitchen door swung open, and Ynez Mendes came bustling in with a tray of steaming food. "Dinner is ready. Let us eat now. Enough of this political talk!"

In the parlor of the Manning home, Dulcy Thomas sat posed prettily, well aware that she made a fetching picture in her blue dress with the lace collar.

Also present in the room were Jessica, Mary, Sally McGill, and Anne Manning, but it was for the one gentleman in attendance that Dulcy preened. Brill Kroger was the handsomest thing, and such a refreshing change from all the boys and young officers of her acquaintance. She knew that Kroger was aware of her, and she knew also that he did not dare show undue interest before the others. Secure in her belief in the power of her charms, Dulcy flirted outrageously, catching Kroger's eyes whenever possible and giving him that slow, provocative look that many men had told her was irresistible.

Paying little attention to the subject under discussion—the details of the benefit ball—Dulcy let her thoughts wander. Perhaps Kroger could be inveigled into taking her home after the meeting. Of course, he might have to see the others home as well, but perhaps she could arrange to be the last one delivered; and after that, who knew what might happen. . . .

"Don't you think so, Dulcy? Dulcy?"

Dulcy became aware that Jessica was speaking to her. She did not have the slightest idea what Jessica had said, but she nodded, and smiled brightly. "Yes. Yes, I do."

"Well, that's settled then," Jessica said, making a note on the tablet in her lap. "Sally, you will be responsible for making up the guest list, and Mary and Dulcy will be in charge of mailing out the invitations. Now remember, it will have to be done quickly, as it's only four weeks until the ball. Well, I guess that takes care of everything, for now."

She looked questioningly at Brill Kroger, and Dulcy noticed that Kroger was looking back with more than normal interest. So he liked Jessica, did he? Well, there was no real competition there. Jessica, Dulcy knew, was thoroughly proper; a virgin, she was certain. As soon as Brill Kroger knew them both better, there could be no doubt which one he would prefer.

Men were interested in only one thing; Dulcy's mother was always saying that—bitterly and often. Well, Dulcy thought, that was all right with her, because she had considerable interest in *that* herself. There must be something wrong with women like her mother, who considered lovemaking something that must be endured by married women, something from which they could not possibly receive any pleasure. It was no wonder that many men, like Dulcy's own father—she had seen him once with one of his "women friends"—sought female companionship elsewhere.

Dulcy had been very young when she first found out about the pleasure that could be discovered through that area of the body that her mother referred to as "the private parts." Her mother, as did all mothers of that time, made much of modesty, preaching against such manifestations of sexuality as looking too closely at oneself nude, touching oneself in the forbidden areas, playing with boys, et cetera, et cetera.

Most of the girls of Dulcy's acquaintance accepted these parental dictates and exhibited little curiosity as to why there were such strictures upon this particular area of behavior; but Dulcy, always rebellious, always curious, began to wonder what there was about this part of her body that caused her mother to rage so violently against it. Cautious investigation proved to her that touching certain parts generated very exciting sensations; and whenever she was alone, in bed or in her bath, she experimented, and so wondered more than ever why her mother was so against this pleasure.

When she was eight years old, she and a neighbor boy, ten-year-old Richard Morton, with whom she was not supposed to play, retired to the stable behind his house, where, hidden in one of the horse stalls, they discovered the baffling but fascinating difference between male and female.

However, despite all the experimenting that went on over the next few years, Dulcy retained her virginity until she was fifteen, when a visiting college youth managed to get her alone long enough to show her the real thing—what it was that men and women really did together.

Since then she had missed no opportunity to sample the pleasures that her mother constantly assured her did not exist.

It was then that Dulcy began keeping a diary, a little book she carried with her almost everywhere. In it she detailed all her experiences with men. Rereading it, watching the entries grow, was her secret delight.

Brill Kroger would make a delicious entry in her diary, she was positive!

Although her mother never spoke to her of sex save in the most vague and disguised terms, and *never* spoke to her of such things as how a woman might prevent pregnancy, Dulcy somehow heard of an herb woman, a Spanish woman who lived in Ybor City, and she proved an excellent source of information and medication. The one time that Dulcy's monthly flow did not arrive on schedule, the herb woman provided some evil-smelling concoction that happily corrected the situation within a few days.

Now, as the girls began to collect their things, Dulcy walked slowly toward Brill Kroger and Jessica, where they stood talking by the door.

Dulcy was about to ask Kroger if he would be so kind as to see her home, when Anne Manning came back into the room and Kroger turned to her, a ready smile appearing on his handsome face.

Dulcy turned away, annoyed. Her self-assurance concerning her own attractiveness was hard to daunt, but Jessica's mother always made her feel awkward and young. It was not only that Mrs. Manning was beautiful, it was her poise and sophistication, and her always near-perfect appearance.

"Mrs. Manning," Kroger said, bowing slightly, "thank you again for letting me use your lovely home for our meeting. I hope that I haven't kept these charming young ladies too long or interfered with your dinner."

Anne Manning returned his smile. "Not at all, Mr. Kroger. Actually, I'm glad that I caught you before you left. I would like to invite you and the girls to stay over for supper. We have plenty."

Dulcy turned her face away so that her displeasure would not show. Drat the woman! But then, perhaps, Kroger would not care to stay.

"How very nice, Mrs. Manning. I would love to stay."

Well, there went that hope!

"Thank you, Mrs. Manning," Sally said, "but my folks are having my aunt over for dinner, and I'm supposed to be there."

Mrs. Manning said, "How about you, Mary? And Dulcy?"

Dulcy smiled sweetly at the woman. Perhaps all was not lost yet. She might still get Brill Kroger to see her home, *after* supper. "I would love to stay."

"And so would I," Mary said.

"Fine! That's settled then. There will be one more dining with us. A young man, a friend of Jessica's."

This last was a cause of astonishment to Dulcy. A friend of Jessica's? Now that was interesting. Who could it be?

The question was answered almost at once, as a loud knock sounded on the open front door.

Mrs. Manning hurried to the door, and Dulcy shot a quick look at Jessica, just in time to catch her blushing furiously.

"Good evening, Lieutenant, do come in," Anne Manning said. "You're just in time."

The screen door opened with a creak, and into the room walked Neil Dancer.

Dulcy, the memory of those few, delicious moments in the garden behind the hotel returning to her, felt her own color rising.

His gaze passed over the room's occupants, passing over Dulcy without acknowledgment, and came to rest on Jessica, and his smile was slow and intimate.

Suddenly Dulcy realized what was going on—these two were sweet on each other! A quick fury raced through her. How could he possibly pick Jessica over her, after she had been so generous to him the night of the ball?

Jessica was very quiet during supper, but there was so much conversation among the others that she did not think anyone noticed.

From time to time she glanced at Neil Dancer, and each time she did, she found him looking at her, even though Dulcy Thomas, who was seated next to him, kept trying to monopolize his attention.

Jessica wished very much that her mother had not been quite so gracious on this particular evening. Usually Jessica would have been pleased to have the extra company for dinner, but tonight she had counted on having just Neil, and he and she were having difficulty even speaking to one another. If it was not Dulcy talking, it was Brill Kroger. And from the way Dulcy was carrying on, you would think that Neil had come to see *her!*

But finally the meal was finished, and they all retired to the parlor for after-dinner coffee. The instant they left the table, Neil hurried to Jessica's side, taking her elbow with his hand as they walked down the hall.

This seemed to annoy Dulcy, who shot Jessica a venomous glance;

then, with a toss of her head, she turned her attention to Kroger. But with Neil holding her elbow, his hard male body so close to her, Jessica found breathing difficult, and she could spare no thoughts for Dulcy and her odd behavior.

"I thought I'd never get a chance to talk to you alone," Neil murmured, so softly that only Jessica could hear. "I didn't know there would be so many other people here this evening."

Jessica smiled up into his face and whispered back, "I didn't, either, Lieutenant. It was sort of a last-minute thing, you see. We had a meeting of the Cuban Benefit Committee here this afternoon, and Mother invited them to stay afterward."

The others were filing into the parlor now, and Neil leaned closer. "Look, I have tomorrow free. Could I see you, Miss Manning? We're only going to be in Tampa a very short time, and, well, it would mean a lot to me."

Jessica's mind was suddenly plunged into a confusion of pleasure and dismay—pleasure at his invitation, dismay over his statement that he would be leaving. So soon? Why, he had only been here a few days! And he would be going to Cuba; to war, where what had happened to the soldiers at the gun emplacement could easily happen to him. All at once, the thought of him hurt, possibly dying, was almost more than she could bear.

Neil was going on, in that low, intimate voice. "If you like sailing, I thought I could rent a sailboat, and we could have a picnic. The water is beautiful here, and I'd love to sail at least once while I'm here. I'm a good sailor, your parents wouldn't have to worry on that score."

Jessica saw Brill Kroger coming toward them. Oh, why wouldn't people leave them alone for even a moment? "I'd love to, Lieutenant," she said quickly, "but you had better ask Father first."

Neil's slow smile of pleasure made her heart skip a beat. "I'll ask him right away." He touched her hand briefly, a touch that sent a quiver through her, and then he moved away.

Kroger advanced on Jessica, with Dulcy following a few steps behind.

"I just wish to thank you, Miss Manning, for having us to dinner," he said, giving her an ingratiating smile. "It was most kind. Yes, indeed."

Jessica, who not long ago had found Kroger attractive, now compared him to Neil Dancer, and found Kroger wanting. He's not sincere, she thought, suddenly disliking him as she gazed up into his handsome face; everything he says sounds like lines from a bad play.

She said, "I'm pleased that you enjoyed the meal, Mr. Kroger, but it's Mother you ought to thank."

Dulcy was standing next to Kroger, far too close actually. Jessica wished fervently that they would both leave her alone with her thoughts of Neil and tomorrow. She was hopeful that her father would say yes, for he seldom refused her anything, and she could see that he liked the young lieutenant.

Kroger, taking a step away from Dulcy, focused his too-bright gaze on Jessica's face and leaned over slightly to accommodate himself to her lower height. "I shall thank your mother as well, yes, indeed. It was a lovely evening. As a single man, who travels a great deal on business, it's not often that I am able to share such warm family evenings."

His white-toothed smile was wide, but Jessica felt that it was false. He turns it on, she thought, like a lantern of some sort, to attract and disarm people; and then she was a bit dismayed by her own unexpected waspishness. She was getting as cranky as an old woman lately. So many things seemed to annoy her—Dulcy; Mary; Brill Kroger; all the things she usually did; the people she usually saw. Why, now, did they all seem so shallow, so artificial? Still, she must not be rude to Kroger, he was her father's acquaintance, and she would try to be courteous.

"Well, we were pleased that you could stay," she said as politely as she could, considering that she was dying of curiosity about whether or not her father would give his consent for the boat trip. She glanced across the room, but neither her father nor Neil was in sight. They must have stepped out onto the porch for a smoke.

"Yes, Jessica, dear, your mother is *so* sweet. She's always doing something nice for people."

Dulcy's simper told Jessica that she was speaking strictly for the benefit of Brill Kroger, and Jessica gave an inward sigh. Dulcy's interest in Kroger was transparent, and Jessica could not help but think that they were two of a kind.

"I wonder, Miss Manning, whether I might ask a favor of you?" Kroger was saying. "Tomorrow I will be seeing various merchants in town, attempting to persuade them to contribute goods and services for the ball. Since your family is so well-known, I was wondering if I might induce you to accompany me and lend the weight of your charming presence to my appeals to their better natures? I'm sure that the presence of a pretty young woman would do much to soften their hearts and loosen their purse strings, and it is all for a good cause. Yes, indeed."

Oh, my, Jessica thought. What should she say? Where *were* Neil and her father? Aware that Kroger was waiting for her answer, she said quickly, "I'm sorry, Mr. Kroger, but I have a previous engagement. I will be gone all day tomorrow. It does sound like an excellent idea." She added sweetly, "I'm certain that, with your talents, you will be able to convince the shopkeepers, particularly when, as you say, it is in such a good cause."

Kroger's smile remained in place, but Jessica could sense that he was far from pleased. He nodded slightly, as if to acknowledge her reply.

Dulcy touched Kroger's arm and gazed up at him with wide eyes. "Mr. Kroger, I think that your idea sounds positively inspired, and since Jessica can't go with you, I would be happy to take her place. The merchants in town know my family, too, and I just happen to be free tomorrow."

Kroger hesitated for a moment, glancing at Jessica again, and then he nodded. "Of course, Miss Thomas. What a splendid idea. I shall pick you up at ten in the morning, if that is satisfactory?"

"Ten is just fine, Mr. Kroger," Dulcy said, giving Jessica a triumphant look from under batted eyelashes, as if she had somehow wrested a great honor away from her.

At that moment Neil came into the room from the porch, with Wyngate Manning behind him. Jessica scanned Neil's face, but his expression told her nothing. What had her father said?

As Neil joined them, however, his face broke into a wide smile. "Your father gave his permission," he said, seemingly not even aware of Kroger or Dulcy, his gaze for Jessica only. "He even said that his friend Royce Layton will lend us a sailboat. We'll leave early in the morning, if you don't mind, so that we will have the whole day to ourselves."

Then, abruptly becoming aware of the others, he looked a bit embarrassed, as if realizing that he might better have spoken to her in private.

Jessica, too, wished that he had waited—the expression that crossed Kroger's face was not pleasant in the least, nothing like his usual suave look. Jessica felt a sudden chill and thought that in that fleeting rearrangement of features, she saw, for a brief moment, the real man beneath the polished exterior. And Dulcy's face, too, showed consternation and jealousy, as she glanced first at Neil and then at Jessica.

Then Dulcy took hold of Kroger's arm possessively. "Well, you two have a nice sail," she said with false sincerity. "Mr. Kroger and I will take care of business." She squeezed his arm. "Won't we, Brill?"

Kroger gave a start and immediately flashed his polished smile. "Yes, we will, Miss Thomas. Yes, indeed!"

As Brill Kroger made his polite goodbyes to the Mannings, he was the very soul of urbanity, but underneath his bland exterior, he was seething with a slow anger.

He did not take well to rejection, and the refusal of Jessica Manning to accompany him on the following day, did more than rankle, it made him furious, particularly as he had sized her up early on as being more than a little interested in, and responsive to, his advances.

And now, to have her spurn his company in favor of that callow young lieutenant! Kroger took it as a personal insult.

The willingness . . . nay, the more than willingness, the eagerness of Jessica's friend, Dulcy Thomas, to take her place was flattering, but that in no way dissipated his anger at Jessica.

It was implicit in Kroger's character that, when done an injustice—or what he considered an injustice—he could not rest easy until he had taken a measure of revenge.

Occasionally, getting this revenge was not easy. Sometimes it took a great deal in the way of time and effort, but he always considered such an expenditure worthwhile, for until he had righted the score, it gnawed at him continually, preventing him from focusing his mind upon more remunerative matters.

And so now, leaving the Manning residence, even though he could feel the silken warmth of Dulcy's thigh pressed close to his side in the buggy, his thoughts clung stubbornly to Jessica Manning and her young lieutenant.

How could he obtain satisfaction for her slight? What could he do to balance the scales? He knew what he would like to do to Jessica, but he dared not risk that sort of thing at the present time. The night of the ball, he would take her, take her savagely, the most perfect revenge and satisfaction, and would be long gone by morning when her irate father came looking for him. But what could he do *now*?

Then the answer came to him. They were going sailing, the lieutenant had said. If Kroger could find out which boat they were using—

and that should not be too difficult—he could perhaps arrange a small accident, nothing dire, just something to embarrass and discomfit them.

Feeling much better, he turned his attention to the woman by his side. She was a pretty creature, blond and slender, much like Jessica and his beloved mother, but sturdier than Jessica, with more rounded curves and a bolder face and manner. She seemed willing enough to be in his company, and it would seem, by her actions, much more than willing. She would do very well, very well, indeed, to pass the time with, and perhaps might be useful in other ways as well.

Much cheered by his decision as to what to do to ease the blow to his wounded pride, Kroger smiled down at Dulcy and put his free hand on her thigh. Her quick, answering smile as she moved even closer told him he had not been wrong in his estimation of her.

When Dulcy, Mary, and Brill Kroger had finally gone, Jessica breathed a sigh of relief. Now, perhaps, she and Neil could be alone together for a bit and have a chance to talk. All at once, she was very curious about him, wanting to know about his past, wanting to know everything about him that she could learn.

Anne Manning, as if reading her daughter's thoughts, smiled understandingly. "Why don't you two go out onto the porch, dear, and sit in the glider? A breeze has come up, and it's much cooler out there."

Jessica kissed her mother's cheek. "That's a lovely idea, Mother. Would you like that, Neil?"

"I would like that very much."

"I just believe I'll sit here by the window and read the evening paper," said Wyngate Manning, seating himself in the huge, overstuffed armchair by the window that looked out onto the porch, thereby making clear his intention of chaperoning his daughter.

Jessica hid a smile behind her hand. At least he won't be watching us directly, she thought. The glider was not in the direct line of sight from the window, but her father would be able to overhear their conversation, if he was so inclined.

The air was still warm, but the breeze, moving gently across the porch and the glider where they sat, made it quite pleasant.

Neil said, "Do you mind if I smoke, Miss Manning? I occasionally smoke a cigar."

"Not at all, go right ahead, sir."

He reached into his inside pocket and took out a cigar. As he

d to put it into his mouth, he swore. "Damn! Oh, I'm sorry, Miss
nning. Half the time they get broken in my pocket. I should have a
gar case, but I never have got around to getting one."

He tossed the broken cigar over the porch railing and sat back, silent.

Jessica, feeling strangely excited and almost giddy, sat primly in the
glider, knees together, hands on her lap, very conscious of Neil, only a
few inches away.

"I'm glad they're all finally gone," he said, sighing.

"Oh, so am I! I don't really care that much for Dulcy, or Mary, either. I can't think why I ever asked them to be on the benefit ball
committee."

Neil laughed at this, but he also seemed a bit embarrassed, and Jessica had to wonder if he found her remark too revealing.

"How about Brill Kroger?" he asked. "It struck me that he seemed
to take a great deal of interest in you."

Jessica felt her cheeks grow hot. "Oh, he fancies himself a ladies'
man, I think," she said in what she hoped was a sophisticated manner.

Once again, Neil laughed. "I suspect that you are right there."

Jessica, emboldened by the effect her repartee seemed to have on
him, grew reckless. "Well, if he is, I imagine Dulcy should be able to
keep him occupied."

As she stared into his face for his reaction, Neil glanced away,
shifted uneasily, and again seemed embarrassed, which Jessica found
puzzling.

He said quickly, "That's probably true. But let's not talk about them,
Jessica, let's talk about you. Tell me about yourself."

Jessica, somewhat taken aback, looked down at her hands in her
lap. "Oh, there's nothing much to tell about me. I'd much rather hear
about you, Neil."

He shook his head ruefully. "Well, there's not a great deal to tell
about me, either."

An awkward pause ensued, which Jessica finally broke. "Do you
know how long you will be in Tampa? I mean, have you any idea
when you will be shipping out?"

His face became grave, and Jessica's heart seemed to skip a beat at
the implications of the look.

"Soon. Just as soon as Colonel Roosevelt can get us some transport.
The rumor is that it won't be more than another day or so."

Jessica turned her head so that she could gaze into his eyes; and as she did so, a feeling of longing mixed with melancholy filled her, bringing the sting of tears to her eyes; and in that instant, as if mesmerized, they leaned toward each other until their lips met gently and warmly, and Jessica found her heart beating wildly, as a sweet weakness pervaded her body. I feel like I'm melting, she thought in wonder, caught up in this strange new sweetness that dizzied her with its implications.

As their lips clung, Neil uttered a soft groan and reached out for her, pulling her upper body close to his and bringing greater pressure upon her mouth.

Dear God, Jessica thought; what is happening to me? And yet she knew that she did not want it to stop.

The rattling of the newspaper from inside the house through the open window jerked Jessica back to reality, and she hastily pulled back, breathing erratically. She knew that her face was flushed, and a quick glance at Neil revealed that he was suffering from the same symptoms.

"Jessica, dear Jessica," he whispered hoarsely, "I've wanted to do that for so long, from the first moment I saw you."

Jessica, still shaken, said nothing. She simply did not know how to reply. She felt him take her hand in his as his eyes searched her face for a reaction.

She smiled tremulously, and Neil seemed to understand her feelings, for his own face wore a smile of such love and sweetness that her whole being longed for his mouth on hers again. What was happening to her? She ought to have been shocked and angry. It was not proper to let a young man kiss you unless you were engaged to him, and here she was kissing a man she had only known for a few days and had only been with a few hours at the very most.

The newspaper rattled again, louder this time, and Neil moved a few inches away from her, although he still retained her hand. "I'd best take my leave now. But I'll be back early tomorrow morning, around eight, if that's not too early for you."

"That will be fine," she whispered, unwilling to break the moment by speaking too loudly. "I'll pack us a picnic lunch."

"Until tomorrow then, dear Jessica."

Quickly he leaned forward and again pressed his lips to hers for the briefest moment; and then he was gone, and Jessica was left with the memory of his mouth warm on hers, a memory that haunted her sleep throughout the night.

Chapter Eight

THE morning dawned clear-skied and hot, and by ten o'clock the humidity was overpowering.

Jessica, wearing a neatly pressed white middy blouse, long, navy-blue skirt, and a straw "boater," already felt wilted as she stood on the dock, looking at the *Sea Flower*, a trim, twenty-foot sloop.

"Well, what do you think of her?" asked Neil, looking at the boat as proudly as if she were his own.

"She's beautiful," Jessica said sincerely.

Her attention was more on Neil than on the boat, however. She kept stealing quick little glances at his face, trying to see if he was as good-looking as she remembered, thinking that their relationship was so new that it was difficult to really be as familiar with his features as she would like.

"Here, let me put that picnic basket into the boat."

Picking up the large straw hamper, which Jessica had packed herself, Neil stepped lightly onto the *Sea Flower*. Then, after stowing the basket in the small cabin, he turned back to help Jessica on board.

The firm grip of his hands on her waist caused her to remember the previous night. She found her body warming with a heat that had nothing to do with the humid day, and she yearned to feel again the touch of his lips on hers. She wondered if he was also thinking of last night, and in the back of her mind the thing that she had been thinking of all night long surfaced—would Neil kiss her again? And if he did, what would happen then?

Both excited and frightened by her speculations, Jessica turned her face seaward, welcoming the coolness of the wind on her fevered skin.

"There's a good wind," she commented. "Where are we going to sail?"

Neil smiled as he checked the lines. He was wearing casual clothing —a white shirt, with the sleeves rolled up to the elbows, and brown twill trousers. Even without the glamour of his uniform, he was devastatingly handsome.

"I thought we might just go where the wind takes us for a while

and then sail to one of the islands off the coast for lunch. How d
that sound to you?"

"That sounds fine. I packed a lot of food. I hope you have a go
appetite, Lieutenant."

Neil laughed heartily. "You don't need to worry about that. Arm
food isn't all that great, and most of us are always hungry, it seems

As Neil talked, he was busy with the sail. Since the wind was good
the sail filled as soon as it was hoisted, bellying out with a soft, pop-
ping sound; and the sloop began to move, at first slowly and then with
gathering speed.

Jessica felt her hat to be certain that it was securely pinned to her
piled-up hair, then relaxed against the seat, enjoying the breeze and
the motion.

"She's a good boat," Neil said enthusiastically, smiling up at the sail
and then over at Jessica. "It feels great to be out on the water again."

And then his face changed and grew melancholy. Jessica leaned toward him. "What is it, Neil? What's wrong?"

Neil tried to smile, but it was a feeble effort. "Nothing, just a random thought. Nothing for you to worry your pretty head about."

Jessica frowned. She hated that phrase, which her father had often
used to her mother and to her. It was as if men thought that women
were merely pretty ornaments, not capable of logical reasoning.

"You looked so sad," she said insistently. "*Something* must have
made you feel that way. Sometimes it's better if you talk about it."

He shrugged. "I don't want to bother you with it. Why cause both
of us to feel unhappy?"

This time the smile came through, and she returned it, but she was
still determined that he should talk to her like an adult, a person.

"But I would really like to know."

Neil moved the tiller, changing the course of the boat somewhat,
and the boom shifted as the sloop began to heel.

Jessica edged closer to him so that she could hear him better over
the sound of the water and the creak of the rigging. "Tell me, Neil,"
she said softly.

He looked at her for a moment, then touched her fingers with his
free hand. "It's nothing, really. Nothing momentous, anyway. It's just
that when I said it was good to be on the water again, it made me
think of our orders."

He paused. "It's not common knowledge yet, but Colonel Roosevelt

...ave finally been given our orders. More than likely, ... tomorrow."

...nd leave for Cuba?" Jessica whispered the words, but ...hem.

...rse, we're leaving for Cuba." Taking her hand, he said ...know, it's what I've been wanting, what we've all been ...out now. . . . Well, things have changed."

...iderstood what he meant. She felt like weeping. She could ...he thought of him leaving. It was not fair! She could not ...id yet she must.

...pression must have revealed what she was thinking, for he ...r hand in his and squeezed it gently. "Hey, no tears now! If ...to be our last day together, for a while, let's make the most of

...ssica smiled wanly. "Our last day together, and it's really our first ...together, as well. That's not very much, is it?"

...etting go of her hand, he reached for her, putting his arm around ...er waist and pulling her toward him so that they now sat quite close.

Jessica, assaulted by a torrent of feelings, did not protest and did not even worry that someone might see them.

"Jessica," he said close to her ear, "let's not think about it now. Let's have a wonderful day. That will leave us with something nice to remember when I'm . . . when I'm far away."

Jessica had to again fight her tears, but she finally won. Neil was right. Since they had so little time together, it would be foolish to waste it crying and worrying about what might happen. She managed a smile, taking comfort from his nearness. Who would have ever thought, the night of the party, that she would feel this way about a man, any man? It was both glorious and frightening. She had never felt this way about anyone, and was sure that she never would again. So this was what it was like, being in love. What a strange emotion, such a mixture of pain and joy, so intense that she felt she might not be able to stand it.

The breeze stayed fine, and they sailed on, talking, holding hands, looking deep into one another's eyes, as lovers have done since time began.

Then Jessica settled back and took out her embroidery and began working on it.

"What are you working on?" Neil asked curiously.

She smiled and held it up so that he could see better.

"It's a cigar case," she said. "I'm making it for you. I noticed you smoke a cigar occasionally, and sometimes they get broken in your pocket. I'm making it in red and gold, and it will have your initials here." She indicated an unfinished oval in the center of the piece.

"That's sweet of you, Jessica." He added with mock gallantry, "I shall carry it always next to my heart."

A little past twelve o'clock, Neil headed the boat toward a small island that promised a nice beach for a picnic. The island boasted a rickety dock, and Neil secured the *Sea Flower* to it, then helped Jessica ashore with the picnic basket. The island was indeed small, with shining white sand, covered with shrubs and palmettos, but it seemed deserted. There were no buildings on the island that Jessica could see.

Jessica spread a blanket under one of the palmettos, to take advantage of the sparse shade, and began laying out the contents of the basket. She had been lavish with the food, and there was enough for at least four people, and they both ate hungrily. Soon, satiated and drowsy, they lay side by side upon the blanket, not quite touching, yet both very much aware of the other.

"I'm stuffed," Neil said, chuckling. "I don't believe I've ever eaten that much at one time in my life."

"Me, too." Jessica patted her stomach. "If I always ate like that, I'd soon be fat as a cow."

Neil raised up, facing her, resting on one elbow, and gazed down into her face. "Even if you were, I'd still love you," he said teasingly. And then, as if suddenly aware of what he had said, he paused, staring deep into her eyes.

Jessica drew a deep breath. "Do you know what you just said?" she said shyly.

"Yes, dear Jessica," he said firmly. "I just said that I love you. My sweet, sweet Jessica!"

His words were a cry, a plea, and then his lips were upon hers, hot and demanding, and she was on her back, holding him to her with a strength that she had not known that she possessed; and her body was trembling, trembling with a feeling that she had only felt a premonition of before. It seemed to her that she could never be close enough to him. She wanted to possess and be possessed by him, to be inside of him, to have him inside her. . . .

Panic suddenly struck. What was she doing? What were *they* doing?

Pushing him away, she leaped to her feet, staring down at him in confusion.

He looked up at her, and reading the expression on her face, Neil groaned. "Oh, God, Jessica! I'm sorry. I didn't mean . . . I didn't want. . . ."

He groaned again and turned over on his stomach, hiding his face in his arms.

Jessica, standing above him, her body a maelstrom of raging feelings, longed to be again beside him, but all that she had been taught, all that she had been told, held her motionless.

Finally turning away, she stared blindly out toward the sea. Nothing in her life prior to this moment had prepared her to cope with the situation or with the feelings she was now experiencing.

The sun was beginning to move lower in the sky, and slowly Jessica became aware of this. We should go, she thought; it's time we got started back. And then she noticed the sloop. There was something wrong with it.

Frowning, she stared for a moment uncomprehendingly, then she gave a cry of alarm and swung about. "Neil, the boat! Neil, please look at the boat. Something's wrong."

Neil turned over and sat up, staring toward the sloop. Then, giving a shout, he sprang to his feet and raced toward it, with Jessica right behind him.

The little sloop, which had been riding high and buoyantly in the water, was, even as they watched, settling slowly into the sea. The tide was beginning to change, and the soft lap of small incoming waves moved the boat sluggishly as it sank lower and lower, until finally, with a loud gurgle, the stern vanished from sight, leaving only the bow above the water.

Jessica, hands to her cheeks, watched in horror and disbelief. "I don't understand, Neil. What happened? What are we going to do now?"

Neil looked at her, his shoulders sagging. "I don't know, Jessica. The boat was in perfect condition when we left Tampa. I checked it over carefully, and we weren't shipping any water on the way over here."

"My parents!" Jessica exclaimed. "They'll be worried sick when we don't come back on time. Maybe we can signal to another boat?"

They both looked out to sea, but there were no other boats in sight.

"We could light a signal fire," Neil suggested. "Surely someone would see it on the mainland."

"I doubt it. I understand that fishermen often camp on these islands overnight. No one would think anything of a fire."

"Well . . ." Neil's face brightened with a grin. "At least we won't starve, since you packed enough food for several days. Are you sure you didn't plan on this happening?"

Jessica flushed. "Oh, Neil! Don't make sport. This is serious. My parents—"

"I know." He sighed. "Your parents and my commanding officers. We'll both have some explaining to do, won't we?"

For a long moment they stared wordlessly at one another, then Neil took her by the hand and led her back to the palmetto.

"We have the blanket," he said comfortingly, "and I have matches. We'll have a nice fire and a nice supper, and in the morning your parents will certainly send someone out to search for us. They have a good idea of where we are."

As they approached the palmetto, Neil stopped and turned her to face him. "Jessica, about what happened before. . . . I didn't mean to frighten you or harm you in any way. It's only that I love you, and want you so much, the thought that I'm leaving so soon, that I won't be able to be with you . . ."

"Shhh." Gently Jessica placed a finger against his lips. "You didn't frighten me or hurt me. Not really. You made me feel like . . . I don't know how to describe how you made me feel, Neil, and *that* frightened me."

"And now?"

She shook her head. "No, not now."

Standing on tiptoe, she pressed her mouth softly to his, knowing that she spoke the truth, that with the sinking of their boat, a sort of inevitability had overtaken her. It was as if it was fated to be, an omen of sorts, somehow sanctioning what she knew was about to happen. All that was important was now, this moment, and all at once she had found the necessary courage.

At first Neil was hesitant, but as her lips pressed more firmly on his and her arms went around him, she could feel his restraint weakening and then vanishing entirely as he pulled her hard against him, so that she could feel the muscular length of his body pressed against her.

A mounting feeling of delight and desire blazed through her, as if a fire was within her burning outward from inside, consuming her in a passion that was a wanting, a demand, a glory.

Taking his mouth momentarily from hers, Neil led her to a more sheltered spot, behind low-growing shrubs; and there on the white sand, still warm from the sun, they sank down together, clinging, touching, making soft sounds of love and desire.

Jessica felt his awkward fingers fumbling with the buttons of her dress, and she hastened to help him, eager to feel his touch upon her body.

As his fingers explored her breasts beneath the fabric of her blouse, Jessica felt that she might swoon from pleasure and excitement. She could feel her heart pounding and feel his as well, beating even harder.

Neil was breathing in short gasps, and the very fact of his intense excitement thrilled her even more; knowing that he wanted her so powerfully was a marvelous feeling.

And then he was lifting her skirts, touching her legs, pulling down her undergarments. For a moment she almost panicked again, but her own need, so long denied and now so suddenly and gloriously awakened, overcame her fears.

Moaning softly, she felt him touch her secret place. He was so gentle, despite his own driving need.

After a moment he pulled away, and she cried out, feeling bereft, reaching for him and then raising her head to see him opening his trousers. She fell back, afraid to see what she had only heard about; but then he was back, and something that was hot and soft and hard at the same time was probing her thighs, and his lips were once more insistent on hers; and then his hardness was broaching her secret place, and she instinctively opened her legs to welcome it, in trembling desire and trepidation.

It hurt, for just a moment, a sharp, burning pain, and Jessica cried out faintly.

Neil, above her, froze, whispering words of endearment, his body trembling mightily; but then the brief pain was gone, forgotten in a spreading warmth of intense pleasure, and she pulled him close again and felt him begin to move, slowly, as if fearful of hurting her again. Within her, she felt that part of him probing and moving, sending waves of ecstasy through her, and she knew that she now had her wish. They were as close as two people could possibly be, his body inside her, and the very thought of it, and his thrusting movements, gave her such exquisite sensations that she rose to him, moving with him, against him, as the hot pleasure grew and grew until she thought that she must scream with the tension, which mounted until a great spasm seized her. Her body clenched as she heard Neil cry out as his own body went rigid, then shuddered mightily.

As they lay spent, Neil whispered her name over and over, covering her face with light kisses. Her body felt tender and exhausted, but she was lazily content. It was beautiful, she thought; the most beautiful thing she had ever known.

"Jessie." Neil was looking at her, his face dim in the growing dusk. "I love you very much, and this was the most wonderful thing that ever happened to me."

"I love you, too," she said simply.

"But I may have done you a great harm. What if you should get—? I mean, what if you should have a baby? We don't have time to get married before I leave for Cuba."

Jessica's heart gave a leap. He wanted to marry her!

And then the rest of what he said penetrated her haze of happiness. She was not completely uninformed; she had heard the girls and women talk. What if she *should* have a baby? It would disgrace her family, break her father's heart, and she would become a pariah. But she had just had her monthly, and somewhere she had heard that a woman could not get pregnant just after her period. Also, the strange inevitability that she had experienced with the sinking of the sloop was still with her. Whatever would happen, would happen; it could not be changed now. Neil would be leaving, going to war, and his mind must not be troubled about her; he must think only of surviving to return to her.

"It will be all right," she told him. "I know it will." And she stopped his further words with her lips.

Deep in the pine woods, Brill Kroger lay on the carriage blanket, which he had spread out under the trees. His hand idly stroked the soft breast of Dulcy Thomas, who sprawled naked beside him, but his thoughts were elsewhere.

Although he had just taken the girl, he felt a vague dissatisfaction. She was a pretty little thing, and Lord knows she was willing enough; yet Kroger could not get his thoughts off Jessica Manning.

He still nursed the smoldering anger her rejection had engendered in him, although it was somewhat mitigated by his contemplation of her posssible circumstances at this very moment.

He wondered where she and that snotty young lieutenant were when the soluble plug, which he had inserted into the hole he had bored into the hull of their boat, dissolved. If they were at sea, they should have at least experienced a great deal of discomfort. He supposed that the lieutenant, since he evidently knew how to sail, would find some means of plugging the hole and limping back to shore.

If it happened while they were ashore someplace, well, they just might be marooned overnight, a possibility that pleased him mightily, for if they *were* marooned, on one of the small islands at the mouth of the bay, for instance, Jessica's reputation was certain to be sullied by the fact that she had been alone with the lieutenant in a secluded place for some period of time, perhaps even overnight. Kroger knew well how women were, how they talked, how eager they were to spread gossip that would harm one of their own.

Kroger stretched, lifting his arms above his head, and thought of taking Dulcy again, then decided against it. He was too tired.

Truthfully, the very fact of her willingness to be seduced lessened her attractiveness to him.

Although Kroger was not much given to introspection, and thus knew little about his own motivations, he did realize that he preferred women who were hard to seduce, women whom he had to woo. Somehow the pursuit made the final surrender that much more stimulating. Jessica Manning, now, at first had seemed interested in him; still, she was a "good" girl, and he would have had to work hard to seduce her. But now, for some reason, probably because of that fancy young army officer, she appeared to have lost interest. Strangely enough, this made her even more desirable in Kroger's eyes, for now he would have to work even harder, be even more charming and devious to attain his desire.

He was already working, planning, toward that end. The night of the ball, yes, the night of the ball. All he needed was a foolproof scheme to get her alone.

And then there was the Cuban wench, the one with the long, heavy hair and big, flashing eyes. She too had spurned his advances, and she too stimulated his passions. If it was not for the fact of the benefit balls, he was sure he could find a way to take her at once. But he dared not do anything to jeopardize his scheme, anything that might threaten to alienate the Cuban community prematurely. Still, there might be a way. A few days before the ball, for instance, he could . . .

Dulcy turned on her side and spoke his name. "Brill," she said softly, seductively, moving closer to him. Taking his hand, she placed it on the warm fullness of her breast again. "Brill, that was lovely. Let's do it again." She slid her hand down the length of his body, to his loins.

Despite his early decision, Kroger felt his member begin to stir under her ministrations, and in a few moments he was astride her once more. His thoughts, however, were still on Jessica Manning and Maria Mendes, his passion fueled by thoughts of their soft limbs and tender breasts.

"That's it, Carlos, just up the street there."

Ramon pointed proudly to the small, brown house, neatly painted and maintained, crouching behind the low, white picket fence. He said, "The headquarters of the Liberty For Cuba Club, donated to us by Manuel Rodriguez, the butcher. His old mother lived here before she died. He is a good patriot, and generous to our cause."

Carlos clapped his friend on the shoulder. "It is a fine building, Ramon, and you are fortunate to have such a place of your own, to use as you wish. Do you have many members?"

Ramon nodded. "A great many. You will meet some of them here today. We take turns, shifts, you might say, doing the work that needs to be done. Printing handbills, collecting and packing guns and supplies. There is much to be done, Carlos. They are all good men. You will like them, I know. Some you may remember from your boyhood here, but many have come here since then."

They were at the gate now. Suddenly Ramon lifted his head, his nostrils flaring. "I smell fire. Something burning. Wood?"

Carlos shook his head, frowning. "Not something burning, my friend, something *burned*, and it seems to be coming from your headquarters there."

They could hear the sounds of movement inside and the murmur of voices, subdued and somehow frightening. The door to the small house stood partly open, and Ramon, running at full speed, burst through it without ceremony, with Carlos close behind him. Both men came to a stunned halt in the small parlor, as the shocking sight inside was revealed to them.

There were several other young men already in the room, their faces and clothes blackened with soot and smoke, their eyes glazed with shock. Their arms were filled with boxes and papers. They were apparently trying to salvage what they could from the fire that had obviously destroyed much of the inside of the building.

"José! What happened here?" Ramon said to one tall, narrow-shouldered young man, who was carrying a metal box. His clothes were singed, his face and hands black with soot.

"Ramon!" José came toward them. "It was awful. The parlor went up like a torch. We were fortunate to be able to save the building and some of the papers. If the fire had reached the back room, where the guns and ammunition are stored. . . ."

He began to tremble, and Carlos, placing large, gentle hands on his shoulders, steadied him. "Take it easy, my friend. Here, put down that box. Rest for a minute. Tell us what happened."

José sighed and set the heavy box on the charred floor.

"Tell us what happened, José," Ramon said in a strained voice. "How did the fire start?"

José swallowed, as if his throat pained him. "It was the *Peninsulares*. They came to the door, and when we opened it, they tossed in a firebomb, then ran. We had no time to chase them, we were too busy fighting the fire."

Ramon's face darkened, and his hands clenched into fists at his sides. "The bastards!" he said in Spanish. "Did you get a look at them? Did you recognize any of them?"

José nodded. "One, at least. I saw him clearly, for it was he who threw the bomb. Ricardo Aragones."

"Ricardo Aragones?" Ramon's lips drew back from his teeth as he spat the name. "The son of a dog!"

Carlos frowned. "I seem to recall the name. Isn't his father the owner of a cigar factory?"

Ramon said tightly, "Yes. El Oro de España. A large company. He has always been against the Cubans, and his son"—he spat the name again—"is a troublemaker, a mad dog. He is a coward, as well, and must prove that he is not, by causing violence. I will find him and tear off the arm he used to throw the bomb, and I will choke him with it." He turned again to José. "Just how much damage was done?"

José's face, already a mirror of pain and dismay, now crumpled, as tears stood in his eyes. "Many papers were destroyed, but the worst of it was young Sergio. He—"

Ramon stared at him with slowly dawning horror. "Sergio? He was hurt?"

José stared down at the blackened floor. "He is beyond hurt, Ramon. He is dead."

Ramon let his breath go with a soft cry. "*Madre de Dios!* They shall pay. I, Ramon Mendes, swear it. They shall pay dearly for this!"

His body began to shake uncontrollably, and Carlos put an arm around his shoulders. "Steady, old friend. You must keep your head. It is a terrible thing that has happened, I agree, but you must think things through before you decide what to do."

"They *must* be punished for this outrage," Ramon said bitterly. "Sergio must be avenged!"

"It shall be done," said Carlos. "He will be avenged, but it must be carefully planned. Nothing will be served if you go running off in a state of rage and confusion. We will have our vengeance, and I will help you. Now we can best help right here, saving what we can."

Ramon pulled his handkerchief from his pocket and mopped his face and eyes. He straightened up and turned to José. "We will get the headquarters here in order, and then we will meet, all of us, and decide what to do about Ricardo Aragones and his dog of a father. We have worked too hard to have all our efforts destroyed by cowards! If we must fight here before we fight in Cuba, then so be it."

Chapter Nine

MARIA placed her hands upon her lower back and leaned backward, trying to ease the ache that had been growing there all afternoon.

It had been a hectic day. Ever since the announcement, the previous day, that the troops were embarking for Cuba on the morrow, outright insanity had reigned. She was extremely glad that her shift was finally over, and that she could now go home. Such confusion and tension were more than a person should have to endure.

As she removed her uniform and put on her own clothing, Maria wondered how this departure of the troops would affect the fund-raising balls. Of course, even though the troops would soon be in Cuba, they would still need the monies being raised; but she did wonder if the immediacy of the appeal would not be dulled by the troops leaving for Cuba.

Dressed now, she exited through the kitchen area door and started down the outside steps. Her mind was on other matters, and so she did not see Brill Kroger until he had touched her arm.

Oh, no! she thought in dismay. Not today. I am simply too weary to cope with another advance from this man.

Kroger raised his hat and smiled broadly. "Ah, Miss Mendes. How fortunate, yes, indeed. I just happened to be passing. May I have the honor of seeing you home?"

Maria hesitated briefly. The situation was not quite the same as it had been the other time. Kroger was now known to her, and to her family, and she remembered her decision not to antagonize the man. Still, she had no desire for his company and certainly did not want him to think that she was encouraging him in any way.

She returned his smile, politely, but shook her head slightly. "Thank you for your kindness, Mr. Kroger, but it is not necessary. I am very tired tonight and would be poor company for anyone."

"Ah, but I insist," he said, his smile widening even more. She could not help but think that his teeth, so white and even, gave his mouth the look of a hungry predator. "I promise not to bore you with conversation, if that is what you wish, but I do need to see your brother, at any rate, and we might as well travel together."

Maria drew a deep breath. His persistence angered her, and she felt that to give in to him would grant him a victory of some sort, and *that* she was unwilling to do.

Again she shook her head. "No, Mr. Kroger," she said firmly. "I don't want to be impolite, but I wish no company. Perhaps another time."

Kroger's smile was still in place, but his expression had changed infinitesimally, and Maria was made acutely aware of his displeasure.

"Why are you so cold toward me?" he asked. "I wish only to share your company. You are a beautiful woman, and a beautiful woman should have a man. Yes, indeed."

As he spoke, Kroger placed his hand upon her arm and gripped it with considerable force. The pressure hurt, yet Maria would not give him the satisfaction of showing it.

"Please remove your hand, Señor Kroger," she said coldly. "I am betrothed, and you must know that Cuban women do not welcome the attentions of other men once they are engaged."

Kroger's smile became a sneer. "Indeed? Strange. I have made some inquiries and have learned that you are unencumbered. Now, why should you lie to me?" He gave her arm a cruel twist.

Maria felt her body begin to tremble with anger. How dare he? What made him think that he had the right to ask personal questions about her? Despite her resolution not to antagonize the man, she was about to voice a scathing retort, when she saw someone approaching them, a young man, a lieutenant in the uniform of the Rough Riders. He was tall and light-haired, with a thin, high-cheekboned face, which now held an expression of disapproval. Maria realized how the situation must appear to him, and she blushed in embarrassment and growing anger.

As the officer came closer, Kroger, seeing him, released her arm and took a step aside, his expression showing a surface amiability that was not reflected in his eyes.

"Are you all right, miss?" the lieutenant asked, looking first at Maria, then at Kroger.

"The young lady is fine," Kroger said easily. "There is nothing to concern yourself about, Lieutenant."

The officer frowned. "I'm afraid that is not for you to say, sir. I was asking the young lady."

Kroger said arrogantly, "I said that she was all right, didn't I? You need not concern yourself. Save your gallantry for the battlefield."

The officer smiled tightly. "I notice that you're not in uniform, sir. Some disability, I must suppose. I would hate to have to strike a disabled man, but if you do not allow the young lady to answer for herself, I may just overcome that reluctance."

Kroger's face flushed dark with anger as the lieutenant turned again to Maria. She was shaking with humiliation. Damn Brill Kroger! How *dare* he put her in this position?

"Do you wish this man to leave, miss?" the lieutenant asked courteously.

She nodded mutely, too embarrassed to speak.

The lieutenant turned to Kroger. "Now then, sir, I suggest that you take your leave before there is any more unpleasantness."

Kroger seemed about to explode with anger, and Maria's heart sank. To have them fight, physically, over her, out here where all could see would be too infuriating for words; but Kroger, apparently realizing that discretion was called for, turned violently on his heel and stalked away, his back stiff as a plank. Maria knew that she had now made a bitter enemy, but at the same time she was glad that she would no longer have to make a pretense of being polite to the man.

The young officer bowed slightly, his wide-brimmed hat in his hand. "Lieutenant Tom Farrel, at your service, ma'am." He waited expectantly, and Maria realized that he was waiting to hear her name.

"Maria Mendes, Lieutenant," she said quickly. "And I do thank you for your help, although you really needn't have troubled yourself. I could have handled the situation."

He shook his head. "Perhaps, perhaps not. You don't know that kind of man, Miss Mendes, like I do. I've seen his kind before, and they are always dangerous. I've seen this one, Brill Kroger, skulking about the hotel, busy as a beaver and sly as a fox. I admit to being puzzled. What connection does he have with you?"

"None, really, sir." Maria sighed. "I'm simply too tired to talk about it now, Lieutenant. I must get home. Perhaps another time."

He grinned suddenly, and the wide smile made him look very young. "I understand, Miss Mendes, but have you considered the possibility that Kroger might waylay you, so to speak, on your way home?

I would be happy to offer you a ride. My horse is tethered on the other side of the hotel."

Maria, feeling depressed and somehow battered by the confrontation with Kroger, experienced a warmth toward this young man with the polite manners and handsome face. "I have my own horse," she said slowly, "but if you'd care to accompany me. . . ."

His face brightened. "Good! I would feel much better if I knew you got home safely."

He went with her to the spot where Miguelito was tied, helped her into the saddle, and then led Miguelito around the hotel to the place where his own horse was tethered.

During the ride to Maria's home, Lieutenant Farrel spoke very little, but the silence between them was not strained, and his presence *was* comforting to Maria.

When they finally reached her gate and Maria had thanked him again for his kindness, he seemed reluctant to leave, twisting his hat in his hands. Maria suddenly knew what he was about to ask, and strangely, she felt pleased that he was going to ask it.

"I don't want to presume," he began. "I mean, I wouldn't want you to think that I'm like Kroger, but, well, I would very much like to see you again, Miss Mendes. Would that be possible?"

Maria thought for a moment before she replied. She was drawn to this fair-haired stranger, and her instincts told her that she had nothing to fear from him. He was a good man, and yet, he was not Latin, and her family and friends would, she realized, disapprove of any relationship between them.

As she hesitated, he got a downcast look, his eyes darkening, and she saw that he was steeling himself for a rejection.

"Yes," she said quickly. "Tomorrow, after work, if you like." And then, remembering, she added, "But won't you be leaving tomorrow? I thought the Rough Riders were leaving for Cuba. The news is all over the hotel."

He looked away, and she could see his body stiffen. "Some of us are leaving, yes." His voice was flat. "General Shafter has decided that there is only room enough on the ships for three-quarters of the men at this time. I was not one of those chosen."

Even as Maria felt relief at this news, she realized how disappointed he must feel.

"It must have been a blow to you," she said sympathetically.

He nodded and looked at her. "Yes, it was. But even those who are going will be in for a disappointment. General Shafter also declared that no horses will be shipped, except those of the senior officers. A fine how-do-you-do, cavalrymen without horses." He shook his head and smiled slightly. "Well, at least being left behind has allowed me to meet you, and now I have tomorrow to look forward to." He tipped his hat. "I bid you good evening, Miss Mendes."

He replaced his hat with a flourish, and his back was straight as he mounted up and rode off.

Maria stood for a few moments, staring after him. How strange men were! How they lusted for battle, for glory, for danger!

Inside the house Maria was met by the sounds of voices raised in a heated discussion. In the parlor she found her brothers and Carlos Chavez deep in conversation. Her heart sank as she realized they were discussing the tactics they should use to get revenge for the attack on their club headquarters and for the death of Sergio.

The men, intent on their conversation, barely noticed Maria's passage through the room. More violence and bloodshed, she thought. Wasn't it enough that Sergio was dead? Did they have to continue, causing more blood to be spilled?

She greeted her mother, busy in the kitchen, and went on to her room, where she closed the door against the sound of the men's voices. She lay down, only to rest for a moment, but she went to sleep at once. When she awakened, the house was quiet, filled only with the savory odors of her mother's cooking.

Splashing cold water on her face and arms, she tidied her hair and started for the kitchen, to see if her mother might need her help.

Opening the kitchen door, she was surprised to see Carlos Chavez seated at the worn wooden table, chatting with her mother. He got to his feet and smiled when he saw her. "Maria! I've been waiting for you."

Maria flushed as she took note of her mother's knowing smile. "How nice of you, Carlos. You and my brothers were so involved when I came in that I didn't think you even saw me."

His smile widened. "Oh, I saw you, Maria. My mother did not raise any blind sons. Stupid, perhaps, but not blind."

Maria had to laugh, her usual energy and good humor restored by her nap; and Carlos did have a way about him, an ability to raise one's spirits. Men like Carlos, and Lieutenant Farrel, were good people, and surely, two such good people were more than enough to balance against the bad ones, like Brill Kroger.

"I wondered," Carlos was saying, "if you would like to take a walk with me, Maria." Seeing Maria's quick glance at her mother, he added quickly, "I have already asked your mother. Isn't that right, Mamacita?"

Ynez Mendes blushed, then laughed heartily. "Yes, yes! Away with both of you now and let me get on with my work. Come back in about an hour, for dinner will be ready by then. You will eat with us, Carlos, no?"

"I shall be delighted. Come on, Maria. Let us make the most of our hour."

Laughing, Maria let him take her hand and lead her from the heat of the kitchen out into the breeze that was bringing some evening coolness to the outdoors.

Arm in arm, Maria and Carlos walked slowly along the street. Carlos's proximity brought with it a feeling of great comfort and security. Maria was aware of the male scent of him, and very much aware of the warmth of the arm holding hers so close to his body.

"Ah, Maria," he said, turning his head to smile at her, "this is so nice. So peaceful. If I had known that you had grown up to be such a great beauty, I would have returned sooner. I promise you, I would have."

Somehow his flattering words, spoken lightly as they were, did not embarrass Maria. In fact, they made her feel cherished. She smiled mischievously. "I too am pleasantly surprised, Carlos. Who would have thought that that awful boy, who once teased me so and who was eternally playing sour chords on that dreadful guitar, would turn into such an acceptable man, who evidently now plays the guitar well?"

Carlos broke into hearty laughter. "Only acceptable? But you're right, of course. You have yet to hear me play the guitar. Well, that can soon be remedied. My group, Los Compañeros, has found a job, starting tomorrow night. You may want to come and hear us. All of your family. I will arrange it with the owner of the restaurant, Las Novedades. Would you like that, Maria?"

Maria nodded her head. "It seems only fair that we should give you a chance to show us what you have now become. But not tomorrow night, Carlos. I have an engagement tomorrow night."

He looked at her with evident disappointment but did not question her, for which she was grateful. Carlos was a gentleman, another nice characteristic to his credit.

They strolled and chatted for the rest of their allotted hour, then turned their steps back toward the Mendes home.

When they were almost there, Carlos paused and drew her under the overhanging branches of a spreading tree that grew in an empty lot.

"What are you doing, Carlos?" she asked, feeling a sudden excitement rising in her, her heart beginning to beat faster.

"I am going to kiss you, Maria," he said calmly, pulling her close to him until she could feel her breasts touching the material of his vest, until she could feel the warmth of his breath on her cheek and seemingly the heat of his body through his clothing.

Maria had plenty of time to protest, or resist, had she been so inclined, but she did not do so. Instead, she let him draw her closer still, until the breath was driven from her body. His mouth descended on hers with a strong yet gentle pressure, and it seemed to Maria that her inner being, her very spirit, was being drawn upward through her lips, to meet his.

The kiss lasted for long moments, and when she finally pulled free, it was not because she wished to, but because she was growing afraid of what might happen if the kiss went on any longer.

"Maria," Carlos whispered against her hair. "Maria, I may be speaking too soon, but I must say what I feel. I love you, Maria. I want you to marry me, to be my wife. I won't demand that you answer right now, this minute. I know it is sudden. But will you consider my proposal? Will you think about it?"

He held her away from him, and she was caught up in a conflict of emotions. She was attracted to this strong, kind, and handsome man, but marriage? Marriage was forever. Did she love him? Her emotions were too muddled to allow her even to guess at her real feelings. But he was not asking for an answer now, only asking that she agree to think about it. How could she *not* think about it?

"Yes, Carlos. You are right. This is very sudden, much too sudden for me to know my own mind. But, yes, I will think about it seriously."

A wide smile crinkled his eyes, and he pressed her to his chest in a convulsive movement. "Ah, Maria, my love! That is all I will ask for the time being."

Almost smothering against his broad chest, Maria felt herself smile. She still felt confused but also very happy.

They walked on toward the house, arm in arm.

❖   ❖   ❖

Jessica awakened from a restless slumber, at first not knowing where she was; then full realization surged back as she became aware of the sharp grains of sand in her clothing. She turned her head quickly to look at Neil, still sleeping beside her on the blanket.

So much, there was so much to remember, all that had happened yesterday and last night; that final intimacy that she and Neil had shared; an intimacy that would, she was sure, change her life forever.

She felt both elated and frightened. The fear was for what her parents would say about her having been alone all night with Neil. For the first time in her life, Jessica would be forced to lie to them, for she certainly could not admit what had happened. But they would realize, they must realize, that being stranded here overnight was not Neil's fault, and certainly not hers, either. It could have happened to anyone.

She turned on her side, the better to study Neil's sleeping face. Asleep, relaxed, his face looked younger, more vulnerable, and very beautiful. Her heart seemed to swell in her breast, and a great tenderness washed over her. If only he did not have to leave! Tears burned her eyes as she thought of the possibility of his being wounded. But I won't think about it, she decided; I'll just think of him being safe, of his coming back.

And then, another thought, an unsettling one, pushed its way into her mind. How would Neil feel about her this morning, after what they had done? Would he still love her, respect her?

Not wishing to continue this line of thought, Jessica got to her feet, brushing the white sand from her dress and legs. As she did so, her gaze went out to the sea, and she noticed a boat drawing near the island. It must be her parents, or at least a search party looking for Neil and her.

Her heart pounding, she leaned down and shook his shoulder. "Neil! Neil, wake up! There's a boat coming this way!"

Neil muttered something unintelligible and rolled over onto his stomach. It took several more shakings and proddings to get him roused. When he finally awakened fully, he looked up at her with a smile that made her heart leap with gladness, banishing any doubts she may have had about his feelings.

"Jessie," he whispered. "Did it really happen, or did I dream it?"

Jessica felt her face flush with heat, and she found that she could not meet his eyes. "There's a boat coming," she whispered, as if there were someone else present who might hear. "I think they may be looking for us."

Neil sobered. "I wish that they would never come, Jessie, so that I could be alone with you forever." He spoke seriously, and his gaze was intent on her face.

"I wish so, too, Neil," she said. And then, to lighten the situation, she added, "Although I believe that we might get very hungry and thirsty after a while. Living on love can probably be rather thin fare."

He grinned and rolled to his feet. "Well, if they're coming for us, we'd best make ourselves as presentable as possible." He took her hands in his. "Before we're rescued, I want you to know that I wish to marry you. As soon as the war in Cuba is over, I'll come back. You *will* marry me, won't you, Jessie?"

Jessica nodded, too overcome to speak, as he pulled her into his arms.

"And about last night. I know your parents are going to be upset. I mean, about our being alone all night and everything. I think we'd better tell them that we are planning on getting married. It might ease their minds somewhat."

Jessica held him to her fiercely, wishing with all her heart that she could hold him this way forever, wishing that there was no war, no boat coming inexorably toward them.

"They'll understand," she said with more certainty than she felt. "They're understanding people."

Neil shook his head. "I'm not so sure, Jessie. Parents, fathers in particular, are funny about things like this. I just hope they won't make things too difficult for you. Dear God! How I wish that I didn't have to leave. When I remember how I prayed that I would be one of those chosen to go. . . ."

Jessica smiled at him, hoping to comfort herself as well as him, and began to straighten her clothes and arrange her hair, using Neil's comb.

When the boat pulled up to the rotting wharf, they both were as neat and presentable as could be expected after a night spent on the beach; and when Jessica's father, pale-faced and rumpled-looking, strode down the wharf toward them, she murmured a short prayer that he would not be too angry and abusive to Neil. Most of all, she prayed that he would not be able to tell that his daughter was no longer quite the same as she had been when she left home.

The scene played out on the beach was both embarrassing and difficult, but not as acrimonious as Jessica had feared.

Wyngate Manning and Royce Layton, the owner of the boat that had been loaned to Neil, both looked at Neil sternly and at Jessica reprovingly, but when explanations were made, they seemed reassured, although both men still looked at Neil now and then with unreadable expressions.

Layton clucked dolefully upon hearing about the sinking of his sailboat. "She was fine, shipshape, when I loaned her to you. I don't understand what could have happened, Lieutenant Dancer. I'll send two of my men out to float her again. Then we can see what the trouble is. You going to be in dutch with your commanding officers, Lieutenant?"

Neil sighed. "I don't know, sir. Probably. We ship out later today, and I should have been in camp early to get my things ready. I hope they will be understanding, when I explain the situation."

"Well, we'd better get back as fast as we can," Wyngate Manning said, as he led his daughter toward their boat, "and get Jessica home and into a hot bath and then into bed." He sighed heavily. "God only knows what she may have caught, sleeping on the beach all night."

Jessica kept her gaze lowered, hoping that he would not notice the color that she knew was staining her cheeks. "I'm quite all right, Father. Really I am. It was quite warm, and we had plenty of food and water."

Her father, disregarding her remark, hustled her onto the boat and wrapped a blanket around her, which, considering that the morning was already warm and humid, Jessica thought quite unnecessary. But recognizing his need to look after her, she made no protest.

The trip back seemed to take forever and was filled by an awkward silence she did not dare break. She dared not even risk a glance at Neil, not with both her father and Layton watching them like a pair of hunting hawks. Although both men had been nice enough, there was a definite climate of suspicion, and under the circumstances, it affected Jessica greatly.

Once back at the house, she barely had time to say goodbye to Neil. He did manage to take her aside long enough to say in a low voice, "I'll write you as often as I can, Jessie. You *will* wait for me?"

She had time to nod and smile encouragingly at him before her father had her by the arm and was hurrying her into the house. On the porch she turned her head for a last look at Neil as he left. Tears came to her eyes as she realized that this might be the last sight she would ever have of him, unless God and the Fates were kind to them.

Chapter Ten

RAMON's head was beginning to hurt. The room was full of cigar smoke, and the sound of voices raised in shrill debate filled every corner of the parlor of the small building that housed the headquarters of the LFC Club. Over all, the sickly, sweet smell of burned wood and cloth hung, a pungent reminder of the firebombing.

Ramon rubbed his eyes tiredly. How long was this going to go on? The same arguments over and over, again and again. They could not seem to reach an agreement. Eduardo had left at least two hours ago, to meet his sweetheart, and Ramon fervently wished that he had left with him.

He looked across the table at Carlos, who was sitting, his chin propped on his hands, his dark eyes mirroring his own weariness.

"We should repay them in kind," shouted Julio Lopez. "Bomb the Spanish Club!"

"But Ricardo Aragones does not represent the Spanish Club. Many of the men who have supported our cause belong to that club," Ramon said. "That would be damning all the Spanish for the acts of a few."

"Then burn the cigar factory!" Julio said, his thin face flushed with the passion of his anger.

"Yes! Burn his father's factory," shouted someone from the back of the room. "His father is no friend of ours. Burn the Aragones out! Justice must be had. We must be revenged for Sergio's death!"

Ramon did not respond. The argument had been raging for so long that he was no longer certain which side he was on, if he ever had been certain. His own fiery spirit wanted, demanded, revenge. The only way to wipe out the shame of Sergio's murder was to avenge him; and yet, part of Ramon, the more sensible part, agreed with Carlos, who had, all evening, argued on the side of restraint. He had repeatedly said, "Our argument is with Ricardo Aragones and the others who helped him do this thing. We must not harm innocent people who had nothing to do with it."

However, feelings ran high, and most of the Cubans present seemed to be on the side of immediate retaliation against any and all Spaniards. Finally, Juan Andrade, the president of the LFC Club, hammered on the table until the voices finally faded away into silence. Andrade announced that it was past midnight and that since the next day was a working day for all of them, they should go home and get some sleep.

"But nothing has been decided," Julio said sullenly.

"That is right," Juan Andrade retorted. "But if you will calm yourselves for a moment, you will realize that nothing is going to be accomplished tonight. We are all too tired and overwrought. We will sleep on it tonight and resume the discussion tomorrow. We will settle it then."

Ramon knew that this was the proper decision. He rose and stretched as the group began to disband into small knots of men, still discussing, still arguing, as they left the building.

Beside Ramon, Carlos shook his head ruefully. "There are some firebrands here. I hope none of them does anything foolish on his own."

Ramon shrugged, his headache growing. "Most of it is talk, Carlos. They will cool down by tomorrow. Come, let's go home. My head hurts."

Carlos picked up his hat from the table. "I don't know, Ramon. Julio worries me. He is too angry to think rationally."

"What can he do by himself?" Ramon, anxious to be out in the night air, led the way out of the building. "A good night's sleep will help clear his head. At least, I hope so. Nothing will ever be resolved if we carry on the way we did here tonight."

Carlos nodded. "It is good to hear you speak so, my friend. All that talk and shouting and nothing settled. And yet, it may have accomplished something after all, for now the men have let their feelings out, and tomorrow night they may be able to approach the subject more calmly."

The night was clear and warm, with a gentle breeze from the sea. The kind of a night that a man should be spending with a beautiful woman, Ramon thought.

He took a deep breath of the fragrant air—the salt smell of the sea; the scent of night-blooming flowers. He felt his headache begin to ease. It had been a long time since he had thought of a woman, really thought of a woman. He had been so busy, so involved—with his job; details of the fund-raising ball; and now with the firebombing of their building. It seemed as if there was no time in his life for a woman nowadays, although at night he often awoke with a burning need for one. But he had to put the subject out of his mind. There were other things more important at this time in his life. Besides, he would soon be going to Cuba to join his compatriots in the fight, and it was always possible that he might not come back.

"Ramon?"

"Yes, Carlos?"

"I wish to tell you something, although it is too soon to know if anything will come of it."

Carlos hesitated, and Ramon sensed that his friend was embarrassed. He gave him his full attention. "What is it, Carlos?"

"It is Maria," said Carlos, after a moment's pause. "I have asked her to marry me. She has not yet accepted. It may never happen, she may not want me, but I wished you to know. I love her very much, Ramon. I think she has always been in the back of my mind, down through the years that I have been away, even though she was only a child when I left. I must ask you. . . . Do you approve?"

Ramon, his headache completely gone now, gave a shout of laughter. "Approve, old friend? I am delighted, and Mama and Papa will be delighted, also. It is perfect!"

"She may not accept me," Carlos said, suddenly gloomy. "But I do have reason to think that she may look upon me favorably."

"She would be a fool not to," Ramon said, clapping Carlos on the shoulder. "She could not possibly find a better man."

"That is kind of you to say, but women don't always see things the way we men do."

"More's the pity," Ramon said, laughing.

Carlos laughed, too, then looked at his friend askance. "I hope you don't really mean that, my friend, for it would be a dreary world indeed if we all thought alike, men and women."

Ramon sank into sleep with the thought of Carlos and Maria in his mind. He began to dream of a wedding, their wedding, when he was rudely roused from sleep.

With a reluctance born of too little sleep, he fought to return to slumber, but the hand shaking his shoulder was relentless. Finally, he realized that it was Carlos's voice that he was hearing shouting his name, and Ramon pulled himself up to awareness.

Through blurry eyes, he saw Carlos's face, white and strained, and behind Carlos, Maria and his mother. Finally he was awake enough to realize that something was terribly wrong.

"What is it?" he demanded, his gaze on his mother and sister. "Has something happened to Papa?"

"It's the Aragones Cigar Factory," Carlos said breathlessly. "It has been set on fire, and the blaze is threatening the houses close to it."

Ramon was completely awake now. He pulled on his trousers and beckoned Carlos closer, whispering, "Julio?"

Carlos shook his head. "We don't know, but I wouldn't be surprised."

"*Madre de Dios!*" Ramon whispered. "Where's Papa and Eduardo?"

"Already on their way."

Standing up, Ramon put on his shirt. "We will be back soon," he said to his mother and Maria, as he followed Carlos from the room, but Maria, he noticed, was right behind them.

When he turned to her and frowned, she said quickly, "I'm coming, too. Perhaps I can help."

Having no time nor inclination to argue, Ramon did not attempt to dissuade her. He hastened after Carlos, out into the night that now glowed red with the reflected glow of the huge blaze dominating the still-dark sky.

Jessica, clad only in a thin voile nightgown, still felt too warm. She had slept only intermittently all night, her mind too busy, too filled with turbulent thoughts to allow her to sleep well.

Sighing, she tossed and turned, attempting to find a more comfortable position, desperately seeking sleep so that she might enjoy forgetfulness for a little time.

After Neil had gone, her mother had hovered over her solicitously, drawing her bath, helping her into a robe, fixing her food; and looking, always looking at her, Jessica, a question in her eyes.

Jessica, sensing the thrust of the unspoken question, felt guilty. What would her mother say, how would she feel, if she knew that her daughter and Neil had made love last night? Jessica could not possibly tell her. It must remain her secret, and yet keeping that secret made her feel shamed, although the act she had committed did not. She found it difficult to meet her mother's eyes and pledged fatigue so that she might be left alone. Her father had returned to the bank for the rest of the day, but his suspicions also, although unvoiced, hung heavy in the air between them.

Neil had suggested that she tell her parents that they wanted to get married, but Jessica had not done so. It seemed to her that such a declaration would only make her parents more suspicious about what had transpired during the time she and Neil had been alone on the island. And Neil, what was he doing now? Would his superior officers be angry about his absence? Would they discipline him? He had said that the Rough Riders would be leaving today. Was he already on his way?

She remained in her room all day and received no news of any kind. She did not even go downstairs for supper, for she felt that she could not face her father and mother, and the questions they might ask. Her mother fetched her supper to her room, and Jessica smiled at her and tried to pretend that everything was as it had always been, that it was only exposure and fatigue caused by the ordeal of the night on the island that forced her to stay in her room.

Wyngate Manning came up to see her after supper, and Jessica felt that his manner, usually so cheerful, was disapproving and distant, although she could not be certain that her own guilt was not coloring her interpretation of his attitude.

He stayed only for a few moments, but he brought some confusing news. "Royce Layton managed to get his boat afloat," he said, his expression serious. "He learned the strangest thing. A hole had been bored in the hull near the stern and plugged with dissolvable material. Since the boat was quite all right the day before, Layton was out in it himself, it had to have been done the night before you went out in it. He's having the harbor master look into the matter."

Jessica could only shrug, remarking that it was indeed strange. Privately she hoped that her father did not think that Neil had done it himself so that they would be stranded on the island. It was just one more thing to worry her mind and disturb her sleep.

Would she ever see Neil again? Would he come back to her, as he had promised, or would he be killed in the hills of Cuba? Or, worse yet, perhaps he would forget her. Perhaps he did not really love her at all. Jessica knew that men often promised women things, made promises they did not mean. . . . No! Neil had meant what he said. She was certain of it. He had been sincere. Surely she would have known if he was not.

The bed felt sticky and hot. Maybe she should open another window. It had to be nearly morning, the sky was growing light already. In fact, it must be near sunrise, for a red glow was beginning to show through the window.

But that could not be! She went quickly to the window, pushing aside the curtain. As she did, she let out a gasp of shock. It was not the sunrise that tinted the sky with red, but a raging fire, flames leaping against the skyline.

Downstairs, the telephone began to ring insistently. She went tense, hanging onto the windowsill until her fingers began to hurt. Theirs was one of the few telephones as yet in Tampa, and she always experienced a sense of dread when it rang. She heard the door to her parents' room open, and then the ringing stopped.

She turned back to the window. The fire seemed to be in the area of Ybor City, and it appeared to be spreading rapidly. She heard the sound of footsteps on the stairs and moved toward her door, mind numb with the horror of fire. A fire always represented a great danger. The last time there had been one, whole blocks of houses had burned before it could be brought under control.

The door opened before she reached it, showing her mother, pale of face and disheveled in her dressing gown, carrying Jessica's medical kit.

"That was the Red Cross calling," Anne Manning said breathlessly. "There's a terrible fire in Ybor City, and people have been hurt. They need you there, Jessica. Be careful, please."

The heat from the fire was intense, and Ramon wet his handkerchief in the bucket of water he was carrying and tied it over his face in an attempt to filter out the hot smoke that was burning his lungs.

The fire had quickly spread from the factory to the surrounding buildings, some of them private dwellings, and the night rang with cries for help and the moanings of the displaced and the injured, rising above the roar and the crackle of the flames.

As Ramon handed the filled bucket to the next man in the human chain, he saw the slender figure of a woman, her hair bound by a light-colored scarf, struggling with a heavy timber, trying to lift it. One end of the timber was ablaze.

At first he wondered what she was doing, and then he heard a wail and saw that the woman was striving to raise the timber from the body of a small child.

Quickly Ramon left his place in line and hastened to help her. In the growing light of dawn, he could see that the child, a little boy of about six years, was lying on his back, surrounded by pieces of broken and charred wood. The heavy timber lay across his thighs, pinning him to the ground. The boy was sobbing, and the sound of his pain and fear served to emphasize, to Ramon, the terror and suffering of the night.

"Here," he said, touching the young woman on the shoulder, "let me help you."

She turned a pale face toward him, a face streaked with soot, and Ramon saw that she was little more than a girl. Her face seemed familiar to him, but under the circumstances, he had little time to ponder it.

Looking about, he found an unburned two-by-four, and he wedged it under the large timber, like a lever. The young woman watched him with worried eyes. Ramon said, "When I pry it up, you pull the little one out."

She nodded, and Ramon bent his back to the task of raising the heavy timber. As the timber rose slightly, the young woman leaned forward, and as gently as she could, she eased the small body of the boy out from under the beam that held him. He cried out once as she moved him, but then subsided again into steady sobbing.

When the boy was free and Ramon had lowered the heavy timber, he saw that the woman was opening a black medical kit, from which she took a roll of bandages and a bottle of medication. It was then that he realized that her white head covering and dress were those of a Red Cross nurse.

He knelt beside her, the better to check the condition of the boy. "How is he?" He smoothed back the tangled hair on the child's forehead.

She did not look at him as she answered, but went on with her task. "I don't believe anything is broken. His legs are cut and bruised, and he has a cut on his cheek, but I think the damage is superficial. I'm only glad that he didn't suffer any burns. I'll bandage the cuts, and then if you would help me carry him to where the temporary medical center has been set up. . . ."

"Of course."

He watched her slim fingers efficiently clean and bandage the boy's wounds. The boy was quieter now, seemingly reassured by her ministrations, but now and then he would call out for his mother and glance around with frightened eyes.

"I wonder where his mother is?" The young woman's voice was low.

"They may have become separated in all the confusion. She may be looking for him now."

"You're probably right. There! He's bandaged now. If you would carry him for me."

Ramon lifted the child, surprisingly light, into his arms, and together he and the young woman headed toward the building in which a makeshift medical station had been set up. It was only after the boy had been settled on a blanket that Ramon remembered where he had seen the woman before. As they left the building and the light of the rising sun clearly defined her features, he knew that she was the pretty blond *gringa* he had met with Maria the night of the officers' ball at the Tampa Bay Hotel.

Of course she looked different now, with her hair pulled back and hidden by the scarf, and her face pale and soot-stained; but she was lovely still, the fine bones of her face and her large green eyes accentuated by her weariness and pallor.

She, at the same time, recognized him, and her eyes widened. "Oh!" she exclaimed. "I know you, you're the brother of the young woman, Maria, who works at the hotel. Ramon Mendes!"

Ramon nodded. "Yes. And you are Miss Manning. Is that not right?"

"Yes. Jessica Manning."

She turned her face toward the burning factory building. "The fires seem to be dying. I certainly hope it is about over. This has been a dreadful night."

Ramon knew that he was staring at her, but could not seem to keep from doing so. Her profile was so pure, so delicate, that it aroused in him a protective instinct that made him uncomfortable. She was beautiful, but she was not for him—she was not one of his people—and it would do him no good to begin to have romantic feelings toward her.

"A dreadful thing, indeed," he said somewhat gruffly, thinking of Julio and the probable cause of the fire. Many people had been hurt, some had died, and property had been destroyed. If Julio had been responsible, did not some of the responsibility lie with their club, with Ramon himself?

As they stood near the entrance to the medical station, there came a cry of alarm from nearby, as a maddened horse, mindless with terror, came crashing past the bucket brigade, eyes wild and hooves clattering in the rubble.

Before either Ramon or Jessica could react, the animal had veered toward them, seemingly unaware of their presence. Quickly Ramon stepped in front of Jessica, trying to shield her, as the horse ran right at them, knocking both of them to the ground. Ramon felt a hoof strike his leg with numbing force and heard Jessica cry out and then go silent.

Then the maddened horse was gone, and Ramon raised himself on one elbow, turning to look at Jessica beside him.

There was a large bruise, growing rapidly into a lump, on her forehead, and her eyes were closed. Ramon's efforts to rouse her failed, and he pressed his fingers to her wrist, searching for her pulse, which was weak but steady.

He sighed in relief, and picking her up carefully, he struggled to his feet. His leg, where the horse had struck him, throbbed and knotted with pain, but he managed to turn with her and go into the medical station. He looked about for a spot to place her, so that she might be attended to.

The place was bedlam. There was no clear space that Ramon could see, and the Red Cross nurses were obviously distracted and overburdened already. Still holding Jessica in his arms, he approached one of the women. "She's been injured," he said, nodding down at Jessica's still form. "She's one of your nurses. You had better see to her right away."

"Oh, dear." The woman, a motherly looking individual, glanced at Jessica and gasped. "Why, it's Jessica Manning! Here, put her—" She looked around the crowded room. "Oh, good heavens, there's no place in here, we'll have to take her outside."

Ramon found a clear space just outside, and he rested Jessica's still body against the wall. The Red Cross woman appeared with her medical kit and began an examination of Jessica.

"Is she all right?" Ramon asked anxiously. "Is she badly hurt?"

The woman said gravely, "She has a bad bump, and she probably has a concussion, but I think that's the extent of it." She bathed the bump on Jessica's forehead with medication, and Jessica moaned and opened her eyes.

"Thank the good Lord!" the woman said, sitting back on her heels. "Can you watch over her, young man? I'm badly needed inside."

Ramon nodded. "Yes, I will watch her."

The woman got to her feet. "Good! It would be best to have a doctor look at her, just in case."

"I'll take care of her. Thanks for your help."

"That's what I'm here for," the Red Cross woman said cheerfully.

Jessica's eyes were fully open now, but she looked dazed and seemed not to be fully aware of her surroundings.

Ramon glanced around, looking for some sort of vehicle that he might borrow to take Jessica to her home, but he could see none.

The fires were dying down now, yet there was still much confusion, and people were milling about in a stumbling daze. This is no place for Miss Manning in her condition, Ramon thought; she should be taken to someplace quiet, and she should see a doctor.

And then he saw Carlos and Maria nearby, talking together, their faces and clothing blackened by soot. He called to them.

Maria knelt beside him and touched the side of Jessica's face. "What happened to her?"

"A horse. Panicked by the fire. We were standing together, and the animal ran us down. Miss Manning struck her head."

"Are you all right, Miss Manning?" Maria queried softly.

"My head," Jessica said faintly. "I don't seem to be able to . . ."

"Shhh, it's all right," Maria said. "We'll take care of you."

Carlos squatted down next to Maria. "Who is this young woman?"

"Jessica Manning. The daughter of a prominent banker in Tampa. She is also a Red Cross volunteer."

Carlos shook his head. "It seems to me that she should be receiving treatment, not giving it."

"She saved a little boy's life," Ramon said. "I helped her, that is why we were together."

Maria looked at him keenly. "There is no need to explain why you were in her company, Ramon. But she must be gotten away from here. Why isn't she inside the medical station?"

Ramon shrugged. "There's no room in there. I thought of taking her to her home, but there is no transportation."

"Then we must take her to our house," Maria said decisively. "It's the only logical thing to do. It isn't far, and you and Carlos can carry her. Later, we will notify her family, and they can come and fetch her."

"My father . . ." Jessica muttered indistinctly.

"Yes," Maria said gently. "We will let your father know, Miss Manning."

*   *   *

They had no way of knowing that Jessica was trying to tell them that her father had brought her here in his buggy and that he should be somewhere in the vicinity.

The fires were about all out now. Only a few small flames still flickered, and those were being doused by the weary firefighters, of whom Wyngate Manning was one.

Finished at last, he straightened up, gazing about for Jessica. He did not see her anywhere, and he began a search of the area. He had dropped her off where the Red Cross station was set up and then had become busy helping fight the fire.

Now he could not find her anywhere. The first-aid station had been dismantled, and questioning of the few people who remained told Manning nothing. No one had seen Jessica for the last hour. Where could she have gone? he wondered. Perhaps someone had been kind enough to take her home, after her work was done, and she could not find him. It seemed the logical conclusion.

He returned to where his horse and buggy were located, and climbed tiredly into the seat. Clucking to the horse, he started for home, reflecting on the fact that his daughter, who had given him almost no trouble for all those years, should suddenly be causing him considerable concern and anxiety.

Of course she was grown up now, as much as he disliked to think so. Yet it was more than that. That young officer, for instance, he and Jessica staying out all night. The young man seemed a decent sort, yet they were both young, and blood ran hot at that age.

There was a question he very much wanted to ask Jessica, but he had not, and he knew the reason—he was afraid of what her answer might be.

Brooding, he flicked the reins and rode on toward home.

Chapter Eleven

IT was ten at night, and the army camp was in a state of chaos. Men were running about in confusion, and the shouts of the soldiers and the whinnies of horses filled the night with a cacophony that made the ears hurt.

To Neil, hurriedly stuffing his clothing and gear into his duffel bag, the effect was heightened by the fact that only half of his mind was on his task. The other half was on Jessica Manning and the events of the previous night.

"Goldang the blasted orders!" fumed Price, as he threw his own bag onto the cot. "How do they expect me to get all of my gear into one goldanged bag? I'm going to have to leave behind my liquor, my Wild West books, and all my other comforts!"

Gage answered this sally with his whinnying laugh, but for once the sound of it did not annoy Neil. He knew that both of his tentmates were laboring under the combined effects of nervousness and excitement.

As Neil finished packing the last of his gear, Tom Farrel, his face downcast, ducked under the tent flap.

Price glanced around at him. "Hey, Farrel! Sorry you weren't chosen to go along. Tough luck."

Tom Farrel nodded glumly. "Yep. I just came over to wish you fellows the best. Get a couple of Spaniards for me, will you?"

"Sure thing, *compadre*," Price said, and he mimicked the parry and death thrust of a bayonet.

Farrel walked over to Neil. "Just wanted to say farewell, Neil."

Neil nodded, embarrassed by the lost look on Farrel's face. "I know how you feel. I mean, I know how *I* would feel if I were being left behind." Yet, at the same time, he knew he was lying. A few days ago he had been eager to go, but things had changed. Now, he realized, if he had a choice, he would be happy to remain behind, to be with Jessica. However, he well knew that he could not say so in so many words; the others would look at him askance and privately think of him as a coward.

Farrel shrugged, his smile melancholy. "I'm all dressed up"—he gestured to his uniform—"with no place to go."

Neil awkwardly clapped the other man's shoulder. "I'll miss you, Tom. You're a good man. I'd be happy to have you fighting alongside me."

Farrel looked down at his boots. "Well, we'll keep in touch, Neil, if we don't meet in Cuba. You have my address in New York. When this war is over, maybe we can get together."

Neil smiled. "I'd like that, Tom. You take care now."

Farrel waved a hand and left the tent.

Neil turned back to his packing, wondering if, when the war was over, he would be able to contact Tom Farrel. Would he, Neil, still be alive; and if he *was* alive, would he be whole?

Thinking of this, of being crippled, perhaps with an arm or leg missing, Neil swallowed painfully. If something like that did happen, how would Jessica feel? Would she still want him, want to marry him?

Good Lord, he thought; I've got to stop being so damned morbid. I'd better get moving and keep my mind on what I'm doing!

Captain Tanner stuck his head into the tent. "Snap it up, you fellows! Move it out!"

Neil finished gathering his things together and joined Price and Gage in the mustering area, where they were to wait to catch a train, which would take them to the docks where they would board their ship.

At midnight, Neil, along with the other Rough Riders who were shipping out, was still standing alongside the railroad tracks, waiting for their train.

Most of the men, much of the excitement now worn off, were grumbling and complaining. Some had broken out decks of cards and were passing the time with impromptu card games; a few others were collected in a small group attempting barbershop renditions of old songs.

Neil, sitting on his duffel bag, felt drowsy and bored. Where in the hell was the train? Maybe it was too much to ask, but he was praying that *something* would go right for once and that the train would arrive soon.

Price, sitting next to him, grumbled, "Hurry up and wait! Hurry up and wait! The story of this man's goldanged army!"

Gage, also nearby, was eating a large bar of fudge, the sight of which stirred Neil's appetite. Had he eaten any supper? He could not remember. Hell, his mind was mush!

Putting his head down on his crossed arms, he closed his mind to the sounds around him and thought of Jessica. He wondered what she was doing now, this very moment. Was she thinking of him? Was she thinking of last night? God, last night! So wonderful, and tonight, this; waiting by the railroad tracks with a pack of other tired and angry men, waiting for a train that never came.

Another hour passed slowly, and still no train appeared. Then, at last, word came down that they should proceed to another track, not too far from the first.

Elated by the possibility of imminent departure, the men picked up their gear and marched to the new track, but there was no train there, either; and once again they resignedly settled themselves down to wait.

Neil, very sleepy now, curled up on the grass near the tracks and pillowed his head on his duffel bag. He awoke an hour later to the sound of complaining voices. Still no train.

It was close to dawn when a train finally chugged into view. The soldiers sent up a cheer, which quickly turned into groans of dismay when they realized that it was not their train, but only an engine pulling a string of coal cars.

Neil got up from his resting place and, shaking his head in disgust, looked over the scene. What a comedy of errors! If this army is as inefficient in combat as it is in organization, he thought ruefully, we're in deep trouble.

And then he heard Colonel Roosevelt's staccato voice over the sound of the others and saw the colonel swing aboard the engine of the coal train.

In a few moments he emerged from the cab and stood on the engine steps, raising his hands for attention. "Rough Riders!" he shouted. "I have commandeered this train. It is filthy, but it will serve our needs. Get yourselves on board."

A ragged cheer went up from the weary Rough Riders, and they swarmed aboard the coal cars.

Neil threw his gear onto one of the blackened cars and clambered over the side. He lost his balance, and by the time he had regained his feet, he was smeared from head to toe with coal dust.

To his astonishment he found himself standing beside Billy McGinty, the tough little southwesterner.

As the press of boarding soldiers pushed Neil against the little man, McGinty grinned up at him. "Hullo, Lieutenant. Fancy meeting you here!"

Neil answered his grin in kind and shook his head. "It must be something about trains, Billy. They seem to draw us together."

Billy guffawed. "Don't they just! 'Course, I'm not sure I'd call this here coal box a train." He leaned closer and motioned for Neil to lower his head. "I didn't want to say nothing out loud and upset the others, but did you happen to notice that this here so-called train is heading in the wrong direction, Lieutenant? Now how do you suppose Teddy intends to handle that?"

Neil, weary now to the point of silliness, burst into bellowing laughter that caused those near him to stare at him and draw back. "My God, you're right!" he gasped out.

Then the train started moving, and McGinty's question was answered—they were moving backward, instead of forward.

"Godalmighty!" McGinty shouted. "Teddy's done it! He's got the engineer to *back* this here train all the way to Tampa!"

And so Roosevelt had. Slowly the steam engine backed the line of coal cars the nine miles to Tampa, and at last the Rough Riders, coal-blackened but undaunted, arrived at the dock area.

The wharf was already crowded with soldiers waiting to board their ships, and new troops arrived every few minutes, until the dock boards began to groan under their combined weight.

Neil counted thirty transport ships, busy with taking on food and equipment, but from what he could overhear, no one seemed to know which army divisions were to go onto which vessel.

Neil looked at those men around him. They were a comical-looking bunch. The coal dust covering their faces, hands, and clothes gave them the look of a minstrel troupe parody of soldiers; yet Neil did not feel like laughing. He was too weary and disgruntled. There was the air of a farce about the whole proceedings. Was the whole war going to be like this?

He saw Price and Gage near him in the crowd and managed to make his way through to them.

Price shook his head dolefully. "God, I'm worn out, and we're not even *started* to Cuba yet!"

Neil smiled to himself. That must be true, for Price for once was speaking without his dreadful mock-western accent.

"This whole thing is ridiculous," Gage grumbled. "Why the hell are we standing here like this? Why can't we go on board our ship?"

Price snarled, "Because we don't know which ship to go aboard, dumbhead! They've fouled things up royally, as usual. From what I've seen, no one knows anything."

At that moment Neil, from the vantage point of his height, caught a glimpse of Wood and Roosevelt deep in conversation at the edge of the wharf. Then the pair separated, going off in different directions.

"Well," Neil said, "I just saw Colonel Wood and Colonel Roosevelt conferring. Now they're going off in opposite directions. Maybe they'll get it straightened out."

"I sure as hell hope so," Price said sourly. "I'm hungry, tired, and mad as hell. I joined this man's army to do some fighting, not to loll around on some goldanged dock!"

An uncomfortable hour passed, as more and more soldiers arrived at the already overcrowded wharf; and then, at last, Neil, who was now near the edge of the dock, saw Colonel Wood leap from the edge of the dock into a motor launch. The launch roared away, toward a large ship that was just entering the harbor. Neil could make out the name, *Yucatán*, painted on the side, and he wondered what Colonel Wood was up to.

Then he heard Colonel Roosevelt's familiar voice, "Rough Riders! Here! Form up. Get into formation. Make haste now."

As quickly as possible, the Rough Riders struggled to get into formation on the crowded wharf. At last they stood at the ready, and Colonel Roosevelt marched them to the very edge of the wharf. Those on the outer edge had to fight not to be shoved into the water.

Neil, his fatigue completely forgotten in the mounting expectancy, watched the *Yucatán* make her ponderous way to the dock. When she was alongside, her gangplank was run out, and Colonel Roosevelt urged his men on board. Neil and the others followed, hurrying up the gangplank. When they were all aboard, Roosevelt ordered the gangplank taken up.

Neil wondered at the haste, but his question was soon answered as an officer stormed to the edge of the dock and shouted up at Roosevelt: "You've made a mistake, sir! This ship is meant for the Second Regular Infantry, and the Seventy-first New York Volunteers."

Neil could see Roosevelt's grin and the look of triumph on his face. "I'm terribly sorry, old chap," he shouted down in reply, "but, well, we do seem to have it, don't we?"

The officer on the wharf shook his fist up at the ship, his face growing red. At last he stormed off with his troops, accompanied by a shower of coal the Rough Riders scooped out of the *Yucatán's* bunkers.

Colonel Roosevelt turned on his men. "Well, we have our ship, Rough Riders," he announced cockily.

As the men gave him a rousing cheer, Roosevelt's attention was caught by something on the wharf. Neil moved nearer the railing to see what was happening. Standing on the dock among the soldiers were two men in civilian clothes, standing next to a huge tripod and camera.

Roosevelt leaned over the railing. "What are you fellows doing?"

One of the men cupped his hands around his mouth and shouted up, "We are the Vitagraph Company, Colonel Roosevelt, and we want to go to Cuba and take moving pictures of the war."

Roosevelt waved a hand. "On board with you then!"

The gangplank was again lowered, and Neil and the Rough Riders watched in astonishment as the photographers hustled their equipment on board.

As Roosevelt and the newcomers passed by him, Neil heard the colonel chuckle and say, "I may not be able to move a whole army of men, but I should be able to handle two more."

Gage, standing next to Neil, shook his head admiringly. "I don't know how Teddy is going to be as a leader in battle, but he certainly knows how to get publicity."

As Colonel Roosevelt and the two photographers moved away along the deck, Neil heard the colonel shout, "On to Cuba, boys!"

Jessica awoke to considerable pain and to surroundings she did not recognize. For a moment she thought she might be dreaming, and she experienced that peculiar, disoriented feeling that comes with awakening abruptly in an unfamiliar place.

She drew in her breath quickly and tried to sit up, but the pain in her head struck forcibly. A loud moan escaped her, and she fell back down. Where was she? What was she doing in this place? And how had she gotten here? Strange, she could remember none of the details.

At the sound of her loud moan, a door opposite the bed opened, and a young woman entered, carrying a lamp. Jessica, squinting against the light, did not recognize the woman's face.

"Where am I?" she asked weakly.

"Hush, don't try to talk." The woman set the lamp down on a small dresser, and Jessica could see that the room was small, but neatly and nicely furnished, and that the young woman was well-dressed and very pretty.

Jessica spoke again. "How did I get here? What happened to me?"

The young woman sat down beside Jessica on the bed. "Don't you remember? You were hurt at the scene of the fire. A runaway horse knocked you down and hurt your head."

Jessica cast her thoughts back. Fire? Runaway horse? Why couldn't she remember? A feeling of panic seized her.

Her confusion must have shown in her face, for the other young woman looked concerned. "Don't you remember anything?" she asked gently.

Jessica cautiously shook her head.

"But you must remember me? Maria Mendes. We met at the Tampa Bay Hotel, at the officers' ball. Your partner caused me to spill a glass of punch on your dress."

Jessica felt tears stinging her eyes and tried to blink them back. It was as if a thick mist obscured all thoughts of the past.

"A doctor is coming," Maria said. "Don't be afraid. We are your friends. You are at our home in Ybor City. My brother and a friend carried you here, as we live close to the area of the fire. The electricity is off in Ybor City because of the fire, and the telephones are not working. But we have sent word to your parents, by messenger. They should be here soon." She peered closely at Jessica. "You can't remember anything about the fire?"

Jessica shook her head again.

"What *do* you remember?"

"I—I know who I am, I know my parents." Frantically Jessica searched her mind for other memories, definitely remembered things upon which to anchor, and to her dismay, she could not find them. What had she been doing before this fire? What had she been doing the past few days? The ball that this young woman had mentioned; yes, now she could remember the ball, vaguely, and Maria also. And something else, a handsome young officer. . . . The memory tickled her mind and then was gone.

She said slowly, "I remember the ball. I remember you, now. But I still don't remember what happened to me last night, or anything about the past few days. What's wrong with me?"

Jessica felt the treacherous tears again and forgetting the pain, turned her head quickly away. A wave of pain strong enough to make her cry out struck again.

Maria leaned down and began to wipe her face with a cool, wet cloth. The coolness felt good, but it did not help to take away the fear that was growing inside Jessica.

The door opened again, and two young men came into the room. One, slender and darkly handsome, looked much like Maria, and Jessica remembered that she had met Maria's brother, Ramon, the night of the ball. If she could remember that much, why could she not remember everything else?

The other man was heavier than Ramon and perhaps a bit older. He spoke to Maria, "Well, how is our pretty *gringa?* Dr. Velasquez will be here soon. He was busy treating the victims of the fire."

Both men stood looking down at Jessica, and she felt embarrassed to be seen like this. She must look a sight.

"She doesn't remember the fire," Maria said. "She doesn't remember anything of the past few days. It has upset her, of course, and her head pains her."

Jessica had closed her eyes, but now she opened them again and stared up at the two men. Even through her pain and confusion, she could not help noticing that Maria's brother was very attractive and that he was gazing at her with frank concern.

"Thank you for bringing me here and looking after me," she said. "Your sister has told me what you did."

Ramon smiled down at her, and the transformation in his face was astonishing. It was as if a light had been flicked on behind his eyes. For some reason she decided that he was not a man who smiled often, and for this reason his smile was all the more charming.

"It was the least I could do, after you, yourself, had been so heroic."

"I?" She felt panic rising again. What did he mean? What had she done?

"You don't remember?" he said in a soft voice.

She shook her head mutely.

"That is a great pity, Miss Manning, for you were very brave. You rescued a small boy pinned under a heavy beam."

Jessica stared in disbelief. How could she have lifted a heavy beam?

He waved a hand in a self-deprecatory gesture. "Oh, I helped you a bit with the timber. And then, when the boy was safe, we were run down by a frightened horse. A rather embarrassing way to crown a feat of heroism, I must agree, but that is the way of the world. Did Maria tell you that we have sent for your father?"

Jessica nodded weakly.

Maria pushed a tendril of hair back from Jessica's face. Her fingers were soft and cool and comforting. "You two will have to leave now. We must let Miss Manning rest until her father and the doctor get here."

Chapter Twelve

Brill Kroger, a full glass of whiskey in one hand and a fuming cigar in the other, sat staring balefully at the wall of his room in the Tampa Bay Hotel. His mood was foul, and there was little chance, as far as he could see, of it improving anytime soon.

First of all there had been the orders for the troops to depart for Cuba, an event that would likely take some of the edge off the interest in the fund-raising balls; and now, last night, the fire in Ybor City.

It was damned bad timing, and no doubt about it. The fire had caused considerable damage and aroused a lot of bad feeling between the Spaniards and the Cubans; and in the midst of all the uproar, no one was thinking of the coming ball in Ybor City. Oh, it could probably be salvaged, it would go on as planned, but some of the monies that might have gone to the Cuban fund would likely now be used to rebuild the area destroyed by the fire.

Kroger took a deep swallow of the whiskey and grimaced as the liquor burned down his gullet and set his belly aflame. He could not remember when a scheme of his had gone so awry, unless it was another time in Florida, some ten years back. . . .

Kroger had experienced few failures in his lengthy career as a confidence man, and on one of those rare failures he had used a female confederate, the *only* time that ever occurred.

However, a woman was necessary to work the scheme, the badger game, one of the oldest confidence games, if not *the* oldest. It was not too long after the untimely end of his relationship with Randy Squires, and Kroger's faith in himself was not yet strong enough to risk more daring, more involved schemes. An expertly executed badger game was lucrative, if the victim was selected with care.

Kroger's confederate was Rena Karso, a Gypsy woman he had found telling fortunes. She was young, voluptuous, with dark, flashing eyes, hair black as ink, and with the morals of an alley cat. She had one drawback—a temper as explosive as Kroger's own.

He wooed her, seduced her, and then recruited her. She was a willing confederate; in fact, it could be said that she was *too* willing. She often brought the sexual act with their victims to a rapid conclusion, so rapid that it sometimes threw their timing off.

"But I like to make love, Brill," she told him, pouting. "That part's almost as good as the money we make. Besides, it's not taking anything away from you, lover. I still have plenty of time left for you. You have no complaints on that score, do you?"

"That's not the point here," he said angrily. "This is a business partnership. Business comes first with me."

"That's where we're different, lover," she said, gliding toward him. She was wearing nothing but a gauzy negligee, and her ripe body was almost fully visible. "And I can always make you forget business for a little while, can't I, Brill?"

She came close to him, the points of her breasts touching his chest, and then her lower body was pressing against him. Her face broke into a pleased, smug smile. "You see?" she crowed. "I can make you forget business!"

She could, of course. Within minutes they were locked together on the bed. They were in her hotel room; the badger game required that they inhabit different domiciles, although Kroger had a key to her room.

But when their coupling was satisfactorily concluded, Kroger was still left with a residual anger. She was little more than a slut—a woman of her heritage could be nothing else—but to allow it to interfere with their business was more than he would stand for. Leaving her room, he determined that he would break off their relationship the minute their con game was successfully concluded. He would always operate alone in the future; he would never again trust a woman.

Their base of operations at that time was the east coast of Florida, an area that was beginning to flourish as a resort area, where the wealthy came to escape the severity of northern winters.

Their mark was a shoe manufacturer from New York, Dennis Hartman, a fairly young man who had inherited the family business and had managed to go through much of the family fortune; but the business still flourished, and a little discreet snooping by Kroger had revealed that Hartman not only was still wealthy but also was married to an angular, cold woman, who spent most of her time in Florida socializing and playing cards, leaving her husband pretty much to his own devices. Hartman had a fondness for women and was quite a handsome man; he had a history of discreet affairs.

Everything that Kroger had learned pointed to Dennis Hartman as the ideal victim: he had money; he lusted after women but had to sneak around to have them; and he had a wife who would likely leave him if she learned of his affairs.

It was not difficult for Rena to make contact. She played the neglected wife to the hilt, a role she had played before. Her husband was always off somewhere, leaving her lonely and starved for love.

Hartman was instantly in full pursuit, pressing ardent suit in those odd moments when he could escape his wife's eye. As per Kroger's instructions, Rena played coy for several days, alternately tempting Hartman, then putting him off, waiting for his high point of frustration.

Kroger and Rena met a couple of times, when she made her reports on her times with Hartman, and Kroger finally judged that the time was about ripe. As they parted he said, "We'll give him three more days."

One day before the scheduled time for their scheme to reach fruition, Kroger tried all day to contact Rena to plan the last-minute details, but his efforts were unsuccessful. Finally, in exasperation, he went to her hotel late in the evening. Instead of knocking, he let himself into her room with his key. Entering quietly, he froze just inside the door. A small light burned beside the bed, which was occupied not by one person but two. So engaged was the couple on the bed that his presence was not noted until he made a sound of surprise.

The man on top of Rena stopped moving and then turned a red, startled face—Dennis Hartman.

Rage rose in Kroger until it almost choked him. The slut, the stupid slut! She could not wait!

Trying to salvage the swindle, Kroger strode to the bed, assuming the role of outraged husband. "What is going on here? I come home unexpectedly and find my wife in bed with a total stranger!"

He pulled a derringer from his pocket. It was unloaded; it was never easy to predict what would happen in these confrontations. Early on, Randy Squires had counseled: "Never carry a loaded gun, kid. Marks are unpredictable. One might try to wrestle you for the gun. You could get killed. Or the mark could get killed, and you're up on a murder charge. Big difference between being charged with murder and being charged with running a swindle. An unloaded weapon is just as effective."

Now Kroger took a step toward the bed and waved the derringer menacingly. "You have two choices, mister. I can either tell your wife what you've done, or you can pay me enough to ease my pride, as a man who finds himself being cuckolded."

Hartman seemed remarkably calm as he rolled off Rena and sat up. "How do you know I have a wife?"

Taken aback, Kroger stuttered, "Why, I. . . . A man like you always has a wife." An uneasy feeling was building in him—he was not in control of the situation. He sneaked a look at Rena and saw a faint smile on her lips.

Hartman said, "Oh, you're right, I am married. You have my permission to tell her anything you like."

"If I tell her about this, she'll throw you out."

"I don't care. I'm leaving her, anyway. You see, Rena and I, we're getting married as soon as I can divorce Margaret." Hartman put an arm around Rena's shoulders and pulled her against him.

"What?" His anger boiled up again, and Kroger thrust the derringer at Hartman, forgetting that it held no bullets. "I'll kill you, you cuckolding bastard!"

Hartman laughed. "Not with that gun you won't. Rena has told me that it's not loaded. She's also told me how you forced her into a life of crime. She wants out of it, and I'm going to make an honest woman of her."

Glaring at Rena, Kroger came around the bed. "You slut! You lying bitch!"

"Here now!" Hartman reared up. "You watch what you say about this fine little lady!"

With a sidewise, vicious swipe of his hand, Kroger laid Hartman's head open with the derringer. As Hartman groaned, slumping, Kroger hit him again, driving him from the bed and into a limp, naked sprawl on the floor.

Rena screamed and then cowered back as Kroger came down on the bed on his knees. Dropping the derringer, he fastened both hands around her throat. His rage roared in his head like a giant wind, and her face was only a blur in his vision.

He squeezed, shaking her back and forth, muttering curses under his breath. Rena's eyes bulged, and she clawed at his hands locked around her throat. Then Hartman groaned from where he lay on the floor, and a measure of sanity returned to Kroger. If he killed Rena, he would have to kill Hartman as well, and the people in the hotel knew of his, Kroger's, association with Rena. The police would be after him for murder.

He released his hands from around her throat and got off the bed. Rena, breathing raggedly, massaged her throat with shaking hands, her gaze on his face, eyes wide with terror.

Without another word Kroger left the hotel room. He packed and left town within the hour, and he had never worked a confidence game with a woman after that. Never again would he trust a woman.

Thinking back on that unpleasant episode in his life did nothing to improve Kroger's temper.

He reached for the whiskey bottle, noticing with renewed anger that it was empty. The liquor he had drunk might as well have been water for the effect it was having on him. Damn, he could not even get drunk and forget his troubles!

Well, the next best thing to liquor to enable a man to forget his worries was a woman. You did not have to trust them to use them!

Kroger licked his lips, thinking over the possibilities. Of course Dulcy was available, she was *always* available. All he would have to do was go down to the telephone in the lobby and call her home. He played with the idea but he had little appetite for it. Dulcy's charms had already begun to pall. She was too willing. Too easy. If he did decide to call her, he would be damned if he was going to take his pleasure out in the open again.

Kroger was a man who liked his comfort, and bedding a woman on a blanket spread over the hard ground was not really to his liking, although if the circumstances required it, he would do so. No, if he saw Dulcy this afternoon or this evening, he would make her come to his room. There was plenty of traffic in the hotel; no one would take undue notice if she was careful. And it struck him that she cared little for her reputation, anyway.

He set down the empty whiskey glass with a clatter. No, he did not really want Dulcy. He wanted someone else. Someone new, someone exciting, someone who would offer a challenge.

His inflamed imagination immediately jumped to the thought of Maria Mendes. The image of her dark, seductive beauty danced in his mind, and he touched it with lascivious mental fingers.

He smiled to himself, thinking of what he might do to her, how he might humble her. The prospect was irresistible. After all, did he have so much to lose now by alienating her brother and her family? Besides, if the girl was a virgin, and he suspected that she was, would she want her family to know what had happened?

Yes, indeed! He rubbed his hands together. It would be the Cuban girl, but how to go about it? He had approached her twice when she was leaving the hotel after work—his mind veered away from the knowledge that he had failed in those attempts—and accosting her somewhere on her way home was not a very good idea. But she worked here, in the hotel. Of course, that was it! She worked in the dining room. Why not order something, food or drink, to be brought to his room, and demand that she bring it? It was the ideal solution.

And if she should refuse him, resist him—his excitement mounted at the thought of such a delicious possibility—he would take her by force. If she should cry out, an event that struck him as unlikely, as he was sure she would not wish to stain her good name, who would believe her story over his? She was a mere woman, an employee, and he was a paying guest. He would simply say that she had done something, perhaps broken something or been rude to him, and had made up a story of his advance to her as a defense. Besides, it might be different if she was a white woman, but she was not.

Smiling cruelly, his good humor almost restored, Kroger straightened his clothing, brushed back his hair, and then tugged at the ornamental bell rope that would summon the floor valet.

"This is to go to room two-fourteen. See that it gets there before it gets cold, Maria." Mrs. Nelson, the dining room supervisor, pointed to the service cart and the loaded tray with its silver-covered dishes. Her face, as always, was set in severe lines.

Often Maria wondered if the woman ever smiled. She also wondered why *she* was being sent to deliver the food, as it was not her turn to be assigned to room service, but one did not question Mrs. Nelson's orders, one simply obeyed.

Obediently Maria pushed the serving cart onto the ornate elevator and got off on the second floor. She found the room with no trouble and before knocking on the door, she straightened her apron and cap. Mrs. Nelson was very strict about neatness and manners, and woe betide the woman or man in her employ who flaunted these conventions.

At her knock the door opened, but evidently the occupant of the room was standing behind the door, for Maria could see no one.

Carefully she wheeled the cart into the room, pushing it toward the table. As she reached the table, she was surprised to hear the door being closed behind her, and then the unmistakable click of a bolt being thrown.

A jolt of fear went through her, and she whirled around and was dismayed to see Brill Kroger standing in front of the closed door, his arms folded over his chest. He was smiling coldly.

Maria felt her face flush, and her throat close as panic rose in her. Kroger's expression left no doubt as to what he had in mind. She had known that he was a dangerous man, but she had thought that she could handle him. Now, she was not so certain.

Ideas sped through her mind. Should she scream? If she did and someone came, what could she say? Would they take her word over that of a guest? Also, her parents would forbid her to continue working in the hotel, if they learned of the incident.

Could she reason with him? Talk Kroger out of what he obviously had in mind? Another look at his face told her the answer to that. His eyes had a hard, expectant shine, and his expression was set. Maria, who had never really felt fear of a man before, now experienced the weakness of terror. Still, she must try. Perhaps if she behaved normally, as if nothing untoward was happening?

Attempting to control the trembling of her hands, Maria went about laying the linen cloth upon the table and transferring the dishes of food and the bottle of wine from the serving tray.

While she did so, Kroger stood where he was, without speaking, yet she could feel his presence behind her.

When she was finished with her task, she turned, keeping the cart between herself and Kroger. With forced briskness, she said, "Your meal is laid, sir. I hope that you will find it to your liking. When you are finished, if you will just ring for the floor valet, he will return the dishes to the kitchen." She raised her gaze to Kroger's face in time to see his cruel, gloating smile.

He said, "Oh, I'm certain the meal will be to my liking, particularly the dessert, for it is the sweet for which I have had an appetite for some time, and there is nothing like a delay to whet the appetite. Yes, indeed!"

Maria felt her face and throat flame, but she refused to avert her gaze. Be damned to the man! He could not make her grovel, she would not show her fear of him.

"I would not know, sir," she said steadily. "And now, if you will excuse me, I must return to my duties."

"Oh, I think not," he said lazily, leaning back against the door. "At least not just yet."

"My supervisor will be expecting me. She will send someone to fetch me!" Maria, despite her resolve not to show fear of this man, could not keep her voice from trembling, and Kroger was aware of it. She could see the sadistic pleasure in his eyes. Damn him, damn him!

"Perhaps," he said, now walking slowly toward her. "And then again, perhaps not, at least for a while. I won't take long, not this time. Just a short space of time. You'll never be missed." His walk reminded Maria of a cat stalking its prey.

Maria's hands tightened upon the handle of the serving cart until her knuckles turned white. Hastily she glanced around the room, looking for something, anything, that she might use as a weapon to defend herself. Meanwhile, Kroger was coming toward her slowly, smiling, smugly sure of himself.

"You needn't be afraid," he said calmly. "I won't hurt you, not unless you choose to fight me. And then you can go back to your duties. Of course, if you have more time, you might find it more to your liking, but that can wait until another time."

The look on his face, his self-assurance, made Maria furious. Her anger blazed, burning away the fear. It was clear that he thought she had no resources, that she was helpless before him; it was plain that he felt she was of low status, something to take as he willed. He was one of those men who looked upon any woman of another race, or even of a lower class, as fair game.

Well, he was about to find out differently! She was strong, intelligent, and he was not going to find her all that easy.

He was almost upon her now, only the serving cart between them. Swiftly, without warning, and with all her strength, Maria shoved the cart at his midriff, catching him solidly, knocking him backward. Kroger grunted with surprise and pain.

As he staggered back, Maria rushed past him, toward the door, but quick as she was, he was even quicker. He managed to seize her arm as she darted past. He gripped her wrist painfully and yanked her toward him. Surprise and pain were still mirrored on his features, but black rage was there as well; and Maria, having already witnessed a display of the man's temper, knew that she must do something quickly.

The table, where she had set out the food, was within reach. Struggling against his restraining hand, she was able to reach the unopened wine bottle. She scooped the bottle up by the neck and swung it up and around, striking Kroger alongside the head. He grunted explosively and staggered, eyes rolling upward, and released his hold on her.

Not waiting to see the final result of the blow, leaving the cart behind, Maria fled. As she fumbled with the bolt, she held her breath, expecting his hands on her any second. Then the door was open, and she was outside in the hallway. She did not stop running until she reached the stairway, then slowed to a walk and tried to regain her composure, hoping the guests mounting the stairs would not notice her breathless and somewhat disheveled state.

When she returned to the kitchen, Mrs. Nelson was not there, and Maria breathed a sigh of relief. Since no one required the serving cart at the moment, no questions were asked, and she was able to continue with her work without incident, although her anger left her more silent and distracted than usual.

This was the day she had promised Tom Farrel that she would meet him after work. Now, after what had happened, she wished that she had not made the promise. She felt unclean from Kroger's touch, and all she really wanted to do was go home, take a hot bath, and sort out her feelings and thoughts. Also, when she had agreed to meet the lieutenant, Carlos had not yet made his declaration of love; and Maria had scarcely had time to think about *that* yet, what with the fire and the incident with Kroger. It seemed to her that so many things were piling up, so many decisions to be made, that she felt near the breaking point.

Still, a promise was a promise, and Tom Farrel struck her as a good and kind young man. She could not hurt his feelings by breaking her word. She must keep her promise and meet him. He would take her someplace, for supper perhaps. Briefly, she wondered where. Well, it did not matter; she had best stop thinking about her personal problems and concentrate on finishing the day's work.

When it was time to leave the hotel and meet Lieutenant Farrel, Maria, to all outward appearances, was cool and composed. In honor of the occasion, she was wearing one of her good dresses—a pale pink muslin that she particularly liked, even if it did wrinkle easily. The fitted waist made her own waist look incredibly tiny, and the full, free-falling skirt and full upper sleeves were very stylish, although she usually did not worry overmuch about such things. At any rate, no matter how she felt, she would look nice for the young lieutenant.

As she stepped out onto the steps leading from the kitchen area, she steadied her straw hat with one hand. She had barely reached the first step when she saw Tom Farrel below her, looking at her, a smile on his face and his hat in his hand.

The sight of his pleased expression buoyed Maria's spirits. He was obviously glad to see her.

"I was afraid you wouldn't come," he said softly, as she descended the steps. Then he took her arm in his.

She looked up at him from under the brim of her hat. "I promised I would meet you. Aren't you used to women keeping their promises?"

He flushed slightly and gave her a sheepish grin. "It was just that I was looking forward to seeing you so much, and sometimes something you want very much. . . . Well, it has a way of disappearing."

Both pleased and nonplussed by the depth of his feeling, Maria did not respond. It was clear that this man had considerable interest in her; at the moment, a great deal more than she did in him. After all, she hardly knew him, and then there was Carlos. . . . But she must not think of Carlos now. Now she was with Lieutenant Farrel, and he deserved nothing less than her complete attention.

"I thought," he was saying, "that is, if you don't mind, we might have an early supper, then attend the slide show. Mr. Richards, the man giving the show, has just returned from an extended tour of Europe, and I've been told that the pictures are exciting, very realistic."

Maria had not heard of the slide show, but it did sound intriguing. "That sounds very nice. I've never seen a slide show. Where is it?"

"Right here in the hotel. For that reason I thought we'd dine here. I know you're in the hotel all day, and if you'd rather, we can dine somewhere else. But it would be convenient to have supper here. If you don't mind?"

Mind? Maria's thoughts were suddenly awhirl. She had been familiar with the hotel since its beginnings; as a child she had explored every nook and cranny of the magnificent edifice and of course was now employed here. However, she had never entered it as a guest; she had never even considered the possibility. The idea brought a sudden smile to her face. What fun it would be to go to dinner here as a guest; to have, for a change, someone wait upon *her!*

Tom Farrel, seeing her expression, seemed to relax. "Then it's all right with you?"

"It's fine with me, Lieutenant."

Taking her arm under his, Lieutenant Farrel led her slowly along the walkway around the hotel; and there, under the eyes of the rocking chair brigade, Maria elegantly, head high, mounted the steps, arm in arm with the handsome young lieutenant.

Despite Maria's initial reservations and despite the unpleasantness with Brill Kroger, it was a very enjoyable evening.

Seeing the hotel as a guest, was, for Maria, seeing it with new eyes. She enjoyed the service—she might have been a complete stranger for all the recognition the dining room staff showed, although she did see some of the girls whispering together when they thought she and her escort were not watching—and she even enjoyed the envious stares of the officers and men in the dining room; a tribute to the pink gown, she was sure.

They had an excellent dinner and then proceeded to the slide show, which was presented in one of the smaller public rooms. The show was good and very entertaining.

Afterward, they sat sipping coffee on the wide veranda, rocking as Maria had seen so many dignitaries do. They talked of personal matters, exchanging the kind of information that was customary to newly acquainted couples.

She found Tom—he had asked her to please call him by his given name—very good company. He was bright, pleasant by nature, and possessed an excellent sense of humor. Maria found herself telling him things about herself and her family that she would not have discussed with just anyone.

It was not until they left the hotel that she realized that during their time together she had not once thought of the nasty scene with Brill Kroger or of the tragic fire. She thought, briefly, of telling Tom about Kroger; but then she realized that it could only result in more unpleasantness and could inflate the incident up all out of proportion.

And she also realized, with a pang of guilt, that she had not once thought of Carlos and his proposal.

Ramon Mendes stood hesitantly in front of the large, white, two-story house, dressed in his best and carrying a large bouquet of summer flowers. Now that he was here, he felt ill at ease. Why *had* he come? The little *gringa* was certain to be recovering satisfactorily; and even if she was not, how would his visit help her?

When he had first thought of paying a call on Jessica Manning,

Ramon told himself that it was strictly a courtesy call; after all, he and his family had taken her in, tended her, and informed her father of her situation; yet deep in his heart, Ramon knew that that was not the whole of it. He wanted to see her again; she had captured his imagination somehow, with her golden, fly-away curls, her beautiful, clear eyes, and fine bones.

Uncomfortable, he ran his finger around under his collar. Perhaps he should go home, just forget the whole thing; he had enough on his mind with Sergio's death and the business of the fire. But then he *was* here, and since he was, and since he had brought the flowers, he might as well look in on Jessica. He would only stay for a minute. It was the polite thing to do.

With renewed resolve, he mounted the steps to the wide porch and lifted the heavy bronze knocker.

Jessica, the pain in her head reduced to a monotonous throbbing, was dozing when her mother tiptoed into the room.

Seeing Jessica's eyes closed, Anne Manning turned to leave without speaking, when Jessica, sensing her presence, opened her eyes and said, "What is it, Mother?"

"Nothing important, dear, just a young man come to see how you are. I gather he's from the family that took you in yesterday morning. A Ramon Mendes. But if you're not up to it, I'll just extend your thanks, and he can come back another time."

Jessica sat up gingerly—it still hurt her head if she moved too quickly. "No, Mother. I've done nothing but sleep away the day. Have him come up. He and his family were so kind, and he's the man who stepped between me and that runaway horse. If he hadn't done so, I might have been hurt even worse."

Anne Manning nodded. "All right, Jessica. He's brought some lovely flowers. I'll put them in water and bring them up."

When Ramon was shown into her room, looking ill at ease and uncomfortable at being there, Jessica was struck anew by his dark good looks.

She still could not remember the time period immediately prior to her accident, but she could remember most of what had occurred afterward, and she was very grateful for what Ramon and his family had done for her.

"Please sit down." She indicated a high-backed wicker chair near her bed. "It was so nice of you to come, Ramon. Your whole family was so kind to me yesterday, I don't know how to express my gratitude."

Ramon, seemingly embarrassed by her words, held up a hand as if to fend them off. "It was nothing, Miss Manning. Any decent person would have done the same." He shifted uneasily in the chair. "My mother and sister send their regards."

Jessica nodded, smiling. "You must thank them for me and tell them that I am doing well. The pain in my head is better, and although I still cannot remember much of the past few days, the doctor says it is not uncommon to have such a memory lapse after a blow to the head."

As Jessica ceased speaking, an awkward silence ensued. She could see that Ramon was nervous in her presence, and she had to wonder at the reason.

She made an attempt to revive the conversation. "Tell me about yourself, Ramon, about yourself and your family."

Ramon looked surprised. "There is not a great deal to tell. We are Cubans, as you know. My father came to this country sixteen years ago, looking for a better life for himself and his family. He is a chef, a good one, and fortunately he found work easily. When they built the Tampa Bay Hotel, he went to work there, as head sauce chef, and has worked there ever since. My family is not large. There are only my father, my mother, my sister, Maria, and two brothers, Eduardo, and the little one, Paulo. Eduardo and I work in the cigar factory, and Maria works at the hotel. Not a very exciting family history, I'm afraid."

Jessica was smiling. "Your family sounds very nice, and it must be wonderful to have brothers and sisters. I have none. I have always wanted a sister to share things with. You say your family is not large, but it seems quite large to me."

Ramon flushed slightly. "By Cuban standards, our family is small. You Americans—" He stopped abruptly.

Jessica said, "Some of us have large families, too. The Johnsons, for instance, have ten children. Their house is always in a state of noisy confusion."

She had spoken to put Ramon at ease, and indeed, her last remark did bring a smile to his lips.

He said, "If you think they are noisy, you should visit a large Cuban family. Cubans are a very volatile people, you know. We are more emotional, I think, than you Americans."

"Americans? Aren't you an American, Ramon? You know, I have

never thought of myself like that, as an American. It makes us sound like two different kinds of people."

"That is because we are, Miss Manning."

The smile had disappeared, and again he seemed distant, and even faintly hostile. Jessica wanted desperately to put him at ease. He was so handsome, and he had been so kind yesterday. What was wrong today? Why was he so uncomfortable in her presence? Why so ill at ease? She felt very drawn to him and wanted very much for him to like her.

"We are all human beings, Ramon," she said in a soft voice. "Americans and Cubans alike. Can we be so very different, if that is the case?"

He said stiffly, "Many of your people do not feel that way, Miss Manning. Many people hate and fear anyone and anything that is different."

"Then those people are wrong," she said strongly.

Ramon smiled, and as she had yesterday, Jessica wondered at the illumination it brought to his face. "That may well be, but it does not stop them from persecuting the ones that they call different. Still, I am glad that you feel the way you do, Miss Manning. Perhaps one day more will think as you do, and we will all live together in peace."

"I certainly hope so. And please call me by my first name, Jessica. When you call me Miss Manning, it sounds so formal."

His face closed up again, becoming dark and serious. "It would not be proper. Although I do not wish to offend you, I must refuse."

Jessica was taken aback. What a strange, complex creature he was! So very different from the boys and men she knew. It was not only his dark beauty—for he was beautiful really, not just handsome—but his entire character and personality were differently formed. Perhaps he was right, in a way. His people *were* different, at least in customs and language, yet Jessica still thought that the things they had in common were much greater than their differences. She only wished that she could make him see that.

"I must take my leave now," he said, getting to his feet abruptly and bowing slightly. "I and my family wish you a complete and quick recovery."

"Thank you, Ramon," she said softly, and then brazenly reached out her hand toward his. It was a daring thing to do, and she thought, given the conversation that had transpired between them, that he would refuse to take it, but after a slight hesitation, he accepted her hand.

As her small, white hand was swallowed up in his strong, brown fingers, Jessica felt a tremor run through her. His hand was warm and firm, and for an instant only, his fingers pressed against her palm; and then he hastily released his grip, and his face flushed even darker.

Seeing that he was about to leave, she pressed what she considered her advantage. "Will I see you again, Ramon?"

Again, it was a bold thing to do, but Jessica knew that she might not see him otherwise. He gave her a quick, burning glance, nodded once, and then quickly left the room.

After he was gone, Jessica sank back onto the bed, her emotions a strange mixture of misgivings and delight. According to all that she had been taught, she had behaved rather badly, yet she felt that she had done the right thing. Ramon was a person she wanted to see again, wanted to be friends with. Also, she was sure that he felt the same way about her but for some reason was reluctant or afraid to form a friendship. This reluctance, adding a hint of mystery, made him all the more attractive.

She decided that Ramon was really a most fascinating young man.

When Anne Manning brought the flowers into the room, she found Jessica asleep, a faint smile on her lips.

Anne Manning stood looking down at her daughter thoughtfully. It was nice to see Jessica smiling again, and yet one possible reason for the smile troubled her. The young man, Ramon Mendes, was very handsome and presented an excellent, well-mannered appearance, but he *was* Cuban; and although Anne Manning was an understanding and tolerant woman, she knew of the difficulties that confronted romantic liaisons between people of different cultures. She did hope, for Jessica's sake, that she was not thinking of getting involved with the young man.

Shaking her head, she left the room. Two romances for her daughter within such a short time were more than she felt prepared to cope with. As she went downstairs to help Ruby prepare dinner, she could not help thinking that this war, and the thousands of people it had brought with it, was also bringing problems to Tampa.

And that reminded her that Jessica had not once asked about Lieutenant Dancer since the accident. Evidently Neil Dancer was temporarily gone from Jessica's memory as well. She had thought of bringing up the lieutenant's name to her daughter but had finally decided to let Jessica come around to remembering it herself. After all, Neil Dancer was on his way to Cuba, and that fact alone, should Jessica remember, would cause her anguish.

Chapter Thirteen

BRILL Kroger leaned against the wall, one arm across his midriff, and gasped for breath.

The serving cart had caught him across the abdomen and shins, and both areas were now causing him considerable discomfort; but the physical hurt he was experiencing was in no way comparable to the blow to his pride and vanity.

The little bitch! The insufferable bitch! Who did she think she was? How *dare* she do this to him?

He had really expected no trouble from Maria, despite her coldness toward him. He had never had trouble with women, beyond some initial resistance. Seduction had always been comparatively easy for him; women liked him, were attracted to him—at least that had been his experience. And now this!

A deep, hot rage was bubbling in him; he could feel it in his gut, and he knew, also from past experience, that it would have to have an outlet of some sort, or he would not sleep this night.

Walking over to the table Maria had laid, he kicked at it viciously, sending the dishes and the food to the floor with a clatter of breaking crockery; and then, opening the door of his room, he pushed the serving cart out into the hall.

Slamming the door shut, he went to the closet for his coat, put it on, then smoothed back his hair in front of the dresser mirror. Since the tide of feeling in him demanded some release, he would call Dulcy. Although he did not admit to this thought, he knew Dulcy, with her willingness to please, would at least ease some of his anger and tension. As for paying the Cuban bitch back for what she had done . . . well, that would come in due time.

Dulcy, as Kroger had anticipated, was glad to comply with his request to come to the hotel.

Always ready for new and daring things to do, Dulcy found the idea delightful. To come to the hotel and to sneak up to Kroger's room, unseen, right under the noses of her parents and her friends, so to speak, was both a challenge and a welcome adventure.

Quickly Kroger returned to his room and summoned the floor valet to clean up the mess, offering the lame excuse that he had accidentally tipped the table over, but a large gratuity made the valet more than willing to accept any story Kroger offered.

He then ordered another meal sent up, which was delivered just before Dulcy arrived, by a hotel waiter this time.

Dulcy arrived in a cloud of scent and bubbling enthusiasm. She was laughing as Kroger admitted her.

"Oh, Brill, you should have seen Mrs. Purcell! I met her down in the lobby, and of course the old biddy asked me what I was doing here. I told her I had come for the slide show. I found out first, naturally, that *she* wasn't going. Oh, this is delicious!" She clapped her hands like an excited child. "It's going to be much nicer in bed. I promise you!"

Kroger was annoyed by her chatter, but he managed a thin smile. "And you had supper sent up. How grand!"

Dulcy swayed over to the table. "Roast chicken and wine, and those lovely little cakes. Brill, you are a darling!"

Touching her finger to the frosting on one of the small cakes, she put her finger in her mouth, licked the frosting off, then rushed at Kroger and flung her arms around his neck. "You deserve a big kiss!"

She pressed her hot, young mouth against his, and Kroger kissed her back roughly, pushing the sudden rigidity of his need against her until she drew back, laughing gaily. "We *are* anxious tonight, aren't we? Well, I always say you should never keep a gentleman waiting. After all, the chicken will keep."

In another moment they were on the bed, and Kroger was unbuttoning her dress with urgent fingers, with little regard for the delicate fabric of the garment.

"Wait now, you'll tear my dress, and what will my parents think? Wait, I'll help you."

But Kroger was in no mood for waiting, and several small pearl buttons popped as he stripped the dress from her shoulders and pushed up her skirts.

"My dress!" wailed Dulcy, but Kroger paid no heed as he pulled down his trousers and threw them into a corner. Then, in a rage of lust, he thrust himself into her, ramming fiercely against her, until she cried out, "Brill! Not so rough, you're hurting me. Please, Brill!"

Panting, using his body as a weapon, he battered her so that each new thrust banged her head against the headboard. The sound of their bodies coming together had the sound of a blow upon flesh, as indeed it was; and Dulcy, now reduced to tears, tried to pull away from him.

He held her brutally pinned to the bed by her shoulders, grunting at each lunging stroke, until his lust spilled out of him. But as he collapsed on top of her, his anger was unappeased. The thought that it should have been Maria on the bed, instead of this slut, enraged him further.

Dulcy, still weeping, squirmed out from under the weight of his body, and out of the bed. Hands on hips, she glared down at him from streaming eyes. "You hurt me, damn you, Brill Kroger! What do you take me for? You never treated me like this before."

His stare was baleful and should have warned her, but she seemed too enraged to take heed. "You don't treat people you like that way. It was a mean, terrible thing to do!"

Kroger did not move or answer, just glared back at her with eyes that held a glimmer of something dark and mad.

Heedless, Dulcy ranted on, "You're nothing but an animal! I've never been treated so in my life."

Clearly infuriated by his silence, she began to goad him. "You think you're such a great lover. Hah! You think you really know how to treat women." She tossed her head. "Let me tell you something, Mr. Brill Kroger, you're not so great! I've had much better lovers than you. Men who would make you look like a . . . a puling boy! Neil Dancer, for instance. Did you know that Lieutenant Dancer made love to me? Well, he did. Here at the hotel, out in the garden. And he was better, much better than you, and he showed some respect for me, as a gentleman should. . . ."

Dulcy's words going on and on had been chipping away at Kroger's self-control. His anger mounted, feeding on each phrase until, at last, he could control it no longer. Neil Dancer, was it? She thought that callow lieutenant was better than he? Well, she would soon see!

Quick as a striking snake, before she had time to react, his powerful fingers wrapped around her throat, squeezing until he could feel the cartilage and bone beneath the soft flesh.

His pleasure, as he watched her eyes bulge in terror, was enormous. Then a grain of caution inserted itself into his mind—it would not be wise to leave finger marks on her throat.

Taking one hand away, he groped for a pillow and jammed it over her face, then used both hands to hold the pillow firmly over her mouth and nostrils.

Now that her eyes were not staring at him, his feeling of pleasure returned. As she fought for her life, he observed her flailing, jerking body with an almost sexual thrill. It was a losing battle, and at last her movements faded to weak tremors and then stillness.

Neil stood at the railing of the *Yucatán,* looking toward the quay, scanning the area hopefully for the sight of Jessica. Why had she not come?

Once it had been announced that the ships would not be sailing right away, hundreds of wives and sweethearts had flocked to the wharf, calling and waving up to their loved ones on board the ships. But Jessica was not among them.

Neil sighed and then regretted doing so. The air was foul with the stench of unwashed bodies and dying mules. Even though the *Yucatán* had moved out to midstream four days before, in an attempt to get away from the rotting garbage at dockside, there was no avoiding the smell of the ship itself; its overcrowded cabins stank of too many men too close together, with all too inadequate toilet facilities.

And there was the food, if it could be called food. The army rations of fresh beef proved to be anything but fresh, and much of it had to be thrown overboard, to add to the other floating garbage that clogged the canal running past the wharf. Added to that, the drinking water had turned brackish, and a number of men had come down with stomach and bowel disorders. Swimming, the one diversion that might have been possible here in midstream, was made risky by the presence of sharks attracted by the floating garbage.

It was, Neil reflected, the lowest period of his life, and the worst of it was his worry about Jessica. That day and night on the island had been something special to him, and he thought it had been to her as well. Perhaps he had been mistaken in that. Had her parents found out what had happened and forbidden her to come to the docks to see him? Or perhaps she had simply changed her mind. Was she upset by what had happened, and now thought better of her declaration of love? It was driving him crazy. He could stand the stench, he could endure the food and this infernal, seemingly endless waiting, but he could *not* bear not knowing what Jessica was doing or feeling. It had been six days, six long days since they had all so optimistically boarded the *Yucatán,* ready to sail for Cuba.

And then, when all the men were crammed on board, General Shafter's ship, the *Segurança*, had slipped her moorings, preparatory to leading the fleet out of the harbor. Before she got underway, a tug came shrilling out to the ship with a telegram: "Wait until further orders before you sail. Answer quick. R.A. Alger, Secretary of War."

It appeared that three unidentified warships had been seen in the Gulf, and the assumption was made that they were lying in wait for the American fleet.

The navy hurriedly began an investigation, and General Shafter ordered his fleet back to anchor. No one was allowed ashore, not even for a short time, so for the last six days the troops had been confined to the ships, and Neil had had no opportunity to visit Jessica. He had even considered jumping overboard, and he feared that he would soon be desperate enough to do just that.

All the Rough Riders were bored, impatient with the delay, and grumbling was commonplace. Colonel Roosevelt paced the deck like a caged and hungry tiger. Neil and the others had watched him striding back and forth, back and forth, muttering to himself.

What they had no way of knowing was that at night, in his cabin, Roosevelt poured out his frustration in long letters to Henry Cabot Lodge: "I did not feel that I was fit to be colonel of this regiment— but I am more fit to command a brigade or a division or attend to this whole matter of embarking and sending the army than many of those whose business it is. . . ."

Deep in his own thoughts, ignoring the other Rough Riders milling around him, Neil did not hear Price speaking to him, until the man shook his shoulder.

"Dancer, what the devil? Are you mesmerized by that damned quay? You've been staring at it for days now!"

Neil glanced around, upset at being shaken out of his reverie. "What the hell do you want, Price? I'm in no mood for idle conversation."

Price affected a wounded look. "Idle conversation, is it? Well, just for that I've a notion not to tell you. It would serve you right, talking that way to a fellow officer and gentleman."

Neil let his breath go with an exasperated sigh. He no longer found Price so easy to dislike as he once had; and during the night and day of preparation for boarding the ship, he had found that the other man could be rather pleasant company, particularly since he had now dropped his pseudo-western accent and mannerisms. Although at any given moment, Price might affect another persona, his remarks were usually humorous and occasionally insightful. Even plump Gage, with his unfortunate undergraduate manner and moon face, had his good side. Or perhaps, Neil thought wryly, I'm becoming more tolerant.

He smiled with an effort and said lightly, "All right, fellow officer and gentleman, just what is your momentous news?"

Price laughed. "What would make you the happiest right about now?"

To see Jessica on the wharf, Neil thought; to know that she still loves me and will wait for me. Of course, he could not say that to Price, so he gave the answer that he knew Price expected. "To hear that this blinking ship is about to sail."

"That's it!" Price said, grinning broadly. "I just heard that Teddy has received word that the Gulf is clear and our orders to sail have finally come through. What do you think of that? I didn't see it myself, but Gage was there, and he told me that Teddy performed a real Indian war dance when he heard the news. I would have loved to have seen that!"

And so, at long last, in the late afternoon of June 14, the fleet, consisting of thirty-five vessels, four tenders, and fourteen convoy ships, the largest armed force ever to leave American shores, moved out of the harbor and steamed southeast.

Neil Dancer gave a last, lingering look at the receding dock, but he saw only three black women, three soldiers, and a gang of stevedores watching their departure. Jessica still had not come, but he stood at the rail watching, until distance and the gathering dusk closed behind the *Yucatán* like a curtain, hiding all that was left behind.

Once the fleet was at sea, there was a good deal of improvement in the morale of the men.

Colonel Roosevelt wrote that it was pleasant "sailing southward through tropic seas toward the unknown." And although many of the southwesterners were made apprehensive by the vast expanse of water stretching in every direction and although many suffered bouts of seasickness, the excitement of their venture and the anticipation of finally confronting the enemy kept their spirits generally high.

Even Neil, with a part of his mind still obsessed by thoughts of Jessica, became more cheerful as time passed. During the sea voyage, he became better acquainted with many of his fellow Rough Riders, and despite the overcrowded conditions and the dreadful food, time passed rather pleasantly.

And then, early on the morning of June 22, the fleet came in sight of their objective—Cuba. A short time later, the *Yucatán* steamed in toward shore, and the order came down to disembark.

Amid the confusion of disembarkation, Neil went about collecting his gear with mixed feelings. Part of him tingled with excitement, the urge to do battle, to confront the enemy; but another part of him was thinking of the accident at Tampa when the cannon had exploded. He remembered the torn and bloody limbs and the agonized faces. He might very well die here on this foreign island. He might never see Jessica again, nor his parents.

But such matters should not be thought about at a time like this, he told himself. Concentrating on what he was doing, he quickly gathered his few possessions and joined the others on deck, anxious to get off the ship and onto land once again.

But once on deck, ready to go ashore, they were forced again to wait. The landing, like everything else in this rather comic war, was a scene of vast confusion.

However, the Rough Riders were more fortunate than most. They were part of a brigade commanded by Brigadier General S.B.M. Young, who had promised them that he would show them some fighting, and General Young was a good friend of Major General Joseph Wheeler, who commanded the cavalry. Wheeler cooperated to the utmost in seeing that the Young-Wood-Roosevelt troops were landed early.

Soon Neil, Price, and Gage were settled into one of the small landing boats, and in a few minutes the craft was battling the wild surf as the horses of the officers, which had been thrown overboard to make their way ashore as best they could, struggled painfully alongside the boat. Neil could not see his own mount, Excalibur, but he averted his gaze from one fine animal, its eyes rolling wildly as it struggled to keep its head above the water.

"That's a hell of a thing to do to a good horse," he shouted at Price, who only nodded, his complexion shading to green as the small boat pitched wildly.

As the boat drew near the shore and the surf became rougher, Neil, struggling to keep his seat, saw a man fall out of the boat alongside theirs and instantly vanish into the churning sea. Neil felt horror rise in his throat when no effort was made to rescue the drowning man.

However, he well knew that they could not stop for him; it was all they could do to keep their own boat from capsizing. The man went down without so much as a cry for help. There was nothing left to mark his passing. He was gone as if he had never been.

And then, somehow, they were ashore, with all their gear intact, and the boats were returning to pick up other men from the ships.

As Lieutenants Price and Gage assembled their platoons, Neil searched for their captain, Peter Tanner, but he was nowhere to be found. But Neil did find his horse, Excalibur; he greeted the shivering animal with a hug around the neck and then gave him a brisk rubdown. By the time the platoons were assembled, Neil had Excalibur saddled and ready to go, but there was still no sign of their captain.

The troops had been landed at a small hamlet called Daiquiri, where there had once been a sugar plantation. The little village seemed to be deserted, and the Cuban scouts reported that the Spaniards had just evacuated Daiquiri and were heading for the safety of Santiago.

Soon word came down to Neil that General Wheeler had given General Young the task of pursuing the fleeing Spaniards with all due vigor, and orders were given to begin the march at once, so that they could support General Lawton, who had been dispatched to establish an outpost about four miles to the west, in the direction of Santiago.

Neil, astride Excalibur, who was quivering with eagerness to run, was not sure what he should do. Where *was* Captain Tanner? Leaving Price in charge, Neil rode up to the head of the column, where Major Keaton sat upon his bay horse. Neil told the major about the missing captain, and the senior officer, a tall, sandy-haired officer with a Boston accent, said, "I'm sorry, Dancer. I thought you knew." The major sighed. "It seems everything is fouled up in this war, and that includes lines of communication. Captain Tanner is very ill, some kind of tropical fever. He didn't even come ashore, so I guess it's your troop, Lieutenant. Good luck!"

Neil, in a rather stunned state, wheeled his mount about and rode back to his troop. *His* troop. He was not at all certain that he was up to commanding it. Certainly he had thought of such a possibility, had dreamed of it even, but now that it was a reality, he was not so sure he wanted it. Still, he had little choice in the matter. He was an officer, and as second in command, it was his sworn duty to take Captain Tanner's place.

By the time he returned to his men, the troop in front of them was already moving out, and in as firm a voice as he could manage, Neil shouted out the order to march, and his men began to move forward.

Neil saw that Gage had found his horse, but Price had not and was afoot, as were all the enlisted men and noncommissioned officers.

As the command to move out traveled down the line, the Rough Riders began the eleven-mile march through the sand to Siboney, another small village to the west.

As the already footsore, unhorsed southwesterners of the First Volunteer Cavalry trudged along the soft sand, other infantrymen jeered and catcalled. Neil heard one voice rise above the others, "Ain't it grand to have a horse?"

The southwesterners, faces set in determination, kept their eyes straight ahead and ignored the jibes. Most of them had fought to be here, and with or without horses, they meant to be a part of this war.

"For Christ's sweet sake, Dancer, can't we take it a little easier?" Price, his face red with heat and exertion, and streaming sweat, trotted alongside Excalibur, staring up at Neil in anger.

Neil, feeling almost as uncomfortable as Price looked, shook his head. "I'm sorry, Price, but Colonel Wood has ordered us to employ all haste. I don't like it any better than you do."

"Oh, sure!" Price spat into the sand. "You can say that, but you've got your horse!" He slowed, falling back.

Neil sighed. He knew how Price and the other Rough Riders afoot must feel, but orders were orders, and General Wood had been very specific. General Young, who had decided to take personal command of two regiments of regular cavalry, was approaching his goal, Las Guásimas, from a valley road to the right, as the Rough Riders traveled a hill trail farther inland. This decision by Young had caused a rivalry to spring up between Wood and him; General Wood was determined to reach Las Guásimas before Young and his regiments.

The Cuban advance scouts had reported that the Spaniards appeared to be falling back in the face of the speedy American advance; but all at once, as the Rough Riders neared Las Guásimas, the jungle came alive with the crackle of gunfire.

Neil, swearing, scrambled off his horse and took cover behind a boulder alongside the trail. It was as if they had suddenly fallen into a nightmare as the previously, almost eerily silent jungle erupted with the whine of Mauser bullets and the shouts of startled men.

Neil looked around at the men under his command and was

relieved to see that all had survived the ambush and had managed to find cover of some sort, but some of the other troops were still exposed; and even as he watched, Neil saw Hamilton Fish go down with a bullet in his chest, as another man fell dead nearby.

A tremendous rage seized Neil, smothering his fears, and he began firing steadily into the dense jungle, firing at an unseen enemy. For the first time he called the Spaniards enemies in his mind. He lost all track of time as he reloaded, fired his rounds, then reloaded again and again. Above the sound of gunfire he could hear the cries of the wounded and the dying.

Something moved behind him, and he whirled about in panic, thinking it was the enemy, but it was Captain Capron, who had sprung to his feet and was emptying his revolver at a briefly seen figure who had stepped out from behind a tree trunk to fire, then jumped back to safety.

Neil watched in horror as Captain Capron grunted, clasped his chest, and began to fall. A young trooper rushed at him, shouting, "Captain! Captain!"

Captain Capron waved him back. "Don't mind me, boys. Continue with the fight."

Two medics hurried to the captain's side, and Neil, seeing that there was nothing he could do, returned to his methodical firing.

Slowly, after what seemed an endless time, the barrage of fire from the trees slowed and finally stopped altogether. In the silence that followed, the air was filled with stinging smoke, the acrid smell of gunpowder, and the moans of the wounded. Neil thought that Hell must be something like this. Weary, he propped his rifle and leaned back against the boulder that had protected him; he was too tired and dispirited to even feel glad that he had survived.

In the now silent jungle, the weary troops began burying their dead, which numbered sixteen. Fifty more men had been wounded. Neil, helping to dig the mass grave, wondered if the cost had been worth it.

He heard from Gage that a newspaper correspondent, Edward Marshall, had been seriously wounded and that he had been carried to the rear by Richard Harding Davis and Stephen Crane.

Remembering his meeting with Crane, Neil could only speculate as to how well the slight, frail-looking Crane had stood up to the arduous journey here, and the fierce battle. Neil could understand why the others, as well as himself, were here; they were fighting for a cause, but for a man to place himself in jeopardy so that he might write about it later was beyond his comprehension. Still, they were brave men, that could not be denied.

Neil's own troop had lost only one man, although several had been seriously wounded. As he herded his weary, sweaty band together, he was amazed to find that most of them were in high spirits, seemingly elated that they had gotten the "first crack at the Spaniards."

For days after the skirmish at Las Guásimas, there was little or no food, for the commissary department had virtually collapsed under the stress of battle. The Rough Riders ate, after a fashion, for Colonel Roosevelt, using his own funds, had organized supply parties and dispatched them back to the coast to buy what food was locally available.

And then, due to the fact that General Young had fallen ill, Colonel Wood was elevated to brigade commander, and Lieutenant Colonel Theodore Roosevelt became colonel of the First Volunteer Cavalry.

On June 30, orders came down that they were to advance on Santiago.

Neil was glad to be on the move again. Anything was better than sitting in the steaming tropic heat, waiting and not being privy to what was happening. His nights were filled with dreams, dreams in which a faceless enemy fired at him from the darkness, dreams in which he was wounded or lay dying. These nightmares alternated with dreams of Jessica, but they, too, were unpleasant dreams, for in them he could see Jessica but not reach her. There was always some barrier between them. By day, Neil wondered if she was thinking of him; if she missed him at all; or if she would still be waiting, if she would still care, when he returned.

Then they were again on the march, fighting the jungle, weighed down under heavy camp equipment and ammunition. The jungle, like the Spaniards at Las Guásimas, took its toll. Sharp cactus spines, called Spanish bayonets, cut their flesh and shredded their uniforms; and men fell one after another from the intense heat and the fever.

Neil's first sight of Santiago caused mixed feelings in him. It was lovely, lying in a picturesque valley, surrounded on the north and the east by lofty, green hills that overlooked the city. He thought first of its citizens, the noncombatants, and was dismayed at the thought that their own cannons and guns might be the cause of the death of innocent women and children; but then his soldier's eye discovered the forts and blockhouses on the hillsides, and his mind turned to possible battle strategy, wondering how his commanding officers would plan their attack.

He could readily see that the Spanish position was a strong one, and that the hills, El Caney and San Juan, were as indispensable to the defense as their capture was to the coming attack. Yes, the hills held the key to victory.

When their orders finally came down, Neil was pleased to see that his analysis of the situation had been correct. The regulars were directed to storm El Caney, supported by Colonel Wood, and the word was that they expected little resistance.

Unfortunately this assessment proved to be grossly inaccurate, and soon Neil and his troop found themselves under heavy fire as they lay in the valley below the hill. Insofar as Neil could judge, their orders had been rather vague. The Rough Riders were in an extremely bad location directly in front of the Spanish batteries, pinned down by heavy fire, and any retreat was blocked by masses of their own troops congesting the road behind them. As he saw his men fall under a hail of bullets fired by the Spaniards, Neil cursed the sheer idiocy that had placed them there. The almost smokeless powder that the Spaniards were using made it impossible to pinpoint their positions, while the Americans exposed their position every time they fired.

Then, just when it appeared that things could not be worse, the huge war balloon was cut loose from its moorings and went sailing over the heights until it was exploded by Spanish bullets, accomplishing nothing beyond giving away the location of a column advancing under the direction of General Wheeler.

Neil and his men, still pinned down by fire from the fortifications above them, could not attack or retreat. He had never felt so helpless in his life. In frustration, he emptied his rifle, simply firing at random, with no visible target.

As he crouched down behind his skimpy shelter, he took a moment to catch his breath. He glanced slowly around the area. To his horror he saw Excalibur not thirty yards away, grazing in a patch of sparse grass, bullets whistling all around him. Neil had ridden the animal close to this position, then dismounted, tethering him to a tree, and come the rest of the way on foot. Somehow Excalibur must have gotten loose.

He grazed, seemingly undisturbed by the gunfire. In the beginning the horse had been skittish under fire, but by now he was accustomed to it. It was a minor miracle that he was so far unscathed, but Neil knew that the miracle could not last.

Without further thought he was up and running, keeping low and weaving. He reached Excalibur without being hit. He jammed the rifle into the scabbard and sprang into the saddle, drumming his boot heels on the animal's sides.

Excalibur bolted toward the trees, but before he reached full stride, Neil felt something strike his left shoulder. At first he felt only surprise, but then the pain began, spreading rapidly, a heavy, throbbing ache that quickly sapped his strength. Consciousness began to fade, and he had the presence of mind left to sag forward, wrapping his arms around Excalibur's neck.

Chapter Fourteen

It had not been a very satisfactory meeting, Jessica thought. First of all, Brill Kroger had been very upset when they told him of their decision to cancel the balls, even after her father had explained to him that now, with the troops already in Cuba and with supplies piled high on the docks of Tampa, there was no need for additional funds for supplies and arms. In addition, according to all the newspaper estimates, the war was all but over.

And then there was the matter of Dulcy Thomas, who had been missing for over a week. It was the talk of Tampa, and although the police had been notified after the first night she had not come home, so far they had come up with nothing concrete.

Also, Jessica was not feeling her best. She still could not remember what had happened just prior to the fire in Ybor City. The week before that was still a complete blank, although she could remember everything else about her past life. Her parents had told her, of course, as best they could, about the events that had transpired, but they had not been with her every minute. Occasionally an image crossed her mind of a handsome young man in a military uniform, but she could not put a name to the image, nor think of a reason why he should tickle her memory. And as soon as she thought hard about it, the image would vanish.

Only one good thing had resulted from her experience at the fire—her new friendship with the Mendes family. She really liked Maria, and she was very attracted to Ramon, although the only time she had seen him since he had come to call after the accident was when she met with the Cuban Ball Committee to discuss the possibility of canceling both the Ybor City ball and the one at the Tampa Bay Hotel.

At that meeting, Ramon had been polite but reserved. She had caught him looking at her twice, when he probably thought she was unaware of it. He seemed to like her. Why was he fighting against it so?

And now, with the balls definitely canceled, with the army gone, or at least the part that was doing the actual fighting, the heavy summer heat settled over Tampa, bringing a general feeling of lassitude and weariness.

Jessica, sitting on the front porch glider, watching Mary, the last one to leave, go slowly down the walk with a goodbye wave of her hand, felt the humidity settle upon her shoulders like a great, oppressive weight.

Taking out her linen handkerchief, she wiped her forehead. Why did she feel so sad, so depressed? Was it the loss of memory? She supposed that it was. There was something hidden behind a screen in her mind, something she *should* remember, a teasing memory that was driving her crazy. What *was* it?

The departure of the army had taken much of the excitement from the town. Although there were still some twelve thousand soldiers encamped outside of Tampa, they were a dissatisfied lot, unhappy at being left behind. Since most of them were volunteers, they had had little training and so were less disciplined than the regular troops had been; they were given to drunkenness, disorder, and a disregard for even rudimentary rules of camp sanitation. This unhappy fact, coupled with a shortage of fresh water and the heavy summer heat, contributed to the spread of malaria and typhus, and many people had died. Despite the fact that the war was going in favor of the Americans and the Cubans, it was not a particularly happy time for Tampa, and certainly it was not a happy time for her, Jessica felt.

"I am going, Papa," Ramon said stubbornly. "I am going to Cuba with General Nuñez and his men. Nothing any of you can say will stop me. It is what I have been waiting for!"

His face drawn, Felix Mendes stared at his eldest son. Shrugging, he finally turned away. "If that is so, then I'd best not waste my breath. If that is your final decision, so be it."

The rest of the family, along with Carlos, were silent, their faces solemn.

Ramon turned to Eduardo. "What do you say, my brother? Are you with me?"

Eduardo came to his feet, his cheeks flushed. "Of course. I too have been waiting."

Ramon glanced at Carlos. "And you, Carlos? Will you too go with us?"

Carlos sneaked a look at Maria's set face. "Yes, my friend. I too will go with you. When do we leave?"

"In a little more than a week, with General Nuñez, and Colonel Mendez Miranda."

Maria made a small sound of protest that caused her mother to turn and take her into her arms. "It is the way of men, my daughter. There is nothing we can do, except to let them go, pray for them, and wait patiently for their return."

Maria, feeling hot tears flooding her eyes, pushed her mother's arms away and ran out of the room.

If this was the way of men, then it was a foolish way; and she did not believe for a moment that all women could do was to submit to the men's decision meekly, then wait and pray. She, for one, intended to do everything in her power to persuade Carlos not to go. Persuasion, she well knew, would be useless in the case of Ramon; and Eduardo, of course, would follow his older brother's lead. It was all so futile. They might all be killed. Thank God little Paulo, at least, was too young to go with them!

As she stood in the yard behind the house, inhaling the heavy scent of the night-blooming flowers in the humid darkness and knuckling away her tears, Maria heard the kitchen door open and the footsteps of someone on the crushed rock pathway.

"Do not cry, Maria. Do not cry, my love. We will return. We will all return, you shall see."

Maria, though still angry, could not stop herself from turning into Carlos's extended arms. Burying her face against his chest, she tried to sort out her emotions.

"I know you do not fully understand, Maria, but this is something we *must* do. For ourselves. For Cuba. This will be our last chance. This expedition will probably be the last one sent to Cuba, and it will be a great honor to serve under General Nuñez and Colonel Mendez Miranda."

Maria raised her head. "You're right, Carlos, I do *not* understand. The war is almost won. The newspapers say so. Why do you need to go *now?*"

He shook his head. "I cannot explain it, not so you will really know how it is for us. But we won't be away long, and when we return, perhaps you will have made up your mind about my question, eh?"

Maria stepped out of his embrace, even though it cost her an effort to do so. "And perhaps my decision will be no! Perhaps I do not wish to marry a man who is so foolish as to risk his life in such a way."

He reached for her again. "Maria, you don't mean that!"

She evaded his arms. "Perhaps I don't. I'm not sure of anything. The way I feel this very minute, I do mean it."

"Maria, don't let me go away like this. We can't part this way. Give me some kind of word to take with me, something to warm me while I am away from you."

Maria, her resolve weakening, came again into his arms. "Carlos, I care for you, you must know that. Perhaps I even love you. I do know that being with you gives me great pleasure, that you make me happy, but I do not yet know whether I wish to spend my life with you, whether or not I'm ready to decide such a grave matter. You say you must go. Well, go then, and come back as soon as possible. I will try to have a decision for you upon your return."

Carlos lowered his head and pressed his mouth to hers in a long kiss. Feeling him so close to her, so close and warm, a feeling rose in Maria, a feeling of such depth and yearning that she felt it would cause her heart to burst.

Pulling back again, she looked up at him. "Doesn't it matter that we need you here, Carlos? There is much rebuilding to be done because of the fire. And how about the fire itself? Was it set by Julio? The rumor is that he was responsible. Will the Spaniards retaliate? We need someone like you to take charge, to make decisions."

He rested his cheek against hers. "There is no real proof that Julio set the fire, although he has evidently fled from Ybor City. He cannot be found. And there *is* proof that Ricardo Aragones threw the fire-bomb into our club, but with the war going the way it is, I'm sure that the *Peninsulares* are not anxious to press the matter. I feel reasonably sure that nothing more will be done. As for the rebuilding, there are others who will attend to that, and I'm sure they are more fitted for the task. No, my love, I must go, even though it causes you unhappiness. Forgive me for that."

Again, he drew her into his arms, and Maria offered no resistance. Perhaps her mother was right, in a way. Perhaps this was the way it was meant to be. She had done all she could, now it would be in the hands of God.

Brill Kroger paced his hotel room, scowling blackly, his cigar fuming, his footsteps striking the rug like blows. Goddamnit! What was happening? Why were things going so wrong? He was accustomed to *good* fortune, not bad, and now it looked as if his whole scheme was going down the well. All his efforts, all his expenses, would be for naught.

He was almost out of funds. It had cost a small fortune to set himself up here in this expensive hotel, to live as he had been doing, to entertain and woo people; and now these damned provincials wanted to call off the fund-raisers, were *going* to call them off. There must be a way to salvage the scheme. There had to be *something* that he could do to recoup his expenditures.

Of course, in one way he had been fortunate. He had managed to get rid of Dulcy's body without being detected, and so far no one had connected him with her—or with her sudden disappearance.

His mind turned away from the vivid image that suddenly surfaced in his mind—Dulcy's pale body, limp and lifeless, her vacant eyes fixed on him. He shuddered slightly. Kroger had few compunctions about breaking the law, but he was not accustomed to killing, and the memory of what he had done was not pleasant. Not that he had any regrets about Dulcy's death; she had deserved to die, he thought. But it had happened, although he had not planned it beforehand, and the results had had to be dealt with.

But he must turn his thoughts to what was more important, finding a means of making up his losses, something that would compensate him for the time and money he had spent in Tampa.

There was no help for it, the balls had been canceled, but what about another kind of ball? Where was there a pressing need for money? What would be a good cause?

Pacing, he pondered the situation. And then he had it. The fire in Ybor City, it was a natural! The fire had caused considerable damage, and the rebuilding would be expensive; and although the damage had been confined to the Cuban community, surely the rest of Tampa would be generous enough to contribute to such a worthy cause.

Yes! That was the answer!

He would get on it right away, have some local artist make up posters, possibly depicting a tearstained tot, made an orphan and left homeless by the fire. He would go first to the Mendes family and then to Wyngate Manning. Christ, he would make a good score yet. Yes, indeed!

"Since the other fund-raising balls have been canceled, and for good reason," Kroger said suavely, "we should get busy on this one at once. It should be arranged as quickly as possible, for I'm sure you will agree that the unfortunate people of Ybor City desperately need our help. If you could only have seen firsthand, as I have, the homeless children, the pathetic families. . . ."

Brill Kroger, Jessica thought sourly, looked as if he was about to weep. However, there was something patently false about his dramatic flourishes, and she could not help but wonder why he, who was not even a resident of the area, should be so interested in arranging charitable events here.

Yet the fact that Ramon Mendes was in her house also, diverted Jessica's thoughts from Kroger. The two men had arrived together a short time ago, to speak to her father, and now all the Mannings were gathered in the parlor, over tea and sweet cakes, discussing the matter that Brill Kroger had come to bring to their attention.

Kroger was going on. "Ramon and his family have graciously agreed to organize the affair, and I thought that since the businessmen of Tampa would surely wish to contribute their time and money, your family, Mr. Manning, might wish to work alongside Ramon and his family. It is a worthy cause, I am sure you will agree." He smiled over at Jessica, but Jessica only nodded coolly. "Would you, Miss Manning, be willing to work with Señor Mendes on this project?"

This time Jessica did smile but directed it at Ramon. "Why, yes. I would be most happy to do so."

"Is that all right with you, Mr. Manning?" Kroger asked.

Wyngate Manning pursed his lips, studying his daughter, thinking that this was a fine opportunity to get her involved in something. Ever since the accident, she had not been her usual sunny self and had kept pestering him with questions concerning the days immediately before the fire. He and Anne had filled her in on most of the details, but they had decided not to tell her about Neil Dancer and her friendship with him. If Jessica remembered on her own, well then, there was nothing for it; but if she did not, then it seemed to him unnecessary to burden her with worry over the lieutenant, who was now in Cuba.

He said firmly, "I think it is an excellent idea, Mr. Kroger. My family and I will be all too happy to participate in the arrangements. And I am sure that other businessmen in the city will also cooperate, as well as contribute to this worthwhile endeavor."

During the next several days, despite the heat and the humidity, Jessica's mental state improved considerably.

She met with the Mendes family, and Ramon, almost every day, usually at their home, and she became very fond of the volatile Cuban family.

During these visits, Ramon usually sat near her, and although not much in the way of private conversation was possible, a great deal had been communicated with their eyes.

Jessica no longer worried so much about her memory loss, and she had begun to hope that Ramon would at last come out of his protective shell and open up to her.

The plans for the new fund-raising ball, which was to be held in the Tampa Bay Hotel, naturally, were almost complete. The menu—the same as they had made up for the other balls—was set. The invitations had been mailed, the orchestra hired, and the posters dramatically displayed in the stores all over the area. Jessica was hoping that now that the work was done, Ramon would have time to see her away from the business meetings; and after the last meeting, when they had completed the final details, she dared to suggest as much.

"Ramon," she said to him softly, when the rest of his family was out of earshot, "Ramon, may I speak to you alone? I have something to give you."

Among her things Jessica had, surprisingly, found a piece of needlework, an unfinished man's cigar case. She could not remember for whom she had intended the case. It could not have been her father, since he did not smoke cigars. At any rate, it seemed a fine idea to give the case to Ramon, in gratitude for his many kindnesses. And so she had finished the work on it, carefully putting in his initials, RM, with loving care. She had brought the case with her that day, hoping for a chance to give it to him.

Ramon was staring at her, his face flushed even darker. Finally he said, "Come with me into the garden."

Jessica willingly followed as he led her through the kitchen and out the back door into a large, rather wild garden, where a riot of bright flowers fought for space with a vegetable garden and fruit trees.

When they were seated under an arbor that blanketed them with its cool shade, he turned to her. Before she could speak, he said, "Jessica . . ."

It was only recently that he had finally started calling her by her first name. She said quickly, "Yes?"

"Jessica, I wanted to . . ."

"Yes, Ramon?" Her heart began to beat faster.

"I am going away. I am sailing with the troops that are leaving with

General Nuñez. We will be going to Key West and then on to Cuba."

"Oh, no!" she exclaimed in dismay.

He nodded. "Yes. It is what I have been waiting and working for. We are all going. I, my brother Eduardo, and Carlos Chavez. I thought you knew."

Jessica was silent for a few moments, as she experienced a sense of déjà vu. It seemed to her that she had heard those words spoken before. Had someone else, someone she cared for, said much the same thing to her? The memory was gone as quickly as it had come.

"I—I wish you wouldn't go, Ramon. I like you very much!" The last sentence was blurted out, without forethought, and Jessica lowered her burning face into her hands in an agony of embarrassment.

Ramon gently took her hands into his. "I like you very much also, Jessica."

Jessica looked up in pleased surprise, meeting his glance squarely.

"But, Jessica, I must say something else. Although I do like you, even care for you, any such friendship between us is impossible."

She stared. "But I don't understand."

"Yes, you do." He sighed. "Because you are what you are, and I am what I am."

"You mean because you're Cuban and I'm not?"

He nodded. "Yes. We are too different. Our worlds are too different."

Jessica smiled painfully. "But I like your world, Ramon. I love your family, they are wonderful people."

"Yes, they are. And I like your family, but that has nothing to do with it. Believe me when I say that I, better than you, know of the difficulties such differences can cause between a man and a woman. It has nothing to do with my going to Cuba, that was decided long ago, but now I can see that it is for the best."

Close to tears, she pulled her hands away. "I don't know how you can say that!" She turned her face away. "I think I'd better leave now. My mother is expecting me at home." She had only taken a few steps before she turned back, fumbling in her reticule, finally closing her fingers around the carefully wrapped cigar case. "Here," she said, thrusting it at him. "I made this for you, for helping me the night of the fire."

Before the startled Ramon could respond, she fled, running around the house to where her horse and trap were. The tears that had threatened now came. As she made her way home, guiding the horse through the familiar streets, the memory that had briefly surfaced earlier now returned to nag her, making her feel uncomfortable and disoriented. Just when she had started feeling better, just when she thought Ramon was finally ready to warm up to her, he was going away, and she would be left alone again. *Again?*

Feeling very confused and unhappy, Jessica urged the horse into a faster pace. All she wanted now was the privacy of her bedroom, where her tears would go unmarked and unnoticed.

When Neil opened his eyes, he was at first terrified that he had been blinded, for he could see nothing; and then, he became aware of the dull pain in his chest and left shoulder. Raising his head, he saw the glow of a campfire close by. Thank God, he could see! It was night.

Gingerly he explored his left shoulder, where the pain was the most severe, and encountered something bulky beneath his shirt. A bandage? Had he been shot? It would appear so. But where was he now? There were no sounds of gunfire, so he must be somewhere away from the battlefield.

Concerned, he made an attempt to raise himself from the blanket on which he was lying but could not manage it. He fell back, groaning. Where the devil *was* he?

Turning his head, he stared in the direction of the fire and saw the outlines of several men against the light. They did not look like Rough Riders. He pondered the wisdom of calling out to them. A horrifying thought occurred to him—had he been captured by the enemy? But if that were the case, they would have a guard over him. Also, they must have tended him, bandaging his wound.

And then one of the figures, the smallest, turned and came toward him, carrying something that Neil could not make out in the firelight. As the figure came closer, he could smell food, and his stomach contracted. He could not recall when he had eaten last.

The figure was close now, then was standing over him, peering down. "Ah, so you are awake!" said a soft voice in English, but with a Spanish accent. "Good! I have brought you something to eat."

Neil was startled. The voice belonged to a woman, despite the fact that she was wearing men's clothing. Again, Neil tried to sit up.

"Here, wait. Let me help you."

The girl, or woman, placed the plate she was carrying on the ground and putting her hands under his arms, helped him to sit up. Her slender arms were surprisingly strong.

"There. That is better, no?"

Neil, dizzy from the effort of sitting upright, could only nod weakly.

"How do you feel?"

Neil swallowed. His throat was dry. "All right, I think, considering. I'm very thirsty, though."

"Here." She reached behind her in the dark, producing a canteen. "Drink, but not too much all at once."

Neil took the canteen, which she helped to hold to his mouth. He could feel her fingers, strong and wiry, under his as he drank greedily.

"There, that is enough." She took the canteen away. "You may have more later. Now you must eat and rebuild your strength."

She held the savory-smelling plate out to him. In the firelight Neil could not really see the contents, but it smelled delicious, and his stomach growled in anticipation.

He took the plate and forked the food into his mouth. He took several mouthfuls before he said, "Thank you, thank you very much. But who are you? Where am I? And where is my horse? The last thing I remember was being in the saddle."

"Your horse is fine, señor. He is tethered in the trees, over there." She pointed to a wall of darkness behind the campfire.

"As to who we are, we are Cuban patriots, fighting against the Spaniards, as you are. You are here because your horse brought you here. He came trotting into our camp three days back, with you on his back. You were unconscious to all appearances, but somehow, you had managed to stay on his back. He is a fine animal, señor, and may well have saved your life. Were you wounded in the battle for Santiago?"

Neil swallowed the last of his food. "Yes. Have you heard what happened there? Is the battle over yet?"

She nodded. "A runner came through just today. El Caney and San Juan Hill have been taken. It is considered a great victory."

Neil's thoughts were wry. Fine hero he was, shot and taken out of the battle before it really began! Finished with the food, he handed the woman the plate. "I just realized that I have not introduced myself or asked your name."

She laughed. "Under the circumstances, señor, that is not too surprising."

Neil found himself smiling. Although he had yet to clearly see this woman's face, he liked her and admired her spirit and wit. "I am

Lieutenant Neil Dancer, of the First U.S. Volunteer Cavalry, at your service, ma'am."

She bobbed her head. "How do you do, Lieutenant? I am Margarita Gomez, of the Cuban Freedom Fighters. You are welcome to our camp."

Neil was awakened the next morning by the sound of distant gunfire. He felt somewhat better than he had the night before, and he managed to pull himself up into a sitting position, leaning back against a tree; the effort brought him considerable discomfort and some dizziness.

Closing his eyes against the pain, he took a deep breath and breathed in the scent of damp plants and wood smoke.

"Ah, so you are awake again, Lieutenant. You look much better, I must say. There is even a touch of color in your cheeks this morning."

Neil opened his eyes to see Margarita Gomez squatting in front of him, with another tin dish upon which he could see a pile of beans and rice, topped with a large fried egg.

Despite the egg—he had not had once since they had left the States —he was more interested in the sight of Margarita, for now that he could see her clearly for the first time, he was surprised to find that she was a beautiful woman, if perhaps not in the usual accepted sense.

Dressed in close-fitting leather breeches, calf-high boots, and a loose, belted, long-sleeved shirt, her figure was slender but womanly in all respects; and Neil, who had never seen a woman so attired, could not help but stare at the curve of her thighs in the snug breeches, and the swell of her bosom under the soft material of the shirt. Under a wide-brimmed hat, her hair, long and black, was made into a long braid that hung over one shoulder, falling almost to the ground in front of her as she crouched before him, one knee on the blanket, the other raised and supported by her slender foot in the tight, black boot.

Her face was strong, almost boyish, with a firm chin and wide mouth that looked as if it had been made for smiling. Her eyes were dark and were shaded by luxuriant lashes that made spidery shadows on her cheeks. It was impossible for Neil to guess how old she was; while she looked fairly young, it was clear that she was not a girl.

She smiled impishly, and Neil, abruptly aware that he had been staring, felt himself flush. "I'm sorry, I didn't mean to stare like that."

Margarita shrugged. "It's all right, Lieutenant. You have never seen a woman wearing men's clothing before, eh?"

He nodded, grinning sheepishly, and accepted the plate she extended to him.

She said, "Women's clothes, here, would not be practical. They would be a great bother and would interfere with what I'm doing. There is no time here to worry about such niceties as clothing. There is a war to be won."

"A very practical viewpoint, I agree. But tell me, just what is it that you *are* doing here?"

Margarita moved around to sit beside him, and as Neil ate hungrily, he was acutely aware of the proximity of her slender, trouser-clad leg.

"This is the base camp for the Freedom Fighters. Most of our people are now with your troops outside of Santiago. A few of us have remained behind to keep things in readiness for their return."

"But isn't it unusual for you? . . ." He floundered. "I mean, a woman? . . ."

Margarita threw back her head and laughed, the sound rising delightfully in the already hot morning stillness, like some strange, exotic music. "No, Lieutenant, it is not so unusual. Here, in our country, there are a number of women who, like me, are taking an active part in the struggle to free our country. In your country it is different, yes?"

Neil experienced some embarrassment. In this woman's presence, he found himself feeling rather naive, a feeling he did not at all care for. Again, he wondered how old she was, but of course he could not ask that. However, there was something he could ask and change the subject at the same time. "You speak English well. Where did you learn?"

She smiled. "In the convent school. The sisters found that I had a flair for languages, and they needed people who could speak English, as translators for the American businessmen who come to Cuba."

"And your family?"

She tilted back the brim of her hat and looked at him in some mockery. "You ask a great many questions, Lieutenant, but that is all right, I don't mind telling you. My father was a teacher, and my mother a gifted pianist. They are both dead now, as is my only brother, who was killed by the Spaniards. So, you see, there is no one left who will be shocked by my unladylike behavior."

Neil felt color rise to his face. "I didn't mean to imply. . . . Oh, hell and damnation, I suppose I did! At any rate, I think that you are very courageous."

Her smile turned gentle. "And so are you, Lieutenant. And we appreciate the help you have given us, all of you. Without the Americans coming to our aid, freedom might never have been achieved. Now it looks as if it will only be a matter of days before our freedom from Spain is assured. Santiago is surrounded. General Linares must soon capitulate, if only to save the civilians in the city."

Neil put down his empty plate. "I hope you're right." Gingerly he touched his wounded shoulder. "When do you think I'll be able to ride, Margarita? I should get back to the men under my command. They probably think I'm dead."

She frowned severely. "It will be some time, I should judge. You received a nasty wound. You were unconscious for three days, remember, and we feared that you might not live. You must not hurry things, Lieutenant, and undo all that we have done for you."

Neil leaned back against the tree. Although he would never have admitted it, even to himself, a part of him was glad that he would not have to return to battle. Margarita had implied that the war was all but over. Neil fervently hoped so. The sooner it was over, the fewer men would have to die. In the brief time that he had been in Cuba, he had seen all the dying he ever cared to see.

During the next few days, Neil's strength slowly returned as his wound healed. He still could not use his left arm to any great extent, but he was up and about now, and had made the acquaintance of the rest of the rebels at the base camp.

There were not many—Margarita; old Emmanuel Rojas, who had but one hand, the other having been chopped off by his Spanish master for alleged thievery; Manuel Cruz, a thin, wiry youngster who looked even younger than his twelve years; and Chico Hernandes, a short, stocky, middle-aged man, who was almost as wide as he was tall and who had a gimpy leg.

Not a very formidable army, Neil thought wryly. But they were all friendly, and Neil was glad that Excalibur had carried him here, rather than into the arms of the Spaniards or off into the jungle, where he most certainly would have perished before anyone found him.

Still, as he grew steadily better, he became increasingly restless. He fretted about the men in his command and about Price and Gage. He had thought the day would never come when he would worry about that pair! There had been no more word since the report that El

Caney and San Juan had been taken. What was happening? It was extremely frustrating.

They could occasionally hear the sounds of firing in the distance, but it was not the gunfire of an extended battle. Neil was strongly tempted to ride back toward Santiago, just to see for himself what was going on; but Margarita, sensing his intent, admonished him sharply that although he might be feeling better, he was by no means healed and that such a trip could be very harmful.

And then, one evening as the little group sat around the campfire having coffee, they heard the unmistakable sounds of horses and men approaching. Although it struck Neil that they were rather noisy to be the enemy, he jumped up, reaching for his rifle, as did the others.

But the group of tired and dirty men that approached the fire held no threat. Margarita, at first clear sight of the newcomers, voiced a glad cry of recognition, and in a moment the area around the fire was a confusion of greetings, embraces, and joyous voices.

Neil, standing off to himself, felt out of place, a little foolish, and for a moment, very lonely.

When things had quieted down somewhat, Margarita led over a short, slender man, with mahogany-colored skin, and a large mustache.

"Juan Morales, this is Lieutenant Neil Dancer, of Colonel Roosevelt's Rough Riders. As you can see, Juan, the lieutenant has been wounded, and we have been nursing him. Lieutenant Dancer, this is Juan Morales, the leader of our little group of freedom fighters."

Morales, whose keen, dark eyes seemed to miss very little, gazed at Neil appraisingly, as if making up his mind about him before he spoke. Neil was impressed by the man and could feel the strength of his personality. He could easily see why Morales was their leader.

"I am happy to meet you, Señor Morales," Neil said, speaking first.

Morales nodded formally. "As I am happy to meet you, Lieutenant Dancer. How is your wound?"

"It is much better, thanks to your friends here."

"That is good."

Neil, anxious to hear news of what had been happening, could control his curiosity no longer. "Tell me, Señor Morales, where does the war stand? I was wounded several days ago and have heard nothing since the capture of El Caney and San Juan."

Morales smiled slowly. "We bring good tidings. Santiago has fallen. General Toral is even now signing a treaty with your General Shafter.

Soon the Spanish will be gone, the tyrants will no longer rule us, and Cuba will be *our* country again. Viva Cuba!"

As he spoke the last words, his voice soaring, a chorus of cheers went up from the others around the fire.

"Come," Morales said exuberantly, taking Neil's good arm. "It is a time for celebration! We have baked in the sun, gone hungry, been shot at, wounded, and made generally miserable. But now it is done. Margarita!"

Margarita stepped forward, smiling.

"*Chica*, do we have food?"

She nodded.

"And drink?"

She nodded again, and her smile broadened. "I will start preparing a feast at once. In the meantime, the stream is nearby. Perhaps the men would like to wash themselves?"

Morales gave Neil's good shoulder a hearty clap. "Now that is a woman for you, eh, always thinking of cleanliness. But do not let that confuse you, my friend. Our Margarita can fight alongside a man when need be, cook as well as a man's mother, and make love like an angel!"

Margarita, for the first time since Neil had met her, looked suddenly shy. Ducking her head, she hurried off. Neil, startled at Morales's laughing remark, still enjoyed seeing her discomfited. At last, he thought, the shoe is on the other foot!

The ragged band of guerrillas, some obviously wounded, broke up, most of them heading toward the stream that flowed on the other side of the grove of trees. Neil settled down in a comfortable position where he could watch Margarita.

Leaning over the large iron kettle that was resting on the coals, she looked graceful and very desirable. Was Juan Morales her lover? Or was he just one of those outspoken men who liked to make sport of his friends? But what does it matter to me? Neil wondered. He was curious, just the same. Briefly he wondered how it would be to make love to Margarita. Her body would be slender and muscular, he could see that, even through her clothes. Would she be a passionate lover? He decided that it was more than likely, and that thought triggered memories of Jessica; and the ever-present pain of not knowing about her twisted his heart. God, a woman could hurt a man, without ever striking a blow!

Deep in meditation, Neil paid scant attention as one of the guerrillas sat down beside him. It was only when the guerrilla leaned forward to insert a stick into the flames to use to light a cigar, that Neil took notice of him. The familiar, pungent smell of the cigar made Neil slightly dizzy; he had not smoked a cigar since he had been wounded.

He looked closely at the smoker. He was young, about Neil's own age, well-built, quite handsome in his torn and filthy clothing, and obviously Latin. He had evidently washed in the stream, for droplets of water still clung to his face and hands.

He nodded courteously to Neil as he drew on the cigar, then smiled contentedly. "I brought it with me to Cuba," he said, in English, "to smoke when victory was ours. Now that time has come."

"An excellent idea. But how did you keep it from being smashed up while in battle?"

"I carried it in this," the guerrilla said, taking from his pocket a slender, heavily embroidered cigar case, just the right size to hold two cigars.

When Neil got a good look at it, his heart almost stopped. For a long moment he could not speak, for his throat was suddenly dry. The case was elaborately embroidered in red and gold. It could not be, he must be mistaken!

"Where did you get that case?" he asked tensely, knowing that the question was abrupt and tactless, but he had no time for niceties.

The guerrilla looked mildly surprised but seemingly took no offense. "A young woman gave it to me, a very beautiful young lady."

Neil still had to be absolutely certain. "May I see it, please?"

"Of course, señor."

He offered the case to Neil, who took it in trembling fingers. It looked just like the one Jessica had been making for him, only the place where the initials were to have been—Neil's initials—now bore the letters, RM.

"That is very good work. Did she—?" He cleared his throat. "Did she make it herself?"

The guerrilla nodded proudly. "Yes, and for that reason, it is more precious to me."

Neil was anxious to know the other man's name. "I'm Neil Dancer, by the way, Lieutenant Neil Dancer, of the First Volunteer Cavalry."

The guerrilla exhaled cigar smoke. "I'm pleased to make your acquaintance, Lieutenant. I am Ramon Mendes."

Were there other cigar cases like this one? Neil wondered. Could it be a general pattern that anyone might make? He had to know!

"Have you been with the guerrillas long, Señor Mendes?"

Ramon Mendes shook his head. "Not long at all. Just a short while. My brother and I, and a friend, arrived only a week ago."

"And where are you from, may I inquire?"

"Tampa, sir. And you?"

"Oh, I came from New York State originally, but I was stationed in Tampa for a time. Perhaps we know some of the same people."

Ramon Mendes said thoughtfully, "Perhaps, but it is not too likely. If you will forgive my saying so, your people and mine do not mix socially."

Neil desperately wanted to blurt out the question: do you know Jessica Manning? He managed to restrain himself, however. Surely it was some kind of a weird coincidence, and Mendes would eventually reveal that it had been his sweetheart, no doubt a Cuban girl, who had made the case. Neil said casually, "I became acquainted with a very nice family in Tampa. They were very kind to me. The father was a banker. You may have heard of him. Wyngate Manning?"

As Neil spoke the name, Ramon Mendes gave a start of surprise. "Why, yes. I *have* met Señor Manning and his family. It came about in a rather surprising way. . . ."

Neil said urgently, "The daughter, Jessica. Did you meet her?"

Mendes frowned, and Neil realized that something in his, Neil's, voice, had sounded odd.

"Yes," Mendes said slowly. "I know her slightly. In fact, it was Miss Manning who gave me this cigar case, in return for a small favor I rendered her. It is something of a surprise to me that you, sir, should know the Manning family, as well."

Mendes's last words did not register on Neil. He had only heard the man say that Jessica had given him the cigar case. So that was why she had not come down to the ship to see him! That was the reason he had no word from her!

Abruptly he realized that Mendes was leaning toward him anxiously. "Are you all right, Lieutenant Dancer? You have suddenly gone very pale."

"I'll be fine," Neil said hoarsely. "I was wounded, you know, and I've probably overdone things today, what with all the excitement. I believe I will lie down for a bit. It has been a rather unusual day."

"Yes," Mendes said solemnly. "A day that I, for one, shall never forget."

That is true for me as well, Neil thought, as he made his way slowly to his blanket; but certainly not for the reason Mendes meant.

He lay down on his side, his back to the fire, despair sweeping over him. He tried to close his ears to the sounds of revelry around the fire.

He lay sleepless, a question repeating itself over and over in his mind. Why? Why had Jessica taken up with another man before he was even away from the docks of Tampa?

After a long time, in the deep darkness of the small hours, Neil fell into a restless, disturbed slumber.

He was dreaming, something painful and depressing, and then all at once, he was awake, as a soft touch on his shoulder aroused him from his fevered dream.

"Wha—? Who is it?"

"Shhh, Neil," a soft voice whispered in his ear. "You were calling out a name in your sleep. Are you in pain?"

Neil, recognizing Margarita's voice, relaxed and lay back. "Margarita," he whispered, "I'm sorry if I disturbed you. I was dreaming, I guess."

She sighed. "Thank the saints! I was afraid that you were in pain and that the fever had come back."

Oh, I'm in pain right enough, he thought bitterly; but it's not anything that nursing can help me with.

"You called out a woman's name, Neil. Who is it? Your woman you left behind in the United States, were you dreaming of her?"

It was a moment before he answered. "Yes, a woman I knew in Tampa."

"That is not good," she said sympathetically. "Men in battle are far away from their women. It is difficult, I know."

This time he did not answer. What could he say? If he spoke at all, it would be of Jessica's betrayal, and he could not share that with another person.

And then he felt rather than saw her lie down beside him. In the torment of the dream and the sticky heat, he had removed all his clothes but his undergarments. From the feel of her body next to his, he realized that she was also wearing very little, a sleeping shift made of some coarse material. His first reaction was embarrassment, which increased as he became even more aware of her supple, warm body so close to his.

She felt his forehead with cool fingers. "You are a little warm, Neil. Are you certain you are all right?"

At the soft question Neil felt something in him give way, and he turned, and she was in his arms. He expected resistance, perhaps even an outcry, but after a startled jump, she lay still. He buried his face in the softness of her full breasts. Neil did not even realize that he was weeping until he felt her hand stroking the back of his head and heard her murmuring, "There, there," as she might to a hurt child.

Somehow the maternal embrace began to change into something else. He never knew exactly how it came about, but all at once her warm lips were against his, and he was pressing her body to him fiercely, feeling the soft cushions of her breasts flatten against his chest, the heat of her lower body firm against the thrust of his aroused manhood.

He heard himself speaking her name over and over, like some magical chant, "Margarita, Margarita!" Somehow, there was a comfort in the sound of her name. He sensed that he could find some kind of solace, some kind of charm against the pain and despair that gripped him. He still expected her to resist at some point; but she continued to return his kisses with mounting fervor, and her hands stroked his body, one coming to rest on his tumescence.

In a kind of blind frenzy, he pulled the single garment over her head, and then their bodies, bare of any clothing, came together in the ultimate embrace. She muttered words in his ear, in Spanish, but their meaning was clear.

He had no idea of how long they made love, it seemed to go on and on, but the sky was growing pale in the east when she finally pulled away from him. She slipped the discarded garment over her head, kissed him gently, and whispered, "You will sleep now, Neil."

Then she was gone, and Neil slept—a healing sleep, with no nightmares to plague him.

Chapter Fifteen

JESSICA stared with little pleasure at the beautiful blue gown spread out upon her bed.

Made by the best dressmaker in Tampa, it was in the height of fashion, and, Jessica knew, was very becoming, yet somehow such things did not matter now.

It was the eve of the ball to raise funds for the fire victims of Ybor City, and all of Jessica's friends were wound tight with anticipation and excitement, yet she felt nothing. She knew that her mother was worried about her and disappointed that her daughter did not show more enthusiasm for the social event of the year; but how could she when things were as they were? Yes, it was the night of the grand ball —the first really exciting thing to happen since the troops sailed for Cuba—and she was attending with a young man she scarcely knew, one of the many soldiers who still remained in Tampa.

Listlessly she sat down at her dressing table and stared at her reflection in the mirror. She looked too thin, she knew, and despite the slight touch of rouge she had borrowed from her mother, her face was pale, her eyes seeming too large and the shadows under them too blue.

She thought, Neil, where are you? Are you alive? Or lying wounded somewhere in the Cuban jungle?

It might have been better if her full memory had *not* returned, then she would have only Ramon to worry about. But on that day when Ramon had told her that he was going to Cuba, when she had felt so strongly that she had heard those words before, that something was nudging her mind, trying to surface—on that day she had returned home and retired, with a terrible headache, to her bedroom.

Her mother had fussed around her, clucking, then had given her a headache powder. Jessica had fallen into a deep sleep and had not awakened until late the next morning.

When she had awakened, she had remembered everything. It came to her like a revelation, a terrible, blinding revelation. She remembered Neil, the sailboat, the night spent on the island; she recalled everything in vivid detail. And Neil was gone, without a word from her!

She had heard from friends how the ships had not sailed for several days, how sweethearts and wives had sent notes and gifts on board to their loved ones, and how they had sometimes been able to wave and call to them from the wharf. What must poor Neil have thought when he received no word from her! How he must have felt!

And Ramon Mendes? After what had happened between her and Neil, how could she possibly have felt a strong attraction to another man?

Now, before finishing getting dressed for the ball, Jessica pressed her hands to her abdomen, thinking of Neil and what had occurred on the island. She had just had her monthly, which had greatly relieved her mind, for ever since regaining her memory, in the back of her mind had been a tight knot of fear. Despite her brave words to Neil that morning on the beach, she had felt panic. What if she *had* been with child? What would she do? How could she face her parents and friends?

But now that worry, at least, was behind her.

"Jessica!" Her mother's voice floated up the stairwell. "Jessica, are you almost ready? Your father is bringing the carriage around, and your escort will be here any minute."

Wearily Jessica walked to the door to call down. "Yes, Mother. I'll be ready in a few minutes."

Already dressed except for her ball gown, she lifted the fragile fabric from the bed and slipped the garment over her head, thankful that the bodice buttoned in front.

Facing the mirror again, she studied her image as she fastened the tiny pearl buttons. You should be here with me tonight, Neil, she thought; it should be *you* I will be dancing with, it should be you!

A tear formed in the corner of her eye, and she wiped it away angrily, suddenly weary of her own unhappiness and malaise. Besides, it would not help matters to go downstairs red-eyed and miserable. It would only make her parents unhappy and would certainly solve nothing. She had given them enough worries. No, she must try to put on a good face and pretend to be interested, at least, in the ball.

She had tried to get in touch with Neil, sending him several letters of explanation, pouring out her love. Of course there was no way to know if he had received them, and it was too soon to expect a reply. She had even thought of going to Cuba in search of him, but she knew how appalled her parents would be at such a suggestion. But there *must* be some way to—

"Jessica, the young man is here!"

Gathering up her gloves and fan, Jessica took one last look at herself in the mirror, then hurried to the stairs, managing a smile.

The Mendes house was bustling. Ynez Mendes, resplendent in black silk, a high comb in her elaborately piled hair, was adjusting her fringed shawl; and Felix Mendes, dignified and erect in his black evening clothes, looked, Maria thought, like an old-world aristocrat.

In her room, as she struggled with her own dress—a lovely gown of white lace, with a tiered skirt, tight-fitting bodice, and a wide ruffle that framed the shoulders and bosom and fell just below the elbows—she thought how amazing it was, what clothes could do.

"There!" she said in satisfaction. The dress was adjusted properly at last.

The image in the mirror told her that she looked very well. The white lace made her olive skin glow in contrast, and the red rose in her hair was the only other touch of color.

She was attending the ball with Tom Farrel, and she was looking forward to it with giddy anticipation, although she felt a few pangs of guilt about this whenever she chanced to think of Carlos.

Since Carlos had left, with Ramon and Eduardo, there had been no word from them. The newspapers had been carefully reporting the progress of the war, but rarely were individual names mentioned. Maria had lain in bed, night after night, wondering where Carlos was, and if he was safe. Still, she had been seeing the American lieutenant frequently, and she enjoyed his company enormously, a situation that distressed her mother a great deal.

"You should not be seeing this man, Maria. It is not proper," Ynez Mendes had said disapprovingly. "He is not one of us. You have Carlos, a wonderful man, and one of your own kind. What do you want with this American?"

Maria had attempted to explain that Tom Farrel was just a friend, that he was a good man, and that his company was pleasant, and that he provided her with the companionship she needed.

Her mother had snorted scornfully. "Just a friend! Yes, you may think so, but I have seen this man's eyes when he looks at you. He thinks of you as much more than a friend, you can be sure of that, my foolish daughter. And *that* can only mean trouble."

Her father had been present, and strangely, had voiced no objections to the friendship. "We are Americans now," he had said sternly. "We should get acquainted with more people, people outside of Ybor City."

As for herself, Maria had mixed feelings about the growing friendship. Was it dangerous, as Mama claimed? How did she really feel about Tom? And how did she feel about Carlos?

She sloughed off such doubts. Tonight, she was going to forget about such concerns. Tonight, she was going to simply enjoy herself, enjoy the moment.

Her mother bustled into the room in a cloud of perfume, her round, pretty face aglow. "Maria, are you ready? Your father is anxious to leave. He says that the streets will be crowded."

Smiling, Maria gave her mother a hug and a kiss. "Yes, *Mamacita,* I am ready. And you look beautiful!"

Her mother's cheeks glowed pink, but her eyes sparkled at the compliment. "You talk crazy, my daughter. It is *you* who are beautiful. I can only hope that this American soldier appreciates how fortunate he is to be escorting such a lovely woman. But if Carlos were here. . . ."

"Mama," Maria said gravely, "Carlos is *not* here, and I am not married to him, not even betrothed. I have given no answer to his proposal."

"Just the same," her mother said stubbornly, "he has asked for your hand, and surely you will accept." Her face grew sad. "I wonder how they are tonight, our boys? I wonder if they have enough to eat, if they are wounded, if they are lonely?"

Maria put her arm around her mother's plump shoulders. "Mama, Mama, do not think of this tonight. Our prayers are with them, they are in the hands of God. Tonight, think of yourself and Papa, and have a nice time. Ramon and Eduardo would want you to do this. Believe me."

Ynez Mendes brightened, patting Maria's cheek. "You are a good daughter, Maria. You have a good heart, and now we had better go, before Papa gets cross. Mrs. Cruz is here to watch over Paulo, and the soldier is already here, waiting in the parlor." She made a sour face. "He is prompt, that one. It is not proper, for a caller to be so early."

Laughing, Maria took her mother's arm and swept her out of the room.

In his room at the hotel, Brill Kroger was having trouble adjusting

176 Patricia Matthews

his tie properly. His fingers seemed uncoordinated, and he was trembling slightly. Tonight was the night, the culmination of all his efforts. Tonight would make up for all the trouble, all the money he had laid out, the anger caused by Jessica Manning's rejection, and the humiliation of the scene with Maria Mendes in this very room.

Funds had been pouring in, and the money was downstairs in a strongbox in the hotel manager's office, just waiting for him. His bag was packed, his getaway plans were carefully made, and everything was in readiness.

He had arranged it so that he would count the money personally, soon after the ball got underway. Then he had promised to announce to the assembled guests that exact amount taken in. He had "generously" stated that he would need no one to help him count it, for he did not want anyone else to have to miss the ball. In actuality, matters would proceed somewhat differently. Of course, before he supposedly counted the money, he would make a token appearance in the ballroom, and *that* appearance would be the last anyone in Tampa would ever see of Brill Kroger, for after collecting the money he would leave quickly, before anyone had time to become suspicious.

And when he made his token appearance, before he vanished with the money, he planned to ask Maria Mendes to dance—she could hardly refuse him in front of her family and friends without creating a scene—and when he had her in his arms. . . .

He laughed, too loudly, staring at himself in the mirror. Yes, indeed! First the Cuban wench, and then the haughty Miss Jessica Manning!

He continued to laugh as he finished arranging the tie. After that, with all his debts paid, his injured pride soothed, he and the money would leave, to be seen no more.

Kroger had changed his mind about going directly to New York, particularly after the death of Dulcy Thomas. If her body was discovered and if she was ever connected to him, things might get uncomfortable for him. So, he had decided to go first to Mexico, for the American police had no jurisdiction there; and he had been told that a man could disappear there for years, if necessary.

Also, he had heard some stories while in Tampa, of a town called Mérida, on the Yucatán peninsula, near which were the ruins of an ancient Mayan city.

Kroger cared very little for ruins, or for history, but the stories stated that outside the ancient city was a kind of holy well, where the Indians once made sacrifices to their gods in the form of gold and jewels. This tale intrigued Kroger, and since his informant had also told him that Mérida was a pleasant town, he had decided to go there.

If the police, or the Pinkertons, should manage to get on his trail, somehow learning that he was headed for Mexico, they would expect him to head for Vera Cruz, which was a more likely destination. Living in Mérida, Kroger had heard, was cheap and easy, and the señoritas were beautiful and hot-blooded. He grinned savagely at the thought.

He might even spend six months in Mérida, if he liked it. He could afford it after tonight, he thought, and he deserved a long, relaxing vacation. If it turned out to be profitable, so much the better. The night before, he had traced out his route on a map, which was now tucked away in his bag. Also, he had stolen a steam yacht, one sturdy enough to take him across the Gulf, and had it hidden away where he could reach it easily, later that evening. The yacht's owner was away, so the craft would not be missed for a spell.

Satisfied with his appearance, Kroger went downstairs and to the ballroom. The orchestra was just striking up a waltz, and the well-dressed Tampans were moving out onto the polished dance floor.

Kroger paused just inside the entrance, studying them. They were obviously enjoying themselves. He smiled secretively. Let them, let them enjoy themselves while they could; there would be little joy later, when they discovered the money missing.

As he gazed about for the Mendes family, several people stopped to talk to him, congratulating him for arranging such a gala affair. He was cordial and dignified, accepting the compliments graciously, as befitted the man who had conceived and organized the ball, but his glance kept sweeping over the crowd for the sight of Maria.

And then he saw her. She was dancing with a young officer. Kroger went tense as he recognized the Rough Rider—the insolent young pup who had defied him the night he had accosted Maria for the second time. Too bad there was no way he could pay *him* back for his arrogance. But first things first. When the dance ended, he would approach Maria. He decided that it would be best to wait until her escort led her back to her parents before making his move, so that it would be even more difficult for her to refuse him.

The dance seemed to go on forever, but finally the last note faded away, and there was a pause, while the musicians arranged their music for the next dance.

Just as Maria and the lieutenant approached the spot where her parents were seated, Kroger made his way over, walking quickly, so that he reached the place just as Maria and her partner did.

Kroger bowed slightly, pleased by the sudden blaze of anger in the girl's dark eyes. She was looking uncommonly pretty tonight, in a lacy white gown that set her off to an advantage. Virginal white, he thought, barely restraining a sneer. Well, if she was a virgin, which he strongly doubted, she would be no longer, not after he was finished with her!

"Miss Mendes," he said suavely. "How lovely you look this evening. And you as well, Señora Mendes. Yes, indeed!"

Maria only nodded, but Ynez Mendes smiled broadly. "Gracias, Señor Kroger. The ball is going well. Everyone, it seems, is here. We must have taken in much money."

Kroger smiled. "Yes, indeed, señora, and I will be going to count the proceeds shortly so that later in the evening I may announce the exact amount. But first, with your permission, I should like to ask your lovely daughter for a dance." He turned to Maria. "May I, Miss Mendes?"

Maria's face flushed, and her eyes gave off sparks. She glanced sidelong at her escort, who was frowning, then at her mother, who gestured sharply. Maria nodded reluctant consent.

Good! It was as he had thought. She did not want to create a scene before her parents.

The orchestra struck up another waltz, and Kroger took Maria into his arms and moved with her out onto the floor. Her body was stiff and unyielding in his arms, but that was all right. Soon, she would be at his mercy, and she would be only too happy to yield to his desires before he was finished with her!

Slowly, as they danced, neither speaking, Kroger edged her nearer and nearer to the opposite side of the ballroom, close to the doors opening onto the veranda. When they were at the very edge of the dancers, he suddenly grasped Maria's hand and hauled her through the open doors.

Before she had time to protest or cry out, they were outside, in the semidarkness, where only a few couples stood talking or holding hands in the shadows. Once outside, Kroger took the knife from his belt and placed the point against her back, his own body shielding his action from anyone else. Maria flinched, crying out.

"Quiet, slut!" He increased the pressure on the knife point. "You will keep moving, Maria, and you will keep your mouth shut, or I will slip this knife in between your shoulder blades. Do you understand me?"

Maria nodded mutely, and he hustled her down the steps and along the side of the hotel. As he hurried her along, Maria whispered furiously, "You won't get away with this! Papa will make you pay!"

He laughed gloatingly. "I said, be quiet! And I won't pay for anything, don't worry. It's you who's going to pay, and dearly, for humiliating me. I will soon be long gone, and no one, including your precious papa, will ever find me. Yes, indeed!"

They were near the back of the hotel now, and Kroger pushed Maria ahead of him through a side entrance. There was no one in sight, and quickly he forced her to the stairs, up to the second floor, and to his room.

Once inside, the door bolted, he gave her a mighty shove, sending her tumbling onto the bed. As she started to scramble up, he sat astride her body and held the knife to her throat with one hand while with his other hand, he stuffed his handkerchief into her mouth.

It took only a few minutes more to finish gagging her and to bind her hands behind her back. Then he sat back, and with sadistic enjoyment, he inserted the knife under the bodice of her gown and slowly drew it toward him, splitting the white garment as he might the skin of a fruit. Maria's eyes were huge, alive with blazing anger.

He smiled down into her eyes and turned his gaze to the flesh he was exposing. He chortled as he saw her skin crawl away from the icy blade of the knife. When the dress was split to the nexus of her thighs, he reached down and ripped her undergarments, exposing her body to his burning gaze.

He stared into her eyes again and was pleased to see alarm in them now. She began to struggle, and he laughed harshly, feeling her rear between his thighs. Oh, this was going to be grand! It was going to be the height of pleasure; and when he was done with her, he still had the Manning bitch to look forward to. Kroger had no fears that he would be equal to the task. He had waited too long.

Maria was weeping softly now and gagging against the handkerchief stuffed in her mouth. Slowly Kroger unbuttoned his trousers, raising up so that she could observe as he released his swollen organ. He roared with laughter as her struggles redoubled.

"Now is the moment, Maria," he said hoarsely, leaning forward to tweak one of her nipples cruelly between thumb and forefinger. "Now is the moment that I have been waiting for for so long. Now is the time that you pay the price for flaunting me!"

The sound of lilting music could be heard even as the Manning carriage clattered down the driveway before the hotel, and the lights could be seen for miles.

The hotel, Jessica thought, was at its best tonight; and despite her depression, she experienced a sense of pleasure at its beauty and a small throb of anticipation. It had only been a short time since the last ball, but it seemed as if an eternity had passed. She felt so much older, so much wearier. It sounded strange to her and rather sad, that she would never again be the same girl who had gone so blithely to the hotel the night of the officers' ball. That girl seemed so young now, so naive, and so innocent. Had her friends changed, too?

And Dulcy Thomas, where was she tonight? Although Jessica had never really cared that much for Dulcy, tonight, in her present melancholy mood, she felt somehow sorry for the missing young woman. Was she all right? Had she just run off with someone on an impulse? There were stories circulating that many of the soldiers were deserting. Maybe Dulcy had gone off with one. Or had something happened to her, something much worse?

"Isn't the hotel lovely tonight?" Her mother's voice broke into Jessica's reverie. She smiled wanly in answer and nodded, then included her escort, Don Powers, in the smile. He sat by her side, stiff and nervous.

And then they were pulling up at the entrance and then were inside, among the music and the dazzling lights and the bright colors; and Jessica was dancing with Don Powers and, to her astonishment, enjoying herself.

As they whirled around the floor—Don was an excellent dancer—she smiled at her friends as they sailed past her with their own partners.

And there was Maria Mendes, looking lovely in a white lace gown, dancing with, of all people, Brill Kroger. Although Jessica nodded to her, Maria did not appear to see her. She looked absolutely furious, and Jessica surmised that she was dancng with Kroger out of mere politeness.

I hope he doesn't ask me to dance, Jessica thought. She vowed to do her best to stay out of his way. To think that she had once found him attractive! It was just another example of how much she had changed in the past few weeks.

Then the music ended, and Don Powers escorted her back to the row of chairs on the sidelines; they arrived at the same time as her parents, who had been dancing also.

Anne Manning looked flushed and radiant. Her cheeks were pink, and she was smiling, and Jessica's father looked proud and happy to have her on his arm.

They were scarcely seated—Jessica was just opening her fan so that she might dry some of the perspiration she could feel on her face—when she heard someone call her father's name.

She looked in the direction of the voice and saw Bart Dolan, Tampa's chief of police, making his way toward them. In the doorway to the ballroom stood three more policemen in their uniforms.

Wyngate Manning got to his feet. "Why, Chief Dolan, what brings you here in uniform? I thought you would be attending as a guest."

Chief Dolan's red face was forbidding. He said grimly, "So did I, Mr. Manning, so did I. But something came up earlier this evening that changed all that."

He aimed a rather abashed look at Jessica and her mother, then took Wyngate Manning by the arm and led him aside.

Jessica, her curiosity piqued, attempted to overhear what they were saying, but the music and the babble of conversation made it impossible.

In a few minutes Wyngate Manning, his face somber, came back to them. In a low voice he said, "I'll be back shortly. I must accompany Chief Dolan for a little while."

Jessica wanted to ask why, but the set look on his face warned her to keep quiet.

She watched thoughtfully as her father and Chief Dolan walked away. "What do you suppose that was all about, Mother?"

Anne Manning shook her head, but her expression was puzzled. "I have no idea, dear, but I hardly think it was good news, from your father's expression." And then, as the music started up again, she added, "Go on now, you and Mr. Powers dance and have a good time. I'm sure it's nothing to worry about."

But it was something to worry about. If true, it was too horrible to contemplate, Wyngate Manning thought, as he followed the police chief around the crowd of dancers, toward the other officers across the ballroom.

There had to be some mistake! Brill Kroger could not have been involved in a thing like this! The story Chief Dolan had told him was simply incomprehensible.

The police chief had told him they had found the body of Dulcy Thomas late that afternoon, buried in a shallow grave in the pines near the beach. Young Toby Simpson had been hunting in the woods with his old dog, Blue. The dog had started digging into a pile of leaves and would not stop, no matter how much Toby yelled at him. When Toby finally went to investigate what was so interesting to the old dog, he had seen a partly decomposed hand protruding from the soil and had rushed off to alert the police of his find.

When the body was fully uncovered, it had proved to be that of Dulcy Thomas. Wyngate Manning cringed away from the thought of what condition the body must have been in, after all this time. Chief Dolan had told him that the body had been nude, but all of her clothing and her little velvet bag had been buried with her.

They probably never would have found out who had left her there, Chief Dolan explained, except for the small leather book found in her purse, which her murderer evidently had not seen, or else he had not realized its importance.

The little book was Dulcy's diary, and in it they had found a complete record of her relationshp with Brill Kroger, including a final notation that she was seeing him, in his hotel room, the very day she disappeared.

Chief Dolan had finished his grim tale by saying, "I came to see you, Mr. Manning, because I understand you are acquainted with this Kroger. He arranged this ball, did he not?"

"Yes, Chief Dolan." Wyngate Manning's mind was numb with shock. "I simply can't believe this about Kroger."

Chief Dolan looked at him grimly. "Believe it, Mr. Manning. We have the proof, certainly enough to question him. He knew this Thomas girl was missing, and he had an assignation with her that day. If he has nothing to hide, why didn't he come forward with this information? Have you seen him tonight?"

Wyngate Manning said heavily, "Yes, just a short while ago. He was on the dance floor with the Mendes girl."

Now, at the entrance to the ballroom, Chief Dolan said, "Well, he doesn't seem to be around at the moment."

A sudden chill caused Wyngate Manning to shiver. "You don't suppose? . . ."

The chief's voice was flat. "I don't know, but we'd better find out his room number and hasten up there."

"I know the number, Chief Dolan. It's two-fourteen."

The first knock on the door was light, and Kroger, engrossed in what he was doing, only heard it as a distant, annoying distraction. The second knock was louder, more demanding, and he froze, just on the verge of penetration. He drew back from Maria, looking back over his shoulder at the door. Who the hell could it be?

And then the knock came again, this time accompanied by a loud, commanding voice. "Brill Kroger, are you in there? Kroger!"

Kroger's lust died abruptly, as a cold premonition jolted him. Whoever it was, it did not bode well for him. The voice rang with authority, and that meant that something had gone wrong.

Hastily he scrambled off Maria's recumbent body; his only thought now was for the money in the manager's office and his own safety. He scooped up his trousers and stepped into them.

The voice beyond the door thundered, "Brill Kroger! This is the police! If you're in there, open this door, or we're breaking it down! Do you hear me?"

Kroger was already halfway to the closet, fastening his trousers as he hurried. He grabbed his coat, hat and bag, which he had previously packed. His fingers shook as he fumbled in his pocket for the small tool that he used to jimmy locks. Finding it, he turned to the door that connected with the adjoining room, which was used to turn the two rooms into a suite when the need arose.

"All right, Kroger, we're coming in!" The hall door shuddered as something crashed against it.

Thank God, Kroger thought, that I had the presence of mind to bolt it.

There! The connecting door was unlocked. Now if his luck held, the adjoining room would be empty. Hurriedly he opened the door and stepped through, heaving a sigh of relief when he saw that the room was unoccupied. He closed the door behind him and locked it, just as he heard the sound of a heavy body again striking the hall door to his own room.

Moving on tiptoe to the door, he waited, his hand on the knob until, after several more shuddering blows, he heard his own room door crash inward. Then, as the policemen rushed into his room, Kroger cracked the door and peered out. The hallway was empty. He burst out into the corridor, running toward the stairs.

He did not look behind him, but he could hear the sound of loud voices as the police were no doubt discovering the bound Maria Mendes.

His luck continued to hold—there was no one in the corridor or on the stairs. He hurried down the stairs, taking them two at a time. On the main floor, he used the back way to the manager's office.

Kroger knew that he did not have much time. As soon as they released the girl, she would tell them how he had escaped, and they would be in full cry, searching the hotel thoroughly. He had to be quick; the money, his freedom, perhaps even his life, depended on his haste.

Outside the hotel manager's office, he stopped to catch his breath. There was an armed guard inside, with the strongbox, but he would be no problem. The man knew Kroger was due to count the proceeds of the ball, so there would be no difficulty getting into the room. The problem would be getting rid of the guard so that he could flee with the money.

However, Kroger had taken that into consideration. He fumbled in his carpetbag for the thick stocking, which he had filled beforehand with coarse sand. Placing his bag alongside the door in the hall, he rapped on the door three times—the prearranged signal.

A deep voice inside boomed out, "Yes?"

"It's Brill Kroger. I've come to count the money."

"Right you are, Mr. Kroger," the voice rumbled. "Been expecting you."

The man who opened the door was tall and beefy, with a red-veined face and faded blue eyes. He held a double-barreled shotgun in the crook of his arm. In Kroger's opinion, the man was a little stupid, which was all to the good.

The guard beamed at Kroger. "Come on in. Guess the folks are anxious to know how much we took in."

Kroger nodded. "Yes, indeed. Now, if you'll just fetch the strongbox for me."

"Sure enough," the guard said, placing the shotgun on the manager's desk. "Got it right here in the cupboard."

As the big man bent down to open the cupboard doors, Kroger brought the sand-filled stocking out from behind his back, and holding it in both hands, he raised it high and slammed it down against the back of the guard's head. The man grunted, then sighed, and fell forward onto his face.

Kroger quickly rolled the limp form aside and pulled out the strongbox. Fortunately, he had the key in his possession. Once opened, the box revealed several stacks of bills, as well as a number of checks. Ignoring the checks, Kroger, after retrieving his bag from the hall, began stuffing the money into it.

The money all collected, Kroger left the office and began making his way down the hall toward the rear of the hotel, hoping that he would meet no one along the way. His heart was pounding wildly. He knew that they would be searching the hotel by this time, and he wanted to be outside before the search reached the ground floor.

His hope was in vain. He was halfway down the hall when he heard the sound of pounding feet and loud voices coming toward him. Damn, they were already on this floor! he thought. Panic nibbled at the edges of his mind. He must not be stopped now! But which way could he turn?

The footsteps and voices were coming closer, and Kroger knew that the police would be in the corridor before he could slip out the side entrance. Trying to keep his head despite the mounting panic, he retreated down the hall until he could hear the sounds of music and merriment. He opened a door and found himself in a small salon just off the ballroom. The only way out now without retracing his steps was through the ballroom and to the veranda beyond. That was impossible! He had no hope of getting through the ballroom, carrying a satchel, without arousing suspicions.

As he stood in the empty salon, breathing heavily, a sudden thought came to him. Impossible? Perhaps not. Quickly he removed his hat and threw it aside. Opening the carpetbag, he began stuffing the money into his pockets. When he had it all distributed about his person as evenly as he could, he hesitated over the bag. No, he had no choice—he had to leave it behind. But he did take his knife from the bag and stuck it in his belt.

Drawing a deep breath, he opened the door into the ballroom. The sound of music and chattering voices came at him in waves. He began to make his way through the crowd, his head down; he attracted no notice, as far as he could tell. The feeling of panic began to recede. He was going to make it!

And then, from across the ballroom, he heard a shout: "Stop that man! Brill Kroger, halt in the name of the law!"

Whirling about, he saw people stopping in their tracks to stare at him fearfully. Shocked and indecisive, they seemed not to know what to do. Past the dancers, Kroger could see uniformed men trying to make their way toward him.

Kroger began pushing his way through the crowd, knocking people aside, and panic again threatened to engulf him. Then he saw her, standing a few feet away, staring at him wide-eyed—Jessica Manning!

A wave of anger and hate struck him at the sight of her. It was her fault, she was to blame for the predicament he was in! The illogic of this conclusion did not occur to him, for in that instant he saw the way out for him. A hostage! That was the solution. He would take Jessica hostage, and then they would not dare come after him.

Jerking the knife from his waistband, he was on her in an instant. Her escort tried to bar Kroger's way, but Kroger knocked the man aside with a savage swipe of his hand and then seized Jessica by the wrist. He pulled her against him, turning her so that her body was between himself and the advancing policemen. He touched the knife point to her neck.

"Stand back!" he snarled. "There's a knife against her neck. Stand back, or I'll kill her!"

The policemen skidded to a stop, and those dancers close to Kroger drew back. Then the policemen began moving toward him again.

Kroger raised his voice. "Stand away! I mean what I say. If any of you takes another step toward me, the girl dies!"

As he talked, Kroger began backing toward the veranda doors, open to the night air, pulling Jessica along with him. At his command the police again stopped their advance; and then Kroger was on the veranda, facing several startled people.

"Stand aside and let me through. If anyone tries to interfere or tries to follow me, I'll kill her. I have nothing to lose."

Everyone scrambled out of his path. In his peripheral vision Kroger noticed faces in all the open doorways and windows, but no one made a move toward him as he slowly backed down the steps and to the driveway.

A few moments more, and they were in the shadows of the trees. Over the sound of his own rasping breath, Kroger heard a shout ring out. "After them!"

Another voice rose in a frantic plea. "No, you fools! He has my daughter. He'll kill my daughter! He's already killed once!"

Kroger laughed with glee. It was working! Jessica, stumbling and dazed with fear, was slowing him down; he was almost dragging her. He considered leaving her when he reached the edge of the hotel property, but then he thought better of it. She would still be protection for him if the pursuit got too close; and besides, he had not yet had his vengeance upon her. Taking her at his leisure would make up for the aborted attempt on Maria. Yes, Jessica would accompany him, all the way.

The sounds faded behind them as Kroger ran, hauling Jessica with him, across the hotel grounds. His mind was working coolly now, as smooth and easy as a well-oiled machine. He could not hear any sounds of pursuit now; evidently they believed his threat and were not willing to risk the girl's life. All he had to do was make it to the place where he had left the boat.

He had originally planned to drive his hired carriage to the dock area, but that was out of the question now. Perhaps he would come across a carriage on the road that he could seize. If not, they could make their way on foot. It was not all that far. He grew increasingly confident of making good his escape.

He snapped at Jessica, "You're holding me back, damn you! If you want to live, you'll do exactly what I tell you. Do you understand?"

He brandished the knife, moonlight glinting wickedly off the blade. He heard her breath catch, but she slowly nodded and said in a despairing whisper, "What are you going to do to me?"

"Oh, I have plans for you, my dear," he said gloatingly. "Great plans for you, Jessica Manning. But I'll wait and let you find out for yourself." He touched the point of the knife delicately to her cheek, and she cringed back. "You just do as I say, understand?"

"Yes, yes!"

"Good, good."

And indeed it was good, for now he was in full command again. He had the money, and he had at least one of the women who had humiliated him. Yes, indeed, his luck had turned at last. He was going to make it!

Chapter Sixteen

MARIA, wrapped in her mother's shawl, sat as close to Ynez Mendes as she could get and allowed her mother to hold her and fuss over her, as she had not done since Maria was a child.

As the buggy moved briskly toward home, Maria began to shake. Now that the danger was past, she felt more frightened than she had at the time of the incident. During Kroger's assault, she had been so incensed that she had not had time to be really frightened. Now that she thought of it, thought of Kroger's hateful body astride hers, thought of the cold blade of the knife against her skin and the mad look in his eyes, she shuddered in horror and fright.

Her mother murmured tearfully, "*Pobrecita, mi cariño.*"

"I'm all right, Mama. Really I am. I was fortunate. Think of poor Jessica Manning." Maria shuddered uncontrollably, again. Jessica, in the hands of that madman! Dear God! What would he do to her? Where was he taking her? For a moment Maria was glad that Ramon was not here. She knew something of what he felt toward the American girl; and if he was here, he would probably do something rash.

"I feel so sorry for her parents," Maria said. "Did you see their faces?"

Ynez Mendes nodded somberly, sneaking a quick look at her husband's rigid back as he sat in the driver's seat, flicking the reins at the horse. "I saw your father's face, too, when he learned they had found you in that man's room. Tied up, and naked for the world to see!"

"But I wasn't harmed, Mama. Not really, except perhaps my pride and dignity."

Ynez Mendes shook her head dolefully. "Still, there is the shame of it! Papa will never forgive that. If the man had not fled, your father would have killed him. And yes, the poor *gringa's* parents. Her father must feel the same way as Papa. But how will they ever find them? Who knows where he has gone with her? Oh, he is an evil man, that one! And to think we trusted him."

"There is no denying that he is evil, Mama. I always thought that

he. . . . But no matter." Maria gestured tiredly. "We can only hope
that the police find him, and Jessica, before it is too late for her."

Wyngate Manning held his weeping wife in his arms. He himself
was dry-eyed, despite the pain and helpless rage that consumed him.

The police had followed Kroger and Jessica at a safe distance, fearful of getting too close; and they were fairly certain that Kroger had
headed toward the docks, where he must have had a boat waiting.
The coast guard had been notified, but so far there had been no trace
of a boat, or of Kroger and Jessica.

Wyngate Manning burned to join in the hunt himself, but he knew
that would place an unbearable burden on his wife; and he could not
do that, certainly not when she was in the condition she was in at present. Still, the man must be caught and made to pay for what he had
done to Dulcy Thomas, for the theft of the money, and for the outrage
he had been about to inflict on the Mendes girl. And of course, Jessica. He could not bear to think about what might be happening to his
daughter. All he could do was pray that God, in his infinite mercy,
would look after her and protect her.

What made it even harder for Wyngate Manning to bear was the
part he had played in it all. He had trusted Brill Kroger, taken him
into his confidence and into his home. How could he have been so
blind as to completely misread the man's nefarious character?

The return trip from Cuba was a dreary one for Neil, despite the
fact that the war was all but over and the fact that he was free to
return home; his honorable discharge from the Rough Riders was
pending.

His shoulder was almost healed, but it still twinged and pulled occasionally, graphically reminding him that he was not yet quite the
man he had been when he left Tampa, and he could not get into the
festive mood that was affecting the other men who were returning
with him.

The group of returnees was made up almost entirely of wounded,
and although some of them ranted against a fate that had knocked
them out of the war, most of them were simply glad to be alive and
returning home.

For Neil, the war had lost whatever patina of glory it might have
possessed in the beginning. He had seen too much inefficiency and

just plain stupidity. He had seen too many men die, many of them without reason, to still think of battle as a glorious adventure.

And above all other considerations, there was Jessica. Meeting Ramon Mendes at the rebel camp and learning of the cigar case still had not completely convinced Neil of her perfidy. A part of his mind still hoped, and he still thought of her with love and longing. His nights were haunted with dreams of their time together on the island, and his days with memories of her face. After the first pain of the discovery of her apparent betrayal had worn off, he had decided that he would reserve final judgment until he saw her one more time. He was going back to Tampa first, in any event, so what did he have to lose? Perhaps he was wrong, perhaps there was an explanation.

But if she did care for Ramon Mendes, and not him. . . . Well, at least he would know beyond doubt.

She owed him an explanation at the very least, and by God, he was determined to get it!

Jessica, in the cabin of the yacht, tried to make herself as small as possible in one corner of the lower berth. She could literally not believe what was happening to her. It was too incredible, too impossible! She shook, as if from a chill, as she fought back the hysteria that threatened to overwhelm her.

Brill Kroger was on deck above, at the wheel of the boat. Jessica had no idea where they were headed, no idea of what he intended to do with her, and the suspense concerning this was almost worse than the fact that she had been abducted. And she was terrified of Kroger in a way that she would not have thought possible a short time before. Even though she had grown to distrust and dislike the man, he had possessed a certain polish, a veneer of gentility; but now that veneer was stripped away, and what she saw beneath it was terrifying.

His eyes, she thought; it's his eyes. They look quite mad.

Hugging herself against the chill of her fear, she wondered what her father and mother were doing. And the police, were they searching for her? Surely they must be. Hope began to conquer the fear. Yes, surely there were men out looking for her. Kidnapping, she knew, was a serious offense. And there must be other crimes involved as well, for Kroger had come running through the ballroom in flight; and there was the matter of Chief Dolan speaking privately with her father. Obviously Kroger had done something else, committed some other crime, and she had been a spur-of-the-moment thing. She had just happened to be in the wrong place, and he had seized her as a hostage to assure his escape.

All at once, she noticed that the boat was losing speed, and all of her fears and apprehensions flooded back. Where were they stopping and, more important, why? As long as Kroger was occupied piloting the boat, he was not bothering her. But what would take place once they were stopped?

The chug-chug of the motor grew slower and slower, and then there was a slight bump, as the bow of the boat nudged against something. The engine stopped, and the only sound was that of Kroger's footsteps on the deck, moving back and forth. In a little while came the sound she had been dreading—the thud of his footsteps coming down the ladder into the cabin.

Still shivering, Jessica drew back against the bulkhead as far as she could. Then he was standing in the middle of the cabin, his usually immaculate attire disordered, his hair awry; and strangely, he was smiling, and stranger still, the smile seemed real, not like the flashing show of white teeth that he usually affected.

"Well, we're safe now. I knew we'd make it!" he said jubilantly, looking at her as if he expected her to rejoice with him. "We're anchored in a little cove on one of the keys, and with all the plants around shielding us, no one will even suspect we're here. Even if they search the area, they will pass right by, unaware."

He took a step toward her, rubbed his hands together briskly, and his smile widened. "We'll stay here for a few days, until they've given up trying to find us, and then off to Mérida!"

Again, he looked at her, as if seeking her approval, and Jessica had the feeling that *she* was going mad. How could he speak to her this way, as if she were his accomplice? He had abducted her. He had threatened her with a knife. What reaction did he expect from her? How could he expect *approval* from her?

"You'll like it in Mérida," he said, coming closer, still smiling. And then, as he came close to the bunk where she was crouched, his expression altered, portraying a bewildering array of emotions. First, he looked puzzled, as if he were trying to remember something, and his gaze fixed on a spot above her head. Suddenly his eyes were upon her again, and now his expression was more like the one she was used to.

Leaning down, he reached for her arm and dragged her out from under the upper bunk, forcing her to stand upright, his powerful fingers digging into her arm until she winced.

"Ah, yes! Little Miss Jessica!" he said in a surprised tone, as if he had come upon her unexpectedly. "Yes, little Jessica, who is going to be one of my rewards. You have a lot to make up for, my dear, but I trust it won't be too unpleasant for you."

Pulling her to him, he dipped his head and pressed his mouth to hers, ignoring her attempts to escape. Feeling the loathsome touch of his lips, and his free hand in the small of her back, Jessica realized, belatedly, what his words had meant. Oh, no! Please God, no! She never hated anyone so much in her life.

Then, as his hand moved up her body and around to her breast, which he squeezed cruelly, a wave of despair swept over her. She managed to pull back in the circle of his arms, and she cried out in terror, "Mother!", as if her mother could hear her and come to her aid.

The instant she had uttered the word, Jessica realized how inane and childish it was; and yet, oddly enough, Kroger released her and stepped back. Again, his expression underwent a startling change. The hard, cruel light in his eyes faded, and he looked confused and somehow apprehensive.

When his eyes met hers, they held no trace of a threat. On the contrary, he was again smiling at her as if they were old friends.

"Come," he was saying, his voice gentle, "sit down and rest. You must be very tired." He led her to the bunk. As Jessica, more confused than ever, sat down, Kroger said happily, "Here, I'll show you just where we're going. You see, I have it all planned out, all traced on my map."

As he spoke, he began searching through his pockets, taking out packet after packet of money and dumping them onto the cabin table, humming to himself. "See all the money? There will be more than enough to keep us in comfort. . . ."

Jessica stared at the money in wonder. Where had he gotten it? And then, she knew. The money raised by the ball, Kroger had stolen it; that had been his plan all along. That had to be the reason the police had been after him.

"You'll like Mérida," he was going on. "We'll rent a small house, just large enough for the two of us. We'll stay there for a bit, and then we'll go to New York. That's the big time. I have big plans for New York. I'll have a bankroll large enough to really operate. You'll never know want again. You'll like New York. You can shop, and we can attend the theater together."

Jessica watched him, mystified. What on earth was he babbling about? One moment he appeared ready to rape her, and the next he was chatting away as if they were old and dear friends. A shiver ran down her spine, as she became more and more convinced that he was mad. What other explanation could there be for such behavior? Still, she preferred him this way to the other. Perhaps if she humored him. . . .

"That sounds very—" She almost choked on the words but managed to hurry on. "That sounds very nice."

He beamed at her. "I knew you'd like it!"

His pockets finally seemed to be empty of money, but he continued to search through them, a puzzled look on his face. "I can't seem to find my map. I can't understand what happened to it. Well, no matter." He shrugged. "I remember everything. I told you I had it all planned, yes, indeed."

Leaving the money scattered about on the table, he sat down beside her on the bunk. She shrank back from him but as he showed no indication of wanting to touch her, she relaxed a little.

"Mérida is a pretty little town, I understand. Yucatán is pretty much separated from the rest of Mexico. If they learn, by some chance, that we're headed toward Mexico, they'll expect us to land at Vera Cruz, not Yucatán. So we'll be safe, and we'll be all alone at last. Just you and me, and I'll have enough money so that you won't have to have *friends* ever again. I'll take care of you."

He was staring at her as if expecting an answer, and Jessica, searching her mind frantically for a suitable response, had not the least idea what he was talking about. She finally said what seemed to be the safest thing: "No, I won't need any other friends."

She was relieved to see that she had apparently given the right answer, for his smile widened, and his usually saturnine countenance suddenly appeared vulnerable and much younger.

Before she realized what was happening, he had thrown himself forward so that his face was cradled in her lap. He seemed to be laughing and crying, both at once, and he mumbled something that she could not quite make out.

Completely at a loss, Jessica did not know what to do, and then he raised his tear-wet face for a moment and stared into her eyes. "Oh, Mother," he said in a broken voice. "Mother, I've waited so long for you to say that!"

Mother? *Mother?* Jessica could only stare at him, dumbfounded.

*   *   *

Kroger left Jessica resting in the cabin and went back up on deck to complete the job of camouflaging the boat.

Everything was going according to plan, he thought. Even though things had started going sour right at the end, in Tampa, it was all turning out for the best. And Kroger was confident that everything would continue to go his way.

The only thing that he had lost, really, was his just revenge on Maria Mendes; but he *had* humiliated her, and perhaps that was sufficient.

He had been forced to leave his satchel behind, but that was no great loss. Clothing and personal articles could easily be replaced once they were in Mexico. He had saved what was important, the money, and of course *Her*.

His mind warmed pleasantly when he thought of *Her*. She was with him again, at long last, and he only now realized just how much he had missed her. He could not seem to recall just why she had gone away—his mind was hazy on that point—but at any rate, that did not matter now. Of course, there was something strange and troubling about the way she had changed, but he did not want to think about that, for thinking about it made his head hurt; and so his mind moved away from that line of thought.

It is better not to question some things, he thought; just accept them and be grateful.

He had been feeling so depressed, so pressured, at the hotel in Tampa. So many things had gone wrong, and he was not accustomed to things going wrong. But now it was all right again. It was as if something had broken away, floated free, and he felt fine—wonderful, in fact.

Maybe it's because *She* is with me, he thought; *She* always could make me feel good.

The small yacht was well concealed now, under three overhanging trees and high tropical grasses. There was plenty of food and drink, an abundance of fresh water on board. If matters proceeded as he hoped, they would not have to stay here longer than a few days. By that time, the search for him would have ended. Then it would be safe to leave, heading across the Gulf, and the coast of Yucatán.

Yes, things were turning out fine, yes, indeed!

Alvarado Moreno was feeling on top of the world. This was his lucky week, and no doubt about it. First of all, he had won on the cockfight on Monday—five dollars that he would not have to account for to his mother, as he did his pay envelope. Then Rosa Luza had said yes, she would go to the Saturday night dance with him. And now this, the best of all, a pleasant surprise!

Smiling broadly, Alvarado gazed at the items spread out upon his narrow bed. Two fine suits of clothes, a set of silver-backed brushes, and a silver-plated shaving mug, complete with brush and soap. Four white shirts, four pairs of silk hose, three pairs of underdrawers and undershirts, and four ties. An entire wardrobe! Of course, the sleeves of the coats and the trouser legs were too long for him, but the suits fit fairly well otherwise, and his mother could alter the suits in a few hours.

He had found the large carpetbag sitting in the small salon adjacent to the ballroom, the night of the big charity ball. It had no one's name on it, nor did any of the items inside identify the owner. Everybody was too upset by the theft of the ball funds and the abduction of the American girl, to pay much heed to Alvarado. Alvarado, who worked as a bellhop in the Tampa Bay Hotel, had tried to talk to the manager the night he had found the bag, but the manager had rudely brushed him aside.

Alvarado had taken this as a sign. It was meant for him to have the satchel and its contents. He had even found some money—two five-dollar bills in one corner of the bag.

Now, looking at the items spread out on his bed, he wondered if he should search the bag again, to be sure he had found everything.

Pulling the large bag from under his bed, Alvarado reached a hand down inside and ran it around the bottom. There could be more bills stuck to the lining or folded up in a corner.

Ah, there *was* something! His probing fingers had touched paper, but it did not feel like money. Pulling out his hand, he found that he was holding a small sheet of paper. Swallowing his disappointment, he peered closely at it.

It was a crudely drawn map, he could see that much. There was some writing on it, but most of it was written in English, and Alvarado could read very little English. He was able to decipher one word—Yucatán. It meant nothing to him. Shrugging, he started to crumple it up and throw it away, then thought better of it. Perhaps he should keep it, in the unlikely event that the owner of the bag returned for it. He pushed the map back down into the satchel, closed it, and shoved it back under the bed.

Now he had a small problem—how would he explain his new clothing to his mother? He could tell her that a rich guest had given the things to him. It was not all that unlikely, for besides gratuities, he was often the recipient of leftover candy, fruit, even an occasional bottle of wine when a guest was leaving and did not want to burden himself too much. Yes, he would tell his mother that the clothes had been given to him, but he decided not to tell her about the other things—the silver brushes, the shaving mug and brush. For the time being, that would be his secret.

Smiling, Alvarado gathered up the suits to take to the little room where his mother did her sewing. She would be surprised, naturally, but he knew that she would be pleased at his good fortune. He would wear one of the suits to the dance Saturday night, and Rosa would be unable to resist him.

Tampa looked very different to Neil as the transport ship maneuvered into the channel, preparatory to docking at the quay. The dock area appeared deserted except for the stacks of crates and equipment, which he was certain would now never be shipped to Cuba.

The humid summer heat lay over the harbor like a heavy, deep blanket, and Neil could feel the perspiration running down his back in a steady rivulet. There was no one at the dock to greet them, and the men quickly dispersed, anxious to meet their loved ones or find the nearest saloon or the fastest transportation to their home states.

His wound aching a little, Neil left the dock walking slowly, his duffel bag slung over his good shoulder. Should he go first to the Manning home, or should he find a place to stay? It would probably be best to find a place to stay, so he could get cleaned up, make himself more presentable before going to see Jessica.

Would she be glad to see him? Or would she even dare face him?

He knew the Mannings had a telephone. He *could* call first and make certain that Jessica would see him. He decided not to risk that. If she did not wish to see him, or had told her parents that she did not want to see him, he still would not be certain in his mind. To know, absolutely, how he stood, Neil knew that he must see her face to face, and the only way to accomplish that would be to appear unannounced at her door.

As he made his way through the city, Neil saw many men in uniform, on the streets, and in the cafés and stores. A good share of them seemed to be under the influence of alcohol, and their whole demeanor was very unmilitary. These were the men who had been left behind when the main force went to Cuba; and in all fairness, he thought, they were probably bored and resentful, with nothing to do but wait to be discharged. Many of them struck him as being very young.

He found a decent boardinghouse, not too far from the Manning home, and engaged a room.

It was late afternoon, and he debated waiting until the next day to call upon the Mannings, yet his anxiety and impatience were too strong. He had to know today.

As quickly as he could, he washed and changed into fresh clothing. Studying himself in the wavy mirror of the highboy that stood against one wall of the room, he thought that he looked older and thinner and wondered if Jessica would notice.

Then, for just a moment, he thought of Margarita, and a vague longing filled him. The day following their night together on the blanket, Neil had left the rebel camp, returning to his own unit. He had hardly taken time to say farewell to Margarita. She probably thought badly of him, but there was no help for it—Neil had known that he dared not remain in the vicinity of Ramon Mendes, the man who had taken his place in Jessica's heart.

At last satisfied with his appearance, Neil left the rooming house and headed toward the Manning residence, trying not to anticipate, trying not to speculate about what might or might not happen. By the time he reached the house, the sun was beginning to set, and it was growing somewhat cooler.

As he mounted the porch steps, he could hear the sound of voices through the open front door. As he stopped before the screen door, the voices abruptly ceased; and as he knocked on the door frame, he heard the sound of footsteps hurrying toward the door.

It was Anne Manning. She wore a look of expectancy, which died when she recognized him. She stopped, her face going pale.

"Lieutenant Dancer!" she exclaimed. For an instant she closed her eyes and seemed to sway, and Neil was puzzled by her reaction to his presence. Then her eyes opened, and she smiled with an obvious effort. "Come in, Lieutenant. You must forgive me, but I was hoping for word—" She broke off.

She held the door open. More puzzled than ever, Neil removed his hat and stepped into the darkened parlor, where the blinds had been pulled down to keep out the afternoon sun.

Anne Manning's appearance was shocking. Her eyes and the tip
of her nose were pink, as if she had been crying steadily for some
time, and her usually impeccable appearance had suffered.

Neil, looking quickly about for Jessica, felt a pang of disappointment when he did not see her. But he did see Wyngate Manning, sitting in a high-backed chair. Where was Jessica? And why was Mrs.
Manning so upset? Had something happened to Jessica? The very
thought made his stomach knot. He was almost afraid to ask.

"Lieutenant," said Anne Manning, placing her hand on his arm,
"I'm so glad you are back, and alive and well, but we have. . . .
Something has happened to. . . ."

Her eyes filled, and she turned away. The premonition he had initially felt turned into active fear. He looked over at Wyngate Manning, seeking an explanation. The banker's face was white and drawn.
He looked very little like the self-confident, somewhat complacent
man that Neil remembered.

"What my wife is trying to say, sir, is that something has happened
to Jessica. Something terrible." He swallowed convulsively, then gestured. "Sit down, young man, and I'll try to tell you what happened."

Neil, fearful and confused, perched on the edge of the divan and
leaned forward tensely. "What is it? Is Jessica ill? Is she . . . is she
dead?"

Wyngate Manning winced. "No, no, Lieutenant, she's not dead, at
least not that we know."

"Not that you *know?* That doesn't make much sense, sir."

"I'm sorry." The banker spread his hands in a helpless gesture. "Jessica is missing, you see. She has been abducted. We have no idea
where she is or how she is faring."

Neil shot to his feet. "Abducted! By whom? How?"

"Easy, Lieutenant," Wyngate Manning said. "Suppose you pour us
a glass of sherry from the sideboy there, and I will tell you as much as
we know."

When the story was finished, Neil felt numb. It seemed such an incredible tale, such an unlikely thing to have happened. "And they have
found no trace of them so far? Nothing?"

Anne Manning said listlessly, "Nothing. They have been searching
for the four days she has been gone. They thought that Mr. Kroger
headed for the docks. Checking with the boat owners along the bay,
they found one whose boat had been stolen. The owner discovered it

missing the day after the ball. . . ." She choked up and clapped her hands to her face.

Wyngate Manning said, "And so it's assumed that the blackguard stole the boat, a small steam yacht. But although they have searched every place imaginable, they did not find them. Now they say that it is probably hopeless, for in four days a boat could be far away from Tampa. There are no clues as to where Kroger might have gone. As you can imagine, Lieutenant, we are quite distraught."

With a sick feeling Neil remembered the night of the officers' ball and the erotic episode with Dulcy Thomas in the garden behind the hotel. "Kroger killed Dulcy Thomas? They're certain of that?"

"Quite certain," Wyngate Manning said in a dead voice. "They found her diary, you see, and in it was written a full account of her liaison with Kroger, as well as a note to the effect that she was meeting with him the night she disappeared."

Neil was filled with a helpless rage at the thought of Jessica in this man's clutches. "And so he has plenty of money to travel where he pleases, and a steam yacht as well?"

Wyngate Manning sighed heavily. "And he has Jessica. We have been hoping that he only took her as a temporary hostage, that he would eventually release her, but so far. . . ." He spread his hands.

"What is being done now?" Neil demanded.

"The local police have about given up, claiming that he is probably beyond their jurisdiction by now. The only thing left to do is hire a firm of detectives."

"The Pinkertons?"

The banker nodded. "It is the only thing left that I can think of to do."

Neil got to his feet. "There is one other thing you can do, Mr. Manning. You can let me look for her. I may not be as well trained as a professional, but I have a personal interest in finding her, a much stronger incentive than money."

Wyngate Manning looked slightly embarrassed. "Yes, to be sure." He cleared his throat and glanced at his wife; she gave a slight nod. He looked again at Neil. "I assume you don't know?"

Neil went still. "Don't know what? There's more?"

The banker gestured slightly. "This is something else. My daughter didn't get in touch with you after that night the two of you were marooned on the island. I suppose you wondered about that?"

"I wondered," Neil said tautly. Then he smiled slightly to ease the tension. "I thought she had forgotten all about me."

"She did, son. Literally."

Neil stared. "What?"

"She had an accident, a blow to the head. . . ." Wyngate Manning quickly told Neil about Jessica's loss of memory.

It was all Neil could do to keep from shouting aloud with joy. She had not forsaken him! She still loved him! He said, "There's something you should know, both of you. Before I left, Jessica and I agreed that we would be married when I returned. Did she tell you?"

Anne Manning put her hand to her mouth. "No, she didn't. She must have lost her memory before she had the chance. But may I say that I am happy for both of you, Lieutenant Dancer. You are a fine young man."

"I love Jessica, Mrs. Manning."

"I'm sure you do, Lieutenant." She looked over at her husband. "Let him go, Wyngate. I would have more faith in him than a hired detective. As he said, love is a stronger incentive than money."

Neil paced, pounding his fist into the palm of his other hand. "Now that I know she still loves me, I have more reason than ever to find her." He rounded on the banker. "And you can't stop me, sir. I am searching for her, with or without your permission!"

Wyngate Manning looked from Neil to his wife, then back to Neil. "All right, young man—Neil. You may go, with my blessing. Just find—" His voice broke. "Find our daughter for us. Find our Jessica and bring her home!"

Chapter Seventeen

WRAPPED in a bedsheet, toga style, Jessica stood at the small sink in the galley, rinsing out the dress she had just washed. If she hung it on the railing, it should dry in a couple of hours or so, and she could put it back on.

Kroger was somewhere up on deck, and she would have to risk him seeing her in just her undergarments. However, he had been "peculiar"—as she thought of it—since that first day when he had acted so strangely; and while he was this way, she was not so frightened of him, although she realized that he was not behaving rationally.

It was quite clear that Kroger thought she was someone else. His mother, evidently. This would have been humorous in other circumstances. Jessica had wondered about that a lot these past few days, wondered why he should think of *her* as his mother; but since he at least treated her well and made no attempt to molest her, she could only hope that he would stay this way indefinitely. He was obviously quite mad, but since he functioned well otherwise, she much preferred his mad persona to the real one. This way, he posed no threat to her.

Kroger had told her, that morning at breakfast, that they would probably be leaving their hiding place that night. They would, he had informed her, strike out across the Gulf of Mexico, and to Yucatán, and this town he kept talking of—Mérida.

"And don't worry," he had added. "I know it's a long voyage across the open water, but I have had some experience with navigation. There is nothing for you to fear, I assure you."

And then he had launched into a long, rambling tale of some confidence game he had once operated, conning a wealthy man into financing a treasure-hunting voyage off the coast beyond Key West.

Sighing, Jessica wrung out the light fabric of the dress, upset that there was no iron on board to press it. She would look very odd, going ashore in Yucatán, in a wrinkled party dress. However, there was nothing she could do about it; and at any rate, it was hardly important in the face of all the other things she had to worry about. Her parents, for instance. After the first few days, Jessica had given up hope that they would quickly find her; Kroger had done too good a job of hiding the boat. It had been four days now, and there had been no sign of any rescuers. The little island key where they were anchored was deserted. The mainland was barely visible to the east. Several times Jessica had stood at the railing gazing wistfully at the distant smudge of land. She had contemplated swimming for it, when Kroger was not watching her, but she knew it was hopeless.

And Neil, how was he? Did he think of her at all, and wonder about her, as she did about him? If he was alive and well, he should be returning to Tampa soon. He might return and find her gone. Would he even care? Oh, Neil, she thought; I miss you so!

There was no use in crying, she thought, as she brushed away a beginning tear in her eye. If she gave way to despair, she was lost. She had to remain strong and alert. She had to survive somehow, and return to her family. As long as Kroger was acting in his present manner, all she had to do was play along with him, pretend that she was who he thought she was. What she really had to worry about was that he might go back to being himself. And most of all, she had to keep alert and watch for a chance to escape; he had to relax his vigilance eventually. When that time came, she had to be ready. Since it seemed no one was going to rescue her, it was up to her to rescue herself.

When she went up on deck to hang out her dress, she found Kroger sitting in the shade of a deck chair, smoking a cigar. That cigar made her think of Ramon, but she put that thought away and smoothed the wet dress over the railing, trying to get as many of the wrinkles out as possible.

As she turned away from the rail, Kroger smiled benignly at her. "Are you anxious to get to Mérida?"

She managed to return his smile. "Yes, of course."

"You shouldn't be working so hard, washing your dress. I told you, didn't I, that I would buy you many new dresses once we are in Mérida?"

She nodded stiffly. "Yes, thank you. That will be very nice."

"I'll have to get new clothes, too. I had to leave my satchel back at the hotel. I told you that, didn't I? We'll go shopping together, you'll like that. Remember how carefully you always picked out my clothes? You wanted me to look like 'a little gentleman' you always said."

"Yes," Jessica said with false brightness. "I remember."

But even as she spoke, she wondered how long she could keep up this pretense. It took all her willpower not to scream at him, shout out that he was crazy, that she was not his mother.

On the other hand, what would she do if he went back to being his old self?

The dress finally dried, and Jessica put it on. She and Kroger had eaten a cold supper, and then he had gotten busy and removed the boat's camouflage.

The night was fairly light—there was a gibbous moon—and the sea was calm when they set out across the Gulf. Kroger insisted that Jessica sit with him in the pilot cabin, to keep him company, he said, while he steered the boat. He had found a small Victrola in the main cabin, along with some records, and had brought it to the pilot cabin, so he could play the records for her. One song, "Greensleeves," which was playing now, was, he said, her favorite.

It was a very sad song; and Jessica wondered what she was like, or had been like, this woman who had borne Brill Kroger. Had she resembled her, Jessica? It seemed highly likely. Had Kroger's mother known, when he was small, that he would turn out to be the kind of man he now was? Had there been signs of what he was to become, in his youth? Or had he appeared to be a normal child, just like any other?

It must be a chancy thing, having children, she thought. Even if you raised them right, and taught them to be good, you could never be sure that they would turn out all right in the end. Dulcy was a perfect example. Her parents were law-abiding, church-going people, and yet Dulcy had turned out bad. Jessica wondered what kind of children she and Neil would have—if they ever had the chance. She missed him terribly; she must try to stop thinking so much about the night on the island, for it only made her unhappier.

She was distracted from her thoughts by the sound of Kroger's voice raised in song. She glanced at him, standing at the wheel, and he smiled genially. "Isn't this grand? We have the whole Gulf to ourselves, it seems."

Jessica said carefully, "Yes, it's very nice."

Her thoughts moved ahead to Mexico, to Mérida. Even if it was a foreign city, there would surely be people there who spoke English, people she could converse with. Someone would help her, at least get a message to her parents as to her whereabouts. If Kroger continued to trust her, as he seemed to be doing now, he probably would not keep her under lock and key. Surely, there would be some opportunity to contact someone in authority, who would believe her story.

This thought cheered her up a little and made her feel almost optimistic. She could return Kroger's smile with a measure of sincerity.

Yes, when they got to Mérida, she would try to escape. There certainly would not be any chance until then, out here in this great expanse of open water.

Maria, getting dressed for an evening with Tom Farrel, examined the bruises on her shoulders, where Kroger's brutal hands had left their imprint. There were bruises on her thighs, also, as well as a thin, red line down her midriff, where he had scratched the skin when he was cutting away her clothing.

She shuddered, thinking of how near she had come to being forcibly taken by that horrible man. How close she had come to losing to that repulsive creature that which men seemed to consider so valuable in the women they wanted to marry.

If it had happened, if Kroger had finished what he had started, would Carlos still want her for his wife? Cuban men, she well knew, placed a high premium upon virginity; and yet would she have been so different if she had lost that thin shield of membrane that forever separated the chaste from the unchaste? Would she not be the same person, have the same feelings?

She began buttoning her blouse over the purple marks. Considerations of virginity aside, it would have been terrible to have lost her maidenhood like that, to someone she loathed. She wanted the first time to be beautiful, a sharing of love with someone she cared deeply for.

As she arranged the collar of her shirtwaist, she wondered about Tom Farrel. How would *he* have felt toward her, if Kroger had succeeded in raping her? He had been properly horrified when he learned what had happened, and he had been angry with himself for not succeeding in stopping Brill Kroger when he had asked Maria to dance. Maria knew that Tom wanted her. She could see it in his eyes—remembering her mother's remark, she smiled to herself—and in the way his hand trembled if he happened to inadvertently touch her. And she could feel some of the same hunger in herself when she was with him, or even thought about him. He was a very attractive man, and kind and good as well.

But Carlos, too, was attractive, and his touch, also, had caused her to burn inside. It was not fair that she continue seeing Tom Farrel if she was going to marry Carlos. She knew this, and yet she felt that she needed Tom, needed his company and his friendship, particularly after all the terrible things that had taken place. Besides, she had not definitely made up her mind about Carlos, and his proposal. Perhaps Carlos would not come home from Cuba, perhaps there would be no possibility of a life with him. He might even decide to stay permanently in Cuba, and she certainly had no intention of living there. If this was so, then it would be foolish of her to give up the lieutenant.

She wondered again, as she often did these days, just what Tom's true intentions were toward her. Her mother had warned her repeatedly not to be foolish, that the lieutenant came from a well-to-do family and naturally his parents would expect him to marry one of his own kind. And yet . . .

What would it be like, married to a man like Tom Farrel? Going with him, no doubt, to the city where he had been raised, Philadelphia. It would be difficult, for their ways were different, and perhaps her mother was right—she would not be accepted by his parents and his circle of friends.

Maria shook her head ruefully, annoyed with herself. He had not spoken of marriage. He had not even so much as tried to kiss her.

She stared at herself in the mirror. "It is unlike you to be so indecisive," she said aloud. "You have always prided yourself on knowing what you want, knowing what you must do."

She frowned disapprovingly at her reflection, unhappy over her vacillation and disturbed by the feeling of anxiety that seemed, unaccountably, to hang over her like a dark cloud these days.

It was because of all that happened, she decided. The shocking death of Dulcy Thomas. Her own experience with Brill Kroger. Kroger's theft of the ball funds. And then the abduction of Jessica Manning. All of it, all the awful things, had made her conscious of how fragile life really was, how easily the strands could be broken, and how quickly plans could go awry. Maria had always felt sure of herself, certain that she knew what was best for herself; but now she was fearful that life might be passing her by. Something could happen, she could die tomorrow; and if that happened, she would never experience so many things. She would never know, for instance, how it was for a man to make love to her. She would never know what it was like to be married, to have children; and so much, much more.

The big clock in the parlor struck the hour, and she realized that Tom Farrel would be arriving at any moment. Quickly she finished with her toilet and picked up her bag. They were going to the Tampa Bay Hotel for dinner and to a concert afterward. Maria could not help but think of Jessica Manning again when she thought of the hotel, and the thought of Jessica invariably brought tears to her eyes. She had come to know, and like, Jessica, during those days Jessica was working with her family on the plans for the ball. It almost seemed as if the other girl had paid the price for Maria's own narrow escape; and Maria prayed for her every night, prayed that Jessica would somehow be spared, as she herself had been.

She heard her mother's voice now, in the parlor, and the deeper voice of Tom Farrel. Her spirits soared at the sound of his voice, and she was smiling as she left the room. Tonight, she intended having a good time, forgetting, for a few hours, her problems. That was the way it must be, if she was to survive.

Despite the departure of the troops for Cuba, the Tampa Bay Hotel was still quite busy. There were many officers still residing there—more, it seemed to Maria, than had been sent off—and although most of the newspaper correspondents and other war-connected civilians had departed with the troops, there were a large number of guests in the hotel, and the usual dinners and programs were held weekly.

As Tom's rented carriage rolled up to the hotel, Maria looked at it with her usual appreciation—the strings of lights; the sound of music; and the lovely grounds and landscaping.

As they dismounted from the carriage, she said, "It looks like a picture, a picture representing all the lovely and pleasant things in life."

He gazed down at her, smiling fondly. "You're absolutely right. In fact, I'd say it looks like a palace, a fairy palace at that. And you, you look like a princess. The sleeping beauty!"

She flushed with pleasure, then raised her eyebrows quizzically. "What a strange remark to make, Tom. 'The sleeping beauty.' Why such an image?"

He looked momentarily embarrassed. "I don't know, not really. It sort of slipped out. I guess it's because you always seem a little removed from me, Maria. I hope what I said doesn't upset you?"

"No. No, of course not. Why should it?" And yet, somehow it did disturb her a little. Was that how he saw her? Unawakened? Cool, removed? Was that how she appeared to him?

"I didn't mean it in an uncomplimentary way, you know."

"I'm sure you didn't, Tom." She touched his cheek. "It's all right."

But there was a prince in the story, she recalled. A prince who had awakened the sleeping beauty with a kiss. If Tom saw her as a sleeping beauty, did he see himself in the role of the prince?

She had no time to pursue this line of thought, for she saw a young man coming toward them, a well-dressed man who was waving vigorously at them and smiling. He looked faintly familiar, but Maria did not immediately recognize him.

He stopped before her. "Maria! How do you like my new suit?"

Maria stared in disbelief, then laughed aloud. It was Alvarado, Alvarado Moreno, the bellhop! She had not recognized him in the fancy attire. "Alvarado! You look magnificent! I didn't recognize you. Where are you going, dressed like that?"

"It is my night off. I'm going to the dance in Ybor City, with Rosa Luza," he said proudly. "I am beautiful, no?"

He turned slowly in front of them, preening, and Maria smiled indulgently. The suit had clearly been tailored for a larger man; and although the trouser legs and coat sleeves had been shortened, the shoulders were much too wide, and the hat Alvarado was wearing was too large.

"Lieutenant Farrel, may I introduce you to Alvarado Moreno? You may have seen Alvarado before, he works at the hotel."

Tom shook his head, amused. "Well, if I have seen him, I certainly would not have recognized him, all dandied up like that."

Maria was frowning, staring more closely at the suit. It looked puzzlingly familiar, yet she knew that she had never seen Alvarado in such finery before.

"Well, I had better hurry," Alvarado was saying, lifting the tall hat and bowing slightly in a mock-dignified manner. "I would not want to keep Rosa waiting."

"Of course not," Maria said dryly. As he went down the drive, almost skipping in his haste, she called after him, "Have a nice evening, Alvarado." She turned to Tom. "I have never seen Alvarado so dressed up. I wonder where he got that suit?"

Tom laughed lightly. "I wager he'll be the king of the dance tonight, and that this Rosa Luza will be suitably impressed."

It was not until much later, after an excellent dinner and the concert, when she and Tom were strolling about the hotel grounds, that

Maria suddenly remembered where she had seen the suit before. She stopped short, and a sharp cry escaped her.

Tom said in alarm, "What is it, Maria? What's wrong?"

"The suit, Alvarado's suit! I remember where I saw it, or one just like it." She clutched his arm with strong fingers. "I remember seeing Brill Kroger in a suit just like that. I'm almost willing to swear it's the same one. I remember it so well because he was wearing it when he came to our house to discuss the ball. I noticed everything about him because I disliked him so!"

Frowning thoughtfully, Tom drew to a halt. "Are you certain?"

She nodded quickly. "Yes, yes, it's either Kroger's suit or one just like it. And it seems unlikely that Alvarado, a bellhop, would buy one just like it. It has to be expensive, Tom!"

"But even if it *is* Kroger's suit, what does that mean?"

Maria said thoughtfully, "I don't really know, but we must find out. I have a . . . a strong feeling that it's important, somehow. So far there has been no clue as to where Kroger was heading. I heard that there was no clothing left in his room, and no personal articles. Yet those people who saw him last in the ballroom that night, said that he was carrying nothing, except the knife with which he threatened Jessica. And when the police came to his room that night and frightened him away. . . ."

She broke off for a moment, her thoughts going back. Even thinking about that awful night made her throat tighten, and it was embarrassing to speak of it, particularly to a man. "When Brill Kroger ran out of his room that night, he was carrying a bag, a large carpetbag. I remember that distinctly. Why didn't he have it with him in the ballroom?"

Tom took her hand. "Maria, I know how it pains you to remember that night. . . ." He looked away. "Kroger could have hidden it somewhere, you know, and picked it up later."

She shook her head stubbornly. "No, I don't think he would have had time for that. The time he left, with Jessica, was only a little while after he left me upstairs."

He said dubiously, "Then you think that Alvarado Moreno perhaps found the bag, and that's where he got the suit? That sounds pretty farfetched to me, Maria."

"It's possible, you must admit that. I think it bears looking into."

"I agree, but just how do we do that?"

"We'll go to the dance in Ybor City. I know these dances, they do not break up until dawn. We will find Alvarado, and we will ask him."

The dance that night was being held in the Cuban Lyceum, and as Tom and Maria approached the building, the melodious strains of Cuban music rolled over them like a musical wave. The dance was still going strong, and the sound of voices chattering in Spanish could be heard under the music. When they reached the entrance, Maria spoke briefly to the man stationed there, stating their business, and he let them in without paying admission.

Although it was quite late, the crowd was large, flushed from the heat and the dancing, all attired in their best. The room was a whirl of bright colors. The orchestra, situated on a slight dais, was playing a lively rumba, and Maria began to search among the dancers for Alvarado Moreno.

They were, she soon noticed, attracting a great many stares from the dancers. At first she could not think why, and then she realized that it was because of Tom Farrel. Usually only Cubans attended these affairs, and Tom, with his blond hair and light eyes, was obviously not one of them. Unconsciously, she stood straighter, returning the stares without flinching. Let them wonder, she thought scornfully; she was here on important business.

"You're taller," she said to Tom. "Can you see Alvarado anywhere?"

Tom, who seemed rather nonplussed by the alien, faintly hostile atmosphere, shook his head. "I haven't seen him yet. Maybe he isn't even here."

"No, I know Alvarado. He would be one of the last to leave."

Tom grinned. "But he did mention a young lady. Perhaps they are. . . . Well, you know." And then he blushed furiously.

Maria could not help laughing. "That is true, but believe me, even so, Alvarado would not leave the dance until the last number was played. I have attended dances when he was present, and he— There! Isn't that him, across the room?"

Craning to follow her pointing finger with his gaze, Tom nodded. "Yes, I believe it is. Shall I fetch him for you?"

She took his arm. "No. It's better that we face him together. Come."

Making their way through the thick crowd of dancers took some maneuvering, but they eventually reached the edge of the dance floor, where Alvarado was dancing energetically with a small, dark girl in a red dress.

"Alvarado!" Maria had to shout to be heard over the sound of the music. "Alvarado!"

Alvarado whirled about in surprise. "Maria! What are you doing here? I thought you were attending some affair at the hotel, you and Lieutenant Farrel?"

"We were. But there is something that I must discuss with you."

Alvarado looked dismayed. "Now? It could not wait until to-morrow?"

"No. I know we're imposing on you. I'm sorry for that, Alvarado, but it is very important. Is there somewhere we can talk?"

Frowning, he nodded reluctantly. "Yes, we can go outside, on the veranda." He turned to the girl with him. "Rosa, will you excuse us for a few minutes?"

Rosa Luza nodded, although it was plain that she was far from pleased. She said something sharp to Alvarado in Spanish and walked away, her back straight. Alvarado looked after her, shrugging philo-sophically.

"I'm sorry, Alvarado," Maria said. "I know this seems rude to you, but the matter *is* vital."

Alvarado spread his hands, smiling. "If it is that important, what can I say? You are a friend, Maria."

He led the way out onto the veranda, which was deserted, then stared at Maria questioningly.

Maria turned to her companion. "Tom, it will be much better if I speak to Alvarado in Spanish. I hope you won't think that too rude of us?"

He shook his head. "Not at all, Maria. Get the information the best way you can."

Maria sighed in relief. It *would* be far easier, conversing with Al-varado in their native tongue. As she turned back to Alvarado, she saw that he was suddenly looking uneasy.

"Information?" he said slowly. "What is this information, Maria?"

"Alvarado, first I wish to make clear that I mean no disrespect by the questions I am about to ask you, and neither do I want to imply any wrongdoing on your part."

He nodded, but his expression was guarded now.

"It is about the suit you are wearing. I must know where you got it, Alvarado. It is very important that I know."

His face went pale, and he drew back from her, his glance darting about nervously.

She placed a hand on his arm. "Don't be frightened, it has nothing to do with you personally. Please tell me, and tell me true."

Alvarado swallowed and fumbled in his inner pocket for a small cigar, which he lit with trembling fingers, all the while refusing to meet her gaze.

Maria waited patiently, her heart beating faster. Her feeling about this was right, she knew it now!

"I bought it," Alvarado finally said. "Yes, I bought it from a guest at the hotel."

Maria did not believe him. He was too nervous, too evasive, yet she did not let her disbelief show. "I see. Was the guest Brill Kroger? The truth now, Alvarado. Someone's life may depend on your answer."

Alvarado appeared to be thinking hard. "Yes! Yes, I do believe that was his name. He was leaving. He was in a hurry, he said, and did not wish to be bothered with carrying things. He offered the suit to me for a good price."

Maria knew that he was still lying, but she was afraid she would frighten him if she accused him of it. "Kroger is the man who stole the money collected for the charity ball. He also abducted Banker Manning's daughter, Jessica. You have heard of this?"

Alvarado was turning the cigar over and over between his fingers. "I have heard of these terrible things, yes, but I did not connect them with the man who sold me the suit."

"Yes, well, it seems that the police have no idea where Kroger went with Jessica. There are no clues at all. When I saw your suit, I recognized it as one I had seen on Kroger. I hoped that perhaps you might have found something, say an address, something of that nature, in one of the pockets. *Did* you find anything like that, Alvarado? Anything at all that might hint as to his destination?"

Alvarado seemed to relax slightly, and Maria sensed that he was relieved to learn that she was not accusing him of anything. He looked away, smoking, and she calculated that he was deciding how much to tell her.

Then he nodded abruptly. "There was something, yes. Something that I found in the pocket, like you say, Maria. I did not think it important, the paper. I believe it is a map of some kind, with one word that I could make out. Yucatán."

Maria gave Tom a triumphant glance. "Do you still have it, this map?" she asked, holding her breath for his answer.

"Yes, I was about to throw it away, but did not. You are welcome to it, Maria, if it will be of any help." He was eager to cooperate, now that he knew what she wanted of him.

"Yes, Alvarado. We very much want it. It may lead to Brill Kroger and help to get Jessica back. Just think, you may be a hero!"

Alvarado shook his head quickly. "No, no, I want nothing like that. I will bring the map to the hotel tomorrow, Maria. Now may I go back to Rosa? She is not patient, that one."

"Yes, Alvarado, of course. And I am very grateful for your help. Thank you." Standing on tiptoe, she kissed him on the cheek. "I will see you tomorrow."

As Alvarado walked away, she turned excitedly to Tom. "Oh, Tom! It was just as I thought! It *was* Kroger's suit, and Alvarado found something—"

"Whoa! I think you'll have to explain," he said dryly. "I didn't understand a word that was said here."

"Oh, I am sorry, Tom. Of course you didn't." She told him quickly the essence of what Alvarado had said.

Tom nodded gravely. "I wouldn't get too excited, Maria. It may be a map right enough, but there's nothing that says it's a map showing where Kroger fled to."

Maria was undaunted. "No, but there is nothing to say that it isn't, either. At least it's something, more than we have now, and I have a feeling, a strong feeling, that it *is* a map showing us where Kroger has gone."

Tom nodded grudgingly. "Well, you had a feeling that Moreno was wearing Kroger's suit, and you were right about that. Maybe you're right about this, as well." He smiled down into her face. "I will never laugh at women's intuition again."

His remark pleased Maria so much that she rose up on tiptoe and kissed him on the lips. Immediately appalled by her forwardness, she started to step back; but Tom, his face lighting up, reached out and pulled her into his arms. Maria quickly slipped out of his grasp, adjusting her clothing unnecessarily, and then started down the steps, trying to pretend that nothing untoward had happened.

Tom hurried to catch up; and when he drew level with her, he took her arm. She made no move to evade his grasp but said, "You had best be getting me home now. Mama will think that *I* have been abducted."

Tom was silent as they went down the rest of the steps, and he did not speak until they had reached the hired carriage. "I would *like* to abduct you, Maria," he said, as he helped her into the open vehicle. "I would like to steal you away and never bring you back. Would you mind that very much?"

She stared down into his face as he stood looking up at her. Her first thought was that he was teasing, but his grave countenance told her that he was quite serious. Her heart began to hammer furiously. She did not know what to say, did not even know what she *wanted* to say; but then she realized that she must tell him the truth. She could not in all fairness do otherwise.

"Tom," she said slowly, "you are very dear to me. You have been a good friend, and a wonderful companion—"

He made a face. "That's all I am to you, a companion?"

She said tartly, "Let me finish, please. I haven't been entirely honest with you, Tom. Oh, I haven't lied, but I have not told you that there is someone else. Carlos Chavez, whom I have known since I was a child. Carlos has asked me to marry him."

Tom's face registered pain and dismay. "And you have said yes!"

Maria gave vent to a sigh of exasperation. "I wish you would stop finishing my sentences for me! No, I have *not* said I would marry him. In fact, I have yet to give him any answer, and Carlos is in Cuba now, fighting with the rebels."

Tom's gloomy expression lightened somewhat. "Then I still have a chance!"

Maria felt her pulse quicken again. He was so attractive, and he cared for her; still, she was unsure of his intent. "A chance for what, Tom?"

He looked at her in astonishment. "Why, to ask you to marry *me*. I want to go on record. I hereby formally request your hand in marriage, Maria Mendes. There now, isn't my proposal as good as his?"

She did not know whether to laugh or cry. Staring down into his face so close, she yearned to lean down and touch her mouth to his. "Tom. Oh, Tom! It would not be fair of me to even listen to you, not while Carlos is away fighting in Cuba. I must wait until he returns."

His face closed up again. "I would also be in Cuba, fighting, if it were up to me. It wasn't my decision to remain behind."

Maria felt a pull of anger. Men! Why were they always so eager to charge into battle? Did he think that she thought less of him because he was not fighting? "The fighting does not matter," she said curtly. "What matters is that Carlos is away, and you are here, and it would not be right for me to make up my mind before I see him again."

"At least you haven't said no," he said, suddenly cheerful. "I'll keep on loving you, and I'll keep right on asking you to marry me. Oh, Maria!"

In an instant, he was into the carriage, so quickly that he startled the horse in its traces, and Tom had to haul back on the reins until the animal quieted. But then, instead of starting the carriage in motion, he turned to Maria, his face so close that she could feel his warm breath on her cheek. He gave a muffled groan. "Oh, Maria, my dearest love!"

His arms went around her, and his lips were pressing hers with a sweet, hot insistence that made her body feel as if it were melting. She had forgotten how good a man's arms could feel, and briefly she thought of Carlos's arms around her in the garden the night he had told her he was leaving. Oh, she *was* lonely, she had not realized just how lonely she had been. Would it be so wrong if she let her body and heart hold sway over her mind, just this once? She had never known physical love. Was it so wrong to yearn for such a culmination?

His lips were becoming more demanding, and his hands, which had been around her waist, had now moved up to cup her breasts, making them feel hot and heavy; and then his mouth was at her ear. In a hoarse whisper he said, "Maria, Maria! Let me love you! I've wanted you for so long!"

And then, suddenly, her own words came back to haunt her: "It would not be fair of me to even listen to you, not while Carlos is away fighting in Cuba. I must wait. . . ."

No! She could not allow herself to go any farther, even though she cared for Tom Farrel, even though she ached to open herself fully to him. It would be a negation of everything she had been taught, a violation of everything she believed in. She must wait, and Tom must wait, as Carlos was waiting.

Summoning up the last of her self-control, she pushed Tom away. "No!" she said strongly. "No, I cannot. This is not right."

"But I love you, Maria, you know I do. I want to marry you, so how can it be wrong?" Once again, he placed his hands on her breasts.

She put her hands flat against his chest, holding him off. Now that she had asserted herself, she was calmer. "No, Tom, I am sorry. It's probably my fault, but I did not mean to lead you on, please believe me. I would like to, I even want to, but it would be wrong. Perhaps not for you, but it would be for me. If you love me, as you say, you should be willing to wait."

For just a moment, he looked very angry, his breath coming unevenly. Then his shoulders slumped in defeat. Sighing, he said, "All right, Maria. It isn't easy, for I want you desperately. But I will wait for this Carlos to return, and when he does come back, I shall expect an answer, no matter what it may be. I think you owe me that much."

Chapter Eighteen

As Brill Kroger steered the yacht, the *Maybelle*, into the harbor at Progreso, on the coast of Yucatán, he was in excellent spirits. Since leaving Tampa, everything had been going his way. He was on a roll, and he felt that nothing could stop him. Even the weather was in his favor. They had plowed across the Gulf under a cloudless sky, and without incident.

Of course, much of his good feeling was because of *Her*. Kroger could not get over the fact that she had come back to him, after all this time. The mystery of where she had been during these intervening years was not to be examined. It was enough that she was back, looking younger and prettier than ever. Also, he was pleased about most of the changes in her. The most important thing, to him, was that she no longer seemed to have a need for her "friends." Now she was his alone. There was no need to share her with an assortment of "uncles" and "protectors."

There was, however, one thing that he missed. Although she was amiable, and concurred with everything he said, she no longer seemed as physically affectionate. She used to hold him and fondle him, and sometimes even let him into her bed, to snuggle next to her, when there was no "friend" in attendance; but now she seemed not to want to do this. But when they were settled into a house in Mérida, then perhaps she would resume her affectionate manner toward him. There was one thing certain—he was going to keep all other men away from her, just to be on the safe side. He was going to take no chances on her suddenly deciding that she wanted to take up with some "friend." No, never again! This time it was different, and it was going to stay that way.

When they anchored at Progreso, Kroger planned to have the boat repainted and given a new name, to eliminate the chance of some American boat entering the harbor and recognizing this one as being a stolen craft. Kroger had little fear that he would be tracked this far. So confident was he of this, he was not going to bother using a false name.

After docking the *Maybelle*, he discovered that there was one thing he had not taken into consideration—the language difficulty. It had never occurred to him that he would find no one in the port who spoke English. It had been his experience, in the past, that no matter where a person traveled, there was always someone who could speak *some* English. But Progreso seemed to be the exception to the rule. Of course, it was off the beaten path. It was a bother, but not an unsurmountable problem. He would simply have to find an interpreter, preferably someone who spoke the Mayan language as well as Spanish, since many of the natives still spoke the old tongue.

And so, using the few words of Spanish he had picked up in Ybor City, and with a great many gestures, Kroger tried to convey his need for someone to accompany him to Mérida as an interpreter, and that he would pay well for the service. In the meantime, he could not accomplish much, for he could not make his needs known.

The town of Progreso was not very big, but from what he had been told, Mérida was much larger and much more attractive. He would arrange for a house, somewhere out of town, he thought; so that she would not be tempted by the presence of other people to return to her old habits. Of course, the fact that she did not speak the language would help, and he would instruct the interpreter, whoever he might be, that he was to speak only to him, Kroger, and he was *not* to do any translating for her. That way, she would have to rely totally on Kroger for all necessities. Yes, that was the way it would be.

Two days passed, while they remained on board the boat at the dock, and Kroger began to fret at the delay. He was beginning to believe that his request had been misunderstood, when a man showed up at the wharf, asking for him.

Kroger invited him on board the boat and looked him over carefully. He did not look like much, and that was a fact. He was middleaged, his face shaded by a floppy sombrero. Thin and swarthy, with a long, sharp nose and protruding eyes in a slender, pointed face, he looked fragile and worn; and, if the red veins in his eyes and across his nose were any indications, he was a sot.

"Are you Señor Kroger?" the man asked in slightly accented English.

"Yes, I'm Brill Kroger."

"I was informed that you are looking for an interpreter, to accompany you and your lady to Mérida. Is that right, señor?"

"Yes, that is correct. I plan to stay in Mérida for two or three months, and I do not speak the language. I need someone to deal with townspeople for me, and to help me find a house."

The man grinned widely, showing long, rather yellow teeth. "They say you promise to pay well. Is that also true, señor?"

Kroger narrowed his eyes. He did not take to this man at all; there seemed to be a trace of mockery in his eyes. But he did not have much choice in the matter. He growled, "Yes, I will pay well, but only for good service."

The man doffed the floppy sombrero. "I am Hernando Villalobos, late of Seville, señor, at your service."

Kroger nodded curtly. "Do you happen to speak the native tongue, as well?"

"Mayan? Si. Well enough."

Kroger pondered for a moment. It had been two days, and it did not seem likely that he would find anyone else. Even if he did not like the man, he spoke English well enough. He would have to do.

"Very well, Villalobos. Now we will talk terms."

Jessica, weary from her efforts not to say the wrong thing and upset Kroger, and from the fact that she had not had a good night's sleep since he had taken her from Tampa, was made drowsy by the rocking of the cart and the stifling heat.

Although she was accustomed to the heat and humidity of Tampa, it was different here. The sun burned down with a greater intensity, and the air felt heavier. The countryside, too, was inhospitable—a rough, harsh land with low-growing trees and undergrowth, which, despite the moisture in the air, looked arid. Up above, in the otherwise empty blue sky, she could see vultures circling lazily.

Progreso, where they had landed, had been alien and dirty, and the inhabitants were, to Jessica at any rate, very strange. Although she knew that Yucatán and Mexico were Latin countries, the people little resembled the Cubans and Spaniards of Ybor City. Most of these people were much darker of skin, and many of them had rather pronounced and unusual features—sloping foreheads; large, extremely fleshy noses that seemed to spring directly from the forehead; and slightly receding chins.

She did find their clothing rather attractive. The women dressed very much alike, in short-sleeved, white cotton shifts with bands of colorful embroidery around the necklines, the sleeves, and the hems. The embroidery on each one seemed different, and was quite beautiful. This shiftlike dress was worn over another, longer garment, which showed beneath it. This undergarment was trimmed in lace.

Their feet were often bare, although most of them wore a kind of rough, leather sandal. This typical ensemble was topped by a colorful, long, fringed shawl that was rectangular in shape and that the women used as carry-alls for food, or fat, brown babies, who seemed to thoroughly enjoy this method of transportation.

Another fact that Jessica found fascinating was the way the women carried large and obviously heavy burdens upon their heads, balancing high and wide loads with apparent ease. But the women's clothes did look cool and practical, and Jessica wished that she was so attired, instead of still wearing her wrinkled and awkward ball gown.

Now, as she huddled in the cart, trying to stay under the shawl Kroger had purchased for her for that purpose, she stole a quick glance at the third occupant of the cart, the Spaniard, Hernando Villalobos, whom Kroger had hired as an interpreter. He seemed to be asleep, his head nodding with the choppy motion of the cart.

Hernando had clearly been drunk when he had showed up this morning, and she knew that Kroger was furious with him, for he had intended for Villalobos to drive the cart, while he, Kroger, rode in the back with Jessica.

Thank heaven for small favors, Jessica thought; at least she was spared Kroger's company. And maybe, just maybe, she would get a chance to talk to Señor Villalobos soon!

So far, there had been no such opportunity. Kroger seemed to be taking particular care that she was not left alone in the man's company, and she could see that Kroger was always watching them. Still, he could not watch them constantly, not if Hernando was going to be with them for some time, and she gathered that he was. There had to come a time when she would have an opportunity to talk to him, to tell him her story, and to ask him to help her. Although she had no money, Jessica planned to promise that her father would pay him well, if she was safely returned to Tampa. Surely Señor Villalobos would help her.

Clinging to this comforting thought, she tried to drowse; and finally, despite the heat and the motion of the cart, she managed to fall asleep.

It was the cessation of all movement that woke her. She had slept right through the sounds of the city of Mérida—the clip-clop of horses' hooves; the chatter of voices; and the cries of the street vendors. Much to her surprise, when she opened her eyes, she saw that they were stopped in a courtyard before what appeared to be an inn of some sort, for there were many people coming and going, and carts, carriages, and horses filled the courtyard.

Through sleepy eyes, she gazed at the white building with pleasure, for it was very attractive. Around the inn and the courtyard was a high, white-plastered wall, and in the courtyard itself were numerous green plants and a large tile fountain spouting water. The building had a cool, shaded veranda all around it, and a beautiful red-tile roof.

The sound of lively music poured through the open entranceway, and Jessica's stomach contracted at the odors of cooking food.

"Here now," Kroger snarled, shaking the shoulder of their interpreter. "Wake up, goddamnit! We're here."

Hernando stirred, yawning, and stretched mightily. As he did so, Jessica caught the stink of sour, stale liquor, and she wrinkled her nose.

As Hernando climbed down out of the cart, Kroger came around to Jessica's side of the vehicle and raised his arms to help her down. Reluctantly she allowed him to lift her down onto the hard soil of the courtyard driveway. Feeling ashamed of her wrinkled dress, she tried to cover as much of it as possible with the shawl.

Kroger was talking to Hernando in English, and Hernando in turn was conversing in Spanish to a stocky man in a leather apron, who had emerged from the inn to greet them. After what seemed like a great deal of gesticulating and talking back and forth, Kroger and Hernando were shown into the dim interior of the inn, with Jessica following behind. Kroger was given three iron keys and directed upstairs.

Kroger, taking Jessica's arm, led her toward the stairs, and she resisted the strong urge to pull out of his grasp. She sensed that it would not be wise to create a scene, not at this time and in this alien place. They would not understand a word she said, and it would only succeed in annoying Kroger. At least, she thought with a feeling of relief, the owner or manager, whatever he was, had given Kroger three keys. That must mean that she was to have a room of her own; hopefully, one with a door she could lock. Then, perhaps she could get a decent night's sleep.

As they walked through the large, main room where the guests,

mostly male, sat at wooden tables, eating and drinking, they were the
focus of all eyes, and Jessica, flushing under the bold stares, pulled the
shawl tightly around her.

At last they were up the stairs and on the second floor, and finally at
their rooms. Kroger, stopping in front of a door, selected a key, and inserted it in the large iron lock.

When he swung the door open, Jessica could see that the room was
small but clean, but most welcome of all, was the sight of the big four-
poster bed that took up most of the room space. At last! A real bed, instead of the narrow, uncomfortable bunks in the yacht cabin.

"I'll let you get cleaned up, and then we'll go down to dinner,"
Kroger said, not unkindly, although she could tell that he was still put
out with Hernando Villalobos.

Thinking of her wrinkled dress, Jessica said quickly, "Oh, please!
Could I have supper in my room? My clothes—" She gestured. "And
I'm very tired."

Kroger gave her a penetrating glance, before he turned to the interpreter, who was watching both of them with sardonic, red-rimmed
eyes. "Can you ask them to send something to eat here in the room?"

Hernando said cheerfully, "Of course, señor. It will be no difficulty."

"Good!" Kroger turned again to Jessica. "We will get you some
clothes tomorrow. Villalobos tells me there is a marketplace where we
can purchase clothes and other things we may need, although I suppose the clothes will be Mexican or Indian garments."

"That will be all right," she murmured; and then, trying to sound
grateful: "Thank you."

He smiled at her. "Well, I did promise to take good care of you,
now that you're back. And I mean to do just that. Yes, indeed!"

Jessica, noting Hernando's quizzical look, flushed. What must he
think? What had Kroger told the man about their relationship? How
had he explained her presence? Or perhaps he had said nothing, leaving Hernando to think what he might. But soon, God willing, she
would find a chance to explain to the interpreter herself. Until then, it
did not really matter who he thought she was.

It was not until the men had left her alone and she heard the key
turn in the lock, that she realized that Kroger had not given her a key
to her room.

Despite the clamor downstairs, the noise did not seem to penetrate the thick, white walls of her room; and Jessica, after a heavy supper of beans, rice, and some kind of meat that she could not identify, crawled into the welcome comfort of the large bed. Sometime later, she awoke briefly, thinking she heard the sound of a key turning in the lock. She thought Kroger had already locked the door. She was asleep again before the thought was fully completed.

And then—it could not have been much later—she was abruptly awakened by a heavy weight easing down on the other side of the bed. She sat bolt upright, her heart thudding with frightening intensity, as she realized that someone was sitting on the edge of the bed. Although the room was too dark to see, she knew instinctively that it was Brill Kroger. Dear God! Was he changing his persona again? Had he suddenly remembered who she really was? Was he going to? . . .

The other body raised the covers and slipped in next to her, all the while speaking not a single word. Jessica felt a scream building in her throat. She choked it back as she slowly realized that he had made no move to touch her, but was squirming about, as someone will who is trying to get comfortable before going to sleep.

Gradually her heartbeat slowed, and she lay back down. Then he did touch her, on the hand, tentatively, gently, almost furtively. Tense, not daring to move, Jessica suffered his touch. To her amazement she heard him humming softly—"Greensleeves." If he was going to attack her, he was going about it in a very strange way!

For what seemed an eternity, she lay tense and still, with his hand touching hers, waiting for something to happen, the minutes like hours. And then, at first faintly, but slowly growing louder, a sound filled the room. It was the sound of snoring, and she realized in great astonishment that he had fallen asleep.

Much later, near dawn, she fell asleep herself; and when she awakened, at full light with the sound of a cock crowing in her ears, Kroger was gone.

The incident left her feeling shaken and very confused. How could she keep on dealing with this man who was obviously mad, without going mad herself? She must talk with Hernando Villalobos, and soon!

After a simple breakfast of fruit, coffee, and sweet breads, which was again delivered to her room, Jessica was ready when Kroger knocked at her door. When she opened it to him, he seemed serene, unembarrassed, as if the night before had never happened. Well, she decided, she was willing to go along with that. As far as she was concerned, she would like to be able to forget it *had* happened.

Hernando was with Kroger, and the three of them left the inn together, under the still curious eyes of the other guests. It was early, the shadows long and cool, and the blazing heat of the tropic day was yet to descend upon them, although its promise hung heavy in the air.

Jessica, despite her uncomfortable night, felt better than she had since leaving Tampa. She looked around with active curiosity as the cart, with Hernando driving, and she and Kroger in the back, moved into the inner city.

The city looked very Spanish, much more so than Ybor City, but then, it was clearly very old. There were many large stone houses with red-tiled roofs, great wooden entrance doors, and tall windows protected by wrought-iron grilles, which she was to learn were called *rejas*.

Jessica wondered just how old the city really was and leaned forward to speak to Hernando. "Señor Villalobos, could you tell me how old Mérida is? Do you happen to know when it was founded?"

Hernando turned. "Why, yes, señorita. It is a very old city. Francisco de Montejo, the Younger, conquered Yucatán in 1546 and built the Spanish city that you see here now, but long before that it was a city of the Mayans, called Tiho. There, just on the other side of the plaza, that is called Montejo House. And there, that great yellow building, is the cathedral. It was built two hundred years ago."

Jessica looked with great interest at the huge Montejo mansion. On its façade was a sculptured escutcheon showing two Spanish knights with their armored feet upon the heads of kneeling natives.

"Are those Mayans? Those natives in the carving?" she asked. "They look just like the people I see in the streets."

Kroger whipped around and glaring at Hernando, said, "Did I not forbid you to translate for her, Villalobos?"

Hernando looked surprised. "Si, señor, but I was not translating, only answering a question the señorita asked."

Jessica, shocked out of her study of the city, realized that Kroger did not intend for her to speak with the interpreter at all, and she felt a tug of dismay. How was she to find out anything? And more importantly, how was she to tell Hernando of her situation? She had to persuade Kroger to allow him to talk to her!

Forcing herself to smile sweetly, speaking in a wheedling voice, she said, "Oh, but please, Brill! Let him tell me about the city. I'm really curious and would dearly love to know. After all, neither of us has ever been here before."

Kroger was scowling, but he appeared somewhat mollified. "Yes, I suppose there is no great harm in that." Then he leaned close to her and whispered behind his hand, "But I forbid you to converse with him otherwise, is that understood?"

Hating herself, Jessica simpered. "Yes, of course. Just as you say, Brill. I just want to inquire about the things we see. Is that all right?" She looked at him pleadingly, and then, suddenly divining what he wanted, she placed a hand on his arm and looked meltingly into his eyes.

His expression lightened at once. "I suppose that is all right. Personally, I can't say I care that much for all this ancient history, but if it would please you, you have my permission."

"Thank you, Brill," she said brightly, and squeezed his hand.

Kroger positively beamed. He raised his voice. "All right, Villalobos, you may go ahead with your lecture tour. The lady wants to know about the city."

"Very good, señor." Hernando's voice, Jessica thought, had a twist of sarcasm.

"Well, my lady, Tiho, the old city, was built more than a thousand years ago. It would have appeared very strange to your eyes. When Montejo came, they built Mérida right on top of the ruins of Tiho, using much of the stone in their own buildings, so that there is nothing left of the old city. There are, however, other large ruined cities near here. Chichén-Itza and Uxmal, for instance. Although they are mostly covered with jungle growth now, they are still wondrous to see."

At the mention of the other cities, Jessica noticed that Kroger's interest perked up. "Is this Chichén-Itza far from here?"

Hernando shrugged. "Oh, about a three-day journey, señor. Uxmal is nearer."

"I have heard of Chichén-Itza," Kroger said animatedly. "They say there is some kind of sacred well there."

Hernando nodded solemnly. "Si, señor. There are two wells. One was used for drinking needs, and the other was a holy well, used for sacrifices."

Kroger smiled secretively. "I would like to talk to you about that later."

"Whenever you wish, Señor Kroger," Hernando said formally.

"Oh, señorita, now we are coming to the *mercado,* the marketplace. If you see something you like, we can stop and make our way on foot."

Jessica gazed around wide-eyed, taking in the many open booths, the goods spread upon low tables and upon the ground. Everywhere there was a blaze of color: fruit piled high, oranges, papayas, mangoes, bananas; piles of shawls; and racks of colorful dresses. And all around them were the busy sounds of a marketplace in full swing: calls of vendors; voices haggling prices; and music coming from what appeared to be eating and drinking establishments.

She said to Kroger, "I would like to get some of the native dresses, if I may. They look cool, comfortable, and easy to care for."

Hernando smiled back over his shoulder, and Kroger frowned at him. "They are called *huipils,* señorita. And if I may suggest, a pair of sturdy sandals. You will find that your slippers will not stand up well to those cobbled streets."

The cart was slowing now, as both foot and vehicular traffic had increased threefold.

"Señor and señorita," Hernando said, "I think it would be best if we left the cart and proceeded on foot from here."

With some grumbling, Kroger consented, and soon they were strolling through the marketplace, making their way laboriously through and past the shops, stalls, and street vendors. Jessica felt overwhelmed by the sights, sounds, and smells; so intrigued was she that she almost forgot her predicament.

In a relatively short period of time she was able to find and buy two finely embroidered huipils, a pair of stout sandals, and a beautiful tortoise-shell comb for her hair.

She was quite thrilled with her purchases until she saw an elegant Spanish lady, trailed by her maid, making her way regally through the crowd. It was then that Jessica realized that the clothing she had bought was worn only by the Indians and that she would not be suitably dressed to mingle with the Europeans in Mérida.

"I wonder," she said timidly, "if we shouldn't shop for some regular clothing, as well."

"I know of an excellent dressmaker and tailor, señorita," Hernando said, "but their establishments are on the other side of the city."

"That will have to wait until tomorrow," Kroger said absently. He had stopped to examine an exquisitely wrought dagger, in a leather sheath. "I don't want to spend too much time shopping today. I have to find a house, a place to live."

"If you will permit me, Señor Kroger, I know a man here in Mérida, one Tomas Herera, who deals in property. If there is something available in the city, I am sure he would have knowledge of it."

"I would like something a distance out of town," Kroger said. And then he spoke to the small, brown man behind the row of knives. "I'll take that one." He pointed to the dagger.

Jessica suppressed a shiver of revulsion, vividly remembering the knife that he had pressed to her throat at the hotel.

The transaction completed, they made their way again toward the cart. "Forgive me, Señor Kroger, but it may be difficult to find a Spanish style house outside of the city, and I do not think you would be comfortable in one of the native houses." Hernando indicated a small dwelling some distance away, at the edge of the marketplace. "Do you see that house, the one with the grass roof? That is a typical native house, and it is quite primitive by your standards, I am sure. That is all you will find away from the main part of the city, except for the haciendas, and they are mostly the property of the wealthy."

Jessica studied the small house with some curiosity. It was attractive in its simple way, just an oval of white plaster with a roof of fronds. Its unusual shape made it very graceful.

Kroger was frowning. "Well, if that is the case, perhaps we'll see what we can find in town, although I'd rather not be right in the center."

"Oh, I am certain that Tomas can find you something, for the right price," Hernando said slyly.

Kroger peered at him suspiciously. "For the right price, eh? Well, if he can find something acceptable, I am quite willing to pay, but I would advise you to inform this man that I am no innocent. I will know if he is gouging me."

Hernando laughed softly. "Have no fear, señor. I, myself, would never take you for an innocent."

Kroger peered at him closely. "What is that supposed to mean?"

Hernando widened his eyes guilelessly. "Nothing, señor. It is only that I, Hernando Villalobos, recognize you as a man of the world."

He's not stupid, Jessica thought, hiding a smile; Hernando may be a bit of a sot, but he is far from a fool.

*   *   *

Despite Hernando's warning, Tomas Herera did manage to find them a hacienda outside of town, a fine, large house, whose owner was returning to Spain. Built around an inner patio, it had large, airy rooms and high ceilings that helped to alleviate the humid summer heat.

Kroger hired an Indian woman to cook and clean, and a boy as well, to do the heavier work.

True to his promise, Kroger had taken Jessica to the dressmaker Hernando had recommended, and he had purchased for her two complete ensembles in the modern style and had ordered for himself two suits to replace those he had left behind in Tampa.

Hernando Villalobos was still with them, as interpreter and guide; but so far Jessica had been unable to get him alone for a private conversation. She had been certain that as soon as they were settled into a house, Kroger would relax his guard enough so that she would be able to speak to Hernando alone, but it seemed that she had been wrong.

Kroger had quartered Hernando in a room away from the main part of the house; and when not in his room, the man was almost always with Kroger. They all dined together, but since Kroger was always present, this provided her with no opportunity to talk to Hernando.

Two weeks had passed now, making it over three weeks since Kroger had abducted her in Tampa, and Jessica had been able to do nothing toward making her escape.

At night, lying in her room, she often gave way to tears. Images of her mother and father haunted her. How was her mother bearing up? And then thoughts of Neil would come, slipping into her mind and heart, tugging at her emotions until she would finally fall into an exhausted slumber.

And then there were the nights that Kroger repeated his bizarre behavior of that first night in Mérida and came into her bed, like some great child, to cuddle near her shuddering body. Always he would be gone by first light, and always he seemed not to remember the incident the next day.

Even though he never made the first move to molest her, Jessica dreaded these visits, and the fear of them made all of her nights restless and wakeful.

During the day she had nothing to do. The housekeeper took care of the house and did the cooking, and there was nothing for Jessica to turn her hand to. And since Kroger kept her a virtual prisoner, she soon became very bored, and increasingly despondent.

She grew even more desperate to talk to Hernando alone. She had a strong feeling that her time was running out. Although Kroger continued to treat her with the same strange consideration, Jessica could see that something was working in him. Despite his earlier statement that he had come here to rest and relax, he seemed to be doing neither. There was something preying on his mind, she could tell. He was frequently gone from the house for short periods, with Hernando in attendance, and he and Hernando were forever talking together in the manner of men who had secrets to discuss.

Then there was the matter of the strange equipment they were accumulating in a small shed behind the house. She had observed Kroger storing things out there; and once, while both men were absent, Jessica inspected the shed. It was locked, and peering in through the one dirty window told her very little. All she could see were several objects stacked up, with a concealing tarpaulin over them.

Although this mysterious activity kept Kroger occupied, and therefore away from her, it still made Jessica nervous. She felt that because she had been forced to attune herself to the man's dark moods, she had gained a sort of sixth sense about him; and she was positive that he was growing more and more unstable with every passing day. So far he had not harmed her, but how long would that state of affairs last?

Brill Kroger stared at the gear piled in the shed, then smiled in satisfaction.

Yes indeed, it had been a lucky day when he had decided to flee to Yucatán instead of New York; here he had found the opportunity that he had always yearned for, the chance at the big score, the one that would enable him to retire forever and become a man of wealth and substance, a man to be respected.

He had initially viewed Mérida as a place to rest, to relax, but he had not realized just how primitive it was by American standards. Oh, there were many high-class Spaniards residing here, but they were a snooty lot, who thought themselves very grand; and then, of course, very few of them spoke English. The rest of Mérida's inhabitants were nothing but Indians, and a useless lot *they* were. Yes, the city itself had been a great disappointment to him. There was little entertainment, although he had found a few decent brothels and gambling establishments; but within a few days of their arrival, he had realized that he would have to find some activity to occupy his interest.

Even having *her* with him was not enough. True, she had been behaving well, but now that he had her with him, had her under his control, so to speak, she could not occupy all of his time and interest. It was enough that she was here, that he knew she was his at last.

And so his thoughts had naturally turned to the well at Chichén-Itza and to the treasure he had heard was there. According to the stories, the Indians—crazy bastards, yes, indeed—had thrown all manner of precious objects into the well as offerings to their rain god, Chac. They had thrown in humans, too—young virgin girls, if the tales were to be believed.

Kroger had inquired around, or had Villalobos ask around, and the story was always the same. Countless articles made of pure gold had, for hundreds of years, been tossed into the deep waters of the well.

Of course, being no fool, Kroger had wondered if anyone had ever tried to bring up the treasure. And if not, why?

Villalobos, when Kroger had asked him about this, had laughed heartily. "Oh, si, señor, they have tried! Men, being as they are, greedy for gold and other treasures, have tried many times, but the treasure of the ancients is not so easily retaken from the gods."

"What do you mean?" Kroger had demanded.

"The well is very deep and the currents very swift. Divers have tried to bring up the gold, and some have even found a piece or two, things so beautiful that it would break you heart, señor, to gaze upon them, all of the purest, softest gold. But no one has ever managed to bring up more than a piece or two."

Kroger had been sorely puzzled. "What did you mean, swift current? A current in a well? Why don't they just drain it and pick the treasure off the bottom?"

Villalobos began to laugh again, but he quickly choked it off when he saw Kroger puff up with anger.

"Oh, Señor Kroger! Forgive me, but when I explain, you will see why I am amused. The holy well, you see, is not a well such as you might find in your country. It is a very large, natural well, called a *cenote*, whose waters rise up from the earth's very depths. Perhaps you have noticed that here in Yucatán, there are no rivers upon the surface of the land. Yucatán sits upon limestone, and this limestone is so porous that the water sinks and then runs underground. All our rivers here are beneath the earth, Señor Kroger. But Nature has not been entirely cruel to us. She has made, here and there, natural flumes that rise to the surface, natural wells, that supply fresh water for our peo-

ple. As I told you before, at Chichén-Itza there are two such wells.
One for drinking, the other for holy use.

"Mérida, also, draws her water from just such a well. All the cities
of Yucatán were founded near such water sources, although nowadays
they dig their own wells, too, to tap the subterranean rivers. So you
see, this is not a simple well of which we speak. The walls of the well
are very steep, and the water is many feet below the ground level. A
diver must descend by rope to the water level, then plunge into the
depths. The currents deep in the well are quite swift, and many divers
have gone into the well, never to come up again. Perhaps Chac has
taken them, too, as a sacrifice."

Kroger had grunted at this display of native superstition. Villalobos
had proven to be very valuable to him, but he still did not fully trust
the man—he trusted no man who showed unfailing good humor,
which Villalobos did. Even when the interpreter was drunk, he never
grew abusive or argumentative. He simply became more cheerful. At
any rate, Kroger needed the man, and he was willing to overlook this
failing, as well as the man's fondness for drink.

And so he had confided in Villalobos his plans for getting the treasure. He needed the man until the gold was retrieved, then he could
easily be eliminated. Having already killed once, Kroger knew that he
would not find it so unsettling the second time.

In the meantime Kroger kept himself busy thinking of ways in
which he might harvest the treasure that lay beneath the well's icy
waters. There had to be a way. There was always a way. It was just a
matter of proper planning, and that had always been his forte. Yes, indeed!

He had begun buying equipment, ropes, and tackle, and what diving equipment he could find in Mérida, thankful for the experience at
diving he had gleaned during his one treasure-hunting expedition. Of
course, that time there had been no treasure, it had merely been an
excuse to con the mark out of a tidy sum of money.

This time, Kroger was confident that the gold was there, and he was
equally confident that he was resourceful enough to salvage it.

Chapter Nineteen

As soon as Alvarado Moreno had given her the map, Maria had called Wyngate Manning, and now she and Tom were on their way to the Manning home.

The map was rough, but clear enough. Besides showing the small islands off Florida's west coast, one of which had been marked with an X, it also showed the Gulf of Mexico and the coast of Yucatán, with another large X opposite the city of Mérida.

Maria was certain as she could be that this was where Kroger had fled with Jessica, but Tom was still somewhat dubious. He kept reminding her that the mere fact that the map had been in Kroger's possession did not necessarily mean that it revealed where he had gone. It was quite possible, he contended, that the map could have been left behind as a false clue, to set his pursuers haring off on the wrong trail. Maria had argued that Kroger clearly did not intend to leave the satchel behind, but had done so because he had had no alternative.

At any rate, Maria's intuition told her that the map was vitally important, and she was anxious to get it into Wyngate Manning's hands. When she had spoken to him on the telephone, he had been very excited about the discovery, and he seemed to agree with her that the map offered at least a chance, a starting point, which was something they had not had until now.

When Anne Manning opened the front door and admitted them into the dim parlor, both Maria and Tom stopped short at the sight of a man getting up from the divan to come toward them.

Tom was the first to speak. "Neil! I'll be damned! You're the last person I expected to see. You're back. Lord, am I glad to see you!"

The two men thumped one another on the back, both grinning widely, and Maria finally recognized the man as the young lieutenant who had been so interested in Jessica that night at the officers' ball. He looked somehow different, thin, drawn, somewhat older, and a bit pale. Surprisingly, he was also out of uniform.

Tom echoed her thought. "Neil, you're out of uniform! And what are you doing here?"

"I was wounded. I was sent back early, although many of the others should be returning soon, now that Santiago has surrendered. As for the uniform, I suppose I am a little premature, but I doubt anyone will much care, since my discharge will be coming through any day now."

Maria stepped forward. It was just possible that he had seen Ramon or Eduardo or Carlos. "Did you meet any of the Cuban rebels, Lieutenant?"

Neil looked at her, frowning. Then his face cleared as he evidently recognized her. "As a matter of fact, I did. When I was wounded, I spent some time in a rebel camp. They probably saved my life."

"My brothers," Maria said, "and a—a friend of mine, by the name of Carlos Chavez, are in Cuba, fighting under General Nuñez. I know there are many other Cubans there, but I was wondering if you had come across them. We have heard nothing of them since they left Tampa."

Neil nodded. "It's possible, of course. Your brothers, you say? I recognize you, from the hotel, but I never learned your name."

"Maria Mendes, Lieutenant, and my brothers are Ramon and Eduardo Mendes."

Neil's face went still, his eyes distant. "Ramon Mendes. Yes, I met him. He came to the rebel camp the night before I left, with a group of returning rebel fighters, and I seem to remember him mentioning that his brother was with him. What a remarkable coincidence!"

Maria said eagerly, "Was he all right? Was he well?"

"He seemed fine. He was not wounded, if that is your question. I didn't see your other brother, but Ramon spoke of him as if he were present in the camp."

"And my friend, Carlos," she said hesitantly. "Did you hear of him, also?"

"I don't recall, Miss Mendes. Of course, there were a number of the rebels, and I didn't meet all of them. Also, I left the camp the day after they arrived, as I said. No, wait!" Neil snapped his fingers. "Of course, your brother did mention that he had a friend with him, but he didn't mention his name. But I'm sure he's all right."

"I'm sure he is." Maria sighed softly. Still, she wished that Neil had seen Carlos so that she could be positive that he was alive and well. Tom had stepped to her side, and now gave her hand a gentle squeeze. She was spared looking at him as Anne Manning spoke.

"Won't you all be seated, please? I've made some lemonade and some cookies. . . ." Without warning she started to cry, the tears welling up and running down her cheeks. "I'm sorry." She dabbed at her eyes with a linen handkerchief. "But the cookies I made are Jessica's favorites, and I just—"

Maria stepped forward quickly and put her arms around the older woman's shoulders. "It's all right, Mrs. Manning. We all understand, I'm sure. But now, with this map we've come across, perhaps something can be done about finding Jessica."

"Yes, the map," Wyngate Manning said eagerly. "May I see it, please?"

Maria opened her bag and took out the folded piece of paper. "As I told you on the phone, Mr. Manning, this was found in Kroger's satchel, which he evidently was forced to leave behind when he fled. In my opinion, it reveals his route of escape."

Wyngate Manning took the map with trembling fingers, and Tom and Neil squatted down beside him as he unfolded it on the coffee table.

Tom said, "If this map is to be trusted, it appears that he was headed for Mérida, in Yucatán. To me, it seems like an odd place for him to go."

"Perhaps not so odd, Tom," Neil said thoughtfully. "Mexico has always been a favorite place for American criminals to flee to escape prosecution. We can't bother them there, not legally."

"But don't they usually go to some place like Vera Cruz, where there is more excitement, as well as other Americans of their own ilk?"

"Again, not necessarily. Kroger may have had reasons of his own for choosing Mérida," Neil responded. "I think it's at least worth a try. We have nothing else to go on, after all, except for the fact that he evidently did flee by sea." He looked at Wyngate Manning. "I haven't had a chance to tell you yet, sir, but after I left here yesterday, I went to the police. I learned that a boat, a steam yacht, was indeed stolen just the day before the ball, and so far hasn't been located. The boat was named the *Maybelle*, after the owner's wife. It seems safe to assume that Kroger stole it and used it to get away. He wouldn't have wanted to rent a boat, or even buy one, since then it would have been a matter of record, and would have left *too* obvious a trail. At any rate, I'm going to leave as soon as I can get a boat and supplies together."

Tom sat back on his heels. "Going, Neil? Going where?"

"I'm going after that bas—Uh, sorry, ladies. I'm going after Kroger and Jessica. The police seem to have reached a dead end, and they can't go into Mexico anyway, not officially. But *I* can."

"I can get you a boat, Neil," Wyngate Manning said, his voice quickening with hope. "I just wish I could go with you, but—" He looked at his wife and smiled wanly. "I can't leave Anne alone at this time."

Maria, who had been listening quietly, noticed a thoughtful expression on Tom's face. Abruptly he said, "I want to go with you, Neil." And as Neil started to speak, he cut him off, "No, hear me out. The war is over, and I'll have no trouble getting leave. This inactivity is driving me crazy. You'll need some help, you know that, and we get along well. I want to go with you!"

Maria stared at him in surprise and some dismay. She knew how disappointed he had been at being left behind when the troops were sent to Cuba; but even so, she thought that, feeling as he said he did about her, he would want to remain close to her. She felt a strange, unfamiliar emotion, and she realized that she was hurt by his apparent eagerness to leave her side. Of course, to be fair, she had more or less turned down his proposal, and his going with Neil was certainly in a good cause. But irrationally, she felt hurt and rejected. She did not want him to go!

And then an idea came to her, an idea so outrageous that she immediately rejected it.

The two men were still talking about Tom accompanying Neil on the trip. Finally Neil's face brightened, and he clapped the other man on the shoulder. "All right, old friend! I'll accept your offer and gladly. It certainly won't do any harm to have someone with me that I can trust."

It was a ridiculous idea, Maria thought. What would Mama say, and Papa? Still, if it was so ridiculous, why would it not go away? Why did it keep growing and growing until she suddenly heard herself putting voice to it? "Tom, Lieutenant Dancer—I think you should take me along, as well. I wish to go with you."

A sudden silence fell, a silence as ominous as the heavy, crackling air before the advent of a storm. The others stared at her as though she had suddenly taken leave of her senses.

They were apparently struck speechless, and taking quick advantage, Maria rushed on. "It's not as foolish as it sounds. For instance, do either of you speak Spanish?"

The two men exchanged quick glances, and Neil shook his head. "Speaking for myself, only a few words."

Maria glanced at Tom. "And neither do you, Tom. Remember last night with Alvarado?"

"That's right, I don't."

"Well, then? You will be going into a country where almost no English is spoken. How do you intend to communicate—by sign language? How can you hope to find Kroger if you can't even talk to the natives? You will need an interpreter."

Neil stared at her, his expression puzzled but not unkind. "Miss Mendes—Maria, forgive me, but you're a woman. What you say may be true, but there are others, men in Ybor City, whom we can hire for that purpose."

She said doggedly, "The older men all work and have families to care for, and most of the younger men have gone to Cuba. I'm sure you can eventually find someone, yes, but it will be someone you don't know, someone you may not be able to depend on. Besides, just *looking* for someone else will take up valuable time. I am here, available, and ready to leave whenever you are."

Tom got up and came over to sit beside her, taking her hands in his. "But why, Maria? It will be a rough trip, and it could be dangerous, you know. We already know that Kroger has killed once."

Maria, caught up in her own boldness, said firmly, "For many reasons. First, because you need an interpreter. Second, because I know and like Jessica, and thinking of her in the hands of that man makes me ill." She paused. "And there is something else. The police arrived at Kroger's hotel room in time to save me, but then he took Jessica, and I can't help feeling that, in a way, she was taken in my place. That may sound illogical, but it's the way I feel." She turned to Anne Manning. "Do *you* understand, Mrs. Manning?"

The other woman nodded. "Yes, I think I do."

Neil gazed at Tom in speculation. "What do you think, Tom? We do need someone to interpret for us. I agree there's some element of danger, but with both of us along. . . ."

Tom sighed heavily. "Maria is strong, and she is brave. She is also very stubborn, and I have a feeling that we'd probably expend more energy discouraging her than if we simply agreed to take her along." He laughed suddenly, a joyous sound, and squeezed Maria's hand. "And why should I deny it? I'd love to have her along!"

Neil nodded gravely at Maria. "Then I suppose it's settled, Maria. Welcome aboard."

Maria had known that her announcement to her parents would initiate a terrible scene, and in that she was not mistaken.

Ynez Mendes had been very upset, although perhaps "upset" was too mild a word for the feelings her mother had voiced. Of course, in all justice, her mother had some justification since, with the older boys gone, all her children would be away from her side, with only little Paulo left.

Felix Mendes, usually so tolerant and lenient with Maria, had become very angry with her, and in the end had forbidden her to go.

Amidst all the uproar and the torrent of emotion pouring down on her, Maria had remained calm, doing the best she could to soothe their apprehensions, trying to explain how she felt, why she was going. And all through the emotional storm raging around her, she remained adamant. She was going, no matter what they said; she *was* of age, after all, so they could not prevent her going, unless they tied her to the bedpost.

At long last, worn out, her mother had ceased to rail at her, and her father had stormed off to the hotel. They were finally resigned to the fact that she was going, with or without their permission.

Maria, who had always acceded to her parents' wishes, was saddened by the scene her announcement had caused, but she was nonetheless elated. She was naturally excited that she was embarking on an adventure that would take her away from the humdrum existence she had grown to dislike; but a large part of her excitement, she realized, came from the knowledge that she would be in the company of Tom Farrel for an extended period of time. There was still Carlos to consider, but she would handle that when the time came.

As she stood over the small satchel that she was taking, trying to choose and pack clothing that would be suitable for a trip to Yucatán, Maria could hear her mother in the kitchen, banging pots and pans, slamming cupboard doors.

Maria smiled to herself. Her mother was still furious—she always made loud noises in her kitchen when she was angry. But it would be all right, Maria consoled herself. When it was all over and Jessica was back with her family, her mother would forgive and forget. For all that she was volatile by nature, Ynez Mendes was not a person to hold a grudge or nurse an anger.

Maria's head came up as she heard the sound of a loud knock on the front door, followed by her mother's mutterings and angry footsteps on the floor as she went to answer the door.

As Maria reached for a muslin shirtwaist to pack, a quiet descended on the house, to be broken a moment later by her mother's sharp cry.

Maria whirled away from the bed, running for the front room. What had happened? Her heart almost stopped beating when she recalled how several of the families in Ybor City had received telegrams from the government, telling them that a son or brother or husband had been killed in combat in Cuba. Could this be a telegram about Ramon's death? Or Eduardo's?

As she ran into the parlor, Maria also cried out, but from astonishment, not anguish. In the parlor stood Eduardo and Carlos, bearded and unkempt, but all in one piece.

Ynez was hugging them alternately and crying out: "Oh, *mis hijos! mis hijos!*" She drew back from them and peered around behind them. She voiced the question that had suddenly occurred to Maria. "But where is Ramon? Where is my eldest son?"

Maria, who had reached her mother now, flung her arms around the woman, restraining her, staring at Carlos with dread.

"Ramon, where is he?" Ynez Mendes cried again. "My Ramon, he is dead! He is not coming back to me! Oh, *Madre de Dios!*"

All the while Carlos had been speaking, but her voice drowned his out. Maria said gently, "Hush, Mama. Carlos is trying to tell us something."

Carlos said, "Thank you, Maria. No, *Mamacita,* your son is *not* dead. Ramon is alive and well, and sends his love to you, to all of you."

His words finally penetrated, and Ynez Mendes sagged in Maria's arms. "He is well, my son? Then where is he?" Her voice rose accusingly. "Why is he not with you?"

Eduardo smiled. "Because he is still in Cuba, Mama. He has decided to stay there."

Another wail came from Ynez Mendes. "Stay in Cuba? But why is that? Why does he not come home, to the bosom of his family?"

Eduardo took his mother from Maria's embrace, placed her head on his shoulder, and lovingly stroked her hair. "Because he is a patriot, Mama, and because Cuba needs him. There will be much to do, a new government to set up. He is needed there. You know Ramon. You know he has always felt that Cuba is his real home. He has decided to stay and help rebuild Cuba. He sends his love to you and Papa and says that he will visit from time to time."

Carlos spoke quietly, his gaze now on Maria. "He is doing what he feels he must do, *Mamacita*. Do not begrudge him that. Ramon is a man now and must go his own way."

Maria, studying Carlos, experienced a confusion of emotions that she could not quite sort out. He looked different, leaner and stronger in the dark beard and rough combat clothing, but then her attention was distracted as her mother keened again.

"My son, my Ramon! He will be alone in a strange land. He was too small when he left Cuba to remember it."

"He will not be alone, *Mamacita*," Carlos said soothingly. "He will be with friends. We joined up with a group of rebels, outside of Santiago. They are good people, loyal Cubans, strong and true, and Ramon is with them."

Maria touched her mother's cheek. "Don't be sad, Mama. Ramon is alive and well and doing what he feels he must do. Be glad for him. And stop your tears. Eduardo is here, and Carlos. They have returned. Show them that you are glad of that."

Ynez Mendes straightened up. "But of course I am glad. You have not been eating, the pair of you. You are too skinny," she said in a scolding voice. "Come, I will feed you well."

Carlos cleared his throat. "In a little while, *Mamacita*. First, I wish a few words in private with Maria. Will you come into the garden with me, Maria?"

Her mother gave Maria a sly, triumphant glance, which Maria ignored. She was suddenly shy with Carlos, as if he were a complete stranger. "Of course, Carlos. Mama, we'll be back in a few minutes."

Outside, in the shade of the arbor, Carlos turned to her, his expression serious. He did not attempt to take her into his arms, and she wondered as to the reason.

"Maria," he said slowly, his eyes dark and unreadable, "I wanted to tell you this at once, so you could make your decision. It would not be fair to you otherwise."

Maria shivered suddenly, although the morning was already heavy with heat. His manner seemed somehow ominous.

"Maria, I too have decided to remain in Cuba permanently. I returned only to see you and tell you this, and to ask if you will come with me."

Maria felt a sense of shock. Cuba? Such a possibility had occurred to her, but never seriously.

"If you are thinking that you will know no one there, that you would be a woman alone among men, you are wrong. There are several women already with the rebel group, and one of them, Margarita Gomez, has been with them since the beginning of the rebellion, often fighting alongside the men. I know that you would like her, for she is a strong woman, like you, Maria."

"You are set on this course, Carlos?"

He nodded, his expression still guarded. "Yes, I know now that my life is there. The question is, do you want to share it with me?"

"Carlos," she said, gesturing helplessly. "I don't know what to say. This is so sudden!"

"I know. That is why I had to tell you at once, so that you may get used to the idea, so that you may have time to think about it."

Maria leaned back against the arbor slats. "Carlos . . . is something else wrong? You have not even tried to kiss me. Have your feelings toward me changed that much?"

He flushed and said softly, "I have not changed, Maria. I still love you, still want you for my wife. It is just that I feel it is unfair, what I am asking of you. Although I have thought long and hard on this, to make the decision that this is what I must do with my life, I have no right to ask you to share it with me. Therefore, if you cannot see your way clear to marrying me and living in Cuba, I will accept your decision, with much sadness."

Maria, still shaken by his announcement, stared at him piercingly, for he spoke the words as if he felt they were required of him, as if he felt it was his duty. Somehow, she sensed that the words did not mirror his true feelings.

And yet, it could be for the best, for it would release her of her promise and free her completely for the journey to Yucatán. But she had to have time to consider it very carefully; it would be easy to make a mistake that she might regret for the rest of her life.

She nodded formally. "All right, Carlos, I will think of what you have told me. I think you should leave me now. I need some time to myself."

And then he did take her into his arms, but gingerly, and the touch of his mouth on hers was light and did not ignite any warmth in her. After a moment he stepped back, gave her that same unreadable look, and nodded. Without another word he turned on his heel and entered the house.

Maria sank down onto the stone bench. As she stared after Carlos, a name popped into her mind, a name he had spoken—Margarita Gomez. Thinking back, she realized that a warmth, a hint of sincere feeling, had invaded his voice when he spoke the name. Was that the reason for his change of attitude?

She sat for a long time, her thoughts tumultuous. Did she really love Carlos? Could she go to Cuba with him? And Tom Farrel, how about Tom? She strove for calm, realizing that it was now time for a decision. The thought that Carlos had found another woman in Cuba and had been attracted to her gave Maria a feeling of rejection; and yet, at the same time, she experienced a sense of relief. In his own way Carlos had helped toward her decision. All along, she had been reluctant to hurt him. Now she was sure that he would not really be hurt, even if he did not at the moment know this. If she spurned his proposal, he could return to Cuba, and this Margarita, with a free conscience.

As Maria thought of Tom, a feeling of love and warmth crept over her. Tom was the man she wanted. She knew now that, in the back of her mind, he had been her choice all along, despite their cultural differences and despite the fact that in choosing him she was embarking on a path into the unknown and venturing into a life strange to her. However, she felt that she was strong enough to survive. If nothing else, she was a survivor.

Her resolve made, she arose from the bench. She would tell Carlos at once, so that he could return to Cuba, and his chosen life. Her feeling was strong now that he was attracted to this Margarita and refused to admit it to himself because of his prior commitment to her. Carlos was a good, decent man, and he deserved a good woman beside him, unlike Ramon who, Maria always felt, cared more for his precious causes than he ever would for any woman. She would send Carlos away with her good wishes.

Before going into the house, she stretched, her face turned up to the sun, thinking of the adventure ahead. If what she had heard was true, the sun of Yucatán would be even hotter than it was here in Florida. Her shoulders squared, her mind free of tension at last, she strode into the house.

Maria's parents refused to sanction her adventure by accompanying her to the boat that Wyngate Manning had managed to borrow for their use, but Eduardo and Carlos went along.

Carlos had taken her decision calmly enough, once he was convinced that she meant it, which brought her great relief and convinced her more than ever that his heart really lay with the woman in Cuba.

He even supported her decision to accompany Tom and Neil on the expedition. "I have seen women perform many heroic tasks in Cuba," he had said, smiling. "If I once thought that women were fit only for certain things, I certainly do not think so now."

Eduardo, however, had reservations about the undertaking and tended to side with their parents. Still, he wanted to see her off; and he had given Maria his solemn promise that he would look after their parents, since he intended to remain in Tampa.

The boat, a trim sloop large enough to sleep six comfortably and sleek enough, Neil said, to make fast time with a good wind, was called the *Kelpie,* and Maria thought that she was very beautiful.

She stowed her things below-decks, in the rear of the cabin, which Tom had turned into separate quarters for her by putting up a heavy canvas curtain.

The day was already hot, but there was a good breeze. Maria, attired in a muslin shirtwaist and ankle-length, navy-blue skirt, had her hair tied back in a colorful scarf, and she felt unfettered and free in the simple clothes.

She was imbued with the most marvelous state of excitement, not only because she was going to help someone she considered her friend, but, she had to admit, because of the adventure itself. She, who had never been outside Tampa since her family had moved there, would now be crossing the Gulf of Mexico, to a country she had only heard of; and she would be in the company of the man she now happily admitted to herself that she loved.

She had not told Tom of her decision as yet. There had not really been time, and besides, the occasion had to be just right. Perhaps during the voyage across the Gulf, she would tell him, and then it would be a new life for both of them. She hugged herself and shivered in her delight at the thought.

Her things stowed away, she went up on deck to join Tom and Neil as they prepared to depart.

*   *   *

The trip across the Gulf took them several days, despite fair winds and good weather.

Neil found that the *Kelpie* handled like a dream. The trip had been uneventful, except for the obviously growing closeness between his two shipmates, which Neil watched with indulgent amusement. Good for Tom, he thought. Maria Mendes was an exceptional young woman, her beauty aside. How many other women would have volunteered to set out on such a dangerous and certainly uncomfortable journey? Not many, he was sure. The trouble was, seeing Maria and Tom together, so obviously in love, made his heart ache for Jessica.

He tried not to think of her with Brill Kroger, tried not to think of what Kroger might have done to her, what outrages he might have committed on her person, but it was difficult to keep such speculations out of his mind.

During the long nights, when it was Tom's turn at the wheel—they were sailing day and night—Neil promised himself that no matter what had happened to Jessica, no matter how vilely Kroger might have abused her, he would somehow put it out of his mind and never speak of it to her. If he could find her alive and find that she still loved him, that was enough to expect. They would put whatever else had happened behind them, and never discuss it. Which did not mean, he thought grimly, that Brill Kroger was not going to pay for abducting her!

At last the shoreline of Yucatán came into view, and a short while later, in late afternoon, they anchored in the harbor of Progreso, where they would have to leave the sea and strike inland.

In Progreso, Neil planned to buy either horses or mules, to take them overland to the city of Mérida. Also, he hoped to find someone in the town who had seen the boat, the *Maybelle*, or Kroger and Jessica. If nothing else, it would serve to verify that they were on the right trail.

The morning after docking, they went ashore early, and Maria began to ask her question of everyone they encountered—Had they seen a man of Kroger's description with a pretty blond girl? Or had they seen a steam yacht named the *Maybelle*?

All they received were negative answers, as the natives stared at the three of them as much as *they* stared at the natives. And then, when they had at last found a Spaniard from whom they could purchase horses and pack mules, they received an encouraging reply to Maria's question. The Spaniard admitted to seeing such a man—tall, dark-haired, with a mustache and strange, wild eyes. And yes, the man was accompanied by a beautiful, golden-haired *señorita,* and another man, a Spaniard, as well.

"A Spaniard?" Maria asked in surprise.

"Yes. The *gringo* could not speak our language and hired an interpreter."

"Ask him if he learned where they were going," Neil said, when Maria had translated.

Maria put the question to the man and he shrugged. "He did not say, to me. However, he took the road leading inland, and the road he took only leads to one place, the city of Mérida."

Maria translated to the others.

Neil grinned jubilantly and clapped Tom on the back. "We're on the right trail, by God! It has to be Kroger and Jessica. Maria, ask him how far to Mérida."

Maria relayed the question. "He says that it is twenty-four miles, not far at all. He says that we should be able to make it in one day, on horseback."

After the man left them, they stood grinning foolishly at one another. Neil felt almost giddy with relief, and at the same time highly charged with a flow of adrenaline. How he ached to get his hands on Brill Kroger!

Tom said, "It seems too good to be true. But we'd better get started, if we hope to make Mérida by nightfall. It's almost noon."

Neil's expression turned somber. "We're so *close!*" He smacked his fist into his palm. "I only hope they're still there, in Mérida, and haven't moved on to someplace else."

Maria said, "They're still there, I'm sure of it. I have a feeling about it."

Chapter Twenty

JESSICA awoke as she did every morning, reluctant to face the new day, wanting to escape back into the comforting cocoon of sleep, which gave her some respite from her painful thoughts.

Throwing aside the light sheet that covered her, she gazed dully at the square of light coming in through the high window. The heat was already oppressive, and she could hear the steady, annoying drone of a fly, monotonously crisscrossing the room. Outside, a cock crowed, and she could hear the sound of voices.

Then she remembered. Today was the day they were leaving for the ruined city, Chichén-Itza. She had not been told the reason, and her condition was such that she felt little curiosity.

She shivered, hugging herself with both arms. She had been having these aggravating attacks of shivering for the past three days, and she did not feel at all well. She felt logy and spiritless, as if some malady was draining the strength from her. She knew she should see a doctor; but although she had complained to Kroger about it, he had put her off, saying that she would be fine again in a short while.

"Don't you remember?" he had told her, with that strange, slightly mad smile. "You always used to have these times when you didn't feel well, and the spells always went away. It'll go away this time, just wait and see."

Nothing she could say would make him change his mind. He simply smiled knowingly, shook his head, and told her that she would be fine in a day or two. But three days had passed, and she still felt the same way, weak and easily tired.

And today they were going to start on the journey to Chichén-Itza. At least they were taking the cart, and she would not have to suffer through a lengthy horseback ride. Still, she dreaded the long journey in the enervating heat.

Wearily, she dragged herself from the bed, and slipped one of the huipils over her head. Kroger might just as well have saved his money as far as modern clothes were concerned, she thought. When he had first changed, first began treating her like someone else, someone he seemed to care for and trust, Jessica had thought that he would eventually grant her a certain amount of freedom, but this had not proved to be the case. Although he was kind enough, in his peculiar way, he seldom allowed her out of his sight. She had not been away from the hacienda since the visit to the dressmaker's establishment. She had been as effectively shut away as if she were in prison.

At this thought, she felt the weary weight of depression settle on her again. She thought longingly of Tampa, of her home, her parents, and of Neil. What were they doing? Why had they not come after her? She felt so alone, and so at the mercy of the scary stranger that Kroger had become. The person he now was grew stranger and stranger, day by day, as his madness seemed to accelerate.

She shuddered as she thought of those nights when he slipped into her bed, snuggling next to her like some gross, overgrown child, whispering "Mommie" and humming "Greensleeves." Touching her, asking her to stroke his head, to hold him close—all of which she did, knowing that it was necessary for her survival.

As for her hopes of speaking privately to Hernando, of getting him to help her, that hope was gone. Oh, she had managed to finally talk to him, but that episode had been extremely frustrating.

She became angry as she thought back to that strange conversation. It had occurred on a day when Kroger had had to go into the city, to pick up some more of the items he was storing in the shed.

Kroger had intended to take Hernando with him, but the interpreter, not surprisingly, was drunk and incapable of walking, much less driving the cart. And so Kroger, stiff-lipped with anger at Hernando, locked Jessica in her room, telling her that it was for her own good, especially since she was feeling poorly. He promised to return soon and told her she should rest until then. He left her a plate of food and a pitcher of water.

This crowning indignity upset Jessica so that she began to cry, at first softly, and then, because there was no one to hear her, she let go. All the anger, the hurt and humiliation, and the despair she felt poured out in long, howling sobs, which did not cease until she heard a tentative knock on the door. She sat up, struggling to contain her sobs. If Kroger found her like this, he would be furious.

Then Hernando's slurred voice sounded from the other side of the door. "Are you all right, señorita? Are you in pain?"

"Oh, please!" she cried out. "Let me out! Just open the door and let me out of here!"

She heard him fumble for a few moments with the keyhole. "I cannot, señorita. I do not have the right key. I am sorry."

"The window then," she said frantically. "Perhaps you can get me out through the window."

There was a silence for a long moment as he apparently mulled this over. "Señorita, the window is too high, and far too small, and I am, I am sorry to relate, not in the best of condition. If you need food or water, perhaps I could give that to you through the window, but I fear that is all I can manage. Do you need sustenance? If not, I will leave you, for I am feeling not at all well."

"No, no!" she exclaimed. "Don't go, Hernando, please! I must talk to you. Please don't go yet."

She ran to the door and placed her cheek against it. His voice, sounding weary and weak, replied, "Very well, señorita, I will listen. But have pity and make it very brief, as I feel a great need to lie down again."

"You can hear me? You can hear me well?"

She heard his rasping laugh. "As well as my condition permits, señorita. Please to begin."

Attempting to keep calm and to speak reasonably, Jessica placed her mouth close to the door panel and spoke loudly and distinctly. It was such a bizarre tale, she knew she had to be as convincing as possible, if she expected him to help her. But in spite of her best efforts, the words sometimes tumbled out, as she told of her abduction, Kroger's actions, and her fears that Kroger was mad.

When she was finished, there was complete silence from the other side of the door. "Hernando! Señor Villalobos, did you hear and understand?"

When he finally spoke, he sounded fully sober. "I heard, si. Poor, poor señorita. I am indeed sad for you. I have long thought that all was not well between you and the señor."

Jessica's heart began to hammer with hope. "Then you will help me, Hernando? I have no money with me, but my father has money, and he will pay you well."

Another silence ensued. Then she heard his weighty sigh. "Alas, no, señorita, I cannot. I dare not. I, too, like your Señor Kroger, am in flight from the police, for reasons that would not interest you. But I dare not call attention to myself by going to the authorities with such a tale as yours. They would detain me and question me. Also, señorita, I confess that I am a weak man. I need the money Señor Kroger is going to pay me. Without it, I have nothing. I am indeed regretful. My heart goes out to you, señorita, but I cannot help you."

She heard his voice fade then, like a dying echo, as he went down the hall. "I am sorry. I am sorry. I am . . ."

Jessica clapped her hands over her ears and slid slowly to the floor, her back against the door. Her last hope was gone. She was totally alone, with no one to rely on but herself. Then she *must* do it herself. She had to find a way to escape from Kroger and go to someone in authority in Mérida. Even if she failed in the attempt and aroused his fury, even if he became his other self, the self that remembered who she was and how he really felt about her, even if he killed her, she had to try. Anything would be better than this . . . this limbo she was trapped in!

But then, just when she began to make her plans, she had grown ill with this malady that was so weakening her will and strength that she could scarcely think coherently; and today they were leaving the hacienda, going into the wilderness and to a ruined city with no one she could go to for help, should she manage to escape Kroger's vigilance.

Even so, she was grimly determined to defeat him.

The journey to the ruined city took several days. It was a long distance, and the cart was so heavily laden with supplies, and the items Kroger had been buying the past week, that they could not move very fast. It was so cramped there was only a small place for Jessica to sit.

Hernando drove the cart, and Kroger rode a bay mare he had purchased in Mérida.

Hernando did not speak to Jessica, or even look at her, and she asked no questions about the villages or the other interesting things they passed on the way. She was feeling a little better, but she was still listless and low in spirits. Besides, there was nothing to be gained by striking up a conversation with Hernando; he had made it quite plain that he would not help her.

At night they camped by the side of the road, and Hernando, who was a fair cook when he was sober, prepared simple meals, adding to their own supplies fresh produce and eggs, which he obtained from the villages along their route.

If she had been her usual self, Jessica would have been afire with curiosity about the villages, with their little clusters of oval huts, surrounded by garden patches and fruit trees; but she could only stare at them dully and wonder without much interest what the people's lives were like in such primitive surroundings.

But she stirred out of her lethargy when they finally arrived at Chichén-Itza. After alighting from the cart, Hernando led them down a rock path, through heavy underbrush, and into a large clearing.

Jessica stopped short, gazing around in awe. Rearing up from the edges of the clearing were several huge stone structures, almost smothered in jungle growth, buildings such as Jessica had never seen or conceived of. Great pyramids and templelike structures, made of huge stone blocks, rose from the thick brush; and even though the centuries had covered them with vines and plants, their grandeur was overwhelming.

It was difficult for Jessica to imagine what kind of people once lived in such a city. Even with the structures in partial ruin, and much overgrown, she could still see in them a shadow of the magnificent city that had once existed here.

She drew in her breath. "It's unbelievable! They must have been gods!"

Hernando spoke directly to her for the first time since they had left Mérida. "It was magnificent, si. But they were not gods, the old ones, merely the ancestors of the Mayans you have seen in Mérida and the other villages. But this was not a city of dwellings, you know. If you will notice, they do not build their dwellings here even today, although the buildings could offer them shelter. No, they build their homes on the outskirts, where it is barren, and they come into the old city merely to worship and to give offerings at the holy well. That was the way it was then, also."

Jessica, her anger at him momentarily forgotten, shook her head. "They didn't live here, in the city? Then why was it ever built? What were the buildings for?"

"For worship, señorita. According to the legends passed down, only the priests dwelled here, and the rulers. The main body of the people lived outside, even as they do today."

Kroger, who had been ranging ahead, came striding back toward them. "Well, what are you waiting for, Villalobos? Stop dallying about, and let's get to the well!"

"If you will permit me, Señor Kroger, I would suggest that we make camp for the night and go to the well in the morning. The hour is late, the señorita is tired, and I must confess that I am as well. In the morning we will be fresh."

Kroger peered at him, scowling. "Is it far to the well?"

Hernando shook his head. "Not far, no, but it would not be wise to rush matters. Let the natives get used to our presence, before we proceed to the well. We should proceed with caution and politeness."

Kroger snorted contemptuously. "If you're talking about those raggedy-looking Indians I saw in that last village back there, I can't believe they'll pose any problem."

Hernando gazed about slowly, scanning the area. "Then you would be mistaken, señor. They are all around us now, watching. If you will look carefully, there, near the round temple called the *caracol,* you will see one of them. I suggest that we set up camp outside of the old city, so as not to offend them. Perhaps, as you say, they will do us no harm, but there is nothing to be gained by angering them. Is that not correct?"

Kroger frowned petulantly and then shrugged. "Oh, very well! You're supposed to know these people, and I don't." Then his expression darkened. "But you'd better be steering me straight, Villalobos. If I find out you're lying to me, you'll be damned sorry!"

Hernando nodded dutifully, but Jessica could see that his thin lips held a slight smile, and his dark eyes glittered under the brim of the floppy sombrero. "As you say, señor. Now, shall we find a suitable place to camp?"

He's not as intimidated by Kroger as he pretends to be, Jessica thought. Somehow this insight made her feel better, even though Hernando had refused to help her.

They made their camp on the outskirts of the ruins, as Hernando had suggested, but close enough to see the structures. Once the sun went down, the evening cooled considerably. There was a full moon, and Jessica, watching the outlines of the tall, round temple that Hernando had called the *caracol,* had the uncanny feeling that the spirits of the ancients were there somewhere, drifting about among the ruined temples, watching from the darkness with old and alien eyes. It was an eerie fancy, and she shivered slightly.

As they sat around the campfire, Kroger seemed nervous and tense. He jumped at every sound, every twig crackling in the flames. Jessica, who had formed the habit of watching him closely the better to gauge his moods, grew concerned. He seemed very near to snapping, like an overstretched wire. Just watching him like this made her nervous, too, so that she finally turned to Hernando for distraction.

"How old is Chichén-Itza?" she asked, savoring the sound of the strange name on her tongue. "Do you know, Hernando?"

Hernando spread his hands. "A thousand years, perhaps even two thousand, señorita. It is very ancient, and was already in ruins when my people, the Spaniards, came here over three hundred years ago."

"They must have lived a very strange life, those people," she said dreamily, drawing her knees up and wrapping her arms around them.

He smiled, the firelight throwing flickering shadows on his thin face. He must have been handsome once, she mused; when he was young, and before he drank so much.

"There are pictures," he said quietly. "Carvings in stone, very formal and stiff, but showing how they looked, those old ones. To us today, their dress seems very strange. Short kirtles, or skirts, upon the men, with little covering the torso except for wide pectorals, or collars, which were often made of gold and set with jewels, and bracelets upon their arms and hands. And the headdresses, very high, like a pope's headdress, but decorated with plumes and intricate designs. I have seen artifacts, made of solid gold, beautiful beyond dreaming, and statues as well, that are very strange, nothing like our art or any other art we know today."

"Are there other cities like this one?" Jessica wanted to keep Hernando talking, but she was interested, also, for this unusual place was having a powerful effect upon her imagination. She was feeling much better now, her illness apparently behind her.

"Yes, señorita, I know of at least two more cities. Uxmal, of which I have talked before, is one, and the natives speak of many more."

"It was a whole, great civilization," she said in wonder. "And now it's gone, vanished. Does anyone know why?"

Hernando shrugged. "Civilizations rise, señorita, and they fall. It is the natural way of things. Someday our world, the one we know, may tumble, and men of the future will come and study our ruined cities and speculate on our origins and our end."

"You surprise me, Hernando. You're quite a philosopher."

Hernando ducked his head in embarrassment, but before he could speak, Kroger said crossly, "That's enough of this idle chatter. It's time for sleep. I want to get an early start in the morning." He gazed across the fire at Hernando. "Is it safe here, I mean to sleep without a guard? If those Indians are still wandering around out there . . ."

Hernando smiled tightly. "It is safe, señor. They will not harm us, for we have done nothing to anger them—so far."

Kroger grunted. "Good! Then it's time for us to sleep." He glanced at Jessica. "How do you feel? Do you want me to fix your blankets for you?"

Jessica shook her head. "No, I feel much better for some reason. I can do it myself."

He gave her a penetrating look, then his eyes went out of focus, and he got up without a word and busied himself making a bed away from the fire.

Jessica waited until he had settled down, then made a bed for herself on the opposite side of the fire. She did not think he would venture into her blankets, not with Hernando close by, but she wished to be as far away from him as possible. As she stretched out under a single blanket, she found herself looking forward with anticipation to the next day. Even with Kroger a constant worry in her mind, she was anxious to explore this amazing place. Staring up at the sky ablaze with brilliant stars, now that the moon was down, she felt a nudge of hope. There was absolutely no reason for it, certainly her situation had not changed in the slightest, yet she held the feeling to her like a talisman, as she sank into sleep.

The morning dawned cloudy and humid, but Jessica awoke feeling better than she had in days, and the small flame of hope still burned in her. Kroger was already up, building a fire. As the fire flared, he stepped up to Hernando, who was still asleep, and prodded him roughly with the toe of his boot. Hernando stirred, mumbling, and Kroger prodded him again. "Damn lazy foreigner," he grumbled. "He'd spend his whole life sleeping or sucking on a bottle, if you'd let him."

As Hernando began to stir and then sat up, Kroger turned back to the fire, adding more wood. Seeing Jessica up, he beamed at her. "This is going to be a big day! If that well is full of treasure as all the stories claim, I'll bring you up some fancy trinkets of gold. What do you say to that?"

Jessica was startled. This was the first mention she had heard of any treasure. So that was what he had been so secretive about! Probably if she had been feeling better, she would have been more curious about his reason for coming here.

He spoke harshly. "Well?"

Jessica hastily returned his smile. She had gotten so that she could do it automatically. "Why, that will be wonderful, Brill. I'm proud of you."

He nodded, relaxing. "Yes, indeed! We already have the loot from Tampa, and with what I get from the well, we should be set for life."

Jessica shivered, horrified at the possibility of having to live with Kroger for an extended time. She sneaked a glance at Hernando, who was getting to his feet. The glance he gave her in return was sardonic.

Kroger slammed the blackened coffee pot onto the coals and snarled at the interpreter, "Get a hustle on, Villalobos, and make yourself useful. We'll need a good breakfast if we're going diving for the gold."

Hernando walked over to the supply chest. "Did you say we, señor? Do not expect me to dive. I am not a well man, and I abhor water, in any form."

"That figures." Kroger snorted. "I didn't mean we in that sense. But why do you think I brought you along? If you're going to get a share, you damned well will have to earn it. You'll handle the ropes and the gear. Surely you can manage that much?"

Hernando, struggling with the latch on the supply chest, nodded. "Si, señor. That I can manage well enough. Have no fear."

As Hernando prepared their morning meal of corn cakes, coffee, and bacon, Kroger squatted down beside him. "Now, is there a road to the well? Can we take the cart?"

"There was a road, señor, built by the Mayans, but it is badly overgrown, and I much doubt the cart would make it. It would be best to take the horses. The señorita can ride behind you, and I will walk, with the other horse carrying the equipment."

Kroger was scowling. "It'd be easier with the cart, but if it must be the horses, horses it is then. So, let's get breakfast over with and get started. I can't wait to get my hands on that gold!"

Jessica, who had been watching and listening, saw Hernando give Kroger a strange look that the other man did not notice.

Hernando knows something, she concluded; something that he isn't telling Kroger. This conclusion cheered her up considerably. Even if Hernando had said he could not, or would not, help her, at least he was not completely Kroger's ally.

The sacred well of Chichén-Itza was about two hundred yards from the center of the ancient city. As Kroger's roan picked its way delicately along the stony path, Jessica, riding behind Kroger, gazed around her. There were trees on either side of the path, not tall, but sufficiently high to screen the temples of the city from view. Around them insects darted and droned. There was no other sound, save for the thud of the horses' hooves.

And then Hernando, who was walking ahead of them with the laden cart horse, drew to a halt. "We are here, señor. This is the sacred well."

Jessica, straining to see over Kroger's shoulder, caught a glimpse of a large, round hole in the ground, with walls of sheer stone. It was much larger in diameter than she had expected—the size of a fairly large pond—but she could not see the water, only the opening itself. Across the pool, on the far side, the shaft wall rose much higher.

And then, as their mount moved nearer, Jessica could see the water, many feet below the rim, at the bottom of the strange shaft that the water had undoubtedly carved out of the porous limestone over the long years.

Kroger dismounted and helped her down. As they approached the very edge of the shaft, the clouds suddenly parted, and a ray of sunlight flashed down, illuminating the water in a sudden, golden glow. It was both eerie and beautiful, and Jessica sucked in her breath sharply, wondering if this were an omen of some sort.

Near them, at the edge of the shaft, were a number of large stones in a tumble. When Hernando saw her look of curiosity, he nodded. "Another temple, señorita. Probably where the priests conducted their rites, and from where they threw the sacrifices into the well."

Kroger, kneeling on the rock shelf on the edge, was staring at the dark water, almost black now that the sun was again gone. "It's a devil of a way down to the water, isn't it?" he said nervously. "How deep do you think the water is?"

Hernando shrugged. "I do not know, for certain, but fairly deep, I should judge."

"Well, then." Kroger arose, dusting off his trousers. "My equipment should take care of that. Get busy, Villalobos. Unload the horse and help me put everything together." As Hernando got busy unloading the cart horse, Kroger lit a cigar and strode back and forth, his gaze never leaving the water.

Jessica, seeing that the men would be occupied for some time, found a place for herself on a piece of the ruined temple stone and sat down. The ancient stone beneath her felt warm and strangely comforting.

This place has something, she thought; some kind of power. She could feel it. But oddly enough, the feeling was not frightening in the least, despite the fact that Hernando had explained that the Mayans had tossed human sacrifices into the well, along with gold and jewels. Somehow, the place made her feel calm, and almost at peace.

Then, as she glanced across the well shaft, to the higher rim on that side, she went tense. Standing there, silent and motionless, were a half-dozen figures, all male and all Indian. Their dark faces were inscrutable. Jessica scrambled to her feet.

Were they there out of simple curiosity? Or did they represent a threat?

She glanced at the two men, wondering if she should call out. Kroger was down on one knee beside the stack of equipment and clearly had yet to notice the watching Indians. But Hernando, standing, was staring over at them. Then, as if feeling her gaze on him, his head swung her way. He shook his head ever so slightly and put a cautioning finger to his lips.

Jessica remained silent, slowly resuming her seat on the stone.

Chapter Twenty-One

NEIL, Tom, and Maria reached Mérida just before dark, and all three were tired, hot, and incredibly dusty. Neil's throat felt caked with the dust they had ridden through most of the day. As soon as they entered the city proper, he began to look about for a place to stay the night. It was late to start a search for Kroger and Jessica, as much as it galled him to have to postpone it.

Mérida, he observed, was very Spanish in appearance, with many grand houses and impressive churches. When they came to the main plaza, Maria asked to stop, indicating the cathedral across the way. "On a quest such as ours, it will not do any harm to offer a prayer for our success."

Tom nodded, and Neil also agreed to stop, especially when he saw the fountain splashing in the plaza. They dismounted and tied off the weary horses. At the fountain they brushed as much dust as possible from their clothing, then drank their fill.

"I'm going over to light a candle," Maria said.

She left them and walked over to the cathedral, while Neil and Tom went into a nearby cantina. It was dim and cool inside, and they both ordered *cerveza*. Neither of them spoke until they had drained their first glass.

Then Neil wiped his mouth with the back of his hand. "Lord, nothing tastes better than a beer when you're thirsty, even if it isn't really cold."

Tom nodded, grinning. "Mexico makes good beer." He sobered, glancing around at the men seated at the small tables. They were all studying the new arrivals with varying degrees of interest. "I wonder if anyone here has seen Kroger or Jessica?"

Neil took another swallow of beer. "Well, we can't do much about asking until Maria gets back. My vocabulary doesn't extend much beyond *cerveza* and *Cómo está usted?* But we're here in Mérida, and that's a beginning, anyway. We'll find a decent place to stay and start asking questions the first thing in the morning. This is a small town, and in any small town everybody knows what's going on. If Kroger and Jessica came through here, or if they're staying here, someone will know. They couldn't miss someone like Jessica, with that golden hair."

They had finished two more beers by the time they saw Maria come out of the church and return to the plaza, looking about for them. They paid their bill, not without some difficulty, in American money. Feeling much refreshed, they hastened to join Maria, who was sitting on the edge of the fountain.

When she saw them, she hurried toward them, her face shining in her excitement. "I asked the padre if he knew of any newcomers in Mérida, and I described Jessica and Kroger. He told me that he had not seen them himself, but that his housekeeper's brother knows a woman who works for such a man. She told the brother that she was going to work for a *gringo* and his wife, in a hacienda just outside of town. They are renting the hacienda but did not say how long they were going to stay. She also said that the wife is very young and very beautiful, with hair like the sun. It has to be Jessica!"

Neil said eagerly, "Did the padre tell you where to find this hacienda?"

Maria nodded. "It's not too far, but I do think we ought to rest before we go out there. Personally, I'm too tired to be of much use the way I am."

Tom dropped a hand on Neil's shoulder. "She's right, Neil. It's been a long day, and we don't know what we'll find out there. I'd rather face it after a good dinner and a good night's sleep."

Neil hesitated. They were so close, it was a great temptation to hasten there now, to get the suspense over with. He said reluctantly, "I suppose you're both right. We have come a long, tiring way, and if Brill Kroger is the brute everybody says he is, we'll need to be in top shape, with all our wits about us."

After the long, wearying ride through the dust and the heat, Maria was happy for a chance to bathe and change her clothing. The room in the inn looked very spacious and comfortable, after the days spent on the sloop, and the bed was wide and soft.

Staring at the bed, she could not help but think of the nights spent in the cabin on the boat, she in the curtained alcove and the men in the other section. Lying there at night, listening to the men breathing deeply in sleep, she had often found herself wishing that Tom were on the narrow bunk with her, lying beside her, holding her in his arms.

She had yet to tell him of her decision, mainly because the right moment had not arrived and because there had been little privacy on the boat. Neil had been considerate and had left them pretty much to themselves; yet privacy on a sloop the size of the *Kelpie* had been hard to come by. Still, she and Tom had grown closer during the trip. Being together every day, and so near and yet so far at night, had been both a pleasure and a pain.

Tom, true to his promise, had said nothing further about marrying her; yet his evident happiness when he was with her, and his tender gestures and loving smiles, told her that he refrained from becoming personal only because of his promise.

Maria felt vaguely guilty about not telling him that she had seen Carlos and that her decision had been made. She longed to tell him that she loved him and would marry him, if he still wanted her. And yet there was a certain delicious pleasure in *not* telling him, in prolonging the moment as long as possible.

Well, perhaps tonight she would get the chance she wanted, she thought. She doubted that she could prolong the suspense much longer, even one more day; and it was foolish to keep him waiting, when there was no longer any reason to do so.

They were all meeting for supper, downstairs in the inn. She decided that, after their meal, she would contrive a reason to get him alone. The thought made her glow, and she stared, bemused, at the mirror, seeing not her own image, but the reflection of Tom and her together, as she tried to imagine how he would react when she told him.

Briskly she set about getting ready, taking a bath and then putting on the one good dress she had brought along. Finally satisfied with her appearance, she went downstairs. The men were already at the table.

Tom gave a low whistle as he got up to hold her chair. "Well, look at you! You're beautiful tonight, Maria." As she sat down, he lightly touched the back of her neck in a caress, and Maria felt herself blushing.

She blushed even more furiously when she glanced across the table and saw Neil smiling in amusement. Then he half-turned away to summon the waiter. When the waiter arrived, Neil ordered a bottle of wine. After the waiter had opened the bottle, Neil ceremoniously filled their glasses and raised his in a toast. "To the ultimate success of our undertaking and to Jessica's good health!"

They all drank, sobered for a moment. Setting her wineglass down, Maria reached across the table to touch the back of Neil's hand. "She is fine, Neil, I *feel* it. Tomorrow, the two of you will be reunited."

She hoisted her glass again and smiled fondly at him. During the days at sea, she had grown to know Neil and had found herself liking him immensely. He, like Tom, was a good man, a strong man. She hoped that her assurances to him about Jessica's welfare would prove to be accurate; in truth, she was not all that convinced. She had firsthand knowledge of Kroger's vicious nature, and it was really hard to conceive that Jessica had remained in his clutches unharmed for all this time.

Maria found that she did not need to contrive an excuse to talk to Tom alone. When they were finished eating, Neil stood, smiled down at them, and said, "I'll leave you two. I'm worn out and need to get some rest. To be honest, I suppose I'm not yet completely recovered from my wound. That horseback ride just about did me in."

Maria suspected that he had excused himself to leave them alone together. He was a sensitive man and certainly knew of the strong current of feeling between herself and Tom.

Tom leaned across the table and put his hands over hers. "How about you, Maria? I noticed that the inn has a lovely garden out back. Do you feel up to taking a stroll?"

Maria nodded, suddenly too shy to speak or even look at him. They left the dining room arm in arm and strolled through the dark and fragrant garden, illuminated only by the moon and dim lamplight cast from the windows of the inn.

Maria was nervous, which caused her heart to beat faster and her palms to perspire. Despite living this scene several times in her imagination, it was not going to be as easy as she had thought. She had one consolation—Tom was equally nervous. The hand holding her arm trembled from time to time, betraying his tension.

They stopped at the fountain in the center of the garden, sitting side by side on a stone bench. The sound of the falling water was like music, soothing and somehow comforting.

"It's beautiful, isn't it?" Tom said, his voice low and husky.

Maria nodded, not trusting herself to speak just yet. And then, all at once, she was in his arms, and his mouth was in her hair. Afterward, she was never certain just how it happened, for she could not remember moving or feeling him move. But there they were, pressed fiercely together, each straining to get closer to the other.

Tom moved his mouth down to her ear, his voice a caressing, but urgent murmur. "Oh, Maria! Maria, I know that I promised not to touch you until you gave me the word, but these past few days, being with you every day, have been pure torture. And the nights. . . . Oh, my love, knowing you were there, so close and yet beyond my reach, almost drove me crazy. I don't know how long I can—"

Maria, deeply moved, felt tears spring to her eyes. "Hush, my darling Tom." She put her fingers over his lips. "I understand. Don't apologize. Don't you think I feel the same way? Tom—there is no longer any reason for you not to speak!"

It took a moment for her words to penetrate. He drew back from her, his features showing a conflict of disbelief and dawning hope. "What do you mean? Do you mean that you have made up your mind? But I thought you wanted to wait until this other fellow came back from Cuba?"

"He came back, the day we left Tampa. You remember the men who came with me to the boat? One was my brother, and the other was Carlos Chavez. I wanted to introduce you, but Carlos could not wait." She looked at him out of misty, shining eyes. "You see, Carlos is going back to Cuba. . . ."

He was frowning. "Alone?"

She nodded quickly. "Yes. He asked me to go with him, to live there as his wife, but I told him no."

"You told him no!" Tom threw back his head and let out a whoop that startled a night bird in the tree above them. The bird fluttered off, scattering leaves down upon them.

"I told him no. I wanted to tell you before this, on the boat, but there never seemed to be the right time for it. I hope you're not angry with me?"

"How could I be angry with you, Maria? Not if this means what I want it to mean." He looked at her in apprehension. "Tell me, darling Maria! Tell me you are mine!"

"Yes, yes, yes!" she whispered, her heart thudding wildly with a joy that made her dizzy. "Yes, Tom!"

He surged to his feet, picked her up, and swung her around in a wide circle, then put her down and drew her into his arms. His mouth descended upon hers, hungry yet gentle, and her own lips answered his, speaking all that she yearned and felt, but could not put into words.

They stood thus for a long time, wrapped in each other's arms, their lips demanding and receiving affirmation of their love, until both their hearts were pounding; and Maria felt so giddy, so on fire, that she did not think she could bear it for another moment.

"Oh, my love, my Maria," he said softly, stepping back to gaze with yearning eyes into her face. "I can't let you go tonight. Say that I may love you. Tell me that you won't send me away tonight."

Maria, almost fainting with love and desire, could only nod her silent consent. Tomorrow, who knew what might happen tomorrow? Now, this moment, was important. Tonight, she must be with him. It was right. She felt it, deep in her heart and soul.

Quickly they went up to her room, going separately so as to not attract undue attention to themselves. Once inside, Tom pulled her close, for a long, lingering kiss that heated their blood and made them both breathless.

Then, with trembling, gentle fingers, he unbuttoned her shirtwaist, folding back the fabric from her body as he would open the petals of a flower, to expose the smooth olive skin above her camisole; and then he slipped the camisole off her shoulders until her breasts, smooth and pale, sprang into view. Tenderly he kissed them, caressing the full, pink nipples with his tongue, until Maria was blind and trembling with need. She moaned softly, and he laughed deep in his throat, picking her up in his arms and carrying her to the high four-poster bed.

Placing her gently upon the bed, he proceeded to undress her completely. He took time, despite his great desire and need; and when she was completely unclothed, lying a-tremble under his loving gaze, he kissed and caressed all the tender, secret places of her body, causing her to moan and quiver in delightful torment and then to cry out, murmuring his name. Never had she known such pleasure, such desire, such pounding need! She felt wanton and desperate to have him inside her, so that this blaze of passion could find release.

And then Tom was stripping away his own clothing, no longer patient, no longer able to rein himself in. Maria lay with her eyes closed until she felt his weight come down upon the bed and his body was against her, warm and hard.

Gently he spread her thighs, and she opened them willingly, eager to feel him inside her; and then there was a pain, sharp but of short duration; and she gasped as she felt it, and then felt him, at long last, inside her, filling her, filling an emptiness that she had not realized existed.

He began moving now, thrusting slowly, and soon the pain was forgotten in the rush of sensation, as his body, inside her, ignited a searing pleasure that she could not have even imagined. She wanted it to go on forever, but too soon he gasped and went lax atop her, leaving her still afire with need, so that she gave a small, mewling cry of complaint.

Raising his head, he smiled at her and began to kiss and caress her, and in a few moments he was erect and inside her again; and this time they moved together in timeless rhythm, until Maria, too, felt the explosion of rapture that brought an end to the wild need, and they relaxed together, spent and totally content.

He gathered her into his arms, cradling her head on his shoulder. "It was as I thought it would be. No, it was more, much more. I love you, my sweet, sweet Maria."

Despite Maria's remark that afternoon, that she was tired and needed rest, she did not sleep much that night. She and Tom would drowse for a time, holding one another closely, only to awaken, passions high, eager to love again. Maria lost count of the times they made love. How could she keep count, when each time was more wonderful than the time before!

Finally, not long before dawn, she fell into a deep sleep and slept without dreaming. She awoke in a daze of happiness, clinging tightly to Tom's hand. She gazed in adoration at his sleeping face.

He stirred, opening his eyes slowly. He smiled sleepily. "Good morning, my love." He gave a start when he saw the sun streaming in through the window. "Good Lord, it's late! We promised to meet Neil for breakfast. We'd better—"

Her mouth stopped his word, and it was close to a half hour before they finally got out of bed and began to dress.

Maria felt self-conscious about dressing in front of Tom, which was ridiculous, considering how they had spent the night. Nonetheless, she turned her back.

"Maria," Tom said softly, his voice low. He put his hand on her shoulder and turned her to face him. "I want you to marry me now, today. The church where we stopped yesterday, we can ask the father . . ."

Maria's mouth fell open. "Get married today, *here?* But what about the banns? And my parents—"

He stopped her with a kiss. "Your parents, I know, will want a big wedding at home. But that doesn't mean we can't get married here quickly, then have a big wedding later in Tampa. As for the banns, well, I think that when we explain the situation to the padre, we can persuade him to dispense with the formalities. Dearest Maria, it would make me very happy. Then, no matter what might happen, we would be one in the eyes of God, and man."

"But Neil," she said hesitantly. "Do you think he will be willing to delay any longer, before going to Jessica? You know how anxious he is."

"It won't take that long. And I'm certain Neil knows how we feel. Come on, we'll talk to him at breakfast."

The interior of the huge, yellow stone church was high and vaulted. Above Tom and Maria, the pillars soared to the beautifully ornamented ceiling; and as they knelt before the gilded altar, with candlelight shining upon their faces, Neil felt touched and solemn.

As the priest intoned the words over their bowed heads, his own face reflecting the glory of theirs, Neil felt the sting of tears come to his eyes. If only he and Jessica were kneeling there! His heart was full of love for his two friends, yet there was a pain along with it. He had been upset at their proposal over breakfast this morning—another delay in his search for Jessica, if only for an hour. It was an hour that he did not want to lose, but the shared love on their faces had been too much. He owed it to them; they had accompanied him in his search, happily facing whatever dangers he faced. In the end he had agreed.

If he was fortunate, if they were all fortunate, there would be another wedding in Tampa—a double wedding. But first they had to find Jessica, and the four of them had to return safely to Tampa.

After the brief ceremony was completed, the priest repeated his directions to Maria as to how to get to the hacienda Kroger had rented.

The hacienda was not difficult to find, for it was not much more than a mile from the edge of the city. As the huge, white outer wall came into view, Neil felt his pulse begin to race with excitement and apprehension, and he voiced a silent prayer for Jessica's safety.

"Well, I guess this is it. Let's go!"

Drumming his heels into his horse's flanks, he urged the animal into a gallop, and the others followed suit. Before the high, wooden double gate, Neil slid to the ground and tried the latch. It would not yield. He pushed against the gate with all his strength, but it still did not budge.

He turned to Tom and Maria. "It has to be barred from the inside. The question is, do we try to break it down—or go over the wall?"

"It looks very sturdy," Maria said doubtfully. "And there is nothing around to use as a battering ram."

"You're right. So it's over the wall. I'll go first, Tom, then you follow. Maria, you wait here. If something happens, if we don't open the gate within a few minutes, then you ride like hell for town and bring back the authorities."

Maria started to voice a protest, then subsided, nodding. Neil saw that she was very pale. He smiled encouragingly at her.

He mounted up again, kneed the horse over alongside the wall, then stood up in the saddle. In this position he could just reach the top of the wall. Getting a firm grip, he heaved himself up and over, pausing for just a moment on top, his gaze raking the courtyard, before dropping down inside.

By the time Tom dropped down beside him, Neil had his pistol out and was turned facing the silent house. There was no sound, no evidence of habitation. Neil felt growing dismay. Where were they? Had Kroger taken Jessica somewhere else?

He stepped to the big gate, pushed up the wooden bar locking it into place, and swung the gate open. Maria was waiting just outside.

At her questioning look, Neil shook his head. "Nothing. We're going to the house. You stay back out of harm's way, until we learn what's waiting for us."

With Neil and Tom in the forefront, holding drawn pistols, they advanced on the house. At the entrance Neil put out his hand, testing the knob. To his astonishment, it swung open to his touch. Both men stepped quickly inside, fanning out immediately, one on each side of the door, backs to the wall.

And then they heard it—the first sound. It was a woman's voice, singing softly in Spanish, coming from the back of the house. Quietly the two men moved toward the sound, finally locating its source in the kitchen—a plump, dark woman dressed in native garments. She was stirring something in a clay bowl and singing softly to herself.

At the sound of their footsteps, the woman whirled, her dark eyes going wide with startled fear.

Neil spoke quickly, in English. "We mean you no harm, señora. We're looking for Brill Kroger. Is this his house?"

The woman broke into a torrent of Spanish, with many gestures.

"It's no use," Neil said helplessly. "I don't understand a blasted word."

Behind him Maria said, "Let me talk to her, Neil."

Tom said angrily, "You were supposed to wait, Maria! Who knows what we might have run into in here?"

Maria gestured impatiently and advanced toward the woman, speaking soothingly in Spanish.

Neil put his hand on Tom's arm. "While they're talking, let's go through the rest of the house and make sure there's no one else here."

They went through the house room by room, pistols at the ready. All the rooms were achingly empty. But in one bedroom, the last one they searched, Neil found something that gave him hope. It was a woman's room, and against one wall, hanging from a row of pegs, were two dresses. One was a faded and wrinkled ball gown. Below it rested two worn dancing slippers. Almost reverently, Neil took the dress down. "This must belong to Jessica, I feel it!"

Tom said, "Let me see it. I saw her that night." Taking the dress, he stared at it. "I'm not much on women's clothes, and this dress is in pretty bad shape, but I'm pretty certain this is what she was wearing at the ball."

Neil felt his hopes and his spirits rise. "Let's go see what Maria has found out."

Hurrying back to the kitchen, they found the two women seated at the kitchen table, talking easily, sharing a pot of tea.

Neil said eagerly, "What have you learned?"

Maria smiled up at him. "Kroger is here, and so is Jessica."

"Thank God!" Neil exhaled a gusty sigh of relief. "Is she all right, is Jessica all right?"

"The last time she saw her, she was. She says the *gringa* was often locked in her room."

"The last time?" Neil echoed. "Where are they? There's no one in the house."

"They left two days ago for a ruined city, called Chichén-Itza, with their interpreter, Hernando Villalobos. Something was said about visiting a sacred well there."

"A sacred well?" Tom said in puzzlement. "Whatever for?"

"Never mind that." Neil clapped a hand on Tom's shoulder. "Two days ago, she said? How far is this place? How long will it take us to ride there?"

Maria again addressed the housekeeper in rapid Spanish. After a moment she looked at Neil. "It is a goodly distance, she says. It is a three-day ride, perhaps more, but they will be traveling slowly, for they have a heavily laden cart."

"They have a two-day start on us." Neil struck his palm with his fist. "But if we ride hard, we should make it soon after they do."

The housekeeper engaged Maria's attention again, speaking several words quickly, at the end of which she crossed herself.

Maria drew back, paling slightly.

Neil said urgently, "What is it? What did she say?"

"She says—" Maria looked up, her eyes dark with distress. "She says the *gringo* is. . . . She says he is crazy. Loco." She made a circle at her forehead with a finger, her breath catching. "She thinks that Kroger is slowly going mad, Neil. Dear God! There is no telling what he may take it into his head to do!"

you are away from the ruins, you must find a landmark, in the direction you are headed. When you are past that, pick another, and then another. In such a manner, you will not be traveling in circles."

The rope bell jangled twice. "Will you work the pump, señorita? I must pull the señor up. Do not worry, he will go down again. That one has a fever for the gold."

Jessica, her throat and mouth dry, began to pump the wooden lever that supplied lifesaving air to the man she hated, as Hernando began to pull on the safety rope. If only she possessed enough evil in her to stop the pump!

As Kroger had climbed laboriously down the rope ladder, he had been on fire with anticipation. The water, as he slowly submerged himself, was far colder than he had expected. No matter, he thought; he had no intention of remaining down very long this first time. This dive was exploratory, also a test of his ability to handle the task.

Then he was fully submerged, and the hiss of air began in the crude helmet. He could smell as well as hear it, for it carried the faint scent of rubber. As his head sank beneath the surface, he had a moment of panic, for water rose slightly in the helmet. But it did not rise above his mouth, so he went on.

Down and down he went, deeper into the murky water. If he only had some source of light, the task would be far easier, he reflected. His sense of touch would have to do. The only sound was the hiss of air. Shortly, he began to feel the pull of the currrent that Villalobos had spoken of, yet it was not as strong as the man had claimed. Villalobos was a sot and a fool, and Kroger knew he was not to be trusted. However, he was needed at the moment. As soon as the treasure was brought up, he would be eliminated. Kroger certainly had no intention of sharing the loot with him.

Then his feet struck the bottom, which felt like thick mud. Kroger slowly lowered himself to a squatting position. He could not bend down because of the helmet, and he found that he had a tendency to float. He would need more weights fastened to the belt. Also, the current was quite swift here, pushing and pulling at him. He groped out with one hand and encountered the stone wall of the well. Bracing himself with one hand, he used his other hand to feel through the mud along the bottom. He sifted through the silt as far as he could reach but found nothing.

Slowly, careful to keep his head upright, he moved, still in the uncomfortable crouch, sifting through the mud as he moved. He was growing discouraged and was about ready to head for the surface, when his hand came into contact with something other than the slimy mud. It was round and smooth, and the curve of it protruded out of the mud like the bottom of a bowl. The object came loose from the mud with a sucking sound. Kroger strained to see it in the murky water but could not make it out. It was light in his hand.

Carefully stowing it in the pouch on his belt, he moved again in the same crablike manner, always staying in touch with the wall. Later, he would search toward the center, he decided.

In a little while his fingers hit something smooth and hard. He felt it carefully, then recognizing it as a rock, he pushed it away. But now there was something else—rounded and about an inch long. He put it into the sack.

All at once, as he crabbed forward, the current increased, strong enough to almost topple him off his feet. Panic began to nibble at him, and he turned and made his way back toward the rope ladder, until the pull of the current lessened. He decided that he had been down long enough. It was time to go up, examine his two finds, and add more weights to the belt. He gave two powerful tugs to the rope around his waist. In a few moments the rope tightened around his waist, helping him to maneuver back to the rope ladder.

He found that he had difficulty closing his fingers around the rungs of the ladder, and his feet kept slipping off. The cold water had numbed his hands and feet.

He felt a vast relief when his helmeted head finally emerged from the water. At the top of the ladder, Hernando reached down and helped him climb out. So excited was he that Kroger began talking almost before the helmet was fully off his head. "Everything works fine, except I need to add more weights to my belt. And I found something! Let's see. . . ."

He took out the bowllike object first and found that what he had in his hand was bone—the beautifully rounded and curved arch of a delicate skull. Incredulously, he felt in the pouch for the other item he had scooped off the bottom. It was also a bone—the rounded finger bone from a small hand.

Kroger gasped in revulsion and threw both objects from him, watching in horror as they clattered across the rocky ground.

Hernando was speaking. "I told you, señor, that they often made human sacrifices, maidens, to the rain god, as well as gold and jewels. Perhaps these bones were those of a Mayan princess. It would be interesting to know how long they have been there, eh?"

Kroger was not listening. He rubbed his hands compulsively up and down his wet underclothing. He was thinking of Dulcy Thomas. Her skull must have been as delicate as this one.

And then he shoved such morbid thoughts out of his mind. They were only bones, and old bones at that. How could they harm him? He stepped to the stone where he had left his clothes and dug out a cigar. He lit up and drew deeply on it. "What are old bones to me? I'm going down again, and this time I'll find what I'm looking for. Yes, indeed! Villalobos, add more weights to the belt and hand me that bottle of brandy. It's colder down there than I thought it would be."

Jessica had been horrified when she had seen the bones Kroger had brought up, and her heart began to beat wildly when she saw his look of revulsion. What if she had waited too long? What if he was afraid to go down again? And then he spoke, and she felt relief spread through her.

She glanced at him, then at the bones where he had thrown them, and suppressed a shudder. Before, Hernando's stories had been just that, stories. Now she could almost feel the presence of the victims, the young virgins who had gone to their deaths in the well to appease the rain god. A cruel god, she thought, if he had to exact such a tribute before he would render his services.

Now Hernando handed the brandy bottle to Kroger. As she watched him drink, Jessica knew that she was going. She dared not delay any longer. If, on the next dive, he found nothing but more bones, he might give up. The minute he was down, she was off. Following Hernando's directions, she should be able to find her way to Mérida. Surely *someone* there would help her. If nothing else, she would go to one of the many churches she had seen there and ask sanctuary. Even Kroger would not dare try to take her from a church.

Kroger tossed away the half-smoked cigar, put on the helmet, and marched determinedly over to the rope ladder. In a moment his head disappeared from sight, and Hernando began working the pump.

Jessica went to the stack of supplies and worked her way through it, selecting food items that were light and would keep. In addition, she took a canteen of water and a blanket roll. She knew that Hernando was watching, but he said nothing. Jessica put the supplies into the saddlebag, then hesitated, turning to Hernando.

"I wish you good fortune, señorita," he said softly. "*Vaya con Dios.* May God go with you."

"Thank you, Hernando, and farewell."

Squaring her shoulders, Jessica walked toward where the two horses were tethered. Then she stopped short in dismay. Coming along the road toward her, from the center of the ruined city, were three horses and riders. Who were they? Was this some further threat?

Whoever they were, they effectively blocked her escape. The three horses abreast completely filled the narrow lane, and she could not get around them. They were still too far away for her to make out who they were. Could it be that they were coming for her? She felt a surge of hope, which quickly died. No one knew she was here. Then she remembered that she had heard that there were a number of bandits in this area. . . .

There was something hauntingly familiar about the rider of the lead horse. She shielded her eyes, trying to make out faces. No, it could not be! It was not possible! It had to be some kind of hallucination!

Disbelief and hope struggled in her. She started toward the approaching riders at a stumbling run. Now they were close enough for her to see their faces. It was, dear God, it was!

Her legs were suddenly too weak to carry her. She took two more staggering steps and then slowly crumpled to the ground. For the first time in her life, Jessica fainted.

When she came to, feeling as if she were fighting her way up to consciousness through thick layers of gauze, the first thing she saw was Neil's face looking down at her with tender concern. His face was thin and drawn, very brown; but it looked marvelous to her. She reached out with trembling hands and clutched at him, then buried her face against his chest and wept uncontrollably.

"Jessica, Jessica," he said over and over. "Don't cry, darling Jessie. It's all right now, everything's all right."

She could not seem to stop weeping. All the unshed tears she had held back, all the fear and humiliation she had dared not show, burst from her in a flood.

"Has Kroger harmed you?" Neil asked shakily. "If he's hurt you! . . ."

Still unable to speak, she shook her head in the negative. Finally she pulled back to look into his face. She managed to speak in a trembling voice. "No, I'm all right, darling. I'm fine, now that you're here."

She reached out tentatively to touch his cheek, to reassure herself that he was really there. It was then that she saw two other people behind him, their faces also showing concern. One of them was Maria, Maria Mendes. And the man with her Jessica recognized as the young lieutenant she had seen with Maria in Tampa.

They had come all this distance to rescue her! Had anyone ever possessed such devoted friends!

Maria, seeing that she had stopped crying, came around Neil to kneel down and take Jessica's hand. Jessica was astonished to see that Maria was crying also. "Oh, Jessica, you can't know how happy we are to find you, and alive and well!"

Maria's friend was standing above them, staring at the well and Hernando. "Where's Brill Kroger?"

Neil looked up, his face darkening. "Yes, where is he, Jessie? When I get my hands on that—! And who's the man over there? Is that the Spaniard we were told about?"

Jessica nodded and made a move to get to her feet. Neil helped her up. "He's Hernando Villalobos. Kroger hired him as an interpreter. . . ." She choked up. "Do you have a handkerchief, Maria?"

Maria pulled a handkerchief out of her waistband and gave it to her.

Jessica wiped at her eyes and said, "Kroger is down in the well. He just went down for the second time."

Neil put his arm around her and pulled her against him. "Down in the well? Why, for God's sake? What is he after?"

"They say that for hundreds of years the Indians have thrown treasure of all kinds into the well to appease their rain god. Kroger is after the gold."

Neil's face was set with anger. "Well, when he comes up again, he's going to be in for a nasty surprise!"

Jessica tugged at his sleeve. "Neil, no! Let's just leave, just ride off and leave him. I just want to get away from him and go home, to my parents. Are they all right?"

His expression softened. "They're fine, Jessie. They've been worried sick about you, naturally, but they're strong people, and they never gave up hope. We'll get you back to them, never fear. But Kroger can't be allowed to get away with what he's done. If it was just the matter of theft, it might not be so terrible. But there's more, even beyond his abducting you."

Jessica remembered thinking that Kroger must have committed some crime other than the theft of the ball funds. "Then he *did* do something else. I thought so, because Chief Dolan was looking for him just as the ball began. What was it, what did he do?"

She saw that they were all staring at her in some surprise.

"That's right," Neil said, "you don't know. Jessie, I'm sorry to have to be the one to tell you, but Dulcy Thomas was murdered, and the police are sure that Kroger did it."

Jessica gasped in horror and slumped against Neil's chest. "There was a diary, Dulcy's diary, buried with her, and it described her—uh, relationship with Kroger, and the fact that she was seeing him that night. Kroger must be taken back to stand trial."

"Dear God, how awful!" Jessica was thinking about herself and Kroger, the many nights he had crept into her bed. He could easily have killed her, if she had said or done the wrong thing.

"It's all right," Neil said fiercely. "He can't hurt you now, I'll see to that. We'll wait for him to come up again, and then we'll take him." He glanced at Tom, who nodded grimly.

"Tom, suppose you and Maria go talk to the interpreter, tell him to keep on with what he's doing, and to act natural. I want to talk to Jessica alone for a bit."

Tom and Maria walked over to Hernando. He had been watching the newcomers with curiosity and some apprehension.

Neil said, "Jessica, let's sit down." They sat down together on a great block of stone. "Jessie, you must know by the fact that I am here, that I still love you and want you."

She took his hand and squeezed it. "I know. I'll never forget what you've done, to have come all this way—"

"Shhh!" He put two fingers to her lips. "I did it because I wanted to, because I had to. I don't want anything but to know that you love me as much as I do you, that you don't care for anyone else."

She stared at him in surprise. "Care for someone else? How could you think that? After that night on the island. . . ." She paused. "Are you thinking that because I didn't come down to the wharf to see you before you went to Cuba? Didn't my parents tell you what happened, that I lost my memory for a time?"

He looked away, holding her hand tightly. "Yes, they told me about that, but. . . . Maybe I'd better come right out and tell you what's bothering me."

Jessica felt a shiver of fear. "Yes. Please do."

"In Cuba, after I was wounded, I was taken in by a group of rebels. Just before I left them, another group joined them. One of the newcomers was a man named Ramon Mendes, Maria's brother. . . ."

Jessica was confused. Ramon? Ramon and Neil had met? She felt herself flush, thinking of how she had felt toward Ramon during the period of her memory loss. Had Ramon told Neil about that?

She said, "I'm not sure I understand, Neil."

He put a finger under her chin, tilted her head back, and looked deep into her eyes. "It was the cigar case, the one you showed me on the boat that day. You said you were making it for me."

Realization dawned, and Jessica felt her eyes go wide. Dear God! She had given the cigar case to Ramon. After she regained her memory, she had not once thought of it. How Neil must have felt! Tears threatened to fill her eyes.

"Oh, Neil! Darling, I'm *so* sorry! I found the case while my memory was gone and couldn't remember who it was for. Ramon had saved me from serious injury, perhaps even from being killed, and I wanted to do something for him in return. Oh, my darling, what you must have thought!"

A broad smile blossomed on his face. "That's what I wanted to hear. I was afraid that—"

She leaned toward him tensely. "I love *you*, Neil, no one else. Does that answer your question?"

"That answers my question." He kissed her, a long, searching kiss. When they finally broke the embrace, Jessica said softly, "I'll make you another cigar case. Much prettier, much better. Would you like that?"

"I'd like that, but first things first," he said, and kissed her again.

Down at the bottom of the well, Kroger moved slowly in his awkward crouch, carefully avoiding the area where the current was dangerously swift.

He was growing impatient. Where was the damned treasure? Why had he not found anything? And then, just as he was thinking about going up, his groping hand encountered something small, cold, and heavy. The object was of a size to fit into his hand, and it was carved, for his trembling fingers could trace a shape—vaguely human, with what felt like some kind of headdress.

He raised the item up close to the faceplate, but he still could not make out any details, yet the weight, the very *feel* of it, told him that this time it was not part of a human skeleton, but the real thing.

He stowed his find in the pouch and continued groping in the mud. Just as his fingers touched another, large object, the water level in his helmet suddenly elevated over his nose. He snorted water, and in his panic, he dropped the second piece, which had felt like a small plate. The helmet had sprung a leak. He had to get up, and quickly!

He gave the rope two quick yanks and was gratified when it immediately drew taut around his waist. Holding his breath and keeping his head tilted back to keep his nose out of the water, he followed the tug of the rope to the ladder. He had to remember where he had dropped the other piece so that he could find it when the helmet was repaired and he came back down.

As his head broke free of the surface, he fumbled in the pouch, pausing on the ladder for a moment. He had to examine his find, he could not wait. Holding onto the ladder with one hand, he brought the object up to his faceplate. Light glinted off the surface. Gold! God, it *was* gold! It was the small figure of a man, wearing a high, crown-like headdress that rayed out from his head.

A sob came from Kroger. Wait until she saw this! And this was only the beginning, he just knew it!

Still clutching the tiny statue in one hand, he climbed up the ladder as swiftly as he could manage. At the top, Hernando gave him a hand up.

Once on solid ground, Kroger ripped off the helmet and tossed it aside, his gaze going to *Her*. He started forward, holding the statue reverently in his hands, like an offering.

"Mother! Look what I found! It's solid gold, priceless, and it's for you—"

He skidded to a stop as he belatedly noticed that she was not alone. There were other people with her—two men and a woman. The woman looked somehow familiar. She was dark, a dark woman, an evil woman.

Then all other thought burned away, as rage burst in his head like a bright, hot light. Beside *Her* stood a tall, handsome, young man, his arm around her shoulders.

She had done it again. She had found a new "friend." She had betrayed him again, after all he had done for her.

This was the last time. She must be punished, they must all be punished. Feeling strong and omnipotent, he started for them.

Jessica had gone rigid when Kroger came up out of the well, water streaming off him, looking, in the helmet, like an apparition. And then when he removed the helmet and started toward her, finally seeing Neil with his arm around her, his eyes changed, began to burn like flames. She knew then—he had finally lost all grip on sanity. After weeks of tuning in to Kroger's strange, twisting moods, she knew he was capable of killing them all.

He came at them in a lumbering walk, weighed down by the metal on his belt, his features contorted hideously, with no weapons but his hands, which curled and uncurled at his sides. But Jessica knew what those hands could do.

"Neil," she cried, "watch out!"

Neil stepped in front of her. "Get back, Jessica. You, too, Maria."

As the two women stood side by side, Maria gasped, "Why, he's mad! He's insane!"

Jessica said, "Yes. He's been like this from the time we left Tampa."

Kroger, his hands raised, the fingers curled, was advancing inexorably on Neil. Neil stood his ground, waiting.

"You want to take her from me again!" Kroger shouted. "I won't allow it, not again!" His voice was high and cracked.

Tom, who had been standing off to one side, suddenly rushed at the advancing Kroger. Kroger, quicker than Jessica could have imagined possible, stooped and scooped a heavy stone from the ground at his feet. He hurled it, catching Tom alongside the head, and Tom crumpled to the ground without a sound. A cry came from Maria, and she ran toward his prone body.

The cry distracted Kroger's attention from Neil, and as his gaze found Jessica, he changed direction and came toward her, like some shambling, enraged animal. "You betrayed me again. Well, it's the last time. The last time."

Jessica, her gaze never leaving his face, began to back toward the well. She heard Neil shout something, but she was too frightened to make out his words.

Kroger was muttering, "This time I will put an end to it. This time I will see to it that you never come back."

He was almost upon her, and Jessica realized that she could not back away any farther. The lip of the well was only a few inches behind her.

And then Kroger fell, as Neil leaped onto his back. The two men rolled over and over on the rocky ground, coming dangerously near the edge of the well shaft, Neil clinging to Kroger's back. Kroger was grunting like a maddened beast. Then he managed to get to his feet. He seized Neil's arms, which were wrapped around his chest, and tore them loose, throwing Neil to the ground.

But Neil was up in an instant, ready as Kroger charged, coming at him, hands outstretched. As Kroger came within reach, Neil struck him with his fists, but Kroger, in his madness, seemed not to feel the blows. Then, as his hands reached for Neil's throat, Neil ducked down and came up under Kroger's reaching arms and drove his shoulder, like a battering ram, into the other man's belly.

Kroger, his arms windmilling for balance, teetered on the edge of the well for what seemed an interminable time, his face showing vast astonishment and growing fear. For a few moments it seemed that he might regain his balance. Then he was gone, over the edge, his wailing cry rising up eerily out of the well shaft. In a moment Jessica heard a mighty splash.

The force of the fall, plus the weight of all the metal fastened to his waist, carried Kroger all the way to the bottom of the well, and he was caught in the strong current at once.

Holding his breath, feeling his lungs start to burn with the effort, he struck out with his arms and legs, attempting to free himself from the current's deadly embrace. It was useless. Carelessly, almost contemptuously, the water, very cold now, tossed him about, pulling him relentlessly. As he scraped along the mud on the bottom, Kroger desperately tried to catch onto something, anything that would slow his progress.

One hand, groping wildly, finally struck something solid, and he grasped it, only to have it come free of the mud and into his hand. It was very heavy, very smooth, and as Kroger continued to race with the water, he struck another object, and yet another, so that they, too, were caught by the current and swept along with him.

His lungs, twin sacks of fire now, could sustain no more, and he opened his mouth to gulp air, and water poured in, down his throat and into his lungs.

His hand still clutching the object he had wrested from the mud, Kroger's body was swept out of the well and into the course of the underground river that fed it. His eyes, open but unseeing, took no notice of the priceless items that accompanied him on his last journey, as a part of the treasure he had so greedily sought moved with him into the eternal darkness.

A long silence ensued after Kroger tumbled into the well shaft. Jessica stood frozen, seemingly incapable of speech. Then Maria spoke beside her. "Shouldn't we try to save him?"

Jessica glanced around with a start. Maria and Tom stood together. Tom appeared dazed, and blood flowed freely from a cut on his forehead, but otherwise he seemed all right. Neil, his breath coming in great gasps, came over to take Jessica's hand.

Another voice said unexpectedly, "It would be of no use, just as Señor Kroger is of no use." It was Hernando. "Let him go. Let the gods have him. The current will have taken him now, at any rate."

Neil said curiously, "The current?"

"Si, señor. The river. It runs through the bottom of the sacred well. It is very powerful. It will take the señor away, to his death, as it has countless others. The river protects the treasure for the rain god. I warned Señor Kroger, but he would not listen."

Hernando sighed heavily, then stooped to pick something up from the ground. It was the small golden statue Kroger had brought up from the well. Hernando smiled his sardonic smile and held the statue out to Jessica. "Here, señorita. Do you wish this as a remembrance?"

Jessica shuddered violently. "Dear God, no! I don't want to remember. I only want to forget."

Hernando shrugged philosophically. "As you wish. I will take it, as my payment, if you do not object. Shall we leave now? I will guide you all back to Mérida and take my leave of you there."

Jessica stood for a moment, staring at the well. Then her glance went to the rise across the way. The Indians were still there, as they had been all morning. It was too far to tell, yet Jessica had the strange feeling that they were smiling.

"Jessie?" Neil touched her hand. "Shall we leave this terrible N02 place?"

"Yes, darling."

She faced around, turning her back on the well, and walked away with Neil, holding his hand tightly. She never once looked back, but looked forward to whatever the future might hold for them.

Mr. and Mrs. Wyngate Manning
request the honour of your presence
at the marriage of their daughter
Jessica Anne Manning
to
Mr. Neil Hadly Dancer
Sunday the twenty-fifth of September
at three o'clock
at the Grand Ballroom of the Tampa Bay Hotel
and afterward at the reception

R.S.V.P.

ABOUT THE AUTHOR

A few years ago Patricia Matthews was office manager for The Associated Students, California State University at Los Angeles, and a part-time writer who dreamed of making her career writing.

Married and the mother of two sons, Patricia had to struggle to find time to turn out her poems, short stories and novels which were published under her prior name, Patty Brisco. But the success of her first historical romance, published in 1977, changed all that, and Patricia Matthews' own true life story has proven to have a Cinderella ending. Today she is America's leading lady of historical romance with thirteen consecutive bestselling novels to her credit and millions of fans all over the world.